Mary's Pope

Mary's Pope

JOHN PAUL II, MARY,
and the CHURCH *since* VATICAN II

Antoine Nachef

Foreword by James Cardinal Hickey

Preface by Bertrand Buby, S.M.

SHEED & WARD

Franklin, Wisconsin

As an apostolate of the Priests of the Sacred Heart, a Catholic religious congregation, the mission of Sheed & Ward is to publish books of contemporary impact and enduring merit in Catholic Christian thought and action. The books published, however, reflect the opinion of their authors and are not meant to represent the official position of the Priests of the Sacred Heart.

2000

Sheed & Ward
7373 South Lovers Lane Road
Franklin, Wisconsin 53132
1-800-266-5564

Nihil Obstat:	Imprimatur:
Robert Fastiggi,	Adam Cardinal Maida
Ph.D.	Archbishop of Detroit
Censor Deputatus	March 17, 2000
March 12, 2000	

Quotations from the Vatican II documents are from *Vatican Council II: The Conciliar and Post Conciliar Documents*, Austin Flannery, O.P., General Editor. Northport, NY: Costello Publishing Company, 1992.

Printed in the United states of America
Cover and interior design: Madonna Gauding
Cover art by Christine Granger, used with permission.

Library of Congress Cataloging-in-Publication Data

Nachef, Antoine, 1967–
    Mary's pope : John Paul II, Mary, and the church since Vatican II / Antoine E. Nachef;
    Foreword by James Hickey ; preface by Bertrand Buby.
    p.   cm.
    Includes bibliographical references (p.)
    ISBN 1-58051-077-9 (alk. paper)
    1.   John Paul II, Pope, 1920–20th century. I. Title.

BT613 .N33 2000
232.91'092—dc21

00-033883

1 2 3 4 5 / 03 02 01 00

CONTENTS

Acknowledgments

And so, in the redemptive economy of grace, brought about through the action of the Holy Spirit, there is a unique correspondence between the moment of the Incarnation of the Word and the moment of the birth of the Church. The person who links these two moments is Mary: Mary at Nazareth and Mary in the Upper Room at Jerusalem. In both cases her discreet yet essential presence indicates the path of "birth from the Holy Spirit." Thus she who is present in the mystery of Christ as Mother becomes—by the will of the Son and the power of the Holy Spirit—present in the mystery of the Church. In the Church too she continues to be a maternal presence, as is shown by the words spoken from the Cross: "Woman, Behold your son!"; "Behold, your mother."

Pope John Paul II, *Redemptoris Mater*

Glory Be to the Name of Jesus the Savior!
To Jesus through Mary

✝

In Gratitude to
Almighty God for All His Blessings
and for His Dedicated Servants,
Mike and Nancy Jean

✝

In Recognition of
Father Frederick J. Collins

✝

Dedicated to
The faithful ministry of
Rev. Msgr. John R. McSweeney

The Faithful Community
of Saint Mark's Roman Catholic Church
Burlington, Vermont

Foreword

I AM DELIGHTED to offer a word of introduction to Antoine Nachef's new volume, *Mary's Pope: John Paul II, Mary, and the Church since Vatican II*. This new book follows his previous study on the thought of Pope John Paul II, *The Mystery of the Trinity in the Theological Thought of Pope John Paul II*.

Unfortunately, the Pope's thought is all too often caricatured along narrow ideological lines. In both of his volumes, Nachef does his readers a great service in elucidating the richness, breadth, and profundity of the thought of our Holy Father whose writings will continue to enrich the Church far into the distant future.

In the present volume, Nachef shows how, in the thought of Pope John Paul II, Mary is indissolubly linked to Christ and His mysteries, planned for all eternity in the hidden counsels of the Triune God. Nachef strives to show us not only the content of the Pope's thought about Mary but also its sources, its compelling coherence, and its power to inspire true devotion to Mary.

Over ten years ago, I had the honor to offer the annual spiritual reflections to the Holy Father and his household. Aware of the Holy Father's deep love for Mary, I chose to speak on Mary standing at the foot of the Cross. Nachef's latest volume richly highlights how very deeply Pope John Paul II grasps the Marian dimension of the mystery of salvation.

It is my hope and prayer that a wide audience will carefully read and appreciate Nachef's new work, especially during this great Year of Jubilee.

James Cardinal Hickey
Archdiocese of Washington
January 3, 2000

Preface

ANTOINE NACHEF has dedicated much of his ongoing research to understanding the thought and theology of Pope John Paul II. In this second work on the Pope, Nachef turns to the Marian dimension as seen through the Pope's Marian encyclical, *Redemptoris Mater* and the eighth chapter of *Lumen Gentium* (Dogmatic Constitution on the Church). This excellent analysis and comparison of John Paul II with Vatican II shows how the Holy Father develops Marian doctrine in new ways while always building on the living tradition of the Church. The Holy Father is not merely an interpreter; new ground is being broken not only in thought, theology, and teaching but also in devotion. In a dynamic manner both the Pope and Nachef show the development of Marian research by careful use of the Scriptures, the Fathers, and the magisterial teaching of the Church, especially in Vatican II.

Mary's presence is never separated from that of her Son Jesus, the Christ, nor from the salvific plan of the Father and the sanctifying work of the Holy Spirit, both in the Church and through the mediation of the Virgin Mary. The chief characteristic of the Pope's Marian thought is the divine maternity. Mary is also the first disciple of the Lord, but it is especially her motherhood that connects all of the mysteries of Christ in which she is involved.

Antoine Nachef traces the fundamental principle of Mary's divine maternity throughout John Paul II's extensive writings. Mary's holiness, her ecclesial role, her presence as a theological person within the community, her faith as the model pilgrim for us, and her mediation are carefully and meticulously seen in the citations and works that the author has consulted. It is characteristic of Nachef's zest and enthusiasm for presenting an integrated approach to Mary as seen in the principal Marian writings of John Paul II. Understanding that both creation theology and redemption theology are part of this integration and that Mary has a definite role in this throughout salvation history are clearly seen in the papal teaching page after page.

Antoine Nachef has presented us with a clear and comprehensive insight into this Marian teaching of our Holy Father. The work is both theological and spiritual. It opens up for the faithful reader a deep appreciation of John Paul II's love and knowledge of the mother of Jesus and our mother Mary. Through this work, Mary is better known, loved, and served.

Father Bertrand Buby, S.M.
Professor of Marian Studies
International Marian Research Institute
University of Dayton, Ohio, U.S.A.

The Teachings of Pope John Paul II Concerning Mary

IN MY FIRST VOLUME on the Trinitarian theology of Pope John Paul II, I analyzed his philosophy, his theology of creation and Redemption, his understanding of Christ (Christology), and his theology on the Holy Spirit (Pneumatology).[1] The present study explores his understanding of the Mother of God (Mariology) in relation to *Lumen Gentium* VIII, the document that treats the question of Mary in Vatican II, the Second Vatican Ecumenical Council held in 1962–1965.

The Swiss Marianist Johann G. Roten emphasizes that the Mariology of the Council underwent a structural renewal by focusing on three aspects: Mary's place in salvation history, her faith journey, and her being an archetype of the Church.[2] Chapter VIII of *Lumen Gentium* is, as The Congregation for Catholic Education states, "the fullest and most authoritative synthesis of Catholic doctrine about the Mother of the Lord ever to have been compiled by an ecumenical council."[3] The Council's synthesis entailed both Marian spirituality and Marian doctrine. Sound devotion to Mary is necessarily based on true doctrine. A doctrine not lived in devotional life would be destined to wither and die. Pope John Paul II himself attests to the importance of Vatican II's teaching by saying: "The Second Vatican Council made great strides forward with regard to both Marian doctrine and devotion."[4]

One should be constantly aware that the Fathers of the Council treated the question of Our Lady within *Lumen Gentium,* VIII, inserting it in the Dogmatic Constitution on the Church rather than isolating it as a whole separate constitution. The intention of the Council was to emphasize the role of Mary within the mystery of the Church as well as her instrumentality and cooperation as a human being and Mother of the Lord in God's plan of salvation. As a bishop at Vatican II, Karol Wojtyla favored the inclusion of Marian doctrine within the Dogmatic Constitution on the Church.[5] Later on, as Pope John Paul II, he has clearly stated that the presence of Mary in the mystery of Christ and the Church "is a fundamental dimension emerging from the Mariology of the Council."[6] He adds in his letter *Tertio Millennio Adveniente* (On Preparation for the Jubilee of the Year 2000), 26:

> The Encyclical *Redemptoris Mater* [Mother of the Redeemer], issued on that occasion [occasion of the Marian Year 1987–1988], drew attention to the Council's teaching on the presence of the Mother of God in the mystery of Christ and the Church.[7]

The extraordinary Synod of 1985 has exhorted theologians and the faithful to follow the guidelines of the Second Vatican Council in its teaching about Mary. Both Vatican II and the Synod "embody what the Holy Spirit himself wishes to say to the Church in the present phase of history."[8]

After Vatican II, Mary's relationship with the economy of salvation,[9] her identity as a theological personality, and her representation of the Church became the points of emphasis for the Mariology of Paul VI (Pope from 1963–1978) and John Paul II. Both of them have further developed the Marian doctrine of the Second Vatican Council and implemented its spiritual and pastoral dimensions in the life of the Church. The existential (Paul VI's Apostolic Exhortation "Devotion to the Blessed Virgin Mary," called *Marialis Cultus*), the personalist (John Paul II's encyclical letter *Redemptoris Mater*), and the feminine (John Paul II's "Apostolic Letter on the Dignity and Vocation of Women," called *Mulieris Dignitatem*) approaches to Mary all supplement the theological reflection with a full spirituality.[10]

Pope Paul VI assesses how Mary should influence us in our devotion. In *Redemptoris Mater*, Pope John Paul II says of Paul VI that he:

. . . expounded the foundations and criteria of the special veneration that the Mother of Christ receives in the Church, as well as the
various forms of Marian devotion—liturgical, popular, and private—
that respond to the spirit of faith.[11]

Paul VI's *Marialis Cultus* reflects a strong emphasis on the Tradition of the Fathers of the Church. He states that Marian devotion should
be Trinitarian, Christological, and aware of the role of the Holy Spirit.[12]
The reason behind Paul VI's thought is the centrality of the event of the
Word's Incarnation that was accomplished by the Holy Spirit and the
cooperation of the Virgin Mary. One should never separate Mary from
the Father's plan accomplished by Christ in the Holy Spirit. Mariology is
always Trinitarian. Since Marian doctrine is rooted in the belief that
Mary is *Theotokos* (Mother of God), a truth that is part of the belief in
the economy of salvation (hierarchy of truth), Mariology, in Paul VI's
opinion, would run the risk of becoming an isolated discipline if separated from the general Creed. This risk of isolation would result from
pulling Mary away from the overall picture of the economy of salvation.
If this isolation takes place, Mariology could lose all its interior dynamism that springs from its relationship to the other constitutive elements
of God's plan of Redemption as found in the Creed. For this reason,
Theotokos, a title referring directly to the relationship between Mary
and her Son Jesus, should constitute the fundamental principle for
understanding all other Marian thoughts.

Pope John Paul II's interest in Mary led many theologians and lay
faithful to look at him as a "Marian Pope."[13] It cannot escape any of our
contemporaries that he has a very special devotion to Mary. That special
attachment to the Mother of the Lord is greatly inspired by his experience of Mary in Poland and by Saint Louis Marie Grignion De Montfort
(1673–1716), from whom he takes his motto as Pope, *Totus Tuus* (I am
wholly yours, O Mary!).[14] De Montfort is the only theologian of modern times mentioned in John Paul's Marian encyclical *Redemptoris Mater*.
John Paul II thinks that Montfort's authentic Marian spirituality ranks
among other significant schools of spirituality that were mentioned in
the Second Vatican Ecumenical Council.[15] In *Redemptoris Mater*, 48,
the Pope explicitly mentions only the Second Vatican Council and
Father De Montfort as "points of reference" for the Marian Year

[June 7, 1987 (Pentecost)–August 15, 1988 (Assumption)]. By that reference, the Holy Father intends to point out the value and the actuality of the spirituality of De Montfort in today's life of the Church. Such an important place for De Montfort in the Mariology of the Pope results from the parallel approaches between Vatican II and De Montfort in their outlook on Mary, mainly in her relationship with the mystery of Christ and the Church.[16]

Even though his responsibility to expound the true Marian doctrine became greater with his election to the papacy, John Paul II's relationship with Mary did not come to him only when installed in this high office.[17] In his speech of acceptance of the chair of Saint Peter, John Paul II dedicated his being and his ministry to Mary. He did so because he wished from the very first moment of his pontificate "to enter and penetrate into the deepest rhythm of the Church's life."[18] He understood that the Church's task is "to keep up the link between the mystery of the Redemption and every man," and that the Church is a mother and has a Mother, Mary.[19]

There is always a specific reference to Mary at the end of John Paul's papal documents confirming its purpose from a Marian point of view.[20] The Mariology of Pope John Paul II appears in concentrated form in his encyclical letter *Redemptoris Mater*. This letter deals with the real questions of the present concerning the Mother of the Lord.[21] Besides, the series of seventy Wednesday audience catecheses on Mary delivered between September 6, 1995, and November 12, 1997, has been extraordinarily rich in developing Marian doctrine and Mary's precise place in the economy of Redemption. The Pope's focus on Mary draws its relevance here from the very mechanism of Redemption itself. As the Mariology of John Paul is analyzed throughout his documents, one realizes that this mechanism is a dynamic presence of Mary in Christ's saving activity. Cardinal Ratzinger, Prefect of the Congregation for the Doctrine of the Faith, has rightly stated that John Paul's Mariology, especially as displayed in *Redemptoris Mater*, focuses on the action of Mary and her mission. Her being is made visible clearly through concrete interventions in the history of salvation. Dealt with here is not a mere theoretical presence in the mystery of Christ, but a dynamic action in salvation history.[22]

Throughout his whole pontificate, this "Marian Pope" has been making it his own task and duty to expound the Marian doctrine of the Second Vatican Council.[23] Two theologians from Rome, namely Stefano de Fiores and A. M. Triacca, agree that very frequent reference to *Lumen Gentium* (Vatican II) shows a strong structural relationship to the encyclical *Redemptoris Mater*. In fact, as Triacca states, this encyclical is defined as "the most authoritative comment on *Lumen Gentium*. *Lumen Gentium* is cited ninety-two times only in the footnotes of RM [*Redemptoris Mater*]."[24] John Paul takes as the opening words of *Redemptoris Mater* the very same text that opens the chapter on Mary in Vatican II's Dogmatic Constitution on the Church. Because of his loyalty to the intentions of Vatican II:

> He has thus far been very careful to avoid maximalism and minimalism and to refrain from personally deciding issues that are still subject to theological debate.[25]

Even though, like John XIII (Pope from 1958–1963) and Paul VI before him, John Paul has until now abstained from making any *ex cathedra* pronouncements (infallible dogmatic definitions), his faithfulness to the teaching of Vatican II on Mary constitutes a norm for the Church to follow.

Like all his other theological studies, the Mariology of Pope John Paul II has constantly envisioned the coming of the year 2000. In the opinion of the Jesuit theologian Jean Galot, *Redemptoris Mater* is motivated and dominated by the perspective of the end of the second millennium.[26] Ignace de la Potterie thinks that John Paul II's outlook on Mary's presence in the history of salvation has the year 2000 in mind.[27] The whole Marian encyclical is, according to the Marianist Luigi Gambero, dominated by the proximity of the year 2000.[28] For Avery Dulles, John Paul's Mariology is closely interwoven with his theology of time: "Mary is the primary patroness of the advent of the new millennium."[29] If the bi-millennial Jubilee of the birth of Jesus Christ is the focal point of the Church's celebration, nonetheless:

> ... in recent years, various opinions have been voiced suggesting that it would be fitting to precede that anniversary by a similar Jubilee in celebration of the birth of Mary.[30]

The wish of those "various opinions" was granted with the designation of 1987–1988 as a Marian Year. Such a designation is connected with the great Jubilee of the year 2000 and contains theological underpinnings:

> Two thousand years ago the Son of God was made man by the power of the Holy Spirit and was born of the Immaculate Virgin Mary. The Marian Year was, as it were, an anticipation of the Jubilee, and contained much of what will find fuller expression in the Year 2000.[31]

Just as Mary is remembered each year as the Advent Saint *par excellence*, she also waited with us as we were looking forward to the 2000th anniversary of Jesus' birth. Indeed, *Redemptoris Mater* shares its name with that of the Advent canticle *Alma Redemptoris Mater* that was quoted in the encyclical itself:

> Loving Mother of the Redeemer, gate of heaven, star of the sea, assist your people who have fallen yet strive to rise again.[32]

One can justly say that in the theology of John Paul II, jubilee years are more than sentimental recollections of the past. Nor are they apocalyptic because he does not look at the year 2000 as a sign of *Parousia* (Second Coming) in the sense of the end of the world. The Pope's thoughts are woven into the texture of salvation history. Just as those who heard Christ announcing a year of grace in the synagogue (Lk 4:16–30), we too rejoice and continue to live in this era of Redemption. In and through the jubilee celebration, the Church recalls and reactivates the season of grace and liberation, the arrival of the fullness of time in which God sent His only Son born of a woman. In a word, the year 2000 has been a key point in the pontificate of Pope John Paul II since his election in 1978 and therefore enjoys a Marian dimension.[33]

If Mary occupies an eminent place in his theological thought, the Holy Father does not reduce theology to Mariology even if he chose *Totus Tuus* (I am wholly yours, O Mary!) as the motto for his papacy. The great themes of the life and papacy of John Paul II cannot be limited to his Marian devotion. The human person, devotion in general, discipline, drama, intellectualism, isolation, mysticism, suffering, mystery, and fascination are all dimensions that influenced the child, the young, and the adult Karol Wojtyla (later on Pope John Paul II).[34] Therefore, with this complexity of factors, one should not consider the Pope's Mariology as detached from all those dimensions. Even his very devotion to Mary as inspired by Saint Louis De Montfort is not a superficial relation to her detached from a doctrinal background. The Pope himself attests to this when he says in *Crossing the Threshold of Hope*:

> *Tŏtus Tŭus*. This phrase is not only an expression of devotion. It is more. During the Second World War, while I was employed as a factory worker, I came to be attracted to Marian devotion. At first, it had seemed to me that I should distance myself a bit from the Marian devotion of my childhood, in order to focus more on Christ. Thanks to Saint Louis of Montfort, I came to understand that true devotion to the Mother of God is actually Christocentric, indeed, it is very profoundly rooted in the mystery of the Blessed Trinity, and the mysteries of the Incarnation and Redemption.[35]

It would be a mistake, therefore, to think of Wojtyla's attachment to Mary as the fruit of sentimentality or superficial love. Avery Dulles rightly states that the Pope:

> . . . emphatically denies that Marian teaching is a devotional supplement to a system of doctrine that would be complete without her. On the contrary, he holds, she occupies an indispensable place in the whole plan of salvation.[36]

John Paul's profound devotion to Mary is nourished by a mind that is deeply acquainted with philosophy and theology. Only with a thorough analysis of his thought does one realize that John Paul II's Mariology is not a superficial devotion to Mary based on arbitrary emotional feelings. Rather, his erudition in philosophy and theology influences his vision of Mary and places his Mariology among the disciplines of the very complex body of theology. At the very dawn of his pontificate and with the publishing of his first encyclical letter *Redemptor Hominis* (Redeemer of Man), John Paul immediately made it clear that his understanding of Mary, greatly inspired by the approaches of the Second Vatican Council and Pope Paul VI,[37] is Trinitarian and Christological.[38] In that line of thought and in a very emphatic way, John Paul stated in January, 10, 1996:

> The mystery of Mary is a revealed truth which imposes itself on the
> intellect of believers and requires of those in the Church who have
> the task of studying and teaching a method of doctrinal reflection
> no less rigorous than that used in all theology.[39]

This statement, like many others uttered by the Pope, reflects his
deep conviction that Mariology belongs to Sacred Doctrine in the
Thomistic sense. The mystery of Mary is considered precisely under the
formality of being divinely revealed and, therefore, is a part of the whole
of Sacred Doctrine.[40]

If Pope John Paul II's Mariology enjoys an indispensable Trinitarian
and Christological dimension, Mary is thereby not reduced to an irrel-
evant appendix within God's plan of salvation. The Pope knows how to
avoid an implicit *Gnosticism* (a modern designation for a religious movement of the early centuries A.D. that was radically dualistic and rejected
the material world and all that belonged to it) that has always tortured
the Church with its reduction, sometimes even annihilation, of the human role in the accomplishment of Redemption. To provide a balanced
view on the identity and role of Mary in God's eternal design of salvation seems to be a priority for John Paul since he intends to look at her
according to what God Himself has planned for her. The Pope is more
concerned with communicating the true doctrine and faith of the Church
as transmitted by Holy Tradition than proposing new ideas and theories.
His personal touch in presenting Marian doctrine only adds deeper
insights and wider perspectives to the Church's faith. That is why one
comes across concepts that reflect his own personal insights. In order not
to limit himself to the doctrinal aspect, however, Pope John Paul II has
also developed a Marian spirituality based on this doctrine. Toward the
end of *Redemptoris Mater*, he says:

> Here we speak not only of the doctrine of faith but also of the life
> of faith, and thus of authentic Marian spirituality, seen in the light
> of Tradition, and especially the spirituality to which the Council
> exhorts us.[41]

The relationship between the created order and the uncreated was
presented from a Christological point of view in my earlier volume, *The
Mystery of the Trinity in the Theological Thought of Pope John Paul II*.[42]

It showed the many philosophical and theological difficulties one faced when what is beyond time and history becomes historical in the person of Christ. It all comes down to the question of how one can understand a cooperation between the infinite and the finite. The encyclical letter *Redemptoris Missio* (Mission of the Redeemer) relates the problem of that cooperation in general terms:

> No one, therefore, can enter into communion with God except through Christ, by the working of the Holy Spirit. Christ's one, universal mediation, far from being an obstacle on the journey toward God, is the way established by God himself, a fact of which Christ is fully aware. Although participated forms of mediation of different kinds and degrees are not excluded, they acquire meaning and value only from Christ's own mediation, and they cannot be understood as parallel or complementary to his.[43]

Applied to Mary, this concept is translated into her *mediation* and cooperation in the work of salvation. Just before Vatican II, the doctrine and terminology regarding Mary's mediation was a popular topic for discussion. As an indication of that theological debate, one need only consult the treatment given by Gabriele M. Roschini, founder of the Marianum in Rome.[44] John Paul II's encyclical sheds much light here.

In *Redemptoris Mater*, the mediation of Mary in relation to Christ's universal and unique mediation will be thoroughly analyzed in the chapter on Mary's maternal mediation.[45] The question of relationship between the uncreated and the created emerges again here in its Marian dimension: Mary's participation in the Redemption of humankind entangles itself in a paradoxical context in which Christ is the exclusive Redeemer. The mediation of Mary, understood in the context of her relationship with God, constitutes, therefore, one of the most difficult Marian problems because it shares with the Christological debates the question of *manner of redemption*, that is the relationship between humanity and divinity in accomplishing the work of salvation. It is not by chance that the question of Mary's mediation frequently emerges at this point in the life of the Church and becomes most relevant in Catholic theological circles.

Mary's mediation presents many paradoxical dimensions because it invites human reason to go beyond the limitations of history to explore the logic of interaction between a transcendental God who, by becoming man in history, uses historical people to fulfill His plan.[46] In the English edition of the *Osservatore Romano* of April 16, 1997, Pope John Paul II says:

> Moreover, when the Apostle Paul says: 'For we are God's fellow workers' (1 Cor 3:9), he maintains the real possibility for man to cooperate with God. The collaboration of believers, which obviously excludes any equality with Him, is expressed in the proclamation of the Gospel and in their personal contribution to its taking root in human hearts.

Monsignor Brunero Gherardini, an expert in the history and theology of Vatican II, rightly points out that, at the Second Vatican Council, the Protestant observers recognized the Catholic Church's position on Mary's participation in the work of Redemption. Luther's principle of *solus Christus* (only Christ), however, would seem to not allow any human collaboration in the work of a person's salvation, no matter how secondary and subordinate it might be.[47]

John Paul II's *Tertio Millennio Adveniente* recalls in general terms God's dependency on Mary for the fulfillment of His economy of salvation. When the angel proposed the initiative of God to Mary, she accepted in a way that enables the mystery to take place: "Never in human history did so much depend, as it did then, upon the consent of one human creature."[48] It will take in this present volume a whole section on Mary's mediation to clarify what the Pope meant by such a dependency.

With the historical dimension of God that was revealed in and through Jesus Christ, the question of Mary's mediation does not remain limited to a relationship between her and the divine. It becomes a relationship between her and the divine-human, that is the God who became man in her womb. This logic explains the reason behind the great interest Marian theologians have in shedding new light on the relationship of Mary with Jesus Christ. It is in the context of this relationship that the mediation of Mary should be explored since, in fact, the Marian qualifications receive their ultimate meaning in and through Christ. Her divine maternity, virginity, immunity from original and actual sin, bodily assumption into heaven, and faith, as well as her being an eschatological[49] image of the Church—all these dimensions influence the understanding of her mediation in differing ways and according to various patterns.

Since the Holy Father somehow refers to Mary on almost all public occasions, it becomes impossible to analyze every single Marian statement. On the other hand, even though the focus of our study is the encyclical *Redemptoris Mater*, other major references to Mary will be considered in relationship with this Marian document. Throughout his pontificate, Pope John Paul II returns again and again to the same concepts, but he analyzes them from many different points of view and in relation to many other theological disciplines. Considering his phenomenological method[50] of presenting materials, one should be careful in judging his thought to be too repetitious. Although it seems that the present work repeats the idea, a more careful reading is necessary to realize that it presents the thorough thinking of a pope who is investigating a single idea from many different points of view.

A comparative analysis of the terminology and content of *Redemptoris Mater* with all other documents will help to realize the historical development of the Pope's Marian thought between 1978 and 1999. His dynamic vision and constant search for a better and deeper understanding of the Mother of the Lord relies mainly on Scripture, Vatican II (*Lumen Gentium*, VIII), and the Fathers of the Church.

John Paul II's reference to the Fathers of the Church emphasizes Saint John Damascene and Saint Bernard of Clairvaux. Differing from Davide M. Montagna, who considered the Pope's use of the Fathers' tradition as rather partial and provisional,[51] I think that *Redemptoris Mater* frequently alludes subtly to the Fathers of the Church and analyzes their understanding of the Marian doctrine. Yet, one should keep in mind that this encyclical is a document of the magisterium and, therefore, cannot be limited to the teachings of the Fathers. Inspired by the lasting validity of their work, the encyclical should keep in touch with all of Scripture and with the later teachings of the magisterium as well. The Pope's main target is not a deep analysis of the Fathers of the Church, but exposition of the teaching of the Second Vatican Council. Hence, John Paul II quotes mostly those same Fathers referred to by *Lumen Gentium*, VIII. His choice of certain patristic traditions manifests a cautious approach, since he only refers to those texts that are without controversy in patristic Mariology.

Jean Galot rightly thinks that John Paul II is very interested in the historical development of the Church's Marian doctrine, a doctrine that referred so often to Scripture in the teaching of the Second Vatican Ecumenical Council.[52] The use of Scripture, according to Salvatore Meo, is not a hermeneutic (or an explanation) based on critical scriptural interpretation (exegesis) and linguistic analysis of individual sacred authors. Neither is it a noncritical reproposal of preconciliar theological interpretation. What is dealt with here is a faithful and accurate theological reflection inspired by the Church's interpretation of the Fathers and the Doctors and by the most secure exegetical and theological works of recent scholarship. This does not keep the sharp mind of the Pope from bringing new insights and originality to the methodology of his research. Without any claim of an exhausting presentation, the Holy Father's interpretation of scriptural sources goes one substantial step further than *Lumen Gentium*, VIII and constitutes a fresh doctrinal development in postconciliar Mariology.[53]

The Divine Maternity of Mary as the Fundamental Characteristic of Her Presence in God's Plan of Salvation

THE DIVINE MATERNITY[1] OF MARY AND THE MYSTERY OF THE FULLNESS OF TIME

POPE JOHN PAUL II's main Marian document, the encyclical *Redemptoris Mater* (Mother of the Redeemer) starts with the statement:

> The Mother of the Redeemer has a precise place in the plan of salvation, for "when the time had fully come, God sent forth his Son, born of woman, born under the law, to redeem those who were under the law, so that we might receive adoption as sons. And because you are sons, God has sent the Spirit of his Son into our hearts, crying, 'Abba! Father!'" (Gal 4:4–6).[2]

This was the opening statement of the sixth encyclical of Pope John Paul II, issued March 25, 1987, and of which the Pope says: "I have been thinking of it for a long time. I have pondered it at length in my heart."[3] It is of great importance because it coincides with the opening of Vatican II's Dogmatic Constitution on the Church.[4] We should realize that *Redemptoris Mater* is the expression of the Holy Father's Marian devotion and doctrine that came to maturity after a lifelong devotion to Mary. It is a document that must be viewed as an answer to the questions of the post–Vatican II Church (period after 1965).[5] John Paul himself witnesses to this fact in *Crossing the Threshold of Hope* by saying:

> This mature form of devotion to the Mother of God has stayed with me over the years, bearing fruit in the encyclicals *Redemptoris Mater* and *Mulieris Dignitatem*.[6]

The opening statement quoted above is the *leitmotiv* (or a constant reference) of the entire document because it reveals the Pope's approach to the question of Mary in *Redemptoris Mater* and has a strong influence on his reflections thereafter. It "connects with Vatican II and encounters the theme that interests him and therefore furnishes the leitmotiv for this encyclical: the fullness of time."[7]

The themes of the first statement of *Redemptoris Mater* are Redemption, divine motherhood, Mary's role in God's plan of salvation, and theology of time and history.

That Pope John Paul II emphasizes Mary's motherhood in its relation to Christ the Redeemer is evident from the title of the encyclical letter *Redemptoris Mater* as well as from its opening words. From them emerges his intention to shed light on the Mother-Son image that Mariologists have been elaborating since the Second Vatican Council.[8] Vatican II presented a picture of Mary in essential connection with Christ and the Church, not allowing her to be isolated from the divine mysteries. It is within the framework of this relationship with Christ and the Church that one should search for the Pope's authentic approach to Mary. But that relationship takes place in the historical event of her motherhood. Therefore, as Avery Dulles rightly states, "the key term that unifies the Pope's Mariology . . . is that of motherhood."[9] Luigi Sartori has already mentioned that Incarnation as an event is an eminent theme in *Redemptoris Mater*, a fact that puts more emphasis on the Annunciation than on its implications in the paschal mystery.[10] Mary has a precise place in the economy of salvation because she was destined from the beginning to become the Mother of the Son of God who was born of her in the fullness of time.[11]

In parallel terms John Paul II, in order to express the manner of the Mother-Son relationship, says in *Redemptionis Donum* (The Gift of Redemption), 17: "For she was called by God to the most perfect communion with His Son."[12] *Redemptionis Donum*, 17, shed light on the pneumatological aspect of the Incarnation, yet emphasizing Mary's spousal love that conditions the realization of her motherhood. Saint Augustine, who said that Mary conceived in her mind before conceiving in her womb, is definitely at the basis of the Pope's assertion: "Her spousal love reached its height in the divine Motherhood through the power of the Holy Spirit."[13] Saint Augustine's influence is even more clear in John Paul II's apostolic exhortation *Pastores Dabo Vobis* (I Will Give You Shepherds):

> Mary became both the servant and the disciple of the Word to the point of conceiving, in her heart and in her flesh, the Word made man, so as to give him to mankind.[14]

In *Redemptoris Mater*, 1, the Pope comments on the words of Saint Paul in Gal 4:4: "When the time had fully come, God sent forth his Son, born of woman," rather than on the Annunciation account in Luke:

> For they [the words of the Apostle Paul in Gal 4:4–6] are words which celebrate together the love of the Father, the mission of the Son, the gift of the Spirit, the role of the woman from whom the Redeemer was born, and our divine filiation, in the mystery of the "fullness of time."[15]

The Trinitarian dimension of the *woman's* role in the mystery of the fullness of time will constantly be a point of reference throughout the pontificate of John Paul II.[16] Note that 2 Cor 13:13 ("The grace of our Lord Jesus Christ and the love of God and the fellowship of the Holy Spirit") the inspiration for the three Trinitarian encyclicals— *Redemptor Hominis* (Redeemer of Man), *Dives in Misericordia* (Rich in Mercy), *Dominum and Vivificantem* (Lord and Giver of Life)— assumes in *Redemptoris Mater* a Marian dimension.

The Christological approach to Mary shown in the relationship Mother-Son takes on a new dimension in the context of Redemption. The Mother is the Mother of the Son, the Redeemer. No one can deny that Redemption, from a Marian point of view, is central in the theology of Pope John Paul II.[17] That the Mother has a precise place in the plan of salvation indicates a strictly soteriological[18] function of Mary.

The Pope alludes to that function in the sentences that follow the opening statement of *Redemptoris Mater*. He refers to the Second Vatican Council that had already treated the Blessed Virgin Mary, Mother of God, in the mystery of Christ and the Church.[19] Following in the footsteps of that Council, the Pope asserts:

> I too wish to begin my reflection on the role of Mary in the mystery of Christ and on her active and exemplary presence in the life of the Church.[20]

For the Pope, "nobody else can bring us as Mary can into the divine and human dimension of this mystery [mystery of Redemption]. Nobody has been brought into it by God Himself as Mary has."[21] Does not the opening statement relate the divine motherhood of Mary to the dimension of the mystery that was revealed in the fullness of time? Mary, as Mother of the Redeemer, plays a role in the mystery of Christ and the Church and, therefore, in God's plan of Redemption. The woman spoken of by Saint Paul in Gal 4:4 is brought into contact with the Son precisely in the soteriological context of generation in which he is the Son-Redeemer born of a Woman-Mother. He is the "Redeemer" in the theological sense of John 3:16 and the "Son" in the sense of Saint John's 1:14.[22] Galatians 4:4 is a common denominator for both because it presents the patterns of Christ's Incarnation from a woman, yet with orientation to a soteriological finality. In both encyclicals, *Redemptor Hominis* and *Redemptoris Mater*, John 1:14 and John 3:16 play a pivotal role in John Paul II's theology of Incarnation and Redemption.[23] He prefers John 1:14 to formulate his concept of Incarnation and John 3:16 to describe God's redeeming activity in and through Jesus Christ. Such remarkable consistency in the theology of Pope John Paul is clear to those who follow carefully the historical development of his thought.

Galatians 4:4 is a bridge between Incarnation and Redemption because the "fullness of time" (*pleroma tou chronou*) indicates not only the conclusion of a chronological process, in which the Son of God enters the world, but also points to the coming to maturity and the fulfillment of an expectation in the sense that Christ fulfills the divine promise of salvation. In John Paul's opinion, the time references here in the words of Saint Paul confirm both the entrance of the divine in history and its theological purpose.[24] This is why the encyclical *Redemptoris Mater* is sprinkled with terminology such as "event," a fact that emphasizes the presence of the divine in history in the fullness of time.[25] This double finality of the fullness of time explains the words of the Pope that follow the opening statement of *Redemptoris Mater*:

> This "fullness" indicates the moment fixed from all eternity when the Father sent his Son "that whoever believes in him should not perish but have eternal life" (Jn 3:16). It denotes the blessed moment when the Word that "was with God . . . became flesh and dwelt among us" (Jn 1:14), and made himself our brother.[26]

After connecting John 1:14 with John 3:16 through Gal 4:4, John Paul II uses Gal 4:4 as the moment marked for the Holy Spirit to overshadow the Virgin of Nazareth to accomplish Incarnation. The time of the Incarnation as reported in Luke's Annunciation coincides with the fullness of time in Saint Paul. There is no question that his approach to sacred Scripture follows the patterns of the *sensus plenior*[27] that permits identifying, from an exegetical[28] point of view, the "fullness of time" of Galatians with the Incarnation as reported in the Annunciation in Luke.[29] Both accounts have a Trinitarian dimension; both mark a decisive moment in the history of humanity; and both open the new economy of salvation through the Incarnation of the Son in the womb of a Woman-Mother when the fullness of time had finally come.

Pope John Paul II reaches out to philosophy when commenting on Gal 4:4. He sees in the expression *fullness of time* a summary of the theological and philosophical questions of the relationship between time and eternity. Still in *Redemptoris Mater*, 1, he says:

> This "fullness" marks the moment when, with the entrance of the eternal into time, time itself is redeemed, and being filled with the mystery of Christ becomes definitively "salvation time."[30]

It seems that John Paul reflects on a common practice among Jewish apocalypticists that divides human history into periods. That division points to a moment of fulfillment when time arrives at a certain unique completeness. With the revelation of the mystery of Christ, a theology that John Paul implicitly borrows from the Letter to the Ephesians (1:1–14), human time becomes time of salvation because the eternal comes to live in time. This present human period is essentially different from all prior periods because, although God is present in all of them, His presence now occurs in the dimension of space, time, and history. Therefore, with the Incarnation, time is transformed into salvation time.

In *Redemptoris Mater*, "fullness of time," in the perspective of the entrance of the divine into history, does not fall into a simplistic opposition between the "before" and the "after." It is not reduced to a process of time where everything before the "fullness of time" is fall, sin, and death. The period preceding the Incarnation was not just death and darkness; it was also a time of preparation for the moment of the Incarnation and, in that sense, it is, with the culmination of the Incarnation, oriented toward eschatology.[31] "Fullness of time" becomes the realization of expectation that is oriented toward eschatology. This understanding of "fullness of time" permits the Pope to consider the previous period as not exclusively negative, to look at the Incarnation as the fulfillment of expectation, and to orient the whole process toward its eschatological dimension. With such an approach, I have to disagree with the theologian Jean-Nöel Aletti, who thought that the "fullness of time" in the encyclical *Redemptoris Mater* should not refer to an expectation.[32] Even if Gal 4:4 is a subject of continued discussion in contemporary exegesis,[33] this does not mean that the Pope will adopt all of the current exegetical trends.[34] He is very careful to accept only those theories that stand in conformity with the interpretation of the Church's tradition.

Philosophy of time in its Marian dimension is also present in John Paul II's *Reconciliatio et Paenitentia* (Reconciliation and Penance). Here, Mary's consent at the Annunciation constitutes the bridge between Incarnation and Redemption and orients time to its salvific dimension. *Reconciliatio et Paenitentia* shows in general terms the reconciliation between God and humanity as having a Marian dimension, precisely because it started with Mary's positive answer to God's proposal. John Paul trusts the hands of Mary, "whose fiat[35] marked the beginning of that 'fullness of time' in which Christ accomplished the reconciliation of humanity with God."[36]

From still another point of view, the Holy Father's *Christifideles Laici* (The Lay Members of Christ's Faithful People) brought into the picture the three major dimensions of God's intervention in history. "Fullness of time" indicates the link between creation, Incarnation, and their fulfillment in the mystery of Redemption. In reference to the equality of each and every person in the eyes of God, the Pope states here that God's plan, from the very beginning of creation:

> . . . has been indelibly imprinted in the very being of the human person—men and women—and therefore in the make-up, meaning, and deepest workings of the individual.[37]

That plan was unfolded in history as humanity discovered the face of God through Divine Revelation. Such a process would culminate in the "fullness of time" when history welcomed into its bosom the highest expression of God's presence in the world, the Incarnation. Oriented to its fullest expression in the Redemption (Christ's death and resurrection), Incarnation, as the event that took place in the "fullness of time," will extend throughout history. Time became salvation time with the Incarnation and will always be so until the end of history:

> This most wise and loving plan (of God) must be explored to discover all its richness of content—a richness that "from the beginning" came to be progressively manifested and realized in the whole history of salvation, and was brought to completion in "the fullness of time," when "God sent his Son, born of a woman" (Gal 4:4). That "fullness" continues in history . . . [38]

The theological interpretation of the Pauline "fullness of time" allows the Pope to focus on the *Marian dimension of the year 2000*. The bimillennial jubilee of the birth of Jesus Christ "at the same time directs our gaze toward his Mother."[39] The Church has been aware that "Mary appeared on the horizon of salvation history before Christ."[40] The supernatural character of God's presence through His Incarnation when the "fullness of time" had come, was preceded with the supernatural character of Mary's Immaculate Conception. Time started to become salvation time before the historical "fullness of time" was reached because the "fullness of time" has somewhat a Marian dimension. She who was predestined to become the Mother already existed on earth when the "fullness of time" came. This historical dimension of Mary's Immaculate

Conception that preceded the coming of the Savior places her appearance on the horizon of salvation as preceding Christ in the history of the human race.[41] John Paul refers to Saint John Damascene's *Homilia in Dormitionem* (Homily on the Dormition of Mary) and Pope Pius IX's *Ineffabilis Deus* (The Ineffable God)[42] in order to describe that Mary's hidden and discrete presence in the midst of Israel before the Incarnation associates her "with the plan of salvation embracing the whole history of humanity."[43] This historical precedence has always been celebrated by the Church when, in the liturgy of Advent, the Church salutes Mary as "the one who in the 'night' of the Advent expectation began to shine like a true 'morning star' (*stella matutina*)."[44] As the Church turned her gaze upon the year 2000 of the birth of Christ, the Church could not, from the perspective of the history of salvation, ignore the presence and the birthday of the one who, as the Mother, preceded the Son on earth before the "fullness of time" came:

> With good reason, then, at the end of this millennium, we Christians who know that the providential plan of the Most Holy Trinity is the central reality of revelation and of faith feel the need to emphasize the unique presence of the Mother of Christ in history, especially during these last years leading up to the year 2000.[45]

In *Redemptoris Mater*, 3, one should not overlook the theology of history that Pope John Paul II refers to when describing Mary's chronological precedence of Christ in the history of salvation. The emphasis is on the Immaculate Conception and the "unique presence of the Mother of Christ in history." The Pope looks at the presence of Mary in history before and after the Incarnation as the pattern of shaping the manner of her presence in the history of the Church. If Christ's Incarnation happened in the historical moment of the "fullness of time," this fullness came when God sent His Son born of a woman. That mutual historical connection between the Mother and the Son on the historical horizon of salvation becomes a mutual connection also in the history of the Church. The Church has always looked at the event of Christ through the eyes of Mary and at the event of Mary through the eyes of Christ. A mutual interdependence is a healthy approach to avoid a Gnosticism that has always been trying to uproot the presence of the divine according to human categories, and to depreciate the historical dimension of Mary's appearance on the horizon of salvation preceding the Incarnation of Christ.[46] The historical interdependence between Mother and Son should be dogmatized as the history of the Church proceeds in its consciousness of the role and identity of Mary in the mystery of Christ and the Church.

THE MOTHER-SON RELATIONSHIP:
MARY MOTHER OF GOD IN THE MYSTERY OF CHRIST

In *Redemptoris Mater*, 4, John Paul shows that the Church understands its identity better when *she looks at Jesus through Mary and at Mary through Jesus*.[47] In this sense, Mary and Jesus are both indissolubly joined in the Mother-Son relationship, as it was already mentioned in *Redemptoris Mater*, 1. This idea becomes a pattern in the Pope's thinking because the Mother-Son relationship is an axiom that offers a balanced approach to Marian theology.

Redemptoris Mater, 4 quotes one of the Pope's favorite texts from *Gaudium et Spes*, 22: "Only in the mystery of the Incarnate Word does the mystery of man take on light."[48] This principle:

> . . . must be applied in a very particular way to that exceptional "daughter of the human race," that extraordinary 'woman' who became the Mother of Christ.[49]

The Pauline "Woman" (Gal 4:4) manifests the Pope's preference in biblical terminology to express Mary's belonging to the human family. Her being "extraordinary" emphasizes her essential difference from all other human beings because of her being the Immaculate Conception, a character that the Pope has already presented to us at the very opening of *Redemptoris Mater*. It is her Immaculate Conception that makes her an "extraordinary woman."[50]

One draws several consequences from the principle by which the mystery of Mary is understood in the light of the mystery of Christ. In the opinion of Pope John Paul II, the mystery of Christ enlightens the mystery of every man but in a very special way that of Mary because she fully enjoyed what God has intended humanity to enjoy from the beginning of creation. She shares with human beings the constitutive elements of their nature except the foreign element of sin, which in itself does not originally belong to those constitutive elements. If the mystery of Christ is the criterion for understanding the whole mystery of man, the confusion in understanding the mystery of man does not result from the Christological guidelines but from sin. If one intends to understand man, one should look at Christ. But the possible criteria offered by Christ to understand man are present and fulfilled in Mary. Therefore, even though "only in the mystery of Christ is her mystery fully made clear," "this principle must be applied in a very particular way" to this exceptional and extraordinary woman, Mary.[51]

Christ's Incarnation makes clearer the mystery of the Mother of the Incarnate Word. John Paul attests that the Church has always looked at the mystery of the Incarnation of God's Word as the key to penetrate the mystery of His Mother:[52]

> Thus, through the mystery of Christ, on the horizon of the Church's faith there shines in its fullness the mystery of his Mother.[53]

In other words, the mystery of Mary is understood in the light of the mystery of Christ primarily and especially in the context of his Incarnation. Within that context, however, it was Mary's divine motherhood that was being fulfilled. It is in the event of Incarnation, then, that the Mother of Jesus gets from the Incarnate Word the possibility of being understood in the fullness of her mystery. Therefore, such an interdependence implies that the Pope considers the divine motherhood of Mary as the fundamental characteristic in Mariology as far as the Mother-Son relationship is concerned. Incarnation and divine motherhood become two mysteries intimately interconnected. In that sense, the dogma of the Council of Ephesus (431 A.D.) concerning Mary as *Theotokos* (Mother of God) confirms John Paul's interpretation of *Gaudium et Spes*' theology of Incarnation:

> In turn, the dogma of the divine motherhood of Mary was for the Council of Ephesus and is for the Church like a seal upon the dogma of the Incarnation, in which the Word truly assumes human nature into the unity of his person, without canceling out that nature.[54]

The Mother-Son relationship reaches its fullest meaning when presented in a Trinitarian context, especially since the Incarnation initially occurred when the power of the Most High overshadowed Mary and the Holy Spirit came upon her. This original picture reported by Saint Luke the Evangelist at the Annunciation will echo through all the writings of Pope John Paul II whenever the Mother is put into relation with the Incarnate Word.[55]

Dominum et Vivificantem, 51 is a good example of placing Mary's motherhood in the Trinitarian framework. Speaking of the Holy Spirit as the Uncreated Person-Gift, the Pope presents Him as the agent of God's Self-offering to the world.[56] The Spirit is the Divine Person who ensures God's contact with creation and, therefore, the beginning of each economy of salvation. As for Mary's motherhood at the dawn of the New Testament, the Holy Spirit came down to perform the miracle of the Incarnation:

> The Holy Spirit, who with his power overshadowed the virginal body of Mary, bringing about in her the beginning of her divine motherhood, at the same time made her heart perfectly obedient to that self-communication of God which surpasses every human idea and faculty.[57]

In the tradition of the Catholic Church, the text of Luke 1:35 (*Spiritus Sanctus superveniet in te*—"the Holy Spirit will overshadow you") has a long history. From the Middle Ages theologians attributed to the Holy Spirit the formation of the body of Jesus in the womb of Mary but without considering it as a "mission." The concept of "mission" was reserved for the coming of the Holy Spirit on Jesus in baptism or on the apostles at Pentecost. The Second Vatican Council, however, in the Decree on the Church's Missionary Activity (*Ad Gentes*), 4, specifically identified the coming of the Holy Spirit on Mary as a personal mission. In *Redemptoris Mater*, Pope John Paul II similarly shed light on the person–to–person relationship between Mary and the Holy Spirit, as well as the Trinitarian dimension of the Annunciation that enabled Mary to virginally conceive Christ.[58]

Note that John Paul II insists on the expression "divine maternity" (*maternitas divina*) in *Redemptoris Mater*, 4 to designate the mystery of the Mother of God (*Theotokos*). The concept of "divine maternity" appeared for the first time in the writings of the Dominican Italian priest Nazarius at the beginning of the seventeenth century. Whereas Saint Bonaventure constantly used *Mater Dei* (Mother of God), "divine maternity" became a very habitual term in Nazarius's theology. In his commentary on Saint Thomas's *Summa Theologiae*, he sees that in the Virgin Mary the dignity of the fullness of grace is greater than divine maternity in the absolute sense of the word (*absolute et simpliciter*), whereas, in the relative sense, divine maternity is greater than the fullness of grace.[59] Although Saint Thomas Aquinas did not explicitly use the expression "divine maternity," he nonetheless made a clear distinction between *Mother of Christ*, which affirms the human-yet-miraculous generation of Christ by Mary, and *Mother of God,* which immediately connects the Mother with the Son of God who assumed a full and authentic humanity in her womb, making her really and truly Mother of God, *Theotokos.*[60] This distinction in Saint Thomas's theology is of extreme importance because it guards the faith of the Church centered on the miracle of the Incarnation. Mary did not generate a man who was made temple by the Word of God, as affirms Gabriel Biel, a nominalist and disciple of Occam. Biel thought that if the Son of God ceases to assume the man (*homo assumptus*) generated by the Virgin, that man becomes immediately the human Son of Mary. Therefore, as Biel's logic shows, only a human maternity is possible in Mary.[61] In the theology of Nazarius, however, Mary has generated God Himself in His human nature. The relationship of generation reaches persons. There a real, authentic, and true relationship exists between the person of Mary as Mother and the person of the Word as God, even though she generated Him only in His human nature. I would go back even to the Cappadocian Fathers who, after the Council of Nicea (325 A.D.), affirmed such a maternity in Mary without explicitly referring to the expression "divine maternity."[62] Rome confirmed the term "divine maternity" when proclaiming Saint Cyril of Alexandria Doctor of the Church in the seventeenth century. The French school has adopted the theology behind this term.[63]

The Second Vatican Council used the term "divine maternity" one time in *Lumen Gentium,* 63: "Beata autem Virgo *divinae maternitatis* dono et munere, quo cum Filio Redemptore unitur (By reason of the gift and role of her divine motherhood . . .)" and Pope John Paul II used it ten times in *Redemptoris Mater*.[64] Both the Council and the Pope intended to emphasize the parallel not only between the divine and the human generation of Christ from the Father and Mary respectively but also the divine mission of the Holy Spirit in the intra-Trinitarian life of God as reflected in his temporal mission in the Annunciation. In the same way in which the mission or the procession into time of the Son reveals his eternal generation from the Father, the mission or the procession into time of the Holy Spirit reveals the eternal conception of the divine Son (*in sinu Patris*) of the Holy Spirit. The Father generates only the Son and conceives Him of the Holy Spirit, in eternity as well as in time. Since the Second Vatican Council, then, one can say that the Son, divinely conceived of the Spirit (*in sinu Patris*), is humanly conceived of the same Spirit in Mary. This is exactly the reason behind the Council's and the Pope's insistence on the mission of the Holy Spirit not only in the baptism of Christ or at Pentecost, but also in the Annunciation. For the theologian Manteau-Bonamy, such a theology is already present in Saint Thomas Aquinas.[65]

MARY, THE NEW EVE

Ephesians 1:3 reads: "Blessed be the God and Father of our Lord Jesus Christ, who has blessed us in Christ with every spiritual blessing in the heavenly places . . ." Pope John Paul II's comment on Eph 1:3 in *Redemptoris Mater*, 7 shows that he looks at God's plan of salvation as an organic unity. Creation and salvation are two phases of the same plan and both are oriented toward the same goal, that is, sharing in God's eternal life. If God is the exclusive giver of life who invites all to share His life through creation, God is also the exclusive giver of salvation who intends the Redemption of all:

> Just as all are included in the creative work of God 'in the beginning,' so all are eternally included in the divine plan of salvation, which is to be completely revealed, in the 'fullness of time,' with the final coming of Christ.[66]

According to the same Letter to the Ephesians as interpreted by John Paul II, the divine plan of salvation, which is eternal, is also necessarily related to Christ. It is Christological in the sense that it is "eternally linked to Christ."[67] Since that plan is universal, it includes everyone:

> . . . but it reserves a special place for the 'woman' who is the Mother of him to whom the Father has entrusted the work of salvation.[68]

Only with the historical fulfillment of God's plan in Mary will one realize what "special place" meant for Mary and for the Church.

Mary is included in the plan of salvation as a human being and, at the same time, as the Mother of the Redeemer. These two aspects enable the Pope to appreciate an ancient dimension of Mariology in the tradition of the Church, namely the theme of the *New Eve*.[69] In the opinion of the theologian Ugo Vanni, the Pope does not delve into heavy hermeneutical (biblical interpretation) discussions and other recent interpretations when he uses the text of Gen 3:15 ("I will put enmity between you and the woman, and between your seed and her seed; he shall bruise your head, and you shall bruise his heel"). The reason behind such an approach lies in the difficulty of the questions Gen 3:15 raises in contemporary exegesis.[70]

Ugo Vanni thinks that the Pope was very cautious in using the figure of "woman" for Eve as it appears in Gen 3:15. That text was referred to by quoting Vatican II's *Lumen Gentium* (Dogmatic Constitution on the Church), a document that spoke of "prophetical foreshadowing" (*prophetice adumbratur*). Eve prophetically foreshadows Mary, the *New Eve*. Such a way of reference leaves the door open to various biblical interpretations (or hermeneutics). The literal, the *sensus plenior*, and the typological (Mary as type of Eve) are all possible.[71] The texts of Gen 3:15 and Rev 12:1 ("The woman clothed with the sun who is about to give birth to her descendant"), as used in *Redemptoris Mater*, 4, represent an articulated interpretation. The "descendant of the woman" will bring victory to a humanity infected by original sin. The promise of victory is called "protogospel" and is unfolded in history through a series of battles; a final victory is envisioned by the Book of Revelation 12:1. Both texts of Genesis and Revelation occur in the context of encounter between good and evil within the history of humanity. It is not a dialectical conflict (or a conflict without result) because it is dynamically animated by the perspective of an eschatological victory over evil promised by God Himself. Mary stands at the center of such a conflict as it unfolds in human history on earth.[72]

While Mary stands at the center of the enmity between the serpent and humanity, Pope John Paul II does not attribute to Mary the quality of being the direct protagonist of the victory. Even with her position at the center until the final victory, it is the Descendant of Mary who is the direct agent of the victory. The Pope's insistence on seeing the woman at the center does not eliminate her dependence on the action of her Descendant. That the "descendant" of Mary is Christ is an obvious reality in *Redemptoris Mater*. Such an approach, in Ugo Vanni's opinion, places the Pope, in relationship to the history of exegesis, somewhere between the Hebrew text of Gen 3:15 and its Greek translation in the LXX.[73] This is Vanni's assessment, even though John Paul definitely bases his analysis of Gen 3:15 on the original Hebrew text and not on the LXX.

It is necessary to keep in mind that *Redemptoris Mater* did not assume a "naturalistic" position in regard to the enmity between man and the serpent. In fact, such a position reduces the concept of enmity to a result of divine malediction (God's sentence as a result of Adam's and Eve's sin).[74] Nor can the enmity be merely an ethical question, because the battle between the human and the serpent takes place with the serpent as the symbol of evil.[75] The only reasonable approach is from a position that is open to the salvific dimension of the battle.[76] Only in this last case can the second narration of creation be understood in connection with the first account because it explains this account and goes beyond the understanding that the various elements of the first account of creation have brought about, namely a series of malediction. It is only then that the exegesis of the text does not get lost in analyzing particular elements without a sense of the unity of sacred Scripture.[77]

In *Redemptoris Mater*, 7, the emphasis is placed not only on the centrality of Mary's identity as Mother of the Redeemer but also on her human genealogy as a "daughter of the human race."[78] Mary cannot be the New Eve if she is not the descendant of Eve, and she cannot be "Eve" if she is not the offspring of a human being. In this context she is

included in the plan of salvation like every human being, and the
Thomistic theory of universal salvation accomplished by Christ should
be applied to Mary even if in an eminent manner.

Mary's genuine humanity as well as her divine maternity are equally
important in God's plan of salvation. As the Mother of Him "to whom
the Father has entrusted the work of salvation,"[79] Mary enjoys a special
place in that plan. Notice that John Paul never tires of underlining the
divine maternity of Mary as a major criterion for her exemplary and
active presence in the Church. Even her passive presence of being
included in the eternal plan of God draws its constitutive elements from
her being Mother of Christ.

In the opinion of John Paul II, as shown in *Redemptoris Mater*,
37, the Church has always meditated on the words of the *Magnificat* and
seen in them the antithesis of Eve's situation. In the *Magnificat*, one
realizes that the "sin of the beginning" is destroyed and that there is no
room for "little faith" or disbelief in God:

> In contrast with the "suspicion" which the "father of lies" sowed in
> the heart of Eve the first woman, Mary, whom tradition is wont to
> call the "new Eve" and the true "Mother of the living," boldly pro-
> claims the undimmed truth about God: the holy and almighty God,
> who from the beginning is the source of all gifts, he who "has done
> great things" in her, as well as in the whole universe.[80]

In *Redemptoris Mater*, 37, the Eve/Mary parallel reveals in the
theology of Pope John Paul II a remarkable insight. Jesus applied the
title "father of lies" to Satan in the Gospel of Saint John. The Pope
transfers that qualification to Satan's relationship with Eve as it appears in
the Book of Genesis. At the very beginning of human history, Satan lied
to Eve and sowed suspicion in her heart against God. He twisted the
truth about God and creation, and he convinced Eve about that which is
only apparently good. From the very beginning, therefore, Satan has
been lying, and his lies led Eve to disbelief in the word uttered by God
to her and to Adam. Her "little faith" becomes a mark on human history
forever.

In the thought of John Paul, not only is Eve the first woman, but
in the new economy of salvation, Mary is also the first woman because
she is the first to believe fully. In the same way that Eve introduced a

mark on human history because of the sin of disbelief, Mary introduced into that same history a mark of faith because of the virtue of fully believing. The words of Elizabeth, "blessed is she who believed," will mark the beginning of a new relationship between God and humanity and, therefore, a New Covenant. In that sense, Mary is also the first woman because she is the "*New* Eve," and because she is the *true* "Mother of the living."[81] A new beginning of the relationship between God and humanity through Mary is a true beginning. Because it is a beginning, however, Mary is also an "Eve," or the first woman. Since the beginning with Mary is utterly different from the beginning with Eve, it is a new beginning. Because it is a new beginning, Mary is a "new" Eve. The expression "New Eve" is not limited to the chronological process in which Mary replaces Eve. It is extended to the ontological[82] reality of Mary's identity and her role in the economy of salvation. In that salvific context, one can truly speak of *the mystery of the Mother.* The Jesuit Ugo Vanni rightly states that, as far as the parallel Eve/Mary is concerned, *Redemptoris Mater,* 37 presents Mary as antithesis of Eve not only from a functional point of view but also in her personal profile.[83]

Since Mary is called the true "Mother of the living"[84] by John Paul II, does this make Eve not a true mother of the living? The conversation between God and Eve at the beginning of creation ended with the designation of Eve as "mother of the living." Yet, with the suspicion that was sowed in the heart of Eve by the "father of lies," that title receives a mere physical rather than spiritual connotation. Since human beings, even after the Fall, are descendants of Eve, Eve must be called "mother of the living." However, in the creational context, Eve has betrayed the truth about God and humankind through her sin of disbelief and, therefore, lost her chance to be what God intended her to be from the beginning, that is the *true* "mother of the living." When Mary is said to be the *true* "Mother of the living," Eve does not become a *false* "mother of the living," but somehow Eve's spiritual role of motherhood was stifled, whereas Mary "boldly proclaims the undimmed truth about God."[85]

Saint Epiphanius, to whom Pope John Paul II refers when calling Mary "Mother of the living," is not the only Father of the Church who relates that term. Saint Gregory of Nyssa (fourth century) has also described Mary as "Mother of life." With the help of Isa 66:7 ("Before being in labor she has given birth. Before the birth pangs came, she has been delivered of a child") and Gen 3:16 ("To the woman he said: 'I shall give you intense pain in childbearing, you will give birth to your children in pain'"), Saint Gregory of Nyssa takes up the Eve/Mary parallel originally introduced by Saint Justin and Saint Irenaeus, in order to allegorically explain verse 5:10 of the Canticle of Canticles ("My love is fresh and ruddy, to be known among ten thousand").[86] The Eve/Mary analogy demands "that the Mother of Life begin pregnancy with joy and finishes childbearing through joy."[87] The Pope uses the Eve/Mary parallel in this context in a way similar to Saint Gregory of Nyssa.

At the end of the encyclical *Evangelium Vitae*, John Paul points to Mary's role as Mother of life. In the context of the moral debate concerning human life, Mary is seen as "the most closely and personally associated with the Gospel of life."[88] That privilege results from the event of the Annunciation in which the first one "who accepted 'life' in the name of all and for the sake of all was Mary, the Virgin Mother."[89] The concept of motherhood itself involves life and, in the case of Christ, the human life that Mary gave Him at the Incarnation. That very life that Christ intended to give to humanity in abundance started to exist in its human dimension in the womb of Mary. Her divine maternity becomes the point of departure for a long chain of lives mysteriously born into Christ, the life of the world, according to God's plan. Motherhood implies generation and:

> . . . Mary's consent at the Annunciation and her motherhood stand
> at the very beginning of the mystery of life which Christ came to
> bestow on humanity (cf. Jn 10:10).[90]

In the context of her maternity, where Mary lived her motherhood in its fullest human and historical sense, Mary protected the life of Christ who became the Redeemer of humanity. Thus the mystery of Christ's life itself contains the mystery of Redemption of humanity. Mary, on her part, cooperated fully to play her role as Mother according to the natural laws of generation and motherhood. Mary did not generate Christ, the Life, according to His divinity. She gave birth to Him Who is the Life itself, according to his humanity. Therefore, as soon as He was born of her, Christ was able, in His humanity, to bestow the divine Life on every human person. Mary becomes the Mother of Life itself, even though that Life was expressed humanly through the Incarnation. By generating the Life that gives life to humanity, Mary cooperates in the rebirth of all men and women. In her relationship with Life, Mary, too, is the spiritual Mother of humankind. In that sense the Pope refers to Blessed Guerric of Igny saying:

> Through her acceptance and loving care for the life of the Incarnate Word, human life has been rescued from condemnation to final and eternal death. For this reason, Mary, like the Church of which she is the type, is a Mother of all who are reborn to life. She is in fact the Mother of the Life by which everyone lives, and when she brought it forth from herself she in some way brought to rebirth all those who were to live by that life.[91]

In drawing a parallel between Mary and Eve, the theological question of *predestination*[92] emerges. In *Redemptoris Mater*, 7, the reference to Saint John Damascene and the Second Vatican Council concerning the predestination of Mary is an excellent choice on the part of the Holy Father. Damascene says:

> For it is she who, chosen from the ancient generations, by virtue of the predestination and benevolence of the God and Father who generated you (the Word of God) outside time without coming out of himself or suffering change, it is she who gave you birth, nourished of her flesh, in the last time.[93]

Along the same line of thought, the Vatican Council states:

> She is prophetically foreshadowed in that promise made to our first parents after their fall into sin . . . Likewise she is the Virgin who is to conceive and bear a son, whose name will be called Emmanuel.[94]

Predestination is a very complicated problem as it was demonstrated in my previous study on the Trinitarian thought of Pope John Paul II.[95] The reference to Mary's predestination in *Redemptoris Mater*, 7, footnote 19, does not imply a destruction of Mary's will and personal choice in cooperating with God's plan of salvation. Rather, it points to Mary's inclusion in that plan as Mother of the Redeemer, even if that plan still depends on the will of Mary in that specific historic moment when she accepted becoming the Mother of the Redeemer. God's plan without historical dimension loses all its meaning, because such a plan is fulfilled in the unfolding of human history. The principle of the divine's real entrance into history should always be applied to Mary in her historical relationship with her Son in the Incarnation.[96]

The historical dimension of God's relationship with Mary is a strong weapon against an erroneous understanding of a predestination that would eliminate her freedom as a human person in determining her role and identity in God's plan of salvation. On this point John Paul states:

> This truth is already revealed in the words of the Archangel Gabriel, but its full significance will gradually become clearer and more evident as Mary follows her Son in the pilgrimage of faith.[97]

As God's plan is revealed in the unfolding of history, Mary had to use her will and freedom in order to "follow" and accomplish that plan. It is in that same sense also, even though in different context, that Pope John Paul declares in his recent encyclical letter *Fides et Ratio* (On the Relationship between Faith and Reason):

> The truth of Christian Revelation, found in Jesus of Nazareth, enables all men and women to embrace the "mystery" of their own life. As absolute truth, it summons human beings to be open to the transcendent, whilst respecting both their autonomy as creatures and their freedom. At this point the relationship between freedom and truth is complete, and we understand the full meaning of the Lord's words: "You will know the truth, and the truth will make you free" (Jn 8:32).[98]

Thus, the same line of thought as in *Fides et Ratio, Redemptoris Custos* (The Custodian of the Redeemer), 8, states: "Mary is the Lord's humble servant, prepared from eternity for the task of being the Mother of God."

Being open to the Transcendent with respect to an authentic autonomy as well as to freedom is what constitutes for John Paul the philosophical and theological criteria for eliminating predestination in the relationship between the divine and the human. One understands now why the Second Vatican Council, quoted in *Redemptoris Mater*, 7, refers to Mary as the one who is "prophetically foreshadowed" and the one "who is to conceive and bear a son."[99] That foreshadowing respects the sovereignty of God in establishing the plan of salvation and, at the same time, contains an invitation to Mary, as a human being, to be open to the Transcendent and to a potential cooperation in His plan. This is the only way one can accept a foreshadowing of Mary in the Old Testament without falling into the error of predestination. Therefore, John Paul II concludes *Redemptoris Mater*, 7 with the following words:

> In this way the Old Testament prepares that "fullness of time" when God "sent forth his Son, born of a woman . . . so that we might receive adoption as sons." The coming into the world of the Son of God is an event recorded in the first chapters of the Gospels according to Luke and Matthew.[100]

DIVINE MATERNITY AND MOTHERHOOD IN THE ORDER OF GRACE

Redemptoris Mater, 20 analyses Mary's motherhood in relationship to her faith. The words of an unknown woman addressed to Jesus about His Mother are reported by the Evangelist Luke: "Blessed is the womb that bore you, and the breasts that you sucked!" (11:27).[101] Mary, historically speaking, is not described by Luke to have accompanied Jesus in His public ministry. That woman, who apparently did not know Mary personally, praised her "as Jesus' Mother according to the flesh" and "in a way brought Mary out of her hiddenness."[102]

When describing John Paul II's usage of Scripture from the infancy narratives, Richard J. Taylor thought that *Redemptoris Mater* "deals with Scriptures more for their theological and devotional meanings than for express historical purposes." Taylor gives the example of Mary's presence in the messianic mission and thinks that the Pope's assertion, according to which Mary did not accompany Jesus in that mission, is more devotional than historical. For Taylor, in the Gospel of John, Mary did go with Jesus and the disciples to Caparnaum after the marriage feast of Cana. Taylor's logic is based on the conviction that the Pope "wants us to think of Our Lady's hidden life in Nazareth; this is devotional."[103]

I have to disagree with Taylor because the Pope is analyzing the comments of Luke, not John. There is no doubt that John Paul II often refers to the *sensus plenior* to analyze his idea from an exegetical point of view. Even though the *sensus plenior* takes all of Scripture as one inspired word of God and considers all the inspired texts as connected and interwoven, John Paul II respects the report of Luke on the hidden life of Mary at Nazareth. In Luke, the unknown woman who praised Mary did not recognize her specifically because of her connection with Christ's messianic activity. On the other hand, the description of John Paul is surely based on historicity and personalism, a fact that will be thoroughly analyzed in the chapter on Mary's faith and its relationship with the hidden life of Jesus. Therefore, in line with the theologian Stefano de Fiores, I think that discretion and hiddenness define the basic manner of Mary's presence in the mission of her Son on earth. Even with her significant presence at Cana and beneath the cross, the public life of Christ parallels the hidden life of the Mother.[104]

Luke's unknown woman generally sheds light on the infancy narratives and on Mary's motherhood according to the flesh. This physical type of motherhood is essential to understanding Mary because it defines the Incarnation granting her the privilege to be called Mother of God.[105] Mary conceives her Son in her womb, gives Him birth, and nurses Him like every other woman. John Paul II presents here in *Redemptoris Mater* a simple summary of the Christological doctrine of the Councils of Ephesus (431 A.D.) and Chalcedon (451 A.D.). He adopts both patterns, Word-Flesh (*Logos-sarx*) when referring to John 1:14, and Word-Man (*Logos-Anthropos*) when referring to Luke 1:32. The motherhood of Mary is the instrument for accomplishing the Incarnation in which the Son of God truly becomes Son of Man (Word-Man pattern) and the Word truly becomes flesh (Word-Flesh pattern). Through His birth from the Virgin Mary, Jesus, the Son of the Most High, truly becomes the Son of Man: "He is 'flesh,' like every other man: he is 'the Word (who) became flesh' (cf. Jn 1:14). He is of the flesh and blood of Mary."[106]

On the other hand, *Redemptoris Mater*, 20 presents the spiritual motherhood of Mary resulting from her faith and her adherence to the word of God. The answer of Jesus to the praise of the unknown woman in Luke, as well as to the person who told him that "your mother and brothers are standing outside and wish to see you," attempts to:

> . . . divert attention from motherhood understood only as a fleshly bond, in order to direct it toward those mysterious bonds of the spirit which develop from hearing and keeping God's word.[107]

These texts from the Synoptics were fundamental when the Second Vatican Council and many contemporary Mariologists developed the significance of Mary's spiritual motherhood of Christ and humanity, and the true meaning of her being the disciple of her Son.[108] The journey toward understanding the spiritual motherhood of Mary starts with Jesus' statement about his Father's business. Ever after, Christ does not change this attitude because, during His public ministries, His statements:

> . . . seem to fit in with the reply which the twelve-year-old Jesus gave to Mary and Joseph when he was found after three days in the temple at Jerusalem.[109]

This dimension of Mary's motherhood, namely her spiritual motherhood, derives from her faith and cooperation in the economy of salvation. It is the mystery of Christ who "was *completely* and *exclusively* 'concerned with his Father's business,'" that will reveal the mystery of Mary's spiritual motherhood.[110] The centrality of the Kingdom of God and "his Father's business" necessarily influences the relationship of Christ to the human reality. Without denying the goodness and authenticity of the created order or despising it, the Father's business:

> . . . add(s) a new dimension and meaning to everything human, and therefore to every human bond, insofar as these things relate to the goals and tasks assigned to every human being.[111]

Consequently, the motherhood of Mary according to the flesh, since it is a human bond, receives an extra dimension in its relation to the spiritual order established by the economy of Christ. The spiritual dimension does not limit or deny the human bond of motherhood; it just perfects it.[112] In that same sense *Redemptionis Donum* (The Gift of Redemption), 17 reads: "Her spousal love reached its height in the divine motherhood through the power of the Holy Spirit."

Pope John Paul II considers the fatherhood of the Father as the criterion for a sound understanding of spiritual motherhood. The Father is a Father without any sexual relationship according to the flesh. In the same way that fatherhood is possible without the bonds of the flesh, motherhood is also possible without being restricted to the bonds of the flesh. Although Mary did not have any sexual relationship to conceive Christ, Christ grew in her womb according to the natural laws of gestation. Thus Mary is truly the Mother of Jesus and possesses in her relationship with Him the human bond of motherhood. From the parallel between the fatherhood of the Father and the motherhood of Mary, one concludes that not every spiritual fatherhood or motherhood needs to be connected with sexual bonding (e.g. the fatherhood of the Father). Every human motherhood, however, must have a spiritual dimension "insofar as these things relate to the goals and tasks assigned to every human being."[113] In the light of this comparison, it becomes possible to understand the meaning of the Pope's words:

> "Motherhood," too, in the dimension of the Kingdom of God and in the radius of the fatherhood of God himself, takes on another meaning. In the words reported by Luke, Jesus teaches precisely this new meaning of motherhood.[114]

As Pope John Paul II focuses on the importance of Mary's spiritual motherhood in *Redemptoris Mater*, 20, he still knows how to avoid gnostic tendencies that overemphasize a spiritual dimension with, to use the words of Pope Paul VI quoted by John Paul II, an "unnatural tendency to negate the world" and to reject the importance of human bonds.[115] Can the spiritual dimension of motherhood, in the case of Mary, exist without motherhood according to the bonds of the flesh? "Is Jesus thereby distancing himself from his Mother according to the flesh? Does he perhaps wish to leave her in the hidden obscurity which she herself has chosen?"[116] The Pope's answer is negative:

> If this seems to be the case from the tone of those words, one must nevertheless note that the new and different motherhood which Jesus speaks of to his disciples refers precisely to Mary in a very special way.[117]

Thus the answer of Jesus to the unknown woman of Luke confirms her praise of Mary's motherhood according to the flesh and, at the same time, brings the faith of Mary out of its hiddenness because she is "the first of 'those who hear(s) the word of God and do(es) it.'"[118] Both dimensions of Mary's motherhood are praised by Jesus since, on the one hand, he did not deny the words of the woman, "Blessed is the womb that bore you, and the breasts that you sucked" and, on the other hand, He did not fail to emphasize the centrality of His Father's business and the Kingdom of God. His emphasis, however, coincides with the characteristics reported by Saint Luke in the infancy narratives concerning the attitude of Mary towards the Word of God:

> Without any doubt, Mary is worthy of blessing by the very fact that she became the Mother of Jesus according to the flesh . . . , but also and especially because already at the Annunciation she accepted the word of God, because she believed it, because she was obedient to God, and because she "kept" the word and "pondered it in her heart" (Lk 1:38, 45; 2:19, 51) and by means of her whole life accomplished it.[119]

From the conversation between the unknown woman of Luke with Jesus, one deduces that the *Magnificat*, in which Mary prophetically announced that "all generations shall call me blessed," starts to take form. Pope John Paul II sees in the woman's words a confirmation of Mary's words and the beginning of "the *Magnificat* of the ages."[120]

Pope John Paul II continues to tackle the question of divine maternity and spiritual motherhood and gives new insight into the theology of the Second Vatican Council. At the Annunciation, Mary accepted becoming the Mother of God according to the flesh. Yet it is in faith that she consented to such a motherhood. Spiritual motherhood in faith becomes, as it were, a necessary condition for the possibility of motherhood according to the flesh. Then and there, at the Annunciation, Mary became the Mother of Jesus Christ because of her faith. Motherhood according to the flesh and spiritual motherhood are concomitant; spiritual motherhood conditions divine maternity and divine maternity gives spiritual motherhood its significance in the economy of salvation. Mary's faith is necessary for her to become the actual Mother of her Son; and being predestined to become the Mother of God gives her spiritual motherhood existence, content, strength, and meaning. Short of motherhood according to the flesh, all the other dimensions of Mary's spiritual maternity would be just like ours. For John Paul II, the Annunciation becomes the event in which Mary received the two orders of motherhood:

> If through faith Mary became the bearer of the Son given to her by the Father through the power of the Holy Spirit, while preserving her virginity intact, in that same faith she discovered and accepted the other dimension of motherhood revealed by Jesus during his messianic mission. One can say that this dimension of motherhood belonged to Mary from the beginning, that is to say from the moment of the conception and birth of her Son. From that time she was "the one who believed."[121]

If Motherhood according to the flesh took place in that single event of the Annunciation, Mary's spiritual motherhood had just started there and would be developed and further understood in the unfolding of her Son's economy of salvation. The words "I am the handmaid of the Lord," uttered with faith to enable Mary to become the Mother of God, will become ever clearer when Mary as a Mother opens herself more and more to the new dimension of motherhood. Combined together, faith and motherhood according to the flesh lead Mary to new heights of spiritual motherhood. However, since faith is a pilgrimage in which Mary is invited to grow in discovering her human motherhood in its significance and dimensions, her spiritual motherhood also becomes a pilgrimage toward a more perfect understanding of that reality. And since the mystery of the Mother makes present in the world the mystery of the Son because Mary physically introduced Christ to the world through faith, it follows that God's Self-revelation in and through the mystery of Christ becomes clearer throughout Mary's pilgrimage of faith. Mary's growth in understanding the divine revelation through faith made her become, in a certain sense, the "disciple" of Jesus *par excellence*. In fact, at the very moment of the Annunciation and as a Mother, Mary's journey toward a more perfect understanding of Christ's mystery started. If her first act of faith made her the Mother, then only as a Mother can Mary learn more about the details of her motherhood. This learning through faith constituted her role next to her Son. At the same moment in which Mary became Mother according to the flesh, she became the recipient of a new dimension of motherhood through her faith and, as a result, a disciple of her Son. John Paul II is unique in considering the Annunciation as the point of departure of Mary's motherhood in its two dimensions and of her discipleship of Jesus Christ, her Son. In that sense also John Paul concludes *Redemptoris Mater*, 20 by saying:

> Through faith Mary continued to hear and to ponder that word, in which there became ever clearer, in a way "which surpasses knowledge" (Eph 3:19), the self-revelation of the living God. Thus in a sense Mary as Mother became the first "disciple" of her Son, the first to whom he seemed to say: "Follow me," even before he addressed this call to the Apostles or to anyone else (cf. Jn 1:43).[122]

Along the same lines, the Holy Father already referred to discipleship by quoting Saint Augustine in *Catechesi Tradendae* (Catechesis in our Time). Here Mary is, chronologically speaking, disciple before anybody else:

> She was the first in time, because even when she found her adolescent Son in the temple she received from Him lessons that she kept in her heart.[123]

Mary is also the first disciple in her qualities as a Mother: "She was the first disciple above all else because no one has been 'taught by God' to such depth. She was 'both mother and disciple,' as Saint Augustine said of her, venturing to add that her discipleship was more important for her than her motherhood."[124] Saint Augustine connected the privilege of Mary's discipleship with her dedication to motherhood in relation to the Kingdom of God. From that point of view, as mentioned above, the tie to Christ's work of salvation is more important than the bonds of flesh. Whereas in *Catechesi Tradendae* John Paul emphasizes Mary's discipleship as a fundamental determinant in relation to her Son the Teacher, the theology of discipleship is also stressed at the end of *Redemptionis Donum*, yet from a different point of view. Here the Pope goes back to his original concept of divine maternity as the fundamental characteristic of all Marian dimensions, including that of discipleship. In the context of the evangelical counsels, Mary realizes her vocation as a follower of Christ, *because* she is the Mother:

She, who as Mother carries Christ in her arms, at the same time fulfills in the most perfect way His call: "Follow me." And she follows Him—she, the Mother—as her Teacher of chastity, poverty and obedience.[125]

While *Redemptoris Mater* 20 and 23 are a thorough presentation of Mary's physical and spiritual motherhood respectively, Pope John Paul has already analyzed the same concept in *Dives in Misericordia* (Rich in Mercy) from a different angle. The theology of this encyclical focuses on God's revelation of His mercy through the cross and Mary's participation in that revelation. Through the cross of Christ, there is fulfilled that kiss of peace between justice and mercy spoken of in Ps 85:10. God's love manifested its power through the cross when the transcendent dimension of justice was reconciled with His mercy. The event of Calvary, therefore, constitutes the ultimate revelation of God's mercy toward humanity because only then, God being love, was His justice overpowered by His mercy.[126] Neither Vatican II nor Pope Paul VI has considered Mary's presence at the foot of the cross as a sharing in the revelation of that mercy,[127] whereas Pope John Paul II points out:

> Her sacrifice is a unique sharing in the revelation of mercy, that is a sharing in the absolute fidelity of God to his own love, to the covenant that he willed from eternity and that he entered into in time with man . . . ; it is a sharing in that revelation that was definitively fulfilled through the Cross. No one has experienced, to the same degree as the Mother of the Crucified One, the mystery of the Cross, the overwhelming encounter of divine transcendent justice with love: that "kiss" given by mercy to justice. No one has received into his heart, as much as Mary did, that mystery, that truly divine dimension of the Redemption effected on Calvary by means of the death of the Son, together with the sacrifice of her maternal heart, together with her definitive "fiat."[128]

Notice the terminology and the concepts of John Paul in *Dives in Misericordia*, 9, the text we just quoted. The focus is on God revealing His mercy through the mystery of the cross and on Mary's sharing in it. The One who reveals is God; the revelation is Christ through His cross. Every time Mary is mentioned, only her "sharing" is what makes her needed in the overall scenario. Hers is not a sharing in the sense of an absolute necessity like that of God. She shares in the revelation of mercy because her presence at the foot of the cross is a part of the integral plan of salvation. It is a necessary sharing in the sense that she belongs to the divine plan as it unfolds itself in human history to which fulfillment she, on the human level, contributes. Therefore, when the divine transcendent dimension of justice encountered love, there was the revelation of mercy, and Mary was there at the heart of the event as the Mother of the Crucified. The Pope calls her participation and presence "a unique sharing" because she shared, as a Mother, in the absolute fidelity of God to His own love that was manifested in and through the cross. God's covenant with His people defined by the sacrifice of Christ was, on the human level, an event experienced by Mary in a very singular way. Mary did not reveal; rather, Mary shared in the revelation.

Pope John Paul keeps repeating the same logic when he analyzes the presence of all human persons in the divine plan of salvation. If every person is included in the order of creation, every person is invited to be included, on the human level, in the order of Redemption. From the perspective of revelation of mercy, every person is invited to show it and to share in it. In all of the above, Mary enjoys the highest degree of participation. Created as the Immaculate Conception, she shares in the Redemption like nobody else because of her motherhood. When Christ's sacrifice reveals the mercy of God, Mary also shares in a most excellent manner in the revelation of God's mercy.

"The sacrifice of her maternal heart" explains the manner of her sharing and gives to her presence at the foot of the cross a dynamic dimension.[129] Because of that dynamism, Mary shares in the revelation of mercy and experiences the "overwhelming encounter of divine transcendent justice with love: that 'kiss' given by mercy to justice." Such an active role was inspired by the teaching of Vatican II, even though the Council did not explicitly specify her active sharing in the revelation of the mercy of God through the cross of Christ.

John Paul II places Mary, as a human person, at the center of the mystery of Redemption and attributes to her a special consciousness of the events that made up that mystery. The Pope continues:

> Mary, then, is the one who has the deepest knowledge of the mystery of God's mercy. She knows its price, she knows how great it is. In this sense, we call her the Mother of Mercy: Our Lady of Mercy, or Mother of Divine Mercy.[130]

The emphasis on Mary's knowledge recalls John Paul's personalistic approach to Mary and sheds light on the worth of her action as she shares in the revelation of God's mercy through the sacrifice of her maternal heart at Christ's death.[131] That she is invoked as the Mother of Mercy indicates a subjective consciousness on her part of God's design to extend His mercy to humanity. John Paul II describes Mary's experience as a model for what is being prepared for every human person, i.e., their call to share, each according to God's wisdom and design, in His mercy through their participation in the cross of Christ. She is the first to experience it through the cross in the highest possible degree. Mary:

> . . . having obtained mercy in an exceptional way, in an equally exceptional way "merits" that mercy throughout her earthly life and, particularly, at the foot of the Cross of her Son.[132]

This kind of perception is not developed as such in the Mariology of Vatican II and Pope Paul VI:[133]

> In each one of these titles (quoted above) there is a deep theological meaning, for they express the special preparation of her soul, of her whole personality, so that she was able to perceive, through the complex events, first of Israel, then of every individual and of the whole of humanity, that mercy of which "from generation to generation" people become sharers according to the eternal design of the Most Holy Trinity.[134]

If humanity has been experiencing the "merciful" love of God for generations, this experience connects with Mary who knew it as the Mother of the Crucified and Risen One. John Paul emphasizes the personalistic aspect of motherhood in relation to the experience of mercy. One cannot overlook the fact that Mary's experience of God's mercy vis-à-vis moral and physical evil should never be separated from its human dimension of motherhood. The expression of Mary's motherhood in association with God's mercy allows the Pope to say that "in her and through her, this love continues to be revealed in the history of the Church and of humanity."[135] Mary's experience has a universal quality because humanity, no matter how great its experience of that mercy, will never be able to reach the degree reached by the Mother. The reason lies in the fact that motherhood in the order of salvation does not diminish the role and sensitivity of motherhood in the created order. The effect of Mary's motherhood in the order of grace, as she shares in revealing God's "merciful" love from generation to generation, is to perfect her divine maternity as she establishes an irrevocable relationship of Mother-Son in the Incarnation.[136] It is the prerogative of the Christian mystery that the Mother-Son relationship in the context of Incarnation can and should be projected to the Mother-humanity relationship in so far as the revelation of mercy is concerned. Therefore, Mary truly deserves to be called Mother of Mercy:

> This revelation is especially fruitful because in the Mother of God it is based upon the unique tact of her maternal heart, on her particular sensitivity, on her particular fitness to reach all those who most easily accept the merciful love of a mother. This is one of the great life-giving mysteries of Christianity, a mystery intimately connected with the mystery of the Incarnation.[137]

When Mary participated in God's revelation of His mercy as she stood beneath the cross, that participation is identified in John Paul II's *Salvifici Doloris* (On the Christian Meaning of Human Suffering) as a manifestation of Mary's universal motherhood over human suffering. John Paul emphasizes the function of her spiritual maternity in relation to suffering humanity. The same Holy Spirit who made her the Mother of Christ at the Annunciation is now, at the foot of the cross, given to Mary by Christ in order to make her the spiritual Mother of all humanity. This time, however, her motherhood is an instrument to bring the Body of Christ to be united to Christ in His suffering. This function enables Mary to show to humanity that suffering, including her own, is not merely a physical weakness anymore, since the cross of her Son manifests the power of God:

> As though by a continuation of that motherhood which by the power of the Holy Spirit had given Him life, the dying Christ conferred upon the ever Virgin Mary a new kind of motherhood—spiritual and universal—towards all human beings, so that every individual, during the pilgrimage of faith, might remain, together with her, closely united to Him unto the cross, and so that every form of suffering, given fresh life by the power of this cross, should become no longer the weakness of man but the power of God.[138]

John Paul shed light on the same subject again in his encyclical *Veritatis Splendor* (The Splendor of Truth), 118. Here, Mary is considered the "Mother of Mercy" because she is the Mother of Christ who is the revelation of the Father's mercy. The Father's mercy in *Veritatis Splendor* receives a new meaning that complements that of *Dives in Misericordia*. Whereas in *Dives in Misericordia* the focus is on the cross of Christ as the revelation of the Father's mercy, *Veritatis Splendor* adds to that the mystery of the Son's Incarnation itself that constitutes the essence of the Father's revelation of mercy: "And the greatest mercy of all is found in his being in our midst and calling us to meet him and to confess with Peter that he is 'the Son of the living God'" (Mt 16:16). The spiritual gap between humanity and the Father created by the evil of the ages cannot hinder the mercy of God "or prevent him from unleashing all his triumphant power."[139] In order to ransom slaves, as the *Missale Romanum* relates, the Father has sacrificed His Son.[140] The infinite value of the Son's sacrifice has reestablished the moral order overturned by women and men who infinitely disturbed the infinite God. The mercy of God that manifested the Son's sacrifice as the price for Redemption becomes Redemption: "His mercy toward us is Redemption."[141]

Redemption also has a pneumatological dimension that bestows God's ultimate gift on creation: the Holy Spirit. The Holy Spirit who, in John Paul's theology is emphasized as the Person Uncreated-Gift in the Triune God, "makes possible the miracle of the perfect accomplishment of the good."[142] Redemption is thus extended in human history through the continued action of the Holy Spirit Who not only extends Christ's Redemption on earth but also gives people the power to respond to that Redemption through their moral actions. The Spirit's action intervenes in the two areas of faith and morality in order to provide the mechanism of Redemption for them. John Paul continues:

> This renewal (of the Spirit), which gives the ability to do what is good, noble, beautiful, pleasing to God and in conformity with his will, is in some way the flowering of the gift of mercy, which offers liberation from the slavery of evil and gives the strength to sin no more.

In this way, the Holy Spirit accomplishes in us the Redemption of Christ and leads us back to the Father. The action of Mary, as the "Mother of

Mercy" in *Veritatis Splendor*, 118, consists of her maternal presence. The Son, through whom the ultimate dimension of the Father's mercy was revealed and continues to be revealed by the Holy Spirit (who is the giver of the gift of faith and moral good), is the Son of Mary.

Another reason for Mary to be "Mother of Mercy" is her relationship with the Church and with humanity. Both were entrusted to her maternal care in the person of John at the foot of the cross. Yet the Pope brings a totally new dimension of motherhood that he has not treated before, even in *Redemptoris Mater*. He says:

> At the foot of the Cross, when she accepts John as her son, when she asks, together with Christ, forgiveness from the Father for those who do not know what they do (cf. Lk 23:34), Mary experiences, in perfect docility to the Spirit, the richness and the universality of God's love, which opens her heart and enables it to embrace the entire human race. Thus Mary becomes Mother of each and every one of us, the Mother who obtains for us divine mercy.[143]

The idea of John Paul that Mary as Christ's Mother joins Him in asking the Father to forgive the sin of those who "do not know what they do" is totally new in the postconciliar Mariology. Not only in that historical incident but also throughout the history of the Church on earth, Mary will continue, together with Christ, to ask the Father's forgiveness for the sin of humanity. The Pope universalizes all Marian dimensions always in relation to the universality of Christ's action. It seems that everything that Christ does, Mary does also, albeit in association and participation with Him. In the mechanism of Redemption, as it is shown by Divine Revelation, the Christological dimension of God's action in history is accompanied by a Marian dimension. Isn't that what Incarnation is all about in the theology of Pope John Paul II? Since the actions of Christ are universal and show the universality of God's love in relationship to humanity and the Church, Mary has, in relation to Christ, experienced that universality and has become the Mother of every person. It was her experience of God's all-embracing love that opened the door of Mary's understanding of the universality of her motherhood.

Such a personalistic understanding of Mary's experience allows the Pope to look at Mary's universal motherhood as a conscious act on her part.[144] Mary experienced the universality and the richness of God's forgiving act in and through Christ, and became open to participating in that love in the deepest possible way. The words of Christ concerning forgiveness were heard by Mary and she even participated, in John Paul II's opinion, in the petition of forgiveness because she is the associate of Christ ("together with Christ"). Christ's action on the cross becomes for Mary a norm to follow and a dimension that will make her inherit the privilege of a Mother who asked and continues to ask for pardon of humanity's sin. In this sense, the universality of Mary's motherhood in relation to mercy depends entirely on Christ's revelation of the Father's mercy in forgiving sin, even the sin of those who crucified Him.

Mary, Immaculate Conception

MARY AS "FULL OF GRACE" IN THE MYSTERY OF CHRIST AND THE CHURCH

WITH POPE JOHN PAUL II's emphasis on the theology of the Holy Spirit, as it was presented in my first volume,[1] one should not be surprised that, at the beginning of the Pope's Marian encyclical *Redemptoris Mater*, Mary's holiness occupies center stage in relation to the Holy Spirit (pneumatological dimension).[2] Speaking of the "fullness of time" with Saint Paul as in Gal 4:4, John Paul II says:

> It [fullness] marks the moment when the Holy Spirit, who had already infused the fullness of grace into Mary of Nazareth, formed in her virginal womb the human nature of Christ.[3]

Echoing Pope Pius IX who proclaimed Mary Immaculate Conception as a dogma of faith in 1854, Pope John Paul II interprets Luke's *kecharitoméne* (full of grace) in terms of a continuous state of grace.[4] The Holy Spirit, who forms the human nature of the Word in the womb of Mary, "had already infused the fullness of grace into Mary of Nazareth."[5] In the course of analysis, one will find that the idea of a purification that cleansed Mary at the Annunciation for the sake of the economy of salvation does not find support in John Paul's understanding of her immunity from sin.[6] In this sense, the Mariologist Ignace de la Potterie thinks that, for John Paul II:

... way before that historical moment (of the Annunciation), Mary, the daughter of Israel who was elected by God to become the mother of His Son, was already "full of grace" specifically in preparation of that salvific event.

The infusion of the grace of Immaculate Conception in Mary finds its full explanation in perspective of the history of salvation, the fullness of time. "Full of grace" is directly connected to "fullness of time."[7]

It is necessary to note that *Redemptoris Mater*, chronologically speaking, directly follows John Paul II's encyclical letter on the Holy Spirit, *Dominum et Vivificantem* (Lord and Giver of Life). In *Dominum et Vivificantem*, the Pope has already introduced the theology of the Holy Spirit who is in God the Person-Uncreated Gift.[8] In this context, the Holy Spirit, being the mutual eternal Gift between the Father and the Son, becomes also the Uncreated and Eternal Gift of God expressed in creation. God exists in the mode of Gift in the Holy Spirit. Therefore, from the very beginning of creation, the Holy Spirit puts God in contact with creation. One could call the Holy Spirit the relational God. Before and during the Old Testament, and during and after the New Testament, the Holy Spirit assures and realizes God's relation with and His presence in the world. Thus, at the dawn of the new economy of salvation, it was the Holy Spirit who came down upon Mary to start God's New Covenant with His people. The Pope states in *Dominum et Vivificantem*, 51:

> The Holy Spirit, who with his power overshadowed the virginal body of Mary, bringing about in her the beginning of her divine motherhood, at the same time made her heart perfectly obedient to that self-communication of God which surpasses every human idea and faculty.[9]

John Paul II's *Reconciliatio et Paenitentia* (On Reconciliation and Penance) approaches the same question from the point of view of Christ's sacrifice and its salutary influences on humanity. Mary had received the grace of being the Immaculate Conception in order to participate in Christ's self-offering that became the ultimate reconciliation between God and humanity. While in many other papal documents the finality of Mary's holiness is oriented to her divine maternity, *Reconciliatio et Paenitentia* orients her immunity from sin toward her contribution to the sacrifice of Calvary. The Mother of Jesus has:

> . . . received from God the fullness of grace in virtue of the redemptive sacrifice of Christ. Truly Mary has been associated with God, by virtue of her divine motherhood, in the work of reconciliation.[10]

It is in *Redemptoris Mater*, 8 that Pope John Paul II undertakes an accurate analysis of the Greek expression *kecharitoméne* (full of grace) referring to various patristic sources for the term.[11] He has already prepared the framework for such an analysis when, in *Redemptoris Mater*, 1, he considers the "fullness of time" as the hidden beginning of the Church's journey. The Church salutes Mary of Nazareth as the Church's own beginning because "in the event of the Immaculate Conception the Church sees projected, and anticipated in her most noble member, the saving grace of Easter."[12] For the Pope, the Immaculate Conception is a prerequisite for introducing Mary into the Mystery of Christ. While the initial manifestation of Mary's placement in Christ's mystery was the Annunciation, its remote beginning was the Immaculate Conception. The Annunciation was the public manifestation of Mary as the person "full of grace"—foreshadowed in the history of the community of Israel, "the people which first received God's promises."[13] An encounter between Mary and the transcendent God is what constitutes the mystery. It was shown in our first chapter, on Mary's divine maternity, where the revelation of the divine and its entrance into human history made manifest the mystery hidden for all ages. In the case of Mary, the contact between her and the transcendent God that took place in history happened for the first time at the Annunciation. In that sense, the Pope opens *Redemptoris Mater*, 8 with the following words: "Mary is definitively introduced into the mystery of Christ through this event: *the Annunciation* by the Angel."[14] And then the Pope continues in *Redemptionis Donum* (The Gift of Redemption), 13:

> And His Mother, at the decisive moment of the Annunciation-Incarnation, entering from the very beginning into the whole salvific economy of the Redemption, said: "Behold, I am the handmaid of the Lord; let it be done according to your word."

Unlike any predecessor, John Paul II uses the beginning of Saint Paul's Letter to the Ephesians as a background for his analysis of *kecharitoméne* (full of grace). Ignace de la Potterie rightly thinks that John Paul's use of Ephesians to present a better interpretation of Luke 1:28 (full of grace) is motivated by the fact that in the New Testament only Eph 1:6 contains a parallel terminology, that is *echaritosen* (glory of grace or glorious grace).[15] From a philological point of view, the verb *charitóo* (to grace) enjoys an element of causality that suggests the effect produced by the verb on the object in question.[16] In Luke and in the Letter to the Ephesians, that verb refers to grace in the theological sense, that is, to divine grace that changes someone and "makes him or her gracious." God, according to Saint Paul who uses the term *charitóo*, has done a work of purification and sanctification. That is exactly the sense used by John Paul II to interpret the verse of Eph 1:6. He calls it a "seed of holiness" planted by God in each one of us. This will be discussed later in the chapter.

This unique approach that links together the Annunciation of Luke and the Letter to the Ephesians proves that the Pope looks at Scripture as a unity. He applies to Mary, who is "blessed among women," that blessing "with which God the Father 'has filled us in the heavenly places, in Christ.'"[17] That blessing, which bears fullness and universality, which flows from the love that unites Father and Son in the Holy Spirit, is a blessing "poured out through Jesus Christ upon human history until the end: upon all people."[18] Just as John Paul II introduces Mary as Mother of God in the mystery of Christ by presenting the universality of God's action in creation and salvation, so also here Mary receives the blessing of God because that blessing is meant for everyone:

> This blessing, however, refers to Mary in a special and exceptional degree: for she was greeted by Elizabeth as "blessed among women."[19]

Redemptionis Donum, 17 explains "special and exceptional degree" in these terms: "For she was called by God to the most perfect communion with His Son."[20]

In order to explain both "full of grace" and "blessed among women," Pope John Paul II again uses the theology of the Letter of Saint Paul to the Ephesians. No one prior to this Pope has given in a magisterial document a Marian dimension to the "glory of grace" in Eph 1:6. He sees a relationship between the angel's greeting, "full of grace," and Elizabeth's greeting, "blessed among women," on the one hand, and the "glory of grace," on the other. Actually, "full of grace" and "blessed among women" indicate that:

> . . . in the soul of this daughter of Sion there is manifested, in a sense, all the glory of grace, that grace which the Father . . . has given us in his beloved Son.[21]

The expression, in a sense, indicates that Mary cannot quantitatively absorb all the glory of grace that God intends to bestow on men and women throughout the centuries. Otherwise, the saints would be deprived of their degree of grace and glory. It really means that Mary enjoys the highest degree of glory and that "full of grace" becomes her new name in the sense of a total worthiness and a perpetual qualification:

> For the messenger greets Mary as 'full of grace'; he calls her thus as if it were her real name. He does not call her by her proper earthly name, Miriam (=Mary), but by this new name: "full of grace."[22]

Note that the Pope refers to Eph 1:6 (glory of grace) as a biblical foundation for the dogma of the Immaculate Conception. Magisterial documents before John Paul II have always taken the text of Luke 1:28 (full of grace) as the scriptural background for Mary's immunity from sin. Pius IX, who defined the dogma of the Immaculate Conception in *Ineffabilis Deus* (The Ineffable God) in 1854, cited Luke 1:28 as the best biblical foundation for his proclamation. He commented on the Church's tradition regarding Luke 1:28 and emphasized the idea of "fullness" and the various "graces" and gifts present in Mary.[23] Also prior to Pope John Paul II, Pope Pius XII, commemorating the proclamation of the dogma of the Immaculate Conception,[24] quoted the Greek text of Luke 1:28. Pius XII attributed to Mary the qualification of being a sea of all divine graces, referring thus to the plural form of "grace." John Paul II uses the Greek text of Luke 1:28 and the parallel text of Eph 1:6 to explain it, something new in magisterial documents. In addition, he returns to the expression "full of grace" in the singular form showing his deep interest in the original use of "grace" in Scripture.

I agree with Ignace de la Potterie and Luigi Gambero,[25] against J. Fitzmyer and Raymond Brown, that the Latin formula of *gratia plena* (full of grace), used several times by Pope John Paul II, is still a valid translation of the Greek text of Luke 1:28. Fitzmyer thinks that *kecharitoméne* (full of grace) should be translated as "favored woman," and "favor" should be understood simply as God's choice to pre-elect Mary to be the Mother of Christ. The late tradition of the Church, as he argues, has attributed to Luke's text more than what Luke has originally intended. Raymond Brown also follows the same line of thought and argues that the "grace" that will make Mary *kecharitoméne* is the conception of the Son of the Most High. Fitzmyer's and Brown's approach to Luke 1:28 represents the common exegesis (interpretation of Scripture) followed by most Protestant and even by some Catholic scholars such as G. Miegge, E. Campi, G. Barbaglio.[26]

Both Fitzmyer and Brown contradict the biblical text that uses the passive form of the perfect participle indicating that Mary is "already now" full of grace. At the time of the Annunciation, Mary was already "full of grace." It is a reality that has already taken place, not an event that will take place in the future. The *kecharitoméne* indicates a *gratia gratum faciens* (make gracious) because the verb *charitóo* is causal (*gratum facere*, "make gracious") and is used in the passive form of the perfect participle. Luke is definitely talking about the effect already produced in Mary through the divine grace. The *karis* (grace), therefore, cannot be, as Fitzmyer and Brown suggest, an action that will take place in the future through the conception of Jesus in the womb of Mary. It expresses the situation of Mary in the *now*. The present situation of Mary, who was already changed by the grace of God at the moment of her conception in the womb of Anne, is very well described by the Latin formula *gratia plena* (full of grace). M. Jugie, who analyzes the Greek *kecharitoméne* (full of grace), rightly states that the employment of such an expression ultimately confirms a state of holiness in Mary.[27] The emphasis here is mainly on "grace," even though there has lately been a strong insistence on the "fullness" as an absolute and complete "fullness."[28] In the original Greek, as well as in the Latin translation of the Vulgata,[29] one should not forget that the *kecharitoméne* and the *gratia plena* represent the new aspect, typically Christian, of Luke's formula. It is in that direction that John Paul II interprets Luke 1:28, a fact that eliminates any tendency to look at Mary merely as a "favored woman" who received at the Annunciation a *gratia gratis data*, that is, the future grace to become the Mother of the Son of God. For John Paul, such an interpretation of Luke 1:28 contradicts the Church Fathers' interpretation of Luke 1:28 as well as the magisterial use of that scriptural text.

The logic of the Pope, based on Ephesians, goes as follows. Biblically, grace means a special gift that has its source in the Trinitarian life of God who is love. Love is at the origin of God's gift, which is grace. The fruit of this love is election, of which the beginning of the Letter to the Ephesians speaks and that displays the eternal desire of God to make men and women share His own life in Christ. The effect of this grace of man's election as God's eternal gift:

> . . . is like a seed of holiness, or a spring which rises in the soul as gift from God himself, who through grace gives life and holiness to those who are chosen . . . In this way there is fulfilled . . . that blessing "of man with every spiritual blessing."[30]

Addressing Mary as full of grace "places her among the daughters of the human race" because she shares the blessing bestowed upon every person. At the same time, she is the daughter of Sion because her being full of grace "enables us to understand that among all the spiritual blessings in Christ this is a special blessing."[31] The expressions "daughter of Sion" and "full of grace" emphasize that the blessing Mary received falls into the category of God's election of His people throughout the whole history of salvation, Old and New Testaments. Foreshadowed in the Old Testament through her being the "daughter of Sion," Mary's election to motherhood through the Incarnation in the New Testament thus receives the ultimate degree of blessing, that is the "fullness of grace."

Even though the Letter to the Ephesians does not directly talk about Mary, it is still legitimate to include her as the "daughter of Sion" and the Mother of the Son in God's design of salvation.[32] Including her in those mysteries was foreshadowed in the Old Testament. Vatican II's document on the Church, *Lumen Gentium*, 55, refers to Mary as the "daughter of Sion" exactly in the context in which her predestination was progressively revealed in the unfolding of the history of Israel. In the Old Testament, Israel (Sion) was symbolically seen as a woman called "daughter of Sion" or "Virgin Israel." The title was implicitly applied to

Mary in the New Testament.[33] Ignace de la Potterie remarks that, through-out the history of the Church, such a use has never taken place in a magisterial document (*Lumen Gentium*, 55) before, even though it is present in some ancient liturgical traditions.[34] The Council's intention is to provide a picture of the place of the Mother of Christ in the wide range of salvation history in which Holy Scripture describes the destiny of the people of God. John Paul uses the title "daughter of Sion" in the exact same context as the Council, in order to show Mary at the center of the history of salvation (*Redemptoris Mater*, 3). This title is being studied and evaluated more in contemporary exegesis and Mariology.[35]

The special blessing bestowed on Mary that was mentioned in Ephesians has a Trinitarian dimension in *Redemptoris Mater*, 8. Namely, the fullness of grace that Mary enjoyed from the first moment of her conception is based on her pre-election on the part of God to be the Mother of the Incarnate Word. Pre-election introduces Mary in a most eminent way into the mystery of Christ revealed to us in these last days when the fullness of time came. The Father, source and origin of every-thing, is the One who has chosen Mary in Christ. The grace bestowed on her has its source in love and, because it is a fullness of grace, the Father's love reaches its ultimate expression in that "fullness of grace." As fruit of the Father's love for Mary, there emerges her election to share in God's supernatural life and, because the Father's love reaches in Mary its fullest expression, her election introduces her in a unique and special way into the mystery of Christ. But this happens in the framework of divine motherhood. Therefore, the "special blessing" that Mary received among all the "spiritual blessings in Christ" is necessarily connected to her divine maternity. In that context, her presence in the mystery of Christ is fundamentally dependent on her identity as Mother of God. Here the Pope says:

> In the mystery of Christ she is present even before the creation of the world, "as the one whom the Father has chosen" as Mother of his Son in the Incarnation.[36]

Pope John Paul II continues: "And, what is more, together with the Father, the Son has chosen her, *entrusting her eternally to the Spirit of holiness*."[37] This short yet dense statement displays the Pope's deep consideration of the relationship between the Holy Spirit and Mary as far as her "fullness of grace" is concerned. In my first volume on *The Mystery of the Trinity in the Theological Thought of Pope John Paul II*, I extensively investigated the Holy Father's understanding of the Holy Spirit as the Person Uncreated-Gift.[38] Contemplated in the context of intra-Trinitarian life, the Spirit constitutes that mutual eternal Gift between Father and Son. This mutual self-offering is the basis of God's action *ad extra*, outside the divine nature. Being God as Uncreated-Gift in Person, the Spirit is also God's gift expressed through creation. In his divine subjectivity as God Uncreated-Gift in Person, the Spirit grants all possible gifts whether in the natural or in the supernatural order. Now, if grace "means a special gift, which . . . has its source precisely in the Trinitarian life of God himself, God who is love" (cf. 1 Jn 4:8); if the fruit of this love is the election which is God's "eternal desire to save man through a sharing in his own life in Christ;" if the effect and the product of this eternal desire and gift "is like a seed of holiness, or a spring which rises in the soul as a gift from God himself, who through grace gives life and holiness to those who are chosen"[39]—then it is through the Holy Spirit that the grace of a man's or a woman's election by God is bestowed. And so it is through the Holy Spirit that God, through grace, gives life and holiness to Mary, chosen "as Mother of His Son."[40] The Son and the Father together entrust Mary "to the Spirit of holiness" because only the Holy Spirit is able to give her that holiness, which is the grace of her election by the Father to be the Mother of the Son. The Holy Spirit, as the agent of the Father and the Son *ad extra* the Trinitarian life, is the Person Uncreated-Gift who expresses the holiness of the Father and the Son by enabling Mary to share in it through grace. She is exceptionally chosen by the Father in the sense that she is "present even before the creation of the world, as the one whom the Father has chosen as Mother of His Son in the Incarnation."[41] In the mystery of Christ, she enjoys a unique place. The Spirit of holiness has bestowed on her that maximum degree of grace spoken of in the opening words of the Letter of Saint Paul to the Ephesians. John Paul concludes *Redemptoris Mater*, 8 by saying:

> In an entirely special and exceptional way Mary is united to Christ, and similarly she is eternally loved in this beloved Son, this Son

who is of one being with the Father, in whom is concentrated all the glory of grace. At the same time, she is and remains perfectly open to this gift from above (cf. Jas 1:17).[42]

THE RELATIONSHIP OF MARY'S FREEDOM AND HER BEING THE IMMACULATE CONCEPTION

Redemptoris Mater, 8 reads: "At the same time, she is and remains perfectly open to this gift from above" (Jas 1:17). Note that the continuing attitude of being open to the gift of the Spirit shows that Mary, even if she shares in the "glory of grace" in its ultimate measure, still needs to receive grace throughout her life as a human person. For John Paul, the very first moment of Mary's Immaculate Conception in which a "special blessing" was bestowed on her should not be understood as an *automatic* reality that would arbitrarily eliminate her freedom and her human effort.[43] "She remains perfectly open to the gift from above" means that Mary uses her human faculties, such as will, hope, and trust in God, to receive the gift of God's salvation. Being redeemed in so excellent a manner through the Immaculate Conception does not eliminate the necessity of Mary's cooperation in the whole mechanism of salvation.[44] This is why Pope John Paul quotes Vatican II's *Lumen Gentium*, 55 at the end of *Redemptoris Mater*, 8, saying that Mary "stands out among the poor and humble of the Lord, who confidently await and receive salvation from him."

In *Veritatis Splendor* (Splendor of Truth), 120, John Paul treats this same theme of Mary's freedom as applied to *praxis* vis-à-vis God's plan of salvation. Here, Mary is considered as a "radiant sign and inviting model of the moral life."[45] She enjoys such a privileged place in morality because of her exercise of freedom that became an instrument of accompanying the Son in His awesome sacrifice. Although it was God Who accomplished all the necessary steps of His plan, "Mary lived and exercised her freedom precisely by giving herself to God and accepting God's gift within herself."[46] Freedom is not, therefore, an arbitrary move of the human will to carry out an act; it is the free decision to give complete and authentic acquiescence to the will of God and His gift to humanity.

Inasmuch as Mary was filled with the full grace of the Immaculate Conception, in the course of history she did exercise her freedom and saw the need to be open to God's gift as it was given to her during her life with her Son.

Such a confirmation of the necessity of Mary's free act in accepting God's gift helps the Pope to eliminate implicit Gnosticism, a current of thought that tends to belittle the importance of human action in response to God's grace. Gnosticism overspiritualizes the power of the Incarnation and the Redemption to the point of canceling any need for human faith and moral responsibility. The tendency to annihilate the necessary response of humanity to God's initiative of salvation exercises a negative influence on the value of the human person's reaction. Therefore, the Pope continues, to the free act of Christ to lay down His life for humanity there corresponds the free answer of Mary to accept a key role in the economy of salvation. The presence of Mary in the mystery of Christ, from a moral point of view, becomes a continuing free acceptance of God's plan as it unfolds and reveals itself in history, that is, in the concrete life of Mary of Nazareth:

> Until the time of his birth, she sheltered in her womb the Son of God who became man; she raised him and enabled him to grow, and she accompanied him in that supreme act of freedom which is the complete sacrifice of his own life. By the gift of herself, Mary entered fully into the plan of God who gives himself to the world.[47]

In this sense also, *Pastores Dabo Vobis* (I Will Give You Shepherds), 36 states:

> The creature who more than any other has lived the full truth of vocation is Mary the virgin mother, and she did so in intimate communion with Christ: No one has responded with a love greater than hers to the immense love of God.

It all goes back again to the opening statement of *Redemptoris Mater:* "The Mother of the Redeemer has a precise place in the plan of salvation." In many different ways, Mary enters the plan of God, but as far as the moral dimension of her cooperation in God's plan is concerned, Mary is "Seat of Wisdom."[48] This title given to her in *Veritatis Splendor,* 120 directly refers to her freedom in "accepting and pondering in her heart events she did not always understand (cf. Lk 11:28)"[49] Wisdom is the free act of Mary who faces the mystery with faith and accepts God's initiative as it unfolds itself in the history of her life. Mary, according to John Paul II, has always positively reacted by being open to God's Wisdom, which is Jesus Christ Himself, who "perfectly reveals and accomplishes the will of the Father" (cf. Heb 10:5–10).[50] There is a chain of logic in the mechanism of Redemption in its moral dimension: the Father is revealed by Jesus Christ who, fulfilling and revealing the Father's will, through "that supreme act of freedom" became the Wisdom of the Father. Mary, having been invited to be open to the gift of self-offering in and through Christ, did act freely and accepted God's initiative. She exercised her freedom through a free decision to accept the dimension of mystery throughout her life, even with all the dark tunnels that led the mystery to its completion. By her decision to accept what Christ, who is the Wisdom, has accepted, she became the "Seat of Wisdom."[51]

Like all other Marian concepts, the chain of Mary's moral decisions that made her "Seat of Wisdom" should not be restricted only to her relationship with Christ. They should be extended also to Christ's body, the Church:

> Mary invites everyone to accept this Wisdom. To us too she addresses the command she gave to the servants at Cana in Galilee during the marriage feast: "Do whatever he tells you" (Jn 2:5).[52]

Her intervention to apply the will of Christ in human situations becomes a pattern of moral norms. She will always indicate the necessity of accomplishing the will of Christ, who through a "supreme act of freedom" lays down His life for humanity. Here the mystery of the Mother is revealed in its moral dimension. Mary has put herself in the middle between humanity and Christ when it comes to the norms of moral life.

The wedding of Cana manifests a new dimension in the range of Mary's action. "Do whatever he tells you" is a universal call to every human person who is seeking to live life's moral demands. Mary has lived those demands to the ultimate and now, being in the glory of her Son, invites the Church to do the same. Hers is not a superhuman state, because "Mary shares our human condition, but in complete openness to the grace of God."[53] Being human like us except for sin, Mary shared our limited condition and, therefore, "not having known sin, is able to have compassion on every kind of weakness."[54] Such a statement sounds like the Letter to the Hebrews (5:1–4), where the High Priest, being beset by weakness, is able to help and understand his brethren in humanity. Mary's solidarity with every human person, however, results from her immunity from all kinds of sin, and this shows that her state increases her knowledge of the degree of evil lurking in sin. Jesus, who did not experience sin in any possible way, has revealed to us the evil that sin contains. He did not have to experience sin in order to know the essence of sin. Applying this principle to Mary, John Paul bases Mary's perception of a person's sinfulness on her Immaculate Conception. As an immaculate human being, Mary:

> . . . understands sinful man and loves him with a Mother's love. Precisely for this reason she is on the side of truth and shares the Church's burden in recalling always and to everyone the demands of morality.[55]

In the Church's struggle to fulfill the moral norms and demands of the Lord, here stands Mary with a Mother's love and understanding, acknowledging the dimensions of evil contained in sin and witnessing to the truth of moral life revealed by her Son:

> Nor does she permit sinful man to be deceived by those who claim to love him by justifying his sin, for she knows that the sacrifice of Christ her Son would thus be emptied of its power. No absolution offered by beguiling doctrines, even in the areas of philosophy and theology, can make man truly happy: only the Cross and the glory of the risen Christ can grant peace to his conscience and salvation to his life.[56]

The actions of human persons lead their beings to perfection. Their actions are a response to the norms of moral law handed down by Christ through the Church. In themselves and according to their object (*ex objecto*), they are good or evil. The Catholic moral teaching about acts that are intrinsically (*in se*) evil is based on the fact that a person's act is a response to a truth revealed by Christ. John Paul II seems to follow here not only Saint Thomas Aquinas but also Saint Augustine who understood that the divine reality, once perceived, becomes the source of Christian activity.[57] The *praxis*, understood as a response to Christ's revelation, implies either a fulfillment or a shortfall in fulfilling the demands of the moral law. In the case of shortcoming, a person is invited to acknowledge his or her sinful action without complaining that the divine moral law is impossible to apply to concrete situations of life. Every attempt to lessen the measure of evil contained in sin empties the cross of Christ of its power. People can fulfill and lead their being to perfection only through those actions that witness to the revealed truth of moral law. No matter how much somebody tries to excuse the evil he or she has done, the truth will ultimately prevail and they will find "peace of conscience" and "salvation to their life" only by fulfilling the demands of the revealed moral law. No one before John Paul II had ever attributed to Mary a joint presence in witnessing to the truth of moral demands given by Christ in order to keep His cross from being emptied of its power.

At the end of the encyclical *Fides et Ratio* (On the Relationship between Faith and Reason), John Paul calls Mary "Seat of Wisdom," this time in relation to philosophy. He believes that the life of Mary is a true reflection of what he presented in that encyclical: "For between the vocation of the Blessed Virgin and the vocation of true philosophy there is a deep harmony."[58] This parallel is justified by the Holy Father in the context of the Son's Incarnation. Mary has offered her whole being and femininity to be an instrument for the Word to become flesh. In the same line of action, philosophy is invited to use all of its methods for a more fruitful theology. Mary has put at the service of the Incarnation what constitutes the visible and human dimension of the mystery, that is, her whole being. All the faculties, including her reasoning, that make up her being were instruments to facilitate an intervention of higher order. Actually, it seems that John Paul sees in Mary's reasoning about the Incarnation a model for humanity's thinking whenever God intervenes in history and invites men and women to share in that mystery. Therefore, philosophy, i.e., human reasoning on the mystery of God, is validly operating when it follows the example of Mary in her relation to the mystery of God. What a person can reach in his or her thinking necessarily contributes to making evident the one truth revealed by God. As far as her will is concerned, Mary did not lose her authentic freedom and responsibility when she offered her service at the Incarnation. Freedom reaches its perfection when it is conformed with the supreme freedom of

God revealing Himself in history.[59] Moreover, philosophy does not lose its constitutive elements and foundations if it serves theology. The oneness of truth allows John Paul to consider philosophy as a proper tool for better understanding the gospel. Its autonomy will never be jeopardized because the supernatural cannot contradict the authenticity of the natural:

> Just as the Virgin was called to offer herself entirely as human being and as woman that God's Word might take flesh and come among us, so too philosophy is called to offer its rational and critical resources that theology, as the understanding of faith, may be fruitful and creative. And just as in giving her assent to Gabriel's word, Mary lost nothing of her true humanity and freedom, so too when philosophy heeds the summons of the Gospel's truth its autonomy is in no way impaired.[60]

Whereas Mary reacted with full use of intellect and will to give God's plan her "obedience of faith," the reasoning of her intellect served the fulfillment of God's plan, and the freedom of her will, instead of losing its authenticity because of obedience, became more perfect than ever. By giving birth to the Truth and treasuring it in her heart, Mary started the journey into wisdom, the "sure and final goal of all true knowing."[61] Therefore, *reason* and *will*, following in Mary's footsteps, are always the two fundamental pillars on which man's response to God is built. Also, they constitute the main weapon for fighting *Fideism*[62] and *Pelagianism*.[63] Mary's process of reason and will became the pattern of philosophy for the constant thinking of the Church in explaining Divine Revelation. Pseudo-Epiphanius, representative of monks of Christian antiquity, looked at Mary as "the table at which faith sits in thought."[64]

MARY, REDEEMED IN A MORE SUBLIME MANNER

The balance brought about in *Redemptoris Mater*, 8 concerning Mary's human effort and her sharing to the highest degree in the "glory of grace," would seem to be displayed again in *Redemptoris Mater*, 9, yet from a different perspective. Here, the reason for Mary's election to that privilege is her divine maternity. Even in the context of her immunity from original and actual sin, the Pope still considers Mary's motherhood as the fundamental principle for understanding her place in the overall picture of God's plan of salvation. If God's grace is rooted in His love and the fruit of this love is election, and if the effect of that election is the seed of holiness and Mary has received that seed to its highest degree, then the *reason* for that privilege is her election to be Mother of Christ. The divine maternity gives Mary's Immaculate Conception its possibility. In this sense John Paul states: "If the greeting and the name full of grace say all this [what was just explained about the election of every human person in Christ], in the context of the angel's announcement they refer first of all to the election of Mary as Mother of the Son of God."[65]

Establishing Mary's immunity from sin on the basis of God's election, as displayed in Saint Paul's Letter to the Ephesians, affords the Pope the opportunity to build an authentic Marian image in the consciousness of the people. Popular devotion that thinks of Mary's holiness in terms of a goddess who in and by herself enjoys certain privileges does not fit into the Marian thought of John Paul II. Her immunity from sin has to belong to the broader context of God's plan of salvation and should therefore possess a Trinitarian as well as a Christological dimension. At the same time, since grace builds on nature leading it to fulfillment,[66] the "fullness of grace" that Mary has received because of her election to the divine maternity does not eliminate the characteristics of freedom belonging to her human nature. Mary experienced the freedom that every human person experiences and had to cooperate with God's grace to be able to constantly turn away from sin throughout her entire earthly life. Uniqueness and universality balance each other out whenever Mary's merits and her cooperation in God's plan of Redemption are in question. Universality guarantees the comprehensive dimension of Christ's salvation that includes all people without exception. Singularity emphasizes that Mary, falling into the same category of being redeemed, still occupies a different place in God's plan of salvation.[67] Her place is different not only as to its degree but also as to its essence, in the sense presented by the Second Vatican Council according to which Mary never experienced sin in her humanity and is, therefore, redeemed in a more eminent manner. In that sense, the Pope refers to her as "the first of the redeemed" in his letter to the bishops of the United states.[68] And then he elaborates in *Redemptoris Mater*, 9:

But at the same time the "fullness of grace" indicates all the supernatural munificence from which Mary benefits by being chosen
and destined to be the Mother of Christ. If this election is fundamental for the accomplishment of God's designs for humanity, and
if the eternal choice in Christ and the vocation to the dignity of
adopted children is the destiny of everyone, then the election of
Mary is wholly exceptional and unique. Hence also the singularity
and uniqueness of her place in the mystery of Christ.

Analyzing *Redemptoris Mater*, 9, John Paul comes to the conclusion that the singularity of Mary's election to the divine maternity is the
reason for her uniqueness in Christ's mystery. Since "the Annunciation
is the revelation of the mystery of the Incarnation at the very beginning
of its fulfillment on earth," this mystery includes Mary's maternity and
explains her unique role in the mystery of Christ. Creation is the expression of the fatherhood of the Father, a God who has communicated
Himself and the mystery of His life to creation since the beginning of its
existence. That giving of Himself that possesses a salvific dimension *per
se* goes through different stages as the history of humanity's Redemption
is unfolded. The grace of that Self-offering of God:

> . . . in some way to all creation but directly to man, reaches one of
> its high points in the mystery of the Incarnation.[69]

John Paul uses terms "in some way to all creation but directly to man" to
confirm Vatican II's anthropology that a human person is the only creature that God wanted for Himself. The grace of creation was bestowed
on all creatures for the sake of humans who are the primary recipients of
God's grace and infinite life. Only a human person's vocation gives sense
to the existence of the universe. God's grace, however, was poured on
humanity as the history of salvation progressed to its fulfillment.

When the fullness of time came, the Incarnation started a new
expression of God's presence in the world. It allowed God to be present
in an essentially different way in creation because the Son took on the
dimension of time, making it a salvation time.[70] Because humankind is
called to receive the vocation of sharing in God's gifts of creation and
Redemption, that universality found in Mary an exceptional singularity
because in her the contact of God with humanity reached its highest
degree. It is in the unity between the Mother and the Son, a unity based

on her cooperation in granting Him an authentic human nature, that the climax "among all the gifts of grace conferred in the history of man and of the universe" is reached.[71] Her divine maternity has enabled her to be united to God like nobody else in human history. *Redemptoris Mater*, 9 emphasizes the *maternal* not the spousal character of that unity between Mary and God.

If her being the Mother of the Son of God is the context in which the highest union between God and Mary took place, then "Mary is full of grace because it is precisely in her that the Incarnation of the Word, the hypostatic union [that is, the union of the divine and human nature in the One Person of the Son] of the Son of God with human nature, is accomplished and fulfilled."[72] Since the divine maternity of Mary constitutes the axiom that determines her union with God and the highest point of His Self-offering to humanity, then the relationship with the Triune God is the dimension that should be at the root of her personal privileges and holiness. The Annunciation, as described in *Redemptoris Mater*, 9, is the context that displays Mary's relationship with the Three Divine Persons, her divine maternity, and the highest degree of grace she received from God because of her maternal union with the Son. Pope John Paul II concludes *Redemptoris Mater*, 9 with a quote from *Lumen Gentium*, 53:

> [Mary is] the Mother of the Son of God. As a result she is also the favorite daughter of the Father and the temple of the Holy Spirit. Because of this gift of sublime grace, she far surpasses all other creatures, both in heaven and on earth.[73]

In *Redemptoris Mater*, 9,[74] Pope John Paul II refers to Pius IX and *Lumen Gentium* in order to place the "glory of grace" as reported by Eph 1:7 in a context of salvation. Here the results of the "glory of grace" are not only Mary's status as Immaculate Conception but also a Redemption that is applied to Mary "in a more sublime manner."[75] This means that the fruits of the glory of grace bestowed on Mary cause her immunity from sin and necessarily effect the manner of her Redemption by her Son. This language of Redemption assures the universality of the Redemption of Christ and places Mary under his saving action.[76]

Two sources that provide the full glory of grace bestowed on Mary are dealt with in *Redemptoris Mater*, 10. On the one hand, there is the grace of Jesus Christ that imparts a unique holiness to Mary who was chosen to be His Mother. The Pope calls this the "richness of grace" in *Redemptoris Mater*, 10, which was bestowed on Mary in an exceptional way. On the other hand, there are the merits of Christ's Redemption, accomplished exclusively in and through Jesus Christ. Both work together to make Mary enjoy a unique immunity from sin.[77] In the order of *creation* there is a "richness of grace" that is showered on Mary (God the Father has bestowed the glory of grace on us in His beloved Son). In the order of *Redemption* there emerges the exceptional way that Redemption is applied to the Mother of the Redeemer (in Christ we have Redemption through His blood). The theology of Saint Germanus of Constantinople and of Saint Andrew of Crete, already quoted by the Second Vatican Council in *Lumen Gentium*, 56, with reference to Mary's Immaculate Conception, serves as a backup for the idea of her immunity from original sin:

> By virtue of the richness of the grace of the beloved Son, by reason of the redemptive merits of him who willed to become her Son, Mary was preserved from the inheritance of original sin.[78]

One senses the presence of fourth-century Mariology in *Redemptoris Mater*, 10 when Pope John Paul draws a similarity between the mutual love between Father and Son and Mary's sharing in that love. If the eternal generation of the Son by the Father is based on an indescribable love between two eternally co-existent Divine Persons, the temporal generation of the Son by the Virgin happens in that same context of love and draws all of its power from it.[79] To the eternal generation of the Son corresponds His temporal generation of the Virgin; to the Incarnation of the Son that brings the mystery of salvation corresponds the sharing of Mary in the grace of that salvation. Since Mary participated in the salvific (or soteriological) grace of Redemption from her first moment of existence, that participation in itself is for Pope John Paul II the condition of possibility of Mary's Redemption "in a more sublime manner," and therefore of her Immaculate conception. In the order of grace, Mary receives life, that is Redemption or participation in the divine life of God. In the order of earthly generation, she gives life to the One who gave her life both in the order of creation and Redemption. In that sense, the Pope comments, she is called "Mother of her Creator," as in the liturgy, and "daughter of (her) Son," as in Dante Alighieri, who placed it on the lips of Saint Bernard.[80] This is exactly the meaning of her immunity from original sin: Mary was able to participate in the sanctifying grace of the Incarnation in a unique and exceptional way, a fact that enabled her to be without sin from the first moment of her earthly existence, because she was destined to generate the Son on earth in a like way to His eternal generation by the Father. Such a sharing in that eternal mutual love between Father and Son was reflected in her divine maternity at the Incarnation and enabled her to share, as a Mother, in the salvific grace of the Redemption from the first moment of her conception in the womb of Anne. In *Redemptoris Mater*, 10, the Pope sees in the creation of Mary and in her predestination to be the Mother of God a soteriological finality that was fulfilled in a unique way. At the vigil of the Council, L. Bouyer, according to the opinion of Ignace de la Potterie, said that Mary is really "the predestined *par excellence*."[81] Let us take a look at the Pope's text:

> In this way, from the first moment of her conception—which is to say of her existence—she belonged to Christ, sharing in the salvific and sanctifying grace and in that love which has its beginning in the Beloved, the Son of the eternal Father, who through the Incarnation became her own Son. Consequently, through the power of the Holy Spirit, in the order of grace, which is a participation in the divine nature, Mary receives life from him to whom she herself, in the order of earthly generation, gave life as a mother.[82]

Notice the twofold role of the Holy Spirit in the process of creation (in which the Father bestows the glory of grace on us in His beloved Son) and in the process of Redemption (in Him we have Redemption through his blood).[83] Through the power of the Holy Spirit, Mary has generated the Son in history and given Him life through earthly generation. Through the power of the Holy Spirit, the Son has communicated to her the salvific and sanctifying grace, that is, participation in the very life of God. The Holy Spirit, as the relational God and the Person-Gift between the Father and the Son and between both of them and creation, enables the Father and the Son to exist in a real relationship with the world, and especially with humanity.[84] At the summit of this contact activity with creation, there stands Mary filled with the Holy Spirit in order to receive the Father's glory of grace as a creature and to become "redeemed in a more sublime manner" by reason of the redemptive merits of Christ.

Redemptoris Mater, 10 continues to investigate the question of Mary's Immaculate Conception from all angles. Her immunity from sin and evil is now placed in the overall context of the history of salvation. Starting with the Protogospel (First Gospel) as God's promise to Eve in Genesis, John Paul II interprets the "seed of the woman" as clearly referring to Jesus Christ, the seed of Mary. Although he does not look at it frivolously, the Pope does not find the question concerning the identity of the one who was going to "crush the head of the serpent" to constitute an exegetical problem. Neither does the expression "woman," since the Pope sees in it a clear reference to Mary. His view of the overall unity of Scripture allows him to see allegorically in the Protogospel the promise of the Incarnation. At the foundation of the doctrine of Incarnation there stands John Paul II's exegesis of Gen 3:15, which represents the history of the fall and salvation. The doctrine of the Son's Incarnation as God's intervention to remedy the evil created by human beings is already reflected in the unity of Scripture that relates His plan of creation and Redemption. That harmony between dogma and Scripture linking the Fall and Redemption is expressed by John Paul when he states:

> In the salvific design of the Most Holy Trinity, the mystery of the Incarnation constitutes the superabundant fulfillment of the promise made by God to man after original sin, after that first sin whose effects oppress the whole earthly history of man (cf. Gen 3:15). And so, there comes into the world a Son, the seed of the woman who will crush the evil of sin in its very origins: he will crush the head of the serpent.[85]

The very first book of Scripture reveals the "enmity" between the serpent and the woman's seed, a fact that is confirmed in the Apocalypse. Such an enmity extends through the whole history of humanity on earth and is described as an ongoing battle: "the victory of the woman's Son will not take place without a hard struggle, a struggle that is to extend through the whole of human history."[86] Crushing the head of the serpent should not be imagined as a simple mechanism where God arbitrarily intervenes to save man. Rather, man, in his relationship with God, is involved in the whole process, even if salvation per se is an exclusive act of God, the Creator and the Savior.

If man is involved in the struggle against evil and sin from the beginning of human history:

> Mary, Mother of the Incarnate Word, is placed at the very center of that enmity, that struggle which accompanies the history of humanity on earth and the history of salvation itself.[87]

Precisely because she is the "woman" of Genesis and her seed will crush the head of the serpent, Mary occupies a central place in the battle against the evil of sin. She is involved in the struggle like no other human person. John Paul does not count Mary among those who are stained by sin and need to struggle to wipe it away. In the central position she occupies in this enmity, she is totally human, yet without any involvement in evil. Mary enjoys an immunity from sin as a human not as a superhuman. Hers is not a nature that falls between divinity and humanity. In that sense, Ugo Vanni rightly states that throughout *Redemptoris Mater*, Mary emerges from humanity, not vice-versa.[88] In that sense also, only grace could have given a human being—that is, Mary—the capacity and the gift of original holiness, with all the limitations of her human condition:

> In this central place (of enmity), she who belongs to the weak and poor of the Lord bears in herself, like no other member of the human race, that glory of grace which the Father has bestowed on us in his beloved Son, and this grace determines the extraordinary greatness and beauty of her whole being.[89]

The influence of French spirituality, especially that of Saint Louis of Montfort, is evident here in describing Mary's holiness. She who is immune from original sin because of Christ's grace is the daughter of Sion hiding in the midst of the people of Israel and yet shining forth before the Eternal Father who gives her an "extraordinary greatness."[90]

The expression "being" has a metaphysical dimension because it indicates the belonging of Mary to the human race and, at the same time, confirms that the glory of grace that was bestowed on her reached all the "areas" of her human existence. Precisely because Mary enjoyed a full humanity, the grace of God could determine "the extraordinary greatness and beauty of her whole being."[91] That grace penetrated the very depths of her ontological being, that is, of what makes up her entire being as a person endowed with all the human faculties. Far beyond a merely psychological dimension, the grace that pervaded Mary's being had its source in the love that the Father and the Son mutually exchange. The fruit of this love is the election in Christ mentioned in Eph 1:4–5. In turn, the effect of this election to sonship is the seed of holiness that was given to all of us, but especially to Mary, the one standing in the central place of enmity confronting evil in Genesis. That Mary enjoyed such immunity from evil and sin is in itself a prelude of hope because it demonstrates that the grace of God can bestow on a human being the victory over the Fall of the beginning. It shows that it is possible for a human being, one like us, to remain with the Father's glory of grace without sin and become a sign of assurance of God's Redemption, a Redemption that was given to Mary "in a more sublime manner." John Paul II concludes *Redemptoris Mater*, 11:

> Mary thus remains before God, and also before the whole of humanity, as the unchangeable and inviolable sign of God's election, spoken of in Paul's Letter . . . This election is more powerful than any experience of evil and sin, than all that enmity which marks the history of man. In this history Mary remains a sign of sure hope.[92]

CONCLUSION

The holiness of Mary and her immunity from original and actual sin play a major role in the theology of Pope John Paul II. He displays the dogma of the Immaculate Conception and, although referring to its relationship with many contemporary Marian theologies in order to maintain its dynamic aspects, still keeps its essential doctrinal tradition. Holy Mary, as a theological personality who stands in unique and exemplary relationship with the Three Divine Persons, has accomplished her role in God's plan of Redemption.

Mary's utter reliance upon God's grace does not negate her cooperation with that grace. Moreover, it is Catholic teaching that Mary's Immaculate Conception was *sola gratia* (only grace). In fact, there is no opposition between *sola gratia* and free, human cooperation with God's grace. This opposition should not be present if Catholic doctrine is correctly understood. Our total reliance on God's grace for salvation does not negate the reality of our free cooperation with that grace (Council of Trent's Decree on Justification, Canon 4, DH 1554; Joint Declaration on the Doctrine of Justification by the Lutheran World Federation and the Catholic Church, 1999, no. 15, 19). On the other hand, if one attributes exclusively to Mary's human efforts the capacity of attaining that holiness that was intended by God for humanity to have from the beginning, one runs the risk of following the old Pelagian dogma that was bitterly fought by Saint Augustine. The Pope sees in the relationship between the Triune God and Mary the perfect picture of cooperation between God and humanity in the Redemption process. In Mary, the cooperation between the human and the divine reaches perfection in the sense that it took place in the exact way God intends all humans to respond to His call to life, holiness, and salvation from the beginning of human history.

If both aspects of God's intervention and Mary's free and reasonable response are necessary for understanding the mechanism of salvation, this does not mean that God is not the One who took the initiative to start the whole procedure. At the same time, this is also a paradox in theology because, in the framework of the relationship between a Creator-Savior and a human being, there is not only an absolute dependency but also a necessity of cooperation on the part of Mary to accomplish the plan of God. Absolute dependency on God does not minimize or eliminate her cooperation; neither does her human reason and freedom jeopardize His sovereignty and the absolute character of His gift of salvation. Every time theology attempts to fathom the depth of God's mystery in its presence in the world, every time that theology attempts to relate the Uncreated to the created, it will run into the problem of paradoxes and dilemmas. Analogically, the words of Pope John Paul's encyclical letter, *Fides et Ratio*, even though in the context of faith and reason, are pertinent:

There is no reason for competition of any kind between reason and faith: each contains the other, and each has its own scope for action . . . In their respective worlds, God and the human being are set within a unique relationship. In God there lies the origin of all things, in him is found the fullness of the mystery, and in this his glory consists; to men and women there falls the task of exploring truth with their reason, and in this their nobility consists.[93]

Mary in the Mystery of the Church

THE "PRESENCE" OF MARY IN THE MYSTERY OF THE CHURCH: MARY AS A THEOLOGICAL PERSONALITY AND THE COMMUNITY OF THE CHURCH

THE MAIN LINE of the Second Vatican Ecumenical Council's thought on Mary in its relationship with the Church is clear: the Church should look at Mary in order to learn about herself.[1] Such an approach was an obvious tendency to attribute to ecclesiology[2] a Marian dimension and to Mariology an ecclesiological dimension. In *Redemptoris Mater*, 47, Pope John Paul II relates this fact by saying:

> The Council's teaching emphasized that the truth concerning the Blessed Virgin, Mother of Christ, is an effective aid in exploring more deeply the truth concerning the Church.[3]

And again in his encyclical on the Holy Spirit, *Dominum et Vivificantem*, 66:

> The Church perseveres in prayer. This union of the praying Church with the Mother of Christ has been part of the mystery of the Church from the beginning: we see her present in this mystery as she is present in the mystery of her Son.[4]

The dependency the Church has on Mary for a better understanding of its own identity became a pattern of thought in the pontificate of Pope Paul VI.[5] His remark concerning that reality came at an important moment in the life of the Church, namely right after the approval of *Lumen Gentium*, Vatican II's document on the Church. Paul VI states:

> Knowledge of the true Catholic doctrine regarding the Blessed Virgin Mary will always be a key to the exact understanding of the mystery of Christ and of the Church.[6]

Early in *Redemptor Hominis* (Redeemer of Man), John Paul describes Mary's continual maternal presence in the mystery of the Church. That presence is rooted in the way she lived her role in the mystery of her Son as He accomplished the salvation of humankind:

> The Church, which looks to her (Mary) with altogether special love and hope, wishes to make this mystery her own in an ever deeper manner.[7]

Mary's presence in the mystery of the Church is not an optional choice. Rather, it derives from the mechanism of Redemption itself, at whose beginning God the Son was conceived by the Holy Spirit and born of the Virgin. "Consequently, Mary must be on all the ways for the Church's daily life."[8]

At the very beginning of *Redemptoris Mater*, Pope John Paul II describes Mary as enjoying an "*active* and *exemplary presence* in the life of the Church."[9] It will take the Supreme Pontiff many years to display, in many different documents, what he meant by "*active* and *exemplary presence* in the life of the Church." Such a presence is related to space (geography of Marian faith and devotion),[10] time (liturgies of East and West; traditions of various communites),[11] and history of souls (Marian spirituality).[12] This explains why, in announcing the publication of *Redemptoris Mater*, John Paul specified that the encyclical would concentrate on "the consoling argument of Mary's presence in our lives and in the entire human history."[13]

In contemporary culture, the concept of *presence* has been used as a category of interpretation in many fields.[14] It indicates "being in front" or "mere presence" of the being that pertains to the metaphysical and intentional experience, or also "mutual interior relationship of communion" (personalistic perspective).[15] The notion of "presence" is widely used in the philosophical field, where the mutual coexistence of cause and effect leads us to call Saint Thomas Aquinas's metaphysics a "metaphysics of presence."[16] Saint Thomas specifies that God is present everywhere *"per essentiam, praesentiam et potentiam"* (as to Essence, Presence, and Power) because He maintains everything in existence and knows and governs the universe.[17] Saint John of Damascus, to whom the Holy Father refers in *Redemptoris Mater*, affirms the omnipresence of God who "penetrates everything without being conditioned by anything."[18] Presence plays a major role in religious mysticism, in the Old as well as in the New Testament (especially in Saint Paul).[19]

Stefano de Fiores praises the Holy Father's choice of the concept of *presence* as an approach to the theological question of Mary's identity and role in God's plan of salvation. Already in the conciliar document *Lumen Gentium*, the notion of "presence" belongs to the very structure of chapter VIII on Our Lady. It cannot be accidental, therefore, that John Paul refers to such a concept because of Vatican II and because its validity and actuality in all fields of knowledge manifest, in an adequate manner for contemporary readers, the place and mission of Mary in the economy of Redemption.[20] Since Mary is treated by the Second Vatican Council, by Pope Paul VI, and by Pope John Paul II always in relationship with the Trinity and the Church, her *presence* in the mystery of Christ and the Church cannot be isolated. Actually, it constantly should be measured by and compared to contemporary usage in theology, because Mary's presence should not assume an autonomous character in the midst of the whole body of theological disciplines. The *analogia fidei* (analogy of faith) requires a harmonization of all revealed truths to which the truth about the Mother of the Lord belongs. After publishing *Redemptoris Mater*, John Paul II himself invited the Pontifical Theological Faculty of the "Marianum" in Rome to further investigate the meaning of the notion of *presence*. He encouraged Mariologists to widen the field of research and offer more opportunities for contemporary men and women to understand the meaning of Mary's presence in God's plan of Redemption. The Pope considered "the nature of the various ways of the Virgin Mary's presence in the life of the Church" as one of the most delicate questions and arguments.[21]

Since Pope John Paul II opens his Marian encyclical with the subject of Mary's presence in the mystery of Christ and the Church, the theme of "presence," it seems, is a direct goal of that encyclical.[22] This becomes even more evident as the presentation uses the term "presence" fourteen times and the term "present" twenty-one times.[23] B. Billet refers to "presence" as "un thème central de l'encyclique" (a central theme of the encyclical).[24] I agree with I. Scinella, who also considers "presence" as "one of the key categories" in *Redemptoris Mater*[25] because it joins the different stages of Mary's mission. This mission began as a foreshadowing of Mary in the Old Testament, continued as a presence in the mystery of Christ, and is now a presence in the mystery of the Church.

When John Paul emphasizes in *Redemptoris Mater* the notion of Mary's presence in the Church, it seems that he has in mind the scholastic distinction among the circumscribed presence of earthly bodies, the operative contact of spirits with the world that is not circumscribed, and the presence of God who occupies all the parts of the created universe without being limited by anything. The question of the nature of Mary's presence in the Church remains to be identified. In *Redemptoris Mater*, 28, Pope John Paul II used terminology like "encounter" to designate Mary's journey of faith as her manner of presence on earth before the Assumption. Afterwards, the expression "ray of maternal presence" is used to explain the nature of her presence in the Church in her glorious state. In this sense, the sacred space of a Marian sanctuary cannot be objectivized as an autonomous Absolute; rather, it has the anthropological function of a place in which to encounter God through the experience of Mary who is maternally present. For John Paul II, Mary is present in the sanctuary by her maternal activity. The most important aspect of this presence lies in its interpersonal encounter with the "interior space" of the human person opened by Mary's faith and present in the Church (ecclesiastical space) as a covenant with God. Therefore, the "active and exemplary presence" of Mary in the Church refers, as far as space is concerned, to the encounter of the Church with Mary's intervention in the order of grace.[26]

MARY, THE CHURCH'S OWN BEGINNING

In our first section on the divine maternity of Mary, it already has been clarified that the "fullness of time" of Gal 4:4 has a Trinitarian,

Christological, soteriological (or salvific), Pneumatological, Marian, philosophical, and ecclesiological dimension. As far as ecclesiology is concerned,
Pope John Paul II sees in "fullness of time" the beginning of the Church's
journey. This means that the Church's journey began not only when it
was born from the side of the Christ who was sleeping on the cross (as
Lumen Gentium affirms), not only when the Spirit publicly revealed the
Church's identity to the world (Pentecost), but also when the time had
fully come for the Son of God to be incarnate in the womb of Mary.
The content of the "Church's journey" is Christological, but its human
dimension referring to the presence and the union of the divine-human
in Jesus Christ is necessarily Marian.[27] It is beyond doubt that, for John
Paul, Christ is the only and the ultimate reason for the Church's existence and identity. That is to say that Christ is the condition of possibility
of the Church *in* and *per se*. The response of Mary to the Incarnation of
the Son of God in the fullness of time marks the moment of humanity's
positive answer to God that will enable the Church, as far as its human
dimensions are concerned, to start its journey throughout the ages. This is
the reason for the words of the Pope at the opening of *Redemptoris Mater:*

> Finally, this fullness designates the hidden beginning of the Church's
> journey. In the liturgy the Church salutes Mary of Nazareth as the
> Church's own beginning, for in the event of the Immaculate Con-
> ception the Church sees projected, and anticipated in her most noble
> member, the saving grace of Easter.[28]

When John Paul II relates that the Church salutes Mary of Nazareth
in the liturgy as the Church's own beginning, he refers to the Preface of
the Feast of the Immaculate Conception in the Roman Missal, to Saint
Ambrose, and to *Lumen Gentium*, 68. In *Lumen Gentium*, 68, it is
stated that:

> [I]n the meantime the Mother of Jesus in the glory which she pos-
> sesses in body and soul in heaven is the image and beginning of the
> Church as it is to be perfected in the world to come.[29]

The Pope approaches this document of Vatican II from many different
angles and adds several dimensions to it. Whereas Vatican II (*Lumen
Gentium*) refers only to the bodily presence of Mary in the state of glory

and sees in her the image and the beginning of the Church perfected in the world to come, John Paul II brings the event of the Immaculate Conception to the wider context of his ecclesiological Mariology. Mary is the beginning of the Church because her being the Immaculate Conception anticipates the saving grace of the Lord's death and resurrection. What will happen to the Church in its eschatological dimension (end of time) has already taken place in Mary and, therefore, from the point of view of her immunity from original and actual sin, she is the Church's own beginning. This Marian dimension of the Church allows the Pope to express the continuity between the historical (now) dimension of the Church and its eschatological destiny. Mary of Nazareth, a historical person who is herself the Immaculate Conception, anticipates with her day-to-day sinless life the future state of the Church in the *eschaton* (end of time or last things). Thus, time and eternity, life on earth, and endless life with God do not stand in opposition with one another. Although there is a discontinuity between them because of the different categories in which they exist, there is still a continuity brought about by the loving grace of God who bestowed on Mary a life free from the corruption of sin, anticipating the eschatological state of the glorious Church.[30]

John Paul II's encyclical *Evangelium Vitae* (The Gospel of Life), 103 shows that, from an eschatological point of view, the Pope sees in the final destiny of Mary in the glory of heaven her ultimate crossing as well as the Church's pilgrimage. The "great portent" spoken of in the Book of Revelation (12:1) explains the "mutual relationship between the mystery of the Church and Mary."[31] Looking at Mary, the Church sees in her an icon of her own destiny and realizes that eschatological glorification also constitutes the Church's ultimate goal. The mystery of the Church cannot be reduced to its historical dimension alone, even though it is rooted in history:

> In this sign (Rev 12:1) the Church recognizes an image of her own mystery: present in history, she knows that she transcends history, inasmuch as she constitutes on earth the seed and beginning of the kingdom of God (*Lumen Gentium*, 5). The Church sees this mystery fulfilled in complete and exemplary fashion in Mary.[32]

All that the Church expects to be ours in the glory of heaven is already accomplished in Mary who thereby becomes present in the

78

mystery of the Church as a model and an icon.[33] The reason for her being the exemplary model and icon of the Church lies in the fact that "she is the woman of glory in whom God's plan could be carried out with supreme perfection."[34] Here history and eschatology meet in the person of Mary. The Church, being the "seed and beginning" of the Kingdom of God on earth, strives to fulfill in itself the eschatological dimension of its existence and, therefore, should constantly look at Mary. Expressions such as "eschatological tabernacle" and "eschatological icon of the Church" were already frequently applied to Mary at the vigil of the Second Vatican Council.[35]

When the Second Vatican Council introduced Our Lady into the Constitution on the Church (*Lumen Gentium,* VIII), the Council never intended to belittle or ignore the personal qualifications of Mary. It was simply a matter of seeing Mary as a part of the Church.[36] Mary, having built up Christ's physical body as His Mother, continues this role in the mystical body, the Church. Pope John Paul II elucidates the approach of the Council by including all those traits that were attributed to Mary throughout the tradition of the Church. He never fails to emphasize her personal holiness and distinctive characteristics as an exemplary member of the people of God, as was shown in our third chapter on the Immaculate Conception. He describes Mary as the Church's "most noble member,"[37] "exceptional daughter of the human race,"[38] and "extraordinary woman."[39]

The way John Paul looks at the person of Mary in relation to the community of the Church reflects his *philosophy of person.* The conjunction of Mary, as a human subject, and the community of Church follows the pattern of the principle of participation treated in John Paul II's *The Acting Person* and "The Person: Subject and Community."[40] Participation is understood by John Paul as:

> . . . the property of the person which is expressed in the capacity to stamp as personal one's own existence and action when existing and acting together with many people.[41]

It is a positive relation to the humanity of other people. The Pope goes on to explain that "humanity" is not an abstract idea of humankind, neither an abstraction nor a generality. It should be perceived as a "personal self which in each occasion is unique and non-recurrent," and which possesses the "specific gravity of the personal being in each man."[42]

Such a perception of the human person allows the Pope to refute that which constitutes the ultimate conflict in Platonism, the conflict between being and essence. For Plato, the human person is entirely intelligible as an essence but not entirely intelligible as a being. The Platonic ideas are committed to abstract essences when it comes to the origin of humankind's being and its interior economy. In Plato's system, only ideas are true being. According to Saint Thomas Aquinas, the method that led Plato to posit ideas was intended by Plato himself to transcend the imperfection of sensible things. However, in the opinion of the angelic Doctor (Saint Thomas), Plato's method had ultimately impelled him to have a disexistentialized view of the being of humankind. Anton C. Pegis, in his introduction to Aquinas's *Summa Theologiae* and *Summa Contra Gentiles*, says:

> Because the more Plato sought to discover the ultimate conditions
> of reality by means of a reason which had methodically cut itself off
> from the body and from all sensible experience, the more he was
> investing with the name of being the abstract essences which were
> the only objects that such a methodically isolated reason could reach;
> and the more abstract essences became the center of Plato's world,
> the more Plato found himself incapable of explaining those condi-
> tions of actual beings which he could not derive from, or envisage
> within the economy of, the abstract essences which were the exem-
> plars of his world.[43]

The humanity that for John Paul II possesses the specific gravity of the personal being in each person excludes a mere generality in what makes people and everything that reduces them to the abstract idea of human:

> To participate in the humanity of another man means to continue
> in a living relation to the fact that he is precisely this man, and not
> merely to what, *in abstracto*, makes him a man.[44]

For both Saint Thomas Aquinas and Pope John Paul II, Plato's dilemma was a flight from existence. For John Paul, to understand humankind abstractly means to deny the existence of specific humans who, as a personal self unique and nonrecurrent, contribute to the perfection of their being in acting and existing among others. The whole philosophy and theology of self-fulfillment of John Paul II would be automatically jeopardized if one would consider humankind in the Platonic sense of an abstract essence that is intelligible only in the world of ideas. In the Pope's opinion, this points to the indispensable metaphysical priority of the personal subject in regard to the community. Since it is metaphysical, it is a factual and methodological priority:

> This means not only that people do exist and act together as a plurality of personal subjects, but also that we are not able to say anything essential about this coexistence and cooperation in the personalistic sense, that is, by way of community, if we do not begin with man precisely as a personal subject.[45]

This short presentation of John Paul's understanding of the being of one human as he exists and acts among other human beings sheds light on Mary's relationship with the community of the Church. In this regard he states:

> As an individual, a person is not a number or simply a link in a chain, nor even less, an impersonal element in some system. The most radical and elevating affirmation of the value of every human being was made by the Son of God in his becoming man in the womb of a woman, as we continue to be reminded each Christmas.[46]

The Church is not a mere plurality of personal subjects coexisting and cooperating arbitrarily; rather, it is a community that, in order to function as such, needs to start with the human being as an individual. Mary, precisely as a personal human subject, is the most noble member of the Church. Her active and exemplary presence in the Church,[47] although it draws all of its vitality from belonging to the Body of Christ, nonetheless enjoys a personalistic dimension that results from her subjective identity as a theological personality cooperating in God's plan of salvation. In such an unparalleled intervention, John Paul brings the Immaculate Conception, a dogma that is primarily concerned with the personalistic aspect of Mary's holiness,[48] to the framework of the Church's destiny as an immaculate, eschatological, and redeemed community. He is very careful not to arbitrarily emphasize the role of the Church as a community at the expense of the role of Mary as a personal subject. Therefore, one notices the emphasis on the historical dimension of Mary's personal subjectivity when the Pope states that "in the liturgy the Church salutes Mary of Nazareth as the Church's own beginning."[49]

With this kind of approach, John Paul II elucidates what Vatican II brought out in regard to the question of the relationship between Mary and the Church in so far as individuality-community is concerned. One realizes better, as the Pope emphasizes, that the introduction of Mary in the Constitution on the Church (*Lumen Gentium*) by the Fathers of the Second Vatican Council was never intended to deprive Mary of the privileges attributed to her by the tradition of the Church throughout the centuries. Neither was their intention to develop a theology of collective community at the expense of a personalistic contribution on the part of this "most noble member" of the Church.[50]

Mary of Nazareth is saluted as the beginning of the Church's journey in the sense that the Church draws from the Mother-Son relationship the prototype of the Church-Son relationship:

> And above all, in the Incarnation she (the Church) encounters Christ and Mary indissolubly joined: he who is the Church's Lord and Head and she who, uttering the first *fiat* of the New Covenant, prefigures the Church's condition as spouse and mother.[51]

The Church encounters Jesus and Mary standing in mutual relationship with each other in the sense that they are indissolubly joined. This means that encountering Jesus includes an *a priori* encounter with Mary, and encountering Mary includes an *a priori* encounter with Jesus. To display this idea, the Pope refers to Christ as *Lord* and *Head* and to Mary as *spouse* and *Mother*. The Church encounters Christ and Mary indissolubly joined because both of them are "parts" of the Church. To Christ's Lordship over the Church corresponds Mary's spousal state; to Christ as the Church's Head corresponds Mary's motherhood. However, it is Mary as spouse and Mother who prefigures the basis for the Church.[52]

Mary prefigures the Church as *spouse* in the sense of her intimate union with the Lord. Mary prefigures the Church as *Mother* in the sense of generating sons and daughters of God through the administration of the sacraments. If Mary has humanly generated the Son of God, then the

Church analogically generates sons and daughters of God.

In the encyclical *Dives in Misericordia* (Rich in Mercy), 15, the Pope extends that act of generating to God's revelation of mercy. Like Mary, the Church is invited to be "spiritual mother of mankind"[53] by manifesting God's merciful love through the cross of Christ. In that type of motherhood, the Church expresses "her maternal solicitude" for all human beings to whose service she is invited to be herald.[54]

In *Redemptoris Mater*, 5, Pope John Paul II explains further what he started in *Redemptoris Mater*, 1, namely, in what sense Mary is the hidden beginning of the Church's journey. The Second Vatican Council is now the source of his meditation. This Council presented Mary in the mystery of Christ and, by doing so, "also finds the path to a deeper understanding of the mystery of the Church."[55] The Pope continues to refer to the Council that draws a parallel between the Church as the Body of Christ and the conception of the Son of God in the womb of Mary through the power of the Holy Spirit. Since the Council places these two truths of faith "in close proximity," Mary assumes in the eyes and in the midst of the Church a very special position. Namely, she "as the Mother of Christ, is in a particular way united with the Church, which the Lord established as his own body."[56] The Incarnation of the Son of God in the womb of Mary is a historical reality that took place through the power of the Spirit. This historicity which marks God's physical presence in the world is irrevocable. One should not de-historize God because then the Incarnation would lose its redemptive and eschatological character and would also reduce the presence of Christ in our world to that of any other spiritual guru who came, accomplished a mission, and then disappeared. The infinite value of God's action demands His uninterrupted presence in history. This is the reason, in John Paul's opinion, that:

> . . . the reality of the Incarnation finds a sort of extension in the mystery of the Church—the Body of Christ. And one cannot think of the reality of the Incarnation without referring to Mary, the Mother of the Incarnate Word.[57]

The expression "sort of extension" indicates that there is no onto-logical identity between the two realities because the Church is not the Body of Christ in the same sense Christ received His body from Mary in the Incarnation through the power of the Holy Spirit. Being incarnate in the womb of Mary is a historical event with full physical dimensions connected with it. The Church, as the Body of Christ, is a historical reality but in a spiritual way because the Church cannot be physically identified with the body Christ received from Mary. The analogy of the expression "Body of Christ" allows the Pope to look at Mary as the connection between Christ and the Church. The body of Christ, physically conceived in the womb of Mary, and the Body of Christ, the Church, are two different yet analogous realities, with Mary as the common denominator. The Fathers of the Second Vatican Council, as John Paul II shows, found in this theology an excellent opportunity to place Mary into the mystery of the Church because they knew that by introducing Mary into the mystery of Christ, they would find the path to a "deeper understanding of the mystery of the Church."[58] Since, as it is well known, the Fathers of the Second Vatican Council intended to deepen the knowledge of the Church about its own identity and role, Pope John Paul shows that their approach using Mariology is a positive contribution toward that knowledge.

PILGRIMAGE OF MARY AND PILGRIMAGE OF THE CHURCH

In *Redemptoris Mater*, 25, Pope John Paul II presents the teaching of the Second Vatican Council concerning the pilgrimage of the Church and draws a parallel with the pilgrimage of Mary. The Church "presses forward amid the persecutions of the world and the consolations of God,[59] announcing the Cross and death of the Lord until he comes (cf. 1 Cor 11:26)."[60] As Israel according to the flesh, the Church of God was bought by the blood of Christ and filled with His Holy Spirit, "and provided it with those means which befit it as a visible and social unity."[61] Vatican II emphasizes that "God has gathered together as one all those who in faith look upon Jesus as the author of salvation,"[62] and that this Church is a pilgrim Church journeying toward the kingdom. Such a journey possesses an external character, "visible in the time and space in which it historically takes place." For the Church "is destined to extend to all regions of the earth and so to enter into the history of mankind."[63]

The essential character of that pilgrimage, however, is still interior because it is a pilgrimage of faith in which the Church moves forward empowered by the risen Lord and the Holy Spirit, the invisible Comforter.[64]

This short presentation of Vatican II's concept of "pilgrimage" in *Redemptoris Mater*, 25 prepares the necessary ground for its Marian counterpart. Pope John Paul takes as his point of departure the reality of the Church. He describes in a few words the specific ecclesiological aspects of the Second Vatican Council (*Lumen Gentium*, 8, 9) and then proceeds to examine the identity and place of Mary in that context. Ecclesiology becomes the principle on which much Mariology is built. This method shows the Pope's faithfulness to the principles laid down by Vatican II regarding the Church as a point of departure for studying the presence of Mary in the mystery of Christ and the Church.[65]

If the Church is on a pilgrimage through the present life, so was Mary when she was accompanying Jesus. If the Church is "destined to extend to all regions of the earth and so to enter into the history of mankind,"[66] so does Mary's pilgrimage transcend history in order to walk at the center of the Church and reach out to all humankind.[67] Both the Church and Mary are on interior as well as external pilgrimages. However, there is still a significant difference between the two pilgrimages because Mary had advanced in the most perfect way in her pilgrimage of faith. It has been established in the chapters on divine maternity and the Immaculate Conception that she, as the Mother of God, is the most eminent member of the Church who, faithfully preserving the faith in her Son even to the foot of the cross, was introduced into the mystery of Christ in the deepest possible way:

> It is precisely in this ecclesial journey or pilgrimage through space and time, and even more through the history of souls, that Mary is present, as the one who is "blessed because she believed," as the one who advanced on the pilgrimage of faith, sharing unlike any other creature in the mystery of Christ.[68]

Pope John Paul II refers to the teaching of the Second Vatican Council in order to explain, from the perspective of faith, the meaning of "sharing unlike any other creature in the mystery of Christ." In its relationship to the mystery of Christ, the faith of Mary becomes a model, pattern, and the highest expression of human response to, and cooperation with, the economy of salvation. All that God expects from humankind as far as faith is concerned is present in Mary. Her model embraces all the dimensions that the faith of all human persons of all times had in their intellectual and voluntary responses to God. In that sense, quoting *Lumen Gentium*, 65, the Pope says:

> Mary figured profoundly in the history of salvation and in a certain way unites and mirrors within herself the central truths of the faith. Among all believers she is like a mirror "in which are reflected in the most profound and limpid way the mighty works of God" (Acts 2:11).[69]

Redemptoris Mater, 26 shows that the external as well as the interior pilgrimage of the Church started with the descent of the Holy Spirit on the apostles during Pentecost. It will end when the pilgrim Church and the glorious Church meet together in heaven. Mary was present with the apostles when the visible journey of the Church started, and Mary will always be journeying with the Church until the final coming of Christ.[70] However, because Mary had already started her personal pilgrimage at the Annunciation, "in a sense her journey of faith is longer."[71] It is longer because it covers the entire period of Mary's presence in the entire life of her Son, and because "the Holy Spirit had already come down upon her, and she became his faithful spouse at the Annunciation."[72] Mary precedes the apostles in her journey of faith; she "goes before them" and "leads the way" for them.[73]

Lumen Gentium, 53 has referred to Mary in terms of "*temple* of the Holy Spirit." Pope John Paul II uses terms such as "faithful spouse"[74] when describing the coming down of the Holy Spirit upon Mary at the Annunciation. In his opinion, the spousal character of the pilgrimage of faith strengthens the foundations of the unity between Mary and the mystery of Christ and the Church. By being united to Mary, the Spirit, whose work extends the presence of Christ in the Church, makes Mary constantly and most profoundly an active participant in Christ's mystery. A spousal character, based on "full submission of intellect and will," provides a secure pilgrimage of faith with all the necessary conditions to make it a model and pattern for the Church's pilgrimage. It is that spousal union between Mary and the Holy Spirit that guarantees an uninterrupted presence of Mary in the mystery of Christ, in the mystery of the Church, and in the history of humankind.[75]

Before the Second Vatican Council one finds the Church following the theology of Saint Thomas Aquinas in which Mary has a role in the mission of Pentecost along with the infant Church. As for a special mission of the Holy Spirit in His coming upon Mary at the Annunciation, the special grace possessed by Mary does not mention something similar to Pentecost because she did not receive the apostolic mission to found the Church through the preaching of the doctrine and through the administration of the sacraments.[76] With the Second Vatican Council, one notices a fuller picture of Mary in the Cenacle. There, "we also see Mary by her prayers imploring the gift of the Spirit, who had already overshadowed her in the Annunciation."[77] The parallel between Annunciation and Pentecost is, in Manteau-Bonamy's opinion, the Council's way of underscoring the true coming of the Holy Spirit as a Divine Person on Mary at the Annunciation.[78] Especially in the document on the missionary activity of the Church, the Council clearly indicated that the Holy Spirit had a personal mission not only when He came on Christ or on the apostles, but also when He came on Mary at the moment of the Son's Incarnation:

> Without doubt, the Holy Spirit was at work in the world before Christ was glorified. On the day of Pentecost, however, he came down on the disciples that he might remain with them forever . . . The 'acts of the Apostles' began with Pentecost, just as Christ was conceived in the Virgin Mary with the coming of the Holy Spirit and was moved to begin his ministry by the descent of the same Holy Spirit, who came down upon him while he was praying.

"In the Upper Room Mary's journey meets the Church's journey of faith. In what way?"[79] Also, what are the implications of Mary's journey for the Church's, since hers is a "longer" journey than that of the Church? The Church has always considered the apostles as those who received the command of Christ to go "to the whole world to teach all nations" (Mt 28:19) and to be witnesses of His death and resurrection. Mary, however, "did not directly receive this apostolic mission"[80] even if she was present in the Upper Room with the apostles as the "Mother of Jesus" devoted to prayer and awaiting the descent of the Holy Spirit. The Pope continues:

And that first group of those who in faith looked upon Jesus as the author of salvation, knew that Jesus was the Son of Mary, and that she was his Mother, and that as such she was from the moment of his conception and birth a unique witness to the mystery of Jesus, that mystery which before their eyes had been disclosed and confirmed in the Cross and Resurrection.[81]

Mary receives a very different interpretation in the eyes of the apostles from the very first moment the Lord was risen from the dead. Now in the Upper Room, all the words of the angel at the Annunciation found fulfillment. Mary's faith born at the Annunciation "found confirmation." Her pilgrimage of faith acquired a realization of the unseen hope because, with the Resurrection, "the promise had begun to be transformed into reality."[82] The fulfillment of the promises of salvation that took place through the work of Jesus now places Mary at the center of attention. There certainly arises a sense of interest in investigating the hidden years in which Mary experienced Christ, her Son. The apostles are not searching now for the mystery of Jesus apart from Mary; rather, they now are watching her, because Jesus is the author of salvation. Mary's mystery is revealed through the mystery of Christ, and the mystery of Christ is also enlightened by the mystery of Mary. Both mysteries condition each other in the context of the Mother-Son relationship. In that sense, the Pope continues in *Redemptoris Mater*, 26:

Thus, from the very first moment, the Church looked at Mary through Jesus, just as she looked at Jesus through Mary.[83]

"Looking at" Mary through Jesus has both a historical and an eschatological meaning in the life and vision of the Church. Both the historical dimension of Scripture and all the salvific events fulfilled by the words and actions of Christ are essential. Through that historicity, the Pope avoids an agnostic approach to Scripture that would tend to question the true historicity of the infancy narratives and other Scriptural documents.[84] It is important to note that John Paul's personalistic approach to Mary of Nazareth enables him to draw a picture based on historical events that Mary experienced as she lived with Christ. Historicity vivifies the mystery; it does not diminish its transcendence.[85] However, without an anagogical dimension (this dimension refers to the last things) in the scriptural description of Mary's historical relationship with Christ, the mystery would be reduced to its mere human aspects. Therefore, the Church of Mary's time and of all times, in its search for understanding Christ's mystery, has come and must always come back to look at Mary. This transhistorical aspect of Mary as the Mother witnessing the mystery of her Son *par excellence* is rooted in her historical and concrete identity as Mary of Nazareth and as the Mother of Jesus "who first believed."[86] There are treasures of knowledge hidden in the heart of this one who walked step by step with Jesus from the very first moment of His Incarnation. Perhaps now is the moment, in the Pope's opinion, to turn to Mary for answers to questions about the years she spent with Him and her presence in the awesome mystery of her Son. Therefore, historicity and transhistoricity go hand by hand in order to display what the Church experienced and will always experience whenever it looks at Mary through Jesus:

> For the Church of that time and of every time Mary is a singular witness to the years of Jesus' infancy and hidden life at Nazareth, when she kept all these things, "pondering them in her heart" (Lk 2:19, cf. Lk 2:51).[87]

In *Redemptoris Mater*, 27, Pope John Paul II continues to meditate on the presence of Mary in the midst of the Church at Pentecost. As the Church started its long journey through the generations, Mary was with those who were "the seed of the new Israel"[88] as an "exceptional" witness to the mystery of Christ. To Mary's situation at Pentecost the Pope applies the famous text of Vatican II (*Gaudium et Spes*, 22), according to which the Church contemplates Mary "in the light of the Word made man."[89] But her presence in the mystery of Christ is now, at Pentecost, extended to a presence in the mystery of the Church, since, from the first moment of the Church's birth, Mary's identity and role were the pattern of all that the Church is invited to be in her relationship to Christ:

> At the basis of what the Church has been from the beginning, and of what she must continually become from generation to generation, in the midst of all the nations of the earth, we find the one who

believed that there would be a fulfillment of what was spoken to her from the Lord (Lk 1:45).[90]

What the Church is invited to be and to do now has already taken place through the obedience of faith of the one who, from the beginning of God's new presence in the world, cooperated with His plan to reach the point of Pentecost. Since Mary is the first one who believed in the mystery of the Incarnation proposed by the angel, her faith becomes the first step in cooperating with God's entrance into the dimension of time. In this sense, she opened the door for the New Covenant between God and humanity. That new manner of God's presence among His people of which Mary was an instrument, indicates that her faith will always be a criterion of authenticity for the Church's pilgrimage of faith. Chronologically as well as qualitatively, her presence in the mystery of Christ and the Church preceded the apostolic mission. Therefore, in a manner beyond historical investigation, the faith of Mary will always enjoy an originality that is a source of a constant amazement for the Church. What the Church will experience throughout history is necessarily a reflection of the faith of the first one who lived it right beside her Son. All by herself, she started her journey of faith, and when the Church was born on Pentecost to fulfill the promises of the Lord, the Church looked at Mary to share in her personal faith.

In the opinion of Pope John Paul II, the Marian dimension of the faith of the Church is not an appendix or arbitrary qualification. Somehow, the Church necessarily must have a Marian dimension when it responds to the Lord with faith, because Mary preceded the apostolic witness of the Church and has become for it a source of living faith in the mystery of Christ, to be accomplished in history and throughout eternity. Mary and the Church, therefore, walk side by side in responding with faith to God's revelation as it unfolds in history. The faith of Mary is a model and example that nourishes people throughout all time who accept the faith of the Church. On its part, the faith of the Church witnesses, meditates on, and studies the personalistic dimensions of Mary's faith as the witness *par excellence* of the mystery of Christ.[91] The mystery of the Church that is ultimately based on how it must respond to God's plan of salvation in faith becomes intimately connected with and dependent on the mystery of the Mother. Mary is not only the eschatological image of the Church; she is the icon of the Church even in the very concrete historicity where Mary lived and experienced the mystery of Christ in a way known only to God. Thus Elizabeth's words, "Blessed is she who believed," have a historical dimension as far as the personal faith of Mary is concerned, and a transhistorical dimension as far as the faith of the Church, in its relationship with the faith of Mary, is concerned. These ideas are summarized by John Paul when he says:

> It is precisely Mary's faith which marks the beginning of the new and eternal Covenant of God with man in Jesus Christ; this heroic faith of hers precedes the apostolic witness of the Church, and ever remains in the Church's heart hidden like a special heritage of God's revelation. All those who from generation to generation accept the apostolic witness of the Church share in that mysterious inheritance, and in a sense share in Mary's faith.[92]

As shown in *Redemptoris Mater*, 28, the Second Vatican Council has already described the faith of Mary in its relationship with the mission of the Church:

> Mary figured profoundly in the history of salvation ... Hence when she is being preached and venerated, she summons the faithful to her Son and his sacrifice, and to love for the Father.[93]

This statement of Vatican II, in John Paul's opinion, implies that the faith of Mary is thus being proclaimed as the faith of the Church. Throughout its history, the Church born at Pentecost will never cease to venerate and praise Mary, because the Church's praise reflects on its own identity as the faithful people of God. When Mary is praised she summons the faithful to the Son's sacrifice and to the love of the Father, because she is the very first one who cooperated by her obedience of faith in God's plan and so "figured profoundly in the history of salvation." Every time Mary's faith is praised, the faith of the people of God joins with the mystery of the Mother who, at Pentecost, met in her own journey the journey of the Church:

> For this reason, Mary's faith, according to the Church's apostolic witness, in some way continues to become the faith of the pilgrim People of God: the faith of individuals and communities, of places and gatherings ...[94]

This identification should not be understood in the absolute sense of the word, because the faith of Mary, in its personalistic and historical dimension, is a unique qualification that no other human being will ever fully experience. God's People, however, are invited to look at Mary's faith, imitate it, and try to share in it as deeply as possible. The Church makes the faith of Mary its own only to a degree of participation. There should be careful note of the existing analogy between Mary's faith as a dimension of the historical personality, and the faith of the Church understood as the developing faith of individuals and communities. Both individualistic and collective aspects of the Church's faith are a reflection of Mary's faith. In that sense, the Pope continues:

> [I]t is a faith [the faith of Mary] that is passed on simultaneously through both the mind and the heart. It is gained or regained continually through prayer.[95]

Both Mary and the Church generate Christ to the world through faith. Mary generated Him physically in the historical event of the Incarnation and continues to generate Him spiritually throughout the whole history of the Church. The Church does not generate Christ physically because the Incarnation, historically speaking, happened once and for all. The Church generates Christ spiritually and gives Him to the world. Hence the analogy between the faith of Mary and the faith of the Church. However, one should not understand it as an absolute identification or undifferentiated similarity. Hence, John Paul quotes *Lumen Gentium,* 65:

> The Church in her apostolic work also rightly looks to her who brought forth Christ, conceived by the Holy Spirit and born of the Virgin, so that through the Church Christ may be born and increase in the hearts of the faithful also.[96]

The Church, as a communion of the people of God "with each other in the Holy Spirit,"[97] extends the mystery of Pentecost in space and time. Or, in the Pope's words, "we can therefore say that in this union the mystery of Pentecost is continually being accomplished."[98] If the mystery of Pentecost is unceasingly being fulfilled and Mary was united to the apostles in prayer when that mystery was revealed in history, then, throughout the history of the Church, Mary will always be united to the people of God in prayer in order to extend Pentecost on earth throughout human history.[99]

If the Church and the whole of humanity look at Mary as the one who first believed, it is because of the newly established relationship between God and humanity. There is a parallel between *Redemptoris Mater*, 28 and *Salvifici Doloris* (On the Meaning of Christian Suffering) that analyzes the spiritual space created between humankind and the Father. In *Salvifici Doloris*, the evil of humankind creates a spiritual space between God and humanity. To delete that evil from the spiritual space and fill it again with goodness, Christ took upon His own shoulders the sins of all humanity, and in His unity with the Father He eliminated humankind's estrangement from God. When the Father looked at Christ on the cross, He saw the sum total of evil committed by humankind from the beginning of creation until the end. However, the Father also saw His Only Beloved Son. The estrangement from humanity was not possible any longer because the unity between Father and Son is far stronger than the division between the Father and humanity. In this way, the Redemption accomplished by Christ becomes a substitute Redemption.[100]

From a Marian perspective, the faith of Mary becomes the first opportunity to provide a spiritual space between God and humankind that is not filled with evil. By "evil" is meant the evil in all its forms—diabolical, physical, and moral. This space, which is not a physical space, describes the manner of the relationship between God and humankind based on the distance and the difference between them as a transcendent God and a limited human person. This spiritual space is called "interior space" in *Redemptoris Mater*, 28. When the Father looks at the faith of Mary in obeying the plan of the Incarnation, a new spiritual space is opened that can be filled with the blessing mentioned at the beginning of the Letter to the Ephesians. Pope John Paul II refers again to that letter in order to picture the blessing of Christ bestowed on Mary because she believed and her faith became in Christ a source of blessing:

> For in Mary's faith, first at the Annunciation and then fully at the foot of the Cross, an interior space was reopened within humanity which the eternal Father can fill with every spiritual blessing.[101]

The interior and spiritual space created by the faith of Mary in her response to God becomes the site where a new expression of God's relationship with the world takes place. It is a dynamic relationship for both God and Mary. For God, because He is faithful in expressing Himself in relating to the world; for Mary, because of her obedience of faith which will be constantly renewed until the end of her earthly pilgrimage. That space filled with every blessing opens a new possibility of union between God and humanity through Mary and extends that possibility to the Church. Therefore, because of its dynamic nature, the new interior space of union between God and Mary becomes a Covenant that will remain as such until the consummation of the ages. The Church, which extends the pilgrimage of Mary on earth and continues to reopen the spiritual and interior space between God and humanity, becomes the unfailing sacrament of union between God and man. In that sense, Pope John Paul quotes *Lumen Gentium*, 1 and says: "It is the space of the new and everlasting Covenant," and it continues to exist in the Church, which in Christ is "a kind of sacrament or sign of intimate union with God, and of the unity of all mankind."[102]

THE MAGNIFICAT OF MARY, AS THE NEW EVE, IN RELATIONSHIP TO THE MYSTERY OF THE CHURCH

In *Redemptoris Mater*, 36–37, Pope John Paul II analyzes the *Magnificat* of Mary in relationship to the Church. Elizabeth has blessed Mary because of "the fruit of her womb" and her faith. This twofold blessing bestowed on Mary by Elizabeth is the first step that clarifies "that which remained hidden in the depths of the obedience of faith at the Annunciation . . ."[103] Mary's kinswoman has confirmed the event of the Incarnation and brought a new dimension into Mary's knowledge. The pilgrimage of faith was not an obstacle for a growing consciousness of God's plan as it unfolds in the events of Mary's life. That personalistic aspect allows the Pope to emphasize the historical link between the Annunciation and the Visitation:

> Now, at the visitation, when Elizabeth's greeting bears witness to that culminating moment, Mary's faith acquires a new consciousness and a new expression.[104]

The *Magnificat* of Mary is the new expression of her consciousness of God's plan and her involvement in it. It is "an inspired profession
of faith" based on the sacred texts of the people of Israel and a "response
to the revealed word."[105] Mary manifests her own personal experience
of the mystery of God and speaks of "the glory of his ineffable holiness."[106] Above all, the new expression of God's presence in the world
constitutes the essence of Mary's words in the *Magnificat*. The whole
history of salvation as lived by the people of the Old Covenant is now
displayed and fulfilled because of God's "eternal love which, as an irrevocable gift, enters into human history."[107] Chronologically and
qualitatively, Mary, as the Annunciation and the *Maginificat* relate, is the
witness *par excellence* who experienced the new dimension of God's communication with humanity. That new manner of God's expression in
the world was thoroughly analyzed in my study on the Trinitarian thought
of Pope John Paul II.[108] In the present work, the Marian dimension of
God's new Self-giving to the world is the focus of study:

> Mary is the first to share in this new revelation of God and, within
> the same, in this new Self-giving of God.[109]

If God, in His own divine initiative has decided to enter human history,
Mary is the first to experience it (Annunciation) and to share it
(*Magnificat*).

Being the first to experience and to share God's new revelation to
the world, Mary, on the human level and in the context of the human
dimension of Redemption, becomes the fulfillment of the promises made
to Israel. Pope John Paul II applies to Mary the theology of revelation of
Vatican II (*Dei Verbum*, 2):

> The deepest truth about God and the salvation of man is made
> clear to us in Christ, who is at the same time the mediator and the
> fullness of revelation.[110]

If Christ is the agent of fulfillment of the whole history of salvation,
Mary stands in direct relationship, as a Mother, with that fulfillment. If
Christ is the mediator of all revelation, Mary is connected, as a Mother,
to the mediation of that revelation. The whole economy of salvation is
concentrated on Christ as the author of a definitive revelation of God
and humankind's salvation. The whole economy is also concentrated on

Mary who, as the Mother of Christ, fulfills in herself the history of salvation. The Pope does not want to leave out any player involved in the fulfillment of God's definitive revelation to the world. On the divine level, the Holy Spirit operates the Incarnation and reveals the initiative of God. Also on the divine level, the Son fulfills the revelation of God. On the divine-human level, the divine Son is humanly expressing the truth about God and humanity's salvation. And on the purely human level, in the drama of God's new Self-giving, is Mary who, as the Mother of Christ, stands at the center of the event and witnesses to its fulfillment in her *Magnificat:*

> In her exultation Mary confesses that she finds herself in the very heart of this fullness of Christ. She is conscious that the promise made to the fathers, . . . , is being fulfilled in herself. She is thus aware that concentrated within herself as the Mother of Christ is the whole salvific economy, in which from age to age "is manifested he who, as the God of the Covenant, remembers his mercy.[111]

MARY MOTHER OF THE CHURCH, MODEL OF VIRGINITY AND MOTHERHOOD

Already in *Redemptor Hominis*, 22, Pope John Paul II considered the Church's motherhood as being the result of its duty to constantly "keep up this dynamic link between the mystery of the Redemption and every man."[112] The aim of the apostolic, pastoral, priestly, and episcopal service of the Church makes her a Mother who cooperates in the generation of the sons and daughters of God. This brings us to the reason the Church needs a Mother, especially at our time.[113] We find the answer in Vatican II, especially in *Lumen Gentium*, 52–69. Inspired by the Council's teaching, Pope Paul VI, as mentioned above, calls Mary "Mother of the Church."[114] In *Redemptor Hominis*, Pope John Paul II recalls that the title "Mother of the Church" is based on the Trinitarian mystery of God:

> Mary is *Mother of the Church* because, on account of the Eternal Father's ineffable choice and due to the Spirit of Love's special action, she gave human life to the Son of God, for whom and by

whom all things exist (Heb 2:10) and from whom the whole of the people of God receives the grace and dignity of election.[115]

The Pope's logic is strong: if Mary is the Mother of the Son who was incarnate in her womb on account of the Father's plan and action of the Holy Spirit of Love, then Mary is also the Mother of the people of God constituted as such by the One who is her Son. Such a Trinitarian dimension of the motherhood of Mary results from the Trinitarian dimension of the Church's identity and constitution. *Lumen Gentium* was very attentive to the need of presenting a vision of the Church that is based on the action of the Trinity in history. This action reflects what God is in Himself: a Trinity of Persons in eternal communion. What the Church is in herself, a work of the Trinity, influences Mary's relationship with the Church in so far as motherhood is concerned. By the work of the Trinity, Mary is the Mother of the Son; by the work of the Trinity, the Church exists and receives identity; by the work of the Trinity, the Church is a Mother who keeps up the link between men and women and the mystery of Redemption; by the Trinity, therefore, Mary is the "Mother of the Church," the Body of Christ, since she is the Mother of Christ.[116]

Already by the thirteenth century, the title "Mother of the Church" was often applied to Mary. The Venerable Bede (+735) was aware of the biblical background that attributes to the Holy Spirit a spiritual maternity regarding the Church. For Bede, the Holy Spirit is, in a transcendental way, the Mother of the Church, a fact that inspired him to give the title to Mary in relation to and in absolute dependence on the Holy Spirit.[117]

At the Second Vatican Council and for certain reasons, the commission did not accept the proposal to formally designate Mary as "Mother of the Church." A similar formula was used instead: "The Catholic Church, taught by the Holy Spirit, honors her (Mary) with the affection of filial piety as a most loving mother."[118] It is a fact, however, that the expression "Mother of the Church" was explicitly attributed to Mary by Pope Paul VI who, inspired by the teaching of the Second Vatican Council, declared Mary formally to be "Mother of the Church" at the end of the third session of the Council on November 21, 1964. Paul VI "proclaimed the Mother of Christ Mother of the Church, and that title has become known far and wide."[119] Paul VI also decided to speak further of the Blessed Virgin in many of his documents.[120]

Throughout his pontificate, Pope John Paul II has often referred to Mary as "the Mother of the Church"[121] and has developed the theology behind that concept. This mainly presents the mysterious correspondence that exists in Mary's maternal relationship to Jesus and to the Church. That mysterious correspondence belongs to the very plan of God the Father who:

> . . . choosing her as Mother of all humanity, . . . wanted to reveal the maternal dimension of his divine tenderness and care for men and women of every age.[122]

By saying that, John Paul confirms that Mary's spiritual motherhood of the Church and of humanity is not merely a result of the Church's theology. It is a divinely revealed matter that requires the obedience of faith of those who accept the entirety of the deposit of faith. In this line of thought, the beginning of *Redemptoris Mater* confirms that the Church venerates Mary "as her beloved Mother."[123]

The analysis of *Redemptoris Mater*, 42 presents a different and deeper argument for the relationship between Mary and the Church from the point of view of maternity and virginity. That from most ancient times Mary is invoked under the title God-bearer is a fact that "expresses the profound link which exists between the Mother of Christ and the Church."[124] Being *Theotokos* (Mother of God) is the fundamental characteristic that enables the Church to think of the relationship between her and Mary. Yet, the whole reality of Incarnation, in which Mary became Mother of God the Son, happened in the context of motherhood and virginity. Therefore, "as Virgin and Mother, Mary remains for the Church a permanent model."[125] As a model of virginity and motherhood, Mary, in her relationship with Christ, needs to be present in the mystery of the Church. "Permanent model" is renamed the "first model" in John Paul II's *Redemptionis Donum*, 17. In this document the Holy Father makes sure that, chronologically and qualitatively, Mary is considered the first model of the Church.[126]

Pope John here deals with Mary's presence in the Church based on her virginity and motherhood as the two qualifications attributed to the Church by Scripture and theology:

It can therefore be said that especially under this aspect, namely as a model, or rather as a figure, Mary, present in the mystery of Christ, remains constantly present also in the mystery of the Church. For the Church too is called mother and virgin, and these names have a profound biblical and theological justification.[127]

This statement by the Pope is of extreme importance because he does not in any way separate Church teaching on this question from the teaching of Scripture. In other words, the spiritual motherhood of Mary is accepted by the Church because it is taught by sacred Scriptures. John Paul does not allow the slightest doubt about the historicity of Mary's spiritual motherhood, which is confirmed especially by the Gospel of John. Neither does he refer to the canons of the historical-critical method in order to demonstrate the authenticity of spiritual motherhood as transmitted by the very Word of God.

The motherhood of the Church becomes a reality in its relationship with the Word of God. The Church "becomes herself a mother by accepting God's word with fidelity," so that:

> . . . by her preaching and by Baptism she brings forth to a new and immortal life children who are conceived of the Holy Spirit and born of God.[128]

Already Saint Paul has demonstrates the "maternal" character of the Church when he tells the Galatians that he is in travail until Christ be formed in them (Gal 4:19).[129] It seems that from the very beginning of the Church's life there has been this special dimension in the Church's ministry which nurtures people through preaching and baptism, namely her motherhood. Such a maternal nature enables the Church to contemplate her responsibility in the light of her fidelity to giving life to people in Christ, which leads us to a very important aspect in the Church's ministry: there is an indispensable relationship between the apostolic ministry of the Church, which is regenerating people in God through conception by the Holy Spirit, and motherhood. This relationship should not be looked upon as an addendum to the Church's ministry in the world, but as an essential dimension that completes and fosters the apostolic ministry:

These words of Saint Paul contain an interesting sign of the early Church's awareness of her own motherhood, linked to her apostolic service to mankind.[130]

This relationship (between the Church's motherhood and her apostolic ministry) reaches its culmination when John Paul interprets *Lumen Gentium*, 1 in light of the Church's motherhood. This famous text refers to the Church as "the sign and instrument of intimate union with God."[131] Such a quality of the Church is possible because of her motherhood. Since the Church generates "sons and daughters of the human race to a new life in Christ"[132] when receiving life from the Spirit, the Church must be a sign and instrument of intimate union with God. The Church's motherhood becomes the ground and the framework for her sacramental ministry. Pope John Paul II went beyond Vatican II and Pope Paul VI in attributing a dimension of motherhood to *Lumen Gentium*, 1, and in considering the very sacramental nature of the Church as directly connected with her motherhood.[133]

The whole reality of the Church's motherhood finds its roots and model in Mary who was first to believe at the Annunciation and generated Christ in the world. In exactly the same way, Mary conceived through the Holy Spirit and generated Christ in time, so that the Church, even though not physically or hypostatically (union on the level of person), is invited nevertheless through the celebration of the sacraments to generate Christ in the world and generate the world in Christ. The Church learns her own motherhood from Mary and recognizes "the maternal dimension of her vocation, which is essentially bound to her sacramental nature." Christ will always be "the first-born among many brethren" (Rom 8:29), because no other person will ever conceive Christ again like Mary did. Therefore, the Church's awareness of the link between her motherhood and her apostolic ministry:

> . . . enabled and still enables the Church to see the mystery of her life and mission modeled upon the example of the Mother of the Son, who is "the first-born among many brethren" (Rom 8:29).[134]

In that sense the Pope continues:

> For, just as Mary is at the service of the mystery of the Incarnation, so the Church is always at the service of the mystery of adoption to sonship through grace.[135]

The same theology of motherhood is also addressed at the end of John Paul II's encyclical *Evangelium Vitae*. Here the Pope sees a parallel between the motherly functions of Mary and the Church from a moral point of view. The Church learns her motherhood from Mary in relationship to life. Mary cared for the human life of Christ Who, being the Life itself, revealed Himself as the Savior of the world by laying down His very life for man. The Church, in the footsteps of Mary, generates sons and daughters not only sacramentally but also morally. The Church is invited to embrace them and their right to life in the same way Mary embraced Jesus in the mystery of Redemption. That mystery started when Mary welcomed His human life to exist in her womb at the Annunciation:

> The Church's experience of motherhood leads to a most profound understanding of Mary's experience as the incomparable model of how life should be welcomed and cared for.[136]

Evangelium Vitae also presents Mary as the "woman" of the Book of Revelation (12:1) who was with child. In her eschatological mode, Mary is still with child, an image that becomes a pattern in the Church's consciousness in so far as her mission to regenerate children in time for everlasting life is concerned. Looking at Mary, the Church understands that she is bearing "within herself the savior of the world, Christ the Lord."[137] Both Mary and the Church generate Christ in the world for time and for eternity. In time Mary generated Him physically and the Church spiritually; in eternity both Mary and the Church generate Him spiritually. However, the motherhood of the Church is *caused* by the motherhood of Mary, because without a generation according to the flesh by Mary, Christ could never have been present in the world and thus generated spiritually by the Church for the salvation of all. Therefore, Mary's divine maternity becomes the condition of possibility for all motherhood in the Church. It is even the model for motherhood according to the flesh of every woman who shares God's creative activity in the world. It represents the authentic and true image of Eve's motherhood as it was intended by God from the beginning, a fact that makes Mary, as the document *Familiaris Consortio*, 22 calls her, "model of redeemed woman." It gives reason and meaning to believers' acts of spiritually generating Christ in the world. It replaces Eve with Mary in relation to the generation of life:

> But the Church cannot forget that her mission was made possible by the motherhood of Mary, who conceived and bore the One who is God from God, "true God from true God." Mary is truly the Mother of God, the Theotókos (Mother of God), in whose motherhood the vocation to motherhood bestowed by God on every woman is raised to its highest level. Thus Mary becomes the model of the Church, called to be the new Eve, "the Mother of believers, the Mother of the living" (cf. Gen 3:20).[138]

If the motherhood of Mary happens through the pangs and the labor of childbirth spoken of by the Book of Revelation, so does the Church's spiritual motherhood. This means that the Church, throughout her entire mission, as she gives men and women "new birth into God's own life," will always live "in constant tension with the forces of evil that still roam the world and affect human hearts, offering resistance to Christ."[139] Satan, called "the personal power of evil"[140] by John Paul, along with all the powers of evil, are and will always be at work in history opposing the Church's mission of generating sons and daughters to salvation. The "red dragon" of Rev 12:3 has already attacked Mary's motherhood often, showing his insidious opposition to the Church. That hostility will be working always until the end of human history. If Mary and Joseph fled to Egypt in order to escape a dangerous threat, so also the Church:

> . . . finds "a place prepared by God" (Rev 12:6) in the desert, the place of trial but also of the manifestation of God's love for his people (cf. Hos 2:16).[141]

In her relationship with Christ, the Church is also a *virgin* "who keeps whole and pure the fidelity she has pledged to her Spouse."[142] The Church, as Divine Revelation confirms in the Pauline Letters and in the title found in Saint John's Book of Revelation, is the spouse of Christ.[143] The fidelity to Christ has a virginal character, even though it is a spousal fidelity. It is a total self-giving to God in virginity and, therefore, a virginal-spousal relationship with Him. Pope John Paul calls "motherhood in the Holy Spirit" the Church's virginal motherhood. This paradoxical coexistence of virginity and spousal character in the Church's relationship with Christ draws its modality from Mary who, at the Annunciation, conceived Christ in virginity. "Virgin-Mother" has been the focus of the Church's theology of Mary for the last two millennia:

> Precisely such virginity, after the example of the Virgin of Nazareth, is the source of a special spiritual fruitfulness: it is the source of motherhood in the Holy Spirit.[144]

Virginity as condition of possibility of divine maternity is even clearer in John Paul II's *Redemptionis Donum*, 17. Here the Pope attests that Mary is the Virgin *par excellence* and:

> . . . the one most fully consecrated to God, consecrated in the most perfect way. Her espousal love reached its height in the divine motherhood through the power of the Holy Spirit.

It is such a consecration, made out of responsible love, that enables Mary to conceive. As mentioned in the second chapter on Mary's motherhood, spiritual motherhood conditions divine maternity, and divine maternity gives spiritual motherhood its possibility of existence and its content.

The Holy Spirit connects not only the motherhood of Mary at the Annunciation and her motherhood in the order of grace but also the virginal motherhood of Mary with the virginal motherhood of the Church. At the Annunciation, Mary conceived by the power of the Spirit and become the Mother of the Son of God; throughout the history of the Church, the Church will always bring forth "to a new and immortal life children who are conceived of the Holy Spirit and born of God."[145] That the Holy Spirit is the Divine Person who assures the continuity between the virginal motherhood of Mary and the virginal motherhood of the Church is a fact that has become a pattern in the Pneumatology of Pope John Paul II. The Spirit of the Father and the Son will always make the "initial" contact with humanity whenever God enters the world. If Mary realized at the Annunciation that her motherhood is virginal, so did the Church, in the words of Saint Paul, acquire a consciousness of the virginal character of its motherhood as it serves "the mystery of adoption to sonship through grace."[146] In both instances, it is the Holy Spirit who does the "initial" contact and enters into history in Mary's life as well as in the life of the Church. The Church is:

> ... committed to preserving the word of God and investigating its riches with discernment and prudence, in order to bear faithful witness to it before all mankind in every age.[147]

In the context of virginal motherhood, one should not see just a simple parallel between the situation of Mary and that of the Church. More than a figure or a model, Mary's virginal motherhood actually contributes to the life of the Church. The motherhood of the Church is not only modeled after the example of Mary, *it becomes a reality with Mary's cooperation.* Vatican II, quoted by John Paul, states that:

> ... with maternal love she cooperates in the birth and development of the sons and daughters of Mother Church.[148]

The Pope already prepared for this theology in his first encyclical, The Redeemer of Man (*Redemptor Hominis*, 22):

> Her Son explicitly extended his Mother's maternity in a way that could easily be understood by every soul and every heart by designating, when he was raised on the Cross, his beloved disciple as her son.[149]

The first example of Mary's cooperation in accomplishing the Church's motherhood was clearly manifested at Calvary when Jesus on the cross entrusted John to Mary who, as a member of the Church, became the Mother of humanity through the person of the Apostle John. Every member of humanity, therefore, will have Mary as his or her own mother. In this sense, Mary "embraces each and every one *in* the Church."[150] However, the Church, the fruit of the cross and resurrection, was present at the foot of the cross when Mary received her motherhood in the order of grace. Consequently, Mary "embraces each and every one *through* the Church."[151] In the sense that Mary embraces each and every one *in* the Church and *through* the Church, Mary is the model of the Church. "Model" is not an expression limited to being a random example without substance. Mary is the model of the Church because of her cooperation in generating sons and daughters of the

Church. Such cooperation, revealed at the foot of the cross, enables her to embrace each and every one of us *in* and *through* the Church. John Paul refers to Pope Paul VI who already asked that "the Church must draw from the Virgin Mother of God the most authentic form of perfect imitation of Christ."[152]

CHAPTER FIVE

The Faith of Mary

MARY'S PILGRIMAGE OF FAITH

IN *REDEMPTORIS MATER*, Pope John Paul II has developed the same theme of faith that the Second Vatican Council started in *Lumen Gentium,* VIII. The Marianist Johann G. Roten rightly states that the Council's doctrine constitutes the matrix of all contemporary theological reflection concerning the faith of Mary.[1]

Luigi Gambero and U. Betti think that Mary's faith is the "*leitmotiv* [a dominant and recurring theme] of the encyclical."[2] "Blessed is she who believed" is, in Gianfranco Ravasi's opinion, the key of interpretation to the encyclical.[3] The concept of faith is considered by Salvatore Meo as:

> . . . the connection between the various themes in question and the common pillar that joins the three different parts of the document.[4]

In the opinion of Salvador Muñoz Iglesias, the faith of Mary is central to the point of obsession in *Redemptoris Mater*. Its *leitmotiv* is the "pilgrimage of faith" and the "obedience of faith."[5] Amato also considers the faith of Mary as situated at the center of the encyclical and its overall theme but, for him, the ecumenical goals of the Pope still constitute the fundamental intention of *Redemptoris Mater*.[6] For Leo Scheffczyk, the aspect of "pilgrimage of faith" is intimately connected with the "life" of the Church, and this is evident from the title of the encyclical.[7]

Jean Galot thinks that Pope John Paul II emphasizes Mary's "pilgrimage of faith" precisely because of his interest in the theology of

Vatican II.[8] The Council based its Marian thought on Scripture and on the recognition of the value of historical development. The final text of *Lumen Gentium,* VIII emphasized the truths of Mary's earthly existence as showered with heavenly graces, even though it has the characteristics of being a pilgrimage of faith. Such a figure as the Virgin, continues Galot, is attuned to a historical reality that is able to clarify the situation of humanity of all times. I agree with Galot that the idea of historical journey cannot be applied to Jesus Christ. The Pope never mentions "the faith of Jesus" or the "pilgrimage of faith of Jesus." This abstinence, according to Galot, is due to the fact that Christ was always humanly conscious of His divine identity. He is the founder of faith as the Letter to the Hebrews (see 12:1) relates.[9] In this, Gambero agrees with Galot.[10]

Redemptoris Mater, 2 shows that the Church is in pilgrimage toward the consummation of the ages and goes to meet the Lord who is coming. This whole process of moving from the present toward eschatology has been already successfully accomplished by Mary:

> But on this journey—and I wish to make this point straightaway— she [the Church] proceeds along the path already trodden by the Virgin Mary, who advanced in her pilgrimage of faith, and loyally persevered in her union with her Son unto the Cross.[11]

Throughout *Redemptoris Mater,* the Pope develops the theme of the faith of Mary whom the Church "venerates as her beloved Mother and as her model in faith, hope and charity."[12]

Pope John Paul II quotes *Lumen Gentium,* 58 in *Redemptoris Mater,* 5. The Blessed Virgin advanced in her pilgrimage of faith "faithfully preserving her union with Christ."[13] The union of Mary with Christ throughout her earthly journey is a central theme in the Mariology of Pope John Paul II. Gianfranco Ravasi rightly states that this journey of faith, called by the Pope "pilgrimage of faith" as in *Lumen Gentium,* 58, constitutes the point of departure for a meditation on the whole life of Mary, "the believer" *par excellence.*[14]

John Paul II goes beyond the historical dimension of that faith in order to project it as a model for the pilgrimage of the Church. Mary's faith as the "twofold bond which unites the Mother of God with Christ and with the Church"[15] enjoys a historical dimension and a meta-historical dimension:

> Nor is it just a question of the Virgin Mother's life story, of her personal journey of faith and the better part which is hers in the mystery of salvation; it is also a question of the history of the whole People of God, of all those who take part in the same pilgrimage of faith.[16]

Both historical and meta-historical dimensions, even though they are not absolutely identical, still are not mutually exclusive. There is a paradoxical continuity in Mary's faith as it unfolds in the life of the whole people of God in their pilgrimage of faith. It is paradoxical because the faith of the people of God throughout the history of the Church cannot be absolutely identified with the personal faith of Mary as she advanced in her journey of union with her Son. But the faith of the people of God assumes the same character as that of Mary because of the double bonds: Mary-Christ and Mary-Church. In her relationship with Christ, Mary advanced faithfully, preserving her union with Him; in her relationship with the Church, Mary invites the Church to make her historical faith assume both a historical and a meta-historical dimension in the Church's journey. Historical, because the faith of Mary in her union with Christ is continually present in every historical period of the life of the Church; meta-historical, because the faith of Mary is, so to say, walking with the people of God throughout the centuries. Only in that sense does the twofold bond that unites Mary to Christ and the Church take on a historical significance.[17]

Pope John Paul II continues his investigation of the faith of Mary in *Redemptoris Mater*, 5, referring to *Lumen Gentium*, 63, according to which:

> Mary has gone before, becoming a model of the Church in the matter of faith, charity and perfect union with Christ.[18]

The Mary-Christ pattern of faith develops into the Church-Mary-Christ pattern. John Paul extends this parallel to the reality of the Church as mother and virgin. In its relationship of motherhood and virginity with Christ, the Church advances on the same paths trodden by Mary. Being a model of the Church, Mary illuminates the very mystery of the Church. The Church realizes throughout history what Mary has already realized throughout her own personal history. In that sense, the Pope continues his explanation of the words of *Lumen Gentium*, 64 saying:

> This going before as a figure or model is in reference to the intimate mystery of the Church, as she actuates and accomplishes her own saving mission by uniting in herself—as Mary did—the qualities of mother and virgin.[19]

Both the existential dimension of faith as well as the salvific dimension of Mary's motherhood and virginity play major roles in enlightening the mystery of Mary in relation to the mystery of the Church. Both, however, draw their ultimate existence and meaning from the mystery of Christ. Whereas Pope Paul VI, in *Marialis Cultus,* focused more on the existential dimension,[20] Pope John Paul II, even though he develops at length the theme of Mary's faith, still approaches it from a personalistic perspective.[21] The salvific dimension of Mary's virginity and her divine motherhood are the two main features of John Paul's personalistic approach because they shed light on the identity and role of Mary in the mystery of Christ and the Church. Mary "is a virgin who keeps whole and pure the fidelity she has pledged to her Spouse" and becomes a mother, "for she brings forth to a new and immortal life children who are conceived of the Holy Spirit and born of God."[22]

HISTORICAL AND META-HISTORICAL CHARACTER OF MARY'S FAITH

In *Redemptoris Mater*, 6, Pope John Paul II completes what he started in *Redemptoris Mater*, 5, namely, his reflection on the relationship between the faith of Mary and the faith of the Church. Here he orients his thoughts toward a theology of time and shows the twofold dimensions of faith, its historical as well as its meta-historical character:

> The pilgrimage of faith indicates the interior history, that is, the story of souls. But it is also the story of all human beings, subject here on earth to transitoriness, and part of the historical dimension.[23]

The faith is the faith of people in the present:

> . . . which in itself is not yet history, but which nevertheless is constantly forming it, also in the sense of the history of salvation.[24]

It is also the faith of all people who form the history of humanity. When these two dimensions are contemplated in a Marian context, one must realize that Mary walks at the head of all people of all times as a model of faith. Both the people of the present, who are constantly forming history, as well as those who are already history look to Mary. The unity between the transitory nature of the present and the meta-historical nature of the whole of history allows the Pope to identify Mary with the whole history of salvation. That placement is not an arbitrary consideration of Mary's pilgrimage of faith. Instead, it describes a standard that is rather difficult to measure because Mary was inserted not only into the historical but also into the meta-historical dimension of the Church's faith. Such an approach avoids reducing the history of salvation to a limited historical period in which Mary advanced merely as a theological personality in her pilgrimage of faith. In that sense John Paul says:

> Here there opens up a broad prospect, within which the Blessed Virgin Mary continues to go before the People of God. Her exceptional pilgrimage of faith represents a constant point of reference for the Church, for individuals and for communities, for peoples and nations and, in a sense, for all humanity. It is indeed difficult to encompass and measure its range.[25]

One notes the influence of Cardinal Pierre Bérulle (1575–1629) transmitted to John Paul through Saint Louis De Montfort. Cardinal Bérulle devised the doctrine of *status* (state) in order to explain the actuality of the mysteries of Christ. These mysteries are perpetual, even though they belong to the past. They continue to exist in the present and will exist in the future because of the virtue in which they were executed in the past. The Spirit, the virtue, the state, and the merits of the God-man Jesus Christ bestow on those mysteries a perpetual character. They continue to be communicated to all Christians by virtue of the specific grace given to them.[26] Since in *Redemptoris Mater,* Mary is primarily present in the mystery of Christ as a Mother, the meta-historical character of her presence in the mysteries draws its possibility from Christ's continued presence in the Church. As far as the historical faith of Mary is concerned, that faith is an event that took place in the past. As far as its presence now and in the future is concerned, her association in the mystery of Christ will enable her faith to become unceasingly the faith of the people of God, as John Paul asserts in *Redemptoris Mater,* 28.

Since Mary's pilgrimage of faith surpasses her personal, that is, her historical journey of union with her Son, an eschatological dimension (this dimension points to the end of time) of that faith imposes itself as a criterion for an authentic and true trans-historicity. Without that eschatological dimension, it becomes very difficult to justify the religiosity of the Church when it advances in faith merely to follow the example of a person, Mary, who lived a heroic example of faith two thousand years ago. If Mary walked toward eschatology, the Church has to walk also toward eschatology. It was not for nothing that the Second Vatican Council emphasized that:

> [T]he Mother of God is already the eschatological fulfillment of the Church. In the most holy Virgin the Church has already reached that perfection whereby she exists without spot or wrinkle (cf. Eph 5:27).[27]

Since Mary has already "crossed the threshold between faith and that vision which is face to face" (1 Cor 13:12),[28] the pilgrimage of faith no longer belongs to her. Her state of glory enables her to escape the pilgrimage that falls now on the shoulders of the Church's children. The Pope evokes that continuity between the pilgrimage of Mary and that of the Church. He quotes the Council to confirm the eschatological character of both pilgrimages:

> The followers of Christ still strive to increase in holiness by conquering sin, and so they raise their eyes to Mary, who shines forth to the whole community of the elect as a model of the virtues.[29]

The continuity between Mary's earthly pilgrimage and its eschatological fulfillment is expressed in using Saint Bernard's *Maris stella,* which explains what Mary truly is for all those who are still on the journey of faith. Saint Bernard, quoted by John Paul, says:

> Take away this star of the sun which illuminates the world: where does the day go? Take away Mary, this star of the Sea, of the great and boundless sea: what is left but a vast obscurity and the shadow of death and deepest darkness?[30]

The Pope, however, goes beyond that to seek a Christological dimension at the foundation of that Marian eschatological fulfillment. If the Church's children lift their eyes from their earthly existence to contemplate Mary, they do so because, and John Paul again quotes *Lumen Gentium*, 63, "the Son whom she brought forth is he whom God placed as the first-born among many brethren (Rom 8:29)," and also because in the birth and development "of these brothers and sisters she cooperates with a maternal love."[31] One notices that there is a sudden reference to Mary's divine maternity as a dimension at the roots of her faith. This indicates that, for John Paul, the divine maternity of Mary is still the fountain that nourishes the understanding of her pilgrimage of faith on earth and its eschatological fulfillment in heaven.

MARY AND ELIZABETH

After analyzing the Immaculate Conception in *Redemptoris Mater*, 7–11, Pope John Paul II returns to the theme of faith in *Redemptoris Mater*, 12. Here he draws the picture of the encounter between Mary and her kinswoman Elizabeth.[32] The same Holy Spirit who came upon Mary at the Annunciation to cause the conception, is now confirming through the words of Elizabeth that Mary is "the Mother of the Lord, the Mother of the Messiah."[33] And such an approach should not create wonder in us since the theme of the "Holy Spirit" is prominent in the Gospel of Luke and the Acts.[34] John the Baptist, the son of Elizabeth who will later on point out Jesus as the Messiah, is also sharing in the witness of his Mother because the greeting of Mary made him leap for joy (see Luke 1:44).

John Paul II recognizes the wealth of meaning in every word Elizabeth utters in her encounter with Mary. Yet:

> [H]er [Elizabeth's] final words would seem to have fundamental importance: "and blessed is she who believed that there would be a fulfillment of what was spoken to her from the Lord."[35]

For the Pope, the exegetical question of the relationship between the accounts of the Annunciation and the Visitation does not seem to constitute a problem. As usual, the Pope looks at Scripture as a unity, especially because the two scenes come from the same Gospel of Luke. It is obvious, therefore, that the final words of Elizabeth should be linked to the words of the angel who proclaimed Mary "full of grace." The angel's greeting and Elizabeth's proclamation necessarily imply that "fullness of grace" and "blessed is she who believed" constitute the two key factors of God's relationship with Mary as far as His entrance into the world is concerned:

> The fullness of grace announced by the angel means the gift of God himself. Mary's faith, proclaimed by Elizabeth at the Visitation, indicates how the Virgin of Nazareth responded to this gift.[36]

God's gift of Himself in the mystery of the Incarnation became a possibility through the consent of the Virgin. Therefore, Mary was introduced into that mystery because of her *fiat* ("yes"). The essential truth concerning the identity and the role of the Mother of the Lord took place when she agreed to be involved in the mystery of Christ. Her faith, judging from the Annunciation as confirmed by the final words of Elizabeth during the Visitation, becomes the condition of possibility of her active and unique presence in the mystery of Christ. As an act of the intellect and the will, Mary's response of faith implies her free disposition to accept being present in the mystery of Christ. The subjective dimension of Mary's response to the objective revelation of God is and always will be the definitive criterion for understanding the free decision of the Mother of the Lord to be part of God's plan of salvation. A presence in the mystery of Christ that does not involve Mary's freedom implies a misunderstanding of the truth concerning her identity and role. This is the reason behind the Pope's words that describe Mary not as one who is accidentally present but as one who "has become really present in the mystery of Christ." The words of the angel revealing God's design and Mary's answer display that reality in its ultimate dimension:

> Both of these texts (Annunciation and Visitation) reveal an essential Mariological content, namely the truth about Mary, who has become really present in the mystery of Christ precisely because she has believed.[37]

John Paul II's *Dominum and Vivificantem*, 51 already treated the same theological theme from a different point of view. Here, the Pope analyzes the faith of Mary and Elizabeth in the Annunciation and the Visitation from a Trinitarian point of view:

> Mary entered the history of salvation of the world through the obedience of faith. And faith, in its deepest essence, is the openness of the human heart to the gift: to God's self-communication in the Holy Spirit. Saint Paul writes: "The Lord is the Spirit, and where the Spirit of the Lord is, there is freedom" (2 Cor 3:17). When the Triune God opens himself to man in the Holy Spirit, this opening of God reveals and also gives to the human creature the fullness of freedom. This fullness was manifested in a sublime way precisely through the faith of Mary, through the obedience of faith: "truly, blessed is she who believed.[38]

This quote entails further aspects of Mary's faith and the blessing uttered by Elizabeth. Underlying its theology is the thought of Saint Augustine and Saint Thomas Aquinas. The constitutive elements of God's creative activity presupposes the free response of women and men in relation to their salvation. The opening up of the Triune God to them in the order of creation does not eliminate their freedom in the order of salvation. It sounds like Saint Augustine's concept according to which, "the One who created you without your consent, will not save you without your consent." A person's freedom is a result of the mechanism of Redemption itself. Once the Triune God opens Himself to a person in the Holy Spirit, there automatically emerges the necessity of his or her response because the Spirit of the Lord presupposes the freedom of human beings.[39] In the context of Annunciation, the Spirit already effects God's Self-communication because God became man in the womb of Mary. Her response to that opening up is what constitutes the very essence and definition of *faith* if her response is affirmative yet freely given.[40] Therefore, faith becomes for John Paul II a free yet positive response to God's Self-communication in the Holy Spirit. This aspect is more extensively treated in *Redemptoris Mater*, 13.

MARY'S OBEDIENCE OF FAITH AS SPOKEN OF BY VATICAN II

Pope John Paul II continues to treat the question of Mary's faith in *Redemptoris Mater*, 13, applying to her the "obedience of faith" spoken of by the Second Vatican Council. The Council states in *Dei Verbum*, 5:

> The obedience of faith (Rom 16:26; cf. Rom 1:5; 2 Cor 10: 5–6) must be given to God who reveals an obedience by which man entrusts his whole self freely to God.[41]

Dei Verbum describes in general terms the free response that every human person should have when God reveals Himself and offers Himself as a gift. This principle is eminently applied to Mary because:

> . . . this description (the Council's) of faith found perfect realization in Mary. The decisive moment was the Annunciation, and the Visitation words of Elizabeth—"And blessed is she who believed"— refer primarily to that very moment.[42]

In order to elucidate the "obedience of faith" declared by *Dei Verbum*, the Pope points to the testimony of Saint Irenaeus who draws a parallel between Mary's obedience of faith and Eve's disobedience to God. John Paul II's citation of Saint Irenaeus is not made lightly, however. Saint Irenaeus has been called the Church's first Mariologist because, as the Marianist B. Buby confirms, he "develops and explains the theme of Mary as New Eve to create a Marian teaching from it."[43] Although the theme of the Eve/Mary parallel appears for the first time in Saint Justin Martyr, Saint Irenaeus develops it more deeply focusing on Genesis 3 and delving more into its symbolic and anthropological dimensions.[44] *Lumen Gentium,* 56 has referred to the same theme quoting Saint Irenaeus as John Paul II does:

> And, as by the action of the disobedient virgin, man was afflicted and, being cast down, dies, so also by the action of the Virgin who obeyed the word of God, man being regenerated received, through life, life . . . For it was meet and just . . . that Eve should be recapitulated in Mary, so that the Virgin, becoming the advocate of the virgin, should dissolve and destroy the virginal disobedience by means of virginal obedience.[45]

The central theme of recapitulation in Saint Irenaeus implies that God has restored everything that went wrong in the first creation. The disobedience of Eve is now replaced by the obedience of the New Eve. Mary becomes what Eve was intended to be but lost through her disobedience. Whereas Saint Irenaeus draws the Eve/Mary parallel without a specific reference to a biblical account, Pope John Paul II brings up that parallel in the context of the Annunciation. This indicates that for Saint Irenaeus, what was accomplished throughout the whole life of Mary,[46] was for the Pope, accomplished specifically at the Annunciation and confirmed by the words of Elizabeth. It is then that the decisive moment of Mary's obedience of faith took place.

The "obedience of faith" as described in *Dei Verbum*, 5 becomes clearer when John Paul II explains it in terms of "full submission of intellect and will."[47] The choice of *intellect* and *will* manifests the influence of Saint Thomas Aquinas, and of the First Vatican Council on the Second Vatican Council and Pope John Paul II. For Saint Thomas, the intellect and the will are the two faculties that determine the act of faith of the human person as he or she cooperates with the grace of God in accepting the divine revealed truth.[48] The intellect is necessary for understanding, whereas the will conditions the freedom of the action.

John Paul II adds to the Thomistic theory the necessity of consciousness of the person who is acting. For the Pope, both intellect and will are indispensable conditions for making conscious the act of a human person. In the case of Mary, the act in question is her act of faith. Both intellect and will are necessary to cooperate with God who reveals and offers Himself as a gift to her; both enable her to stay open to the gift of the Holy Spirit who continues to bring to perfection her initial consent to God's initiative. Therefore, Mary's cooperation with the grace of God should be understood as a dynamic attitude on her part. She needs a constant openness to the action of the Spirit in order to perfect the *fiat* she proclaimed at the Annunciation. A perfect *fiat* that expresses her submission of intellect and will should never be considered an automatic *status* that could in any way become separated from the continuing dynamism of Mary's freedom. The initial step of God's communication of Himself as gift at the Annunciation comes to perfection through the continual action of the Holy Spirit who continues to communicate the grace of God to her. In this way the action of God and the response of Mary walk side by side throughout her earthly life to bring her faith to perfection:

> She responded, therefore, with all her human and feminine "I," and this response of faith included both perfect cooperation with the grace of God that precedes and assists and perfects openness to the action of the Holy Spirit who constantly brings faith to completion by his gifts.[49]

Pope John Paul II continues to emphasize the dynamism of Mary's freedom when facing the initiative of God who proposed to her cooperation in the mystery of the Incarnation. In quoting Vatican II—"The Father of mercies willed that the consent of the predestined Mother should precede the Incarnation"[50]—the Pope shows the authenticity of her dynamic freedom.[51] The grace of the Immaculate Conception conditions the dynamic and free attitude of Mary; it neither eliminates it nor compromises its authenticity. This is not an artificial and prearranged conversation between the angel Gabriel and Mary; rather, it is a conversation between the messenger of God, who comes with an unforeseen proposal, and the predestined Mother: "And Mary gives this consent, after she has heard everything the messenger has to say."[52]

The encounter between divine and human freedom is real and represents a long-awaited answer of a humanity that has been invited to say "yes" to God since the beginning of its existence. As for the mystery of Redemption from the divine viewpoint, God already has taken the initiative to save humankind. That initiative is confirmed by the Letter to the Hebrews, quoted by John Paul II, representing that eternal conversation between the Father and the Son regarding the mystery of His Incarnation:

> Sacrifices and offering you have not desired, but a body you have prepared for me . . . Lo, I have come to do your will, O God.[53]

It remains for humanity, represented in the person of Mary, to consent and cooperate in order to bring to completion, from the human viewpoint, the mystery of Redemption. The Letter to the Hebrews and the *fiat* of Mary at the Annunciation are the two decisive moments, "on the human level, for the accomplishment of the divine mystery."[54] Those two moments stand in a perfect harmony with each other because Mary did say "yes." The Pope does not present the consequences of a hypothetical denial on the part of Mary. For him, theology depends on the concrete history of God's presence in the world in His relationship with humanity. Hypothesis cannot be part of the mystery because it does not represent the reality of historical and concrete relationships between God and the human being. "What if Mary said no?" cannot be considered a theological question because Mary said "yes":

> The mystery of the Incarnation was accomplished when Mary uttered her *fiat*: "Let it be to me according to your word," which made possible, as far as it depended upon her in the divine plan, the granting of her Son's desire.[55]

Mary did give her consent after she heard everything the messenger had to say. However, that *fiat* was uttered in faith, because Mary accepted the whole of the mystery by the time of completion of that unusual conversation with Gabriel:

> In faith she entrusted herself to God without reserve and devoted herself totally as the handmaid of the Lord to the person and work of her Son.[56]

But faith, here, seems to be a concept that is not limited merely to a consent to invisible and nonexperimental truths. For John Paul II, the Visitation is a confirmation by Elizabeth of Mary's correct attitude of faith toward the proposal of the angel. Her faith in God's messenger announcing the Incarnation was demonstrated by the words of Elizabeth who greeted her as the Mother of the Lord. This indicated the divine strategy of introducing Mary into the mystery of the Son's Incarnation. She is invited to entrust herself to God in faith and without reserve; yet, God turns around, as it were, and confirms her obedience of faith through historical facts, namely through the words of Elizabeth. Elizabeth provided one of these historical facts that proved Mary to be blessed because she "believed that there would be a fulfillment of what was spoken to her from the Lord."[57] The twofold emphasis in Elizabeth's words is clear. She confirms the objective revelation of God's design, that is, the mystery of Incarnation, and, at the same time, she praises the subjective faith of Mary, that is, her personal and free adherence to all that the Lord has told her through the angel:

> Mary of Nazareth presents herself at the threshold of Elizabeth and Zechariah's house as the Mother of the Son of God. This is Elizabeth's joyful discovery: "The Mother of my Lord comes to me!"[58]

That twofold emphasis explains why Mary, in the thinking of Saint Augustine and Saint Leo the Great, "conceived this Son in her mind before she conceived him in her womb: precisely in faith!"[59] According to Luigi Gambero, this idea was frequently present not only in Augustine and Leo the Great, who were mentioned by the Pope in *Redemptoris Mater*,[60] but also in the Fathers of the Church. Mary was so united in her mind to her Son that He became flesh in her womb. Such a unity, since it will never be repeated throughout the whole history of humanity, becomes the criterion for measuring the degree of faith of the people of God. Every person who comes into the world and believes in God somehow shares in the faith of Mary. Because of Mary's faith that was praised by Elizabeth, one realizes that the words of the Lord have already been fulfilled.

In my first study on the thought of Pope John Paul II, I analyzed the concept of faith in Saint John of the Cross as displayed in the doctoral dissertation of Pope John Paul II.[61] In that analysis it was explained that no subjective mystical experience can supercede or take the place of the objective Divine Revelation fulfilled in and through Jesus Christ. Historical Divine Revelation will always be the criterion of truth as subjectively experienced by any human person. In the case of Mary, her experience of the Annunciation, from a subjective point of view, had to be confirmed by the historical event of the Son's Incarnation, because only in that way could Mary's faith assume a concrete and authentic subjective reality. The subjectivity of faith should always include, in the first place, the truth of objective Divine Revelation. Elizabeth's role in the Visitation was precisely to confirm the harmony between Mary's subjective experience and the objectivity of the Son's historical Incarnation. Therefore, she greeted her as the Mother of the Lord.

FAITH OF ABRAHAM AND FAITH OF MARY

In *Redemptoris Mater*, 14, the faith of Abraham is compared to the faith of Mary. The comparison takes place in the context of an allegorical method in which John Paul II interprets the whole Scripture in its relationship to Christ:

> Mary's faith can also be compared to that of Abraham, whom Saint
> Paul calls our father in faith (cf. Rom 4:12).[62]

One should keep in mind that Abraham, after the creation in Genesis, was the first to receive the blessing from God.

Both the allegorical as well as the *sensus plenior* method let the Pope see in Abraham's faith the beginning of the Old Covenant and in Mary's faith the beginning of the New Covenant.[63] The Old as well as the New Covenant take off through the birth of a child in a supernatural way. In both Covenants we have a collective character (with the chosen people of the descendants of Abraham, the Old Covenant; with all of humanity in Christ, the New Covenant). Both cases display a contract between two parties, but ages apart: God and Abraham on the one hand and, on the other, God and Mary. The Old Covenant and the New Covenant are possible only because God took the initiative to invite human beings to dialogue with Him. Humanity's part consists in accepting the divine initiative and cooperating with the manner of execution of the Covenant. Mary and Abraham went through the same temptation of sacrificing their sons to God, even though both sacrifices, humanly speaking, appeared to contradict the divine promises. Mary's situation is the more difficult because Abraham did not have to go through with the bloody sacrifice. Once Abraham went beyond the temptation, his son Isaac was spared; Mary, however, had to experience the bloody killing of her Son.

Yet one should realize an essential difference between the Old Covenant with Abraham and the New Covenant with Mary. Whereas Abraham "in hope believed against hope, that he should become the father of many nations" (cf. Rom 4:18),[64] God's promise was fulfilled through the process of human generation. The faith of Abraham was historically realized through the conception by Sarah, his wife. In the case of Mary, which is more difficult given the absence of any natural intercourse, a transcendental event took place in the process of a conception that happened "through the power of the Most High, by the power of the Holy Spirit."[65]

The old age of Sarah and Abraham is somewhat parallel to Mary's virginity professed at the Annunciation; it is in the context of an untouched virginity that Mary's faith was productive of the Son's Incarnation in her womb. The adherence of Abraham to God's call enabled him to believe in hope against hope and to be united to God, whereas the faith of Mary enabled her to be united to God so much in her mind that God became flesh in her. The presence of God in the many nations fathered by Abraham will never enjoy the unique experience brought about by the faith of Mary who conceived God in the flesh at the Annunciation. Therefore, even though both Covenants possess a collective character, one should not look at the faith of Abraham as being equal to the faith of Mary. Her faith is the culmination and the perfection of the faith of Abraham and of all people of the Old Covenant. It is a culmination and a perfection not only in the sense of concluding a chronological process but also in the coming to maturity of a period directed toward the fulfillment of an expectation.[66]

The Annunciation is a particular moment of faith in which Mary committed herself to the economy of Redemption. It is "the culminating moment of Mary's faith in her awaiting of Christ."[67] Elizabeth's words, "and blessed is she who believed," must not be applied simply to that event, however; they refer to the beginning of her pilgrimage of faith and her long journey toward God. In the same theological vein as Vatican II, Pope John Paul II considers the Annunciation to be the event that introduced Mary into the mystery of Christ. But the fulfillment of her presence in Christ's mystery would take place in the unfolding of the history of her life in relationship to the revelation of God's plan.[68] Freedom, patience, and discovery of the paths to God were part of Mary's journey of faith:

> And on this road, in an eminent and truly heroic manner—indeed with an ever greater heroism of faith—the obedience which she professes to the word of divine revelation will be fulfilled.[69]

The obedience of faith professed at the Annunciation, then, enjoys a dynamic status that becomes expressed throughout the stages of Mary's journey of faith. Just like Abraham, this Mary "in hope believed against hope," which shows that:

> [E]specially during certain stages of this journey the blessing granted to her who believed will be revealed with particular vividness.[70]

John Paul avoids projecting an idealistic concept of faith in Mary, a concept that eliminates the human process of trusting and renewing the relationship of believing in God. Mary had to entrust herself to the angel's words at the Annunciation and renew that trust with awareness of the difficulties inherent in the limitations of human nature. The paradox of faith that consists in recognizing as truthful the things that are hoped for was an authentic quality of Mary's ongoing experience of God. In this regard, John Paul went beyond Vatican I, for which the faith is a formal act of understanding or perception:

> To believe means to abandon oneself to the truth of the word of the living God, knowing and humbly recognizing how unsearchable are his judgments and how inscrutable his ways (Rom 11:33).[71]

That paradoxical dimension in Mary's faith guarantees the inaccessibility of God's mystery in itself and, at the same time, shows that God, as unreachable as He is in Himself, invites Mary to accept the mystery as a truth and as a reality to be believed and lived. Choosing Mary to cooperate in "obedience of faith" with the mystery of the Incarnation increases the dynamic dimension of her pilgrimage of faith. Mary cannot avoid the narrow road of faith just because she was predestined to journey with her Son toward God. It is the perfect conformity with the whole mystery, a conformity that requires a heroic acceptance of the things that Mary hopes for, that made her journey toward God even more heroic:

> Mary, who by the eternal will of the Most High stands, one may say, at the very center of those "inscrutable ways" and "unsearchable judgments" of God, conforms herself to them in the dim light of faith, accepting fully and with a ready heart everything that is decreed in the divine plan.[72]

MARY FULFILLING THE HOPES OF THE OLD TESTAMENT

Redemptoris Mater, 15 shows without doubt that the historical conversation between Mary of Nazareth and the angel Gabriel at the Annunciation displayed the plan of God and invited her to be open to the great promises. Language such as "you will give him the name Jesus (Savior)," "the Lord God will give to him the throne of his father David," and "he will reign over the house of Jacob forever and of his kingdom there will be no end,"[73] represents the hope of Israel in the long-awaited Messiah. The descendant of David, the king who "will be great" and will save his people, is nobody else but the Messiah. Mary who "stands out among the poor and humble of the Lord," and "who confidently awaits and receives salvation from him," cannot be ignorant of the messianic dimension of the angel's words.[74] She, in fact, "had grown up in the midst of these expectations of her people."[75] At the Annunciation she guessed the vital significance of the angel's words that she was to become the Mother of the "Messiah-King." Pope John Paul acknowledges that the New Testament Marian text is foreshadowed by the Old, whether the human author was specifically aware of it or not. In other words, John Paul is interested in the fact that Mary knew that she was fulfilling the promises made to Israel. The scholarly question—whether the New Testament could be foreshadowed by the Old even without the human author's specific knowledge—does not seem to constitute a problem for the Pope. This is also valid for the relationship between the books of the New Testament. In fact, it has been clear throughout the presentation of his thoughts that he accepts that one New Testament author can be interpreted through the information or theological outlook supplied by another.

Mary's awareness of fulfilling the promises, however, does not stop "obedience of faith" from being a necessary condition in advancing on her journey toward God. The angel's words to her were clear on fulfilling the promises to Israel about the coming of the Messiah, but Mary still had to entrust herself to those words in obedience of faith, because the meaning and detail of the mystery is yet to be revealed in the unfolding history of her life relative to the Messiah-King, her Son.[76]

JESUS' PRESENTATION IN THE TEMPLE

Redemptoris Mater, 16 analyzes the event of Jesus' Presentation in the temple as another factor shedding light on the Annunciation.[77] As far as the scriptural hermeneutic is concerned, John Paul considers the whole Scripture as a unity and seeks to find the meaning of the Presentation in the context of other passages and of the tradition of the Church. No matter what exegetical relationship exists between the texts of the Annunciation and the Presentation, for the Pope both belong to the beginning of the Gospel of Luke, and the *sensus plenior* of Scripture should, therefore, be the tool of interpretation.[78]

"Later, a little further along this way of the 'obedience of faith,' Mary hears the words uttered by Simeon at the Temple of Jerusalem."[79] Simeon the Just is another personality who appeared at the beginning of Mary's "journey" of faith to confirm the words of the angel and of Elizabeth. The same Holy Spirit who accomplished the mystery of the Incarnation in Mary's womb has talked to her through the mouths of Elizabeth and Simeon, both filled with the Holy Spirit (see Luke 2:25–27).[80] As it was analyzed previously, God exists in a manner of Gift in the Holy Spirit, or God offers Himself as a Gift in the Holy Spirit.[81] One may say that in both the order of creation and the order of salvation the Holy Spirit makes the initial contact of God with the created order. This explains why Mary conceived her Son through the power of the Holy Spirit, why Elizabeth was filled with the Holy Spirit when she confirmed His presence and action in fulfilling the Incarnation, and why Simeon the Just was filled with the same Spirit when confirming the truth of the Annunciation and, indirectly, the Visitation.[82] The words of Simeon match the meaning of the Child's name, Jesus (Savior), because he proclaimed that his eyes have seen the salvation of God (see Luke 2:30–32). As far as these words are concerned, Simeon was still speaking in the context of what Mary had already heard from the angel and from Elizabeth.

Another dimension of the angel's words at the Annunciation would be revealed to Mary only when she heard Simeon predicting:

> Behold, this child is set for the fall and rising of many in Israel, and for a sign that is spoken against, that thoughts out of many hearts may be revealed. And a sword will pierce through your own soul also (cf. Lk 2:34–35).[83]

The words of Simeon entangle themselves in a context of contradiction because they differ from what Mary heard from the praise of the shepherds (see Luke 2: 8–20) and the amazement of the Magi (see Mt 2:1–12) regarding the Savior, "the light for revelation." At the beginning of their lives, Mary and her Son experience two different if not opposite dimensions of the same mystery: Christ will be "a sign that is spoken against." The words of Simeon, in John Paul's opinion:

> . . . seem like a second Annunciation to Mary, for they tell her of the actual historical situation in which the Son is to accomplish his mission, namely in misunderstanding and sorrow.[84]

Does not Simeon's attitude show that Mary's "obedience of faith," at least to a certain degree, will put her on a road that requires heroic entrustment to the decrees of God's plan? Do not his words somehow awake in Mary the logic of "how unsearchable are his (God's) judgments and how inscrutable his ways" (Rom 11:33)?[85] Mary is invited by Simeon to understand that her obedience of faith has a sorrowful side to it. But the manifestation of this sorrowful dimension takes place in the context of her divine maternity. At the Annunciation, Mary became the Mother of the Son of God, the awaited Messiah; at the Visitation, that maternity was confirmed by Elizabeth. Now, Simeon reveals that "her motherhood will be mysterious and sorrowful."[86] It is a mysterious motherhood in the sense that all the dimensions related to Mary's divine maternity will be clearly revealed in the unfolding history of her life, even though she knew from Simeon's words at the beginning of her journey that suffering is definitely one of the dimensions of her motherhood. Again, looking at all Scripture as a unity, Pope John Paul II draws a proof for Simeon's prophecy from the Gospel of Saint Matthew: Mary's flight to Egypt is nothing but a first taste of her sorrowful motherhood.[87]

Looking back at some of the Fathers of the Church who interpreted the sword spoken of by Simeon the Just, Saint Basil the Great, for example, used terminology such as *doubt* in order to describe Mary's state of mind beneath the cross. He connected the words of Simeon with the situation of Mary facing the crucifixion. Influenced by Origen, Saint Basil the Great presented Mary as attacked by the temptation of doubt when she saw her Son on the cross. Although aware of the supernatural conception that took place during the Annunciation, Mary will be subject to doubt. Saint Basil applied Mt 26:31 to Mary: "You will all fall away from me." He also gave the reason for that doubt when explaining the doubt of Peter in parallel to Mary's situation: "What was human in him proved unsound, that the power of the Lord might be shown." The universal salvation accomplished by the death of the Lord is a salvation that was necessary for all: the Lord was bound to taste death for every man and woman—to become a propitiation for the world and to justify all people by His own blood. In order to exclude a deficiency in the faith of Mary, Saint Basil immediately restored the whole situation by presenting Mary's faith as being strengthened, right after the event of the cross, through the Resurrection.[88]

The Second Vatican Council, in *Lumen Gentium*, VIII, and Pope John Paul II, in *Redemptoris Mater*, 16, were careful not to attribute to such reasons as doubt or uncertainty the kind of sorrow that Mary sometimes showed on her journey of faith, especially when she was beneath the cross.[89] Mary's sorrowful motherhood in its relationship to the sword of Simeon is not limited to the crucifixion of the Lord in *Redemptoris Mater*, 16. John Paul is extremely cautious not to narrow the suffering and the sword of Mary to the single event of her Son's death. The Pope sees Mary's sorrowful motherhood as extended over all periods of her life, to all the painful stages that "obedience of faith" will experience. This does not mean that at the time of the crucifixion the significance of Simeon's words did not become more vivid than at any other stage in Mary's life. However, not limiting Mary's sword exclusively to the death of Jesus guarantees a true picture of her lifelong striving to advance on the pilgrimage of faith. Mary's progress through life entails many of the usual human misunderstandings and sorrows that demonstrate the concrete, historical, and existential circumstances of a Mother who experienced the sword in many other ways beyond her Son's crucifixion.

John Paul avoids the term *doubt* because it somewhat contradicts the "obedience of faith" professed by Mary at the Annunciation. Yes, that "obedience of faith" will go through many difficult stages, as Simeon foretold. However, the Mother who entrusted and abandoned herself to the truth of the word of the living God[90] will renew her trust even to the point of the sword when she stands beneath the cross of her Son. That constant renewal of the "obedience of faith" that Mary gave as the stages of her pilgrimage of faith unfolded inspired the Fathers of the Second Vatican Council to avoid mentioning *doubt* as a way to describe the attitude of Mary when facing her sorrowful motherhood.[91]

JESUS' HIDDEN LIFE AND MARY'S FAITH

Redemptoris Mater, 17 also does a thorough examination of Jesus' hidden life at Nazareth. After the eventful reported years of Jesus' infancy, "there begins the long period of the hidden life."[92] During this period, there is implied Mary's faith in its dialectical dimension; namely, faith as day and night, as revelation and mystery.[93]

The historicity of Mary's experience as she faces all the situations of her life with her Son, at the beginning as well as during that hidden period, is an important consideration to support the personalism of Pope John Paul II. Mary lived the words of Elizabeth day by day. She "knows" that, when calling her child Jesus, that name was given to him by the angel.[94] She "knows" that her conception happened "without having a husband," by the power of the Holy Spirit, "just as at the time of Moses and the Patriarchs the cloud covered the presence of God."[95] She "knows" that the Son "to whom she gave birth in a virginal manner is precisely that Holy One, the Son of God, of whom the Angel spoke to her."[96] All these "knows" listed in *Redemptoris Mater,* 17 demonstrate Mary's awareness of the events that, even though they are taking place in history, still enjoy a divine dimension.[97] Mary's consciousness of the divine dimension of the historical events taking place in her daily life will constantly affect her actions.

It has been explained in our first volume on the Trinitarian thought of Pope John Paul II that the consciousness of the human person that accompanies his or her actions is an indispensable condition for self-realization and self-fulfillment.[98] To realize and fulfill herself, Mary had to be aware of the divine dimension of the historical events that she experienced. Otherwise, her "obedience of faith" loses its value and dynamism, especially when experiencing misunderstanding and sorrow, at which times she is being invited to live her motherhood at the side of her Son. The "obedience of faith" becomes meaningless in the life of Mary if she is not conscious of the purpose of her actions. Mary not only believes but is conscious that she believes and conscious of what she believes.

Consciousness becomes the bridge between the faith of Mary and her actions. Such a consciousness gives meaning to her actions and dynamically brings her being to perfection and fulfillment. One can apply to the case of Mary, as presented by John Paul II, this Augustinian principle: Mary had faith as if everything depended on God whose gift was evident in her Immaculate Conception, and she acted as if everything depended on her. Mary was aware of her faith and, acting upon it, her conscious actions became the tool for bringing to perfection her being, which was already the recipient of God's generous gift of sinlessness.[99]

Mary's personal consciousness of the divine realities taking place since the Annunciation enabled her life to be "hid with Christ in God" (cf. Col 3:3).[100] This Pauline terminology from Colossians serves to show that Mary, through faith, lived the dimensions of the mystery of the Incarnation like nobody else: "For faith is contact with the mystery of God."[101] That contact happened in the concrete historical situations of her daily life, forming her consciousness in the habit of living the mystery of God in its fullness. Mary, in her personalistic feminine "I," was aware of the essential difference between God's presence among her Jewish people and God's presence as her Son.[102] Her faith was the fundamental factor in the growth of her awareness of the divine mystery, a mystery that had been unfolding in history since her conversation with the angel Gabriel. At the same time, her faith was supported by awareness that her Child was conceived without the cooperation of man. Whereas Mary's faith, as the contact with the mystery of God, was the condition of possibility of her secure and constant awareness of the mystery, her consciousness of the mystery, proved by her simultaneous virginity and maternity, fostered her faith in the mystery:

> Every day Mary is in constant contact with the ineffable mystery of God made man, a mystery that surpasses everything revealed in the Old Covenant. From the moment of the Annunciation, the mind of

the Virgin-Mother has been initiated into the radical newness of God's self-revelation and has been aware of the mystery.[103]

To Mary, John Paul II applies Mt 11:25: "Father, . . . you have hidden these things from the wise and understanding and revealed them to babes."[104] She became the first of those "little ones" to whom the Father will reveal the Son. But, asks the Pope, how can Mary know the Son if "no one knows the Son except the Father" (Mt 11:27)?[105] One senses a taste of patristic style in the comparison between Mary's knowledge of her incarnate Son's mystery and the mystery of eternal knowledge between the Father and the Son. No one can really compare the knowledge of Mary to the knowledge of the Father. Yet Mary is "the first of those to whom the Father has chosen to reveal him" (cf Mt 11:26–27; 1 Cor 2:11).[106] And Mary generates in time the One whom the Father has generated in eternity. For John Paul, the Annunciation is the one specific event in which the Father started to reveal the Son, whom He begets in the eternal "today" (cf. Ps 2:7), to Mary. The Father knows the Son completely and decides to reveal Him to Mary who since that moment was in contact with the mystery of God through faith. Mary comes "in contact with the truth about her Son only in faith and through faith!"[107] John Paul emphasizes the dimension of faith in the context of the Father's revelation of the Son to Mary, because only in faith was Mary able to continue:

> . . . to believe day after day amidst the trials and the adversities of Jesus' infancy and then during the years of the hidden life at Nazareth, where he was obedient to them (Lk 2:51).[108]

The Father's revelation of the Son to Mary at the Annunciation follows the Second Vatican Council: God reveals and Mary adheres to the revelation. Yet, the consciousness of Mary is a dimension that the Pope emphasizes more than the Council because, in his theological anthropology and Christian personalism, the consciousness of the Person is necessary to fulfill the action and bring Mary's being to perfection. That consciousness, at the same time, underscores the historical dimension of her obedience of faith to the revelation of God's mystery and eliminates gnostic tendencies that lean toward excluding from God's revelation the response and cooperation of Mary. Only in this way is John Paul II able to draw the conclusion that Mary was truly aware that her being in contact with God's mystery through faith—her experience, which started with the Annunciation—opens an essentially New Covenant with God:

> The Mother of that Son, therefore, mindful of what has been told her at the Annunciation and in subsequent events, bears within herself the radical "newness" of faith: the beginning of the New Covenant.[109]

The fact that Pope John Paul II strongly emphasizes the consciousness of Mary in *Redemptoris Mater*, 17 is noticeable throughout his Mariology. He proceeds cautiously yet firmly with a historical-personalistic approach to analyze the identity and role of Mary in the mystery of Christ and the Church.[110] Such a historical and personalistic approach to Mary of Nazareth protects his position against some tendencies in Mariology that attribute value to the person and role of Mary in the economy of salvation only as a result of the inventive creation of the Church's theology of Mary. Some of these tendencies have gone so far as to create a serious division between who Mary of Nazareth really was and what the Church thought of her over the last two millennia. However, a radical distinction and separation between the historical Mary and the Mary of faith never finds a place in the logic of the Pope. His most effective tool for analyzing his position is the necessity of consciousness in the actions of Mary throughout her entire life. Consciousness and historicity go side by side to present Mary as that theological personality who, through obedience of faith, was able to accomplish her journey toward God. John Paul II, as far as Mary's consciousness is concerned, has taken a further important step beyond the Mariology of Vatican II.

Investigation of the theology of Pope John Paul II of Mary makes one realize the unity in his thought. His philosophical approach to the human person is essentially tied to his understanding of Mary. If philosophy's primary concern is the search for the truth, that truth enjoys a universality and unbreakable unity.[111] In his encyclical letter *Fides et Ratio* (On the Relationship between Faith and Reason) he asserts:

> In particular, it is necessary to keep in mind the unity of truth, even if its formulations are shaped by history and produced by human reason wounded and weakened by sin.[112]

The magisterium's vocation in service of the truth is stated in his appeal to the bishops:

> We bishops have the duty to be witnesses to the truth, fulfilling a humble but tenacious ministry of service which every philosopher should appreciate, a service in favor of *recta ratio* (right reasoning), or of reason reflecting rightly upon what is true.[113]

In this philosophical context, Pope John Paul II approaches the question of Mary with great care not to fall either into fideism and radical traditionalism, or into rationalism and ontologism.[114] Fideism and radical traditionalism both have distrusted the natural capacities of reason in search for the knowledge of God. Rationalism and ontologism "attributed to natural reason a knowledge which only the light of faith could confer."[115] The positive elements of the debate between these two tendencies were assembled in the dogmatic constitution *Dei Filius* of the First Vatican Council. It was amazing that an ecumenical council—in this case, the First Vatican Council—"pronounced solemnly on the relationship between reason and faith." The essence of the pronouncement of Vatican I, which was quoted by Vatican II, is the following: "There are two orders of knowledge, distinct not only in their point of departure, but also in their object."[116] And:

> [E]ven if faith is superior to reason there can never be a true divergence between faith and reason, since the same God who reveals the mysteries and bestows the gift of faith has also placed in the human spirit the light of reason. This God could not deny himself, nor could the truth ever contradict the truth.[117]

It is exactly the vision of truth as a solid unity that enables John Paul II to apply philosophical principles to Mary, as long as:

> . . . at the deepest level, the autonomy which philosophy enjoys is rooted in the fact that reason is by its nature oriented to truth and is equipped moreover with the means necessary to arrive at truth.

In fact, "a philosophy conscious of this as its constitutive status cannot but respect the demands and the data of revealed truth."[118]

The Trinitarian dimension of the Annunciation affords Pope John Paul II the opportunity to avoid fideism as well as rationalism. To defeat rationalism, on the one hand, the Pope asserts that it was the Father alone who enabled Mary to come into contact with the mystery of His Son. The truth about her Son was revealed to Mary who contacted it "only in faith and through faith."[119] Since the Son is completely known only by the Father, and Mary is "the first of those to whom the Father has chosen to reveal him,"[120] the natural capacities of her human reason would fail to grasp the unfathomable mystery. It is a mystery because it was hidden in the eternal plan of God and revealed in these last days to Mary at the Annunciation. The natural light of Mary's reason, as sharp and oriented toward God as it was, would have been unable to contemplate the truth of her Son had the Father not revealed it through a historical event—the Annunciation—in which Mary came into contact with the ineffable mystery. That approach does not leave any space for rationalism with its idealistic tendencies to transform the mystery of God into dialectical structures that could be grasped by reason.[121]

On the other hand, to defeat fideism, the Pope considers that God invited Mary, through faith, to be conscious of His plan and to use her personal awareness to answer God's unfolding mystery in history. Her consciousness in being in contact with the mystery enables her to develop a deeper understanding of that mystery.[122] The fact that she was introduced into the mystery of Christ at the Annunciation does not imply an automatic and exhaustive perception of the entirety of the mystery. The mystery of God was revealed to Mary in its totality, but the details of that mystery became clearer with the unfolding of history since "every day Mary is in constant contact with the ineffable mystery of God made man."[123] Otherwise, hers would not be a pilgrimage of faith anymore. In fact, faith as defined by John Paul is "contact with the mystery of God."[124] Her reasoning and her consciousness, so much emphasized in *Redemptoris Mater*, 17, demonstrate the Pope's interest in avoiding fideistic approaches that tend to describe Mary as the handmaid of the Lord who accepted contact with the revealed mystery without necessarily using her human reason. Did not Mary have a conversation with the angel Gabriel asking for more explanation of God's message? That questioning will stay with Mary throughout all the stages of her life as the Incarnation mystery unfolds itself through the events and words of persons coming into contact with her. Her "obedience of faith" would lose all its meaning and strength if Mary did not continue to understand and reason out the design in which she is called to share. Saint John of the Cross, about whose concept of faith John Paul wrote his doctoral dissertation, elucidates the question:

> The Mother of that Son, therefore, mindful of what has been told her at the Annunciation and in subsequent events, bears within herself the radical "newness" of faith: the beginning of the New Covenant . . . However, it is not difficult to see in that beginning a particular heaviness of heart, linked with a sort of "night of faith"—to use the words of Saint John of the Cross—a kind of "veil" through which one has to draw near to the Invisible One and to live in intimacy with the mystery. And this is the way that Mary, for many years, lived in intimacy with the mystery of her Son, and went forward in her "pilgrimage of faith," while Jesus "increased in wisdom . . . and in favor with God and man" (Lk 2:52).[125]

The Pope is very careful not to fall into fideism, even when referring to Saint John of the Cross's "night of faith." In the midst of that particular heaviness of heart, Mary needed an intelligent act of the will in order to accept the details of the mystery. Living in the intimacy of the mystery required an act of reason that recognized the total transcendence of God's mystery. Even the decision not to reason, and so live in intimacy with the mystery through contemplation, would need an act of reasoning on the part of Mary. John Paul II refuses even in the context of the "night of faith"—where reason submits itself to live in the intimacy with the mystery—to allow that Mary's faith was, in any way, a blind and unreasonable decision. Therefore, the "pilgrimage of faith" makes sense only if the obedience to the mystery occurs with full consciousness of Mary as she contemplates the mystery of God. If Jesus increased in wisdom, Mary increased in wisdom as well, and advanced in her pilgrimage of faith at every stage of her life.[126] Elizabeth's words, "blessed is she who believed," will echo many times while Mary pursues the final destiny of her journey of faith toward God. Mary did not understand the answer of the twelve-year-old Jesus in the Temple, "Did you not know that I must be in my Father's house?"[127] This shows that, as far as "no one knows the Son except the Father":

. . . even his Mother, to whom had been revealed most completely the mystery of his divine sonship, lived in intimacy with this mystery only through faith! Living side by side with her Son under the same roof, and faithfully persevering in her union with her Son, "she advanced in her pilgrimage of faith," as the Council emphasizes.[128]

Salvador Muñoz Iglesias rightly states that the Pope does not agree with many contemporary Mariologists who deny Mary's consciousness of the mystery of Christ. The Holy Father, without closing the theological investigation of the question of Mary's awareness and consciousness of Christ's mystery, interprets the text of Luke 2:50 in the line of the "night of faith" that Mary humanly experienced. The text characterizes her "advancing in the pilgrimage of faith," of which the Second Vatican Council spoke.[129]

MARY'S FAITH BENEATH THE CROSS

Redemptoris Mater, 18 shows that the blessing contained in Elizabeth's words reaches its peak "when Mary stands beneath the Cross of her Son" (cf. Jn 19:25).[130] There, Mary's intimacy with the mystery of her Son, and her union with Him through the obedience of faith, has its utmost significance. The Pope calls it "union through faith,"[131] because the same faith with which Mary accepted the words of the angel that her Son would be great is the only reason for her to "faithfully preserve her union with her Son even to the Cross."[132] It is a "union of faith" because "standing at the foot of the Cross, Mary is the witness, humanly speaking, of the complete negation of these words."[133] John Paul II does not mention any kind of doubt in the mind or the attitude of Mary. He continues, instead, to analyze the concept of "obedience of faith." Her obedience of faith as she faces the Redemption mystery requires a full consciousness of her decision in the sense that she "completely . . . abandons herself to God 'without reserve, offering the full assent of the intellect and the will' to him whose ways are inscrutable" (cf. Rom 11:33)![134] On the one hand, therefore, her intellect and will are at work to lead her obedience of faith to perfection and, on the other hand, ". . . how powerful too is the action of grace in her soul, how all-pervading is the influence of the Holy Spirit and of his light and power."[135] Parallel to the action of the Holy Spirit in the sacrifice of Christ that I have analyzed in my previous work[136] is this intervention of the same Spirit in the pain of Mary who, in terms of Vatican II as quoted by John Paul II:

> . . . suffering deeply with her only-begotten Son and joining herself with her maternal spirit to his sacrifice, lovingly consenting to the immolation of the victim to whom she had given birth, . . . faithfully preserved her union with her Son even to the Cross.[137]

Two aspects of the pneumatology of the Pope are relevant here regarding the Holy Spirit's presence with and action on Mary. The Holy Spirit, as God existing in the mode of Gift, is the Person-Gift who makes His contact with Mary and enables the grace of God to act in her soul.[138] The other aspect is the union that the Spirit effects between the Father and the Son in the context of the sacrifice of the cross. Because of the eternal union between the Father and the Son, namely, the Person of the Holy Spirit, Christ was able to cry out loud: "My God, my God, why have you abandoned me?" Now, the union of the Son with Mary, who is standing at the foot of the cross, is parallel, humanly speaking, to that divine unity between Father and Son. In both cases, the Holy Spirit is the principle of union and the Person who unites Father to Son (divine level) and Mary to Son (human level). From this double-edged union accomplished by the Holy Spirit there results not only Christ's *Kenosis*, or the self-emptying mentioned in Philippians and commented upon by John Paul II in *Redemptor Hominis*, but also Mary's own *kenosis*, her own self-emptying.[139] Whereas Christ's Self-emptying was done for the sake of the Redemption itself, Mary's self-emptying was done for the sake of her maternal union with her Son. Only in faith empowered by the grace of God was Mary able to lead her obedience of faith to assent to that union of self-emptying. Through that assent, she performed the most perfect act of faith, called "kenosis of faith" by John Paul II:

> Through this faith Mary is perfectly united with Christ in his self-emptying . . . At the foot of the Cross Mary shares through faith in the shocking mystery of this self-emptying. This is perhaps the deepest kenosis of faith in human history.[140]

It is not without reason that in *Redemptoris Mater*, 18, Pope John Paul II underscores the maternal aspect of Mary's faith. If Christ has historically died for the sake of the Redemption, Mary has died through faith, because she is the Mother. The physical bond of Mother-Son is here being compared with that spiritual bond called "union" by Vatican II and Pope John Paul II. That union presupposes the Mother's sharing in the destiny of the Son. If He physically and historically dies to accomplish the salvation of humanity, Mary has no other destiny but to die as well. While her physical death was not possible at that moment of the history of Redemption, Mary still shared in the death of her Son, but only through faith. In that sense, the Pope says:

> Through faith the Mother shares in the death of her Son, in his redeeming death; but in contrast with the faith of the disciples who fled, hers was far more enlightened.[141]

What John Paul did not mention in *Redemptoris Mater*, 16 comes to light in *Redemptoris Mater*, 18: the sword that will pierce the heart of Mary is the cross of Christ, with whom she will be united in the greatest kenosis of faith in human history.

Redemptoris Mater, 19 continues to treat the question of Mary's faith as she stands beneath the cross.[142] The Second Vatican Council saw Mary "freely cooperating in the work of man's salvation through faith and obedience."[143] Vatican II, however, did not speak of Mary's faith in the specific context of her presence at Calvary; neither did it apply the words of Elizabeth, "blessed is she who believed," to Mary's kenosis of faith at the foot of the cross. The Council states:

> Thus the daughter of Adam, Mary, consenting to the word of God, became the Mother of Jesus. Committing herself whole-heartedly and impeded by no sin to God's saving will, she devoted herself totally, as a handmaid of the Lord, to the person and work of her Son, under and with him, serving the mystery of Redemption, by the grace of Almighty God.[144]

Pope John Paul II has analyzed this statement in the more specific context of Mary's faith under the cross. For him, Vatican II's "serving the mystery of Redemption" becomes the sacrifice of Jesus on Calvary:

> From the Cross, that is to say from the very heart of the mystery of
> Redemption, there radiates and spreads out the prospect of that
> blessing of faith.[145]

The culminating point and the heart of the mystery of Redemption is
the cross, and Mary's service of that mystery is her faith as she stands beneath
that cross, fulfilling thus the words of Elizabeth. The two aspects added by
John Paul II to the theology of Vatican II (*Lumen Gentium*, 56), namely,
the mystery of Redemption as the cross and the faith of Mary as a fulfillment of Elizabeth's words, are of extreme importance. They show the
personalistic approach of the Pope to the historical Mary of Nazareth.[146]
The faith of Mary, instead of being one of her abstract qualifications,
becomes a concrete act of intelligence and will that leads her through
the historical stages of her life with her Son up to the foot of the cross.
Such a personalistic approach allows the Pope to interpret Scripture with
a vision of unbreakable unity in the personality of Mary. Unity of message in Scripture will provide a unity among the different aspects of
Mary's faith. For example, the one proclaimed blessed by Elizabeth because of her faith, is also blessed especially at the height of her faithful
career with her Son at the foot of the cross.

Whereas Vatican II (*Lumen Gentium*, 56) did not bring the Eve-
Mary parallel to bear on the context of Jesus' sacrifice on Calvary, Pope
John Paul did see Mary's obedience of faith as counteracting the disobedience of Eve, especially on Calvary. The Council made reference in
general terms, but the Pope did it in specific terms. For him, the blessing
of faith spoken by Elizabeth "goes right back to the beginning," and as a
sharing in the sacrifice of Christ—the new Adam—it becomes in a certain sense "the counterpoise to the disobedience and disbelief embodied
in the sin of our first parents."[147] The blessing of faith uttered by Elizabeth brings Mary back to "the beginning," to Genesis, where she stands
in contradiction to the disbelief of Eve. That blessing of faith also brings
Mary to the foot of the cross, where the contradiction between her
obedience and the disobedience of Eve reaches its high point.

Of extreme importance are John Paul's words "as a sharing in the
sacrifice of Christ," because they demonstrate the consistency of his
thought since the personalistic approach allows the unity of Scripture to
explain Mary's behavior in antithesis to Eve from beginning to end.[148]

Only in the context of such a unity in Scripture could the Pope picture Mary's obedience much later in history as contradicting the picture of Eve as disobedient early on. Saint Irenaeus, a Father of the Church, helps both the Council and the Pope to see this contrast:

> The knot of Eve's disobedience was untied by Mary's obedience; what the virgin Eve bound through her unbelief, the Virgin Mary loosened by her faith.[149]

Yet Saint Irenaeus does not relate the faith of Mary when she counters the disbelief of Eve to the words uttered by Elizabeth, "blessed is she who believed."[150] This is a new concept developed by the theology of John Paul II: that the parallel between Mary's faith at the foot of the cross and the disobedience of Eve at the beginning should be understood as a fulfillment of Elizabeth's blessing of faith.

Pope John Paul II compares the mystery of the Son to the mystery of the Mother in *Redemptoris Mater*, 19:

> In the expression "Blessed is she who believed," we can therefore rightly find a kind of "key" which unlocks for us the innermost reality of Mary, whom the angel hailed as "full of grace."[151]

The mystery of the Son in its relationship to Mary is explained by her Immaculate Conception; that is, her being "full of grace" shows how she is eternally present in the mystery of Christ. When that presence is translated into human and historical terms, her personal faith expresses itself in the unfolding of her life's history:

> If as "full of grace" she has been eternally present in the mystery of Christ, through faith she became a sharer in that mystery in every extension of her earthly journey.[152]

This means that she is eternally present in the mystery of Christ because she is the Immaculate Conception, and the mystery of Christ is present in time because she is the one "who believed." Christ's mystery is made present to humanity in its relationship with Mary as the Immaculate Conception and, in its relationship with Christ, the mystery of Mary is also made clear to humanity through her faith. Mary's historical faith alone is able to translate the mystery of Christ into historical categories, whereas Christ's eternal plan, which includes her being the Immaculate Conception, translates the mystery of Mary into historical categories. The mystery of the Son makes present the mystery of the Mother through her Immaculate Conception, whereas the mystery of the Mother makes present the mystery of the Son through her obedience of faith. Pope John Paul concludes *Redemptoris Mater*, 19:

> She advanced in her "pilgrimage of faith" and at the same time in a discreet yet direct and effective way, she made present to humanity the mystery of Christ . . . Through the mystery of Christ, she too is present within mankind. Thus through the mystery of the Son the mystery of the Mother is also made clear.[153]

Mary's Maternal Mediation

INTRODUCTION

THE PARTICIPATION OF MARY in Christ's work of Redemption has always been an object of discussion within Catholic circles as well as in other Christian churches. The topic has drawn the attention of many theologians throughout the history of the Church and caused many to reflect on its relationship to the absolute primacy of Christ who is the unique mediator between God and man.[1] While all Catholics agree that Christ, as God-man, was the sufficient cause of our Redemption, the question of Mary's mediation concerns the manner in which Christ associated His Mother with Himself in the action of Redemption.

This mediation was widely discussed in theological circles especially before and after the Second Vatican Council (1962–1965).[2] In the opinion of the theologian S. M. Perrella, it was actually the most debated theological theme present at the vigil of the Council.[3] In the preparatory stages of the Council, Episcopal presenters introduced many different concepts to describe Mary's presence and cooperation with Christ's Redemption: *cooperatio* (cooperation), *corredemptio/conredemptio* (coredemption/con-redemption), *corredemptrix* (coredemptrix), *munus* (function), *nova Eva* (New Eve), *officium* (office), *positio structuralis* (position of structure), *redemptrix* (redeemer), *socia Christi* (associate of Christ). Such terms indicate the relationships among mediation and coredemption, the role of Mary in the Church, the universal motherhood, queenship, Immaculate Conception, and bodily assumption. Instead of these terms, Vatican II employed *nova Eva* (New Eve), *socia Redemptoris* (Associate of the Redeemer), *Mater viventium* (Mother of the Living), *Ancilla Domini* (Servant of the Lord), *cooperatio* (cooperation), *munus maternum* (maternal function), *munus salutiferum* (salutary influence), *munus subordinatum* (a subordinate function). In the process of studying the Mariology of Pope John Paul II, one realizes how he uses these terms and in what theological context they appear.

The bottom line is this: magisterial documents have always professed the faith of the Church in the mediation of Mary, a fact whose validity Vatican II has solemnly reaffirmed in *Lumen Gentium* 60–62.[4] Vatican II looked at Mary's mediation in terms of subordinate cooperation and spiritual motherhood.[5] It intended to illustrate her function in the mystery of the Incarnate Word and of the Church. Such an approach to doctrine about the Blessed Virgin Mary has since influenced magisterial documents as well as contemporary theology, especially regarding her mediation.[6] Despite Vatican II's terminology, which included *function, maternal function, salutary influence toward men*, John Paul II still prefers the term *mediation* with the adjectives of *maternal* and *participated*. According to the theologian Salvatore Meo, the Pope intends to implement Vatican II by showing the validity of the many concepts used in the preconciliar period but neglected in the postconciliar Mariology.[7]

The presentation of Mary's mediation in its dogmatic and scriptural dimension represents the main thrust in the postconciliar period, especially in the writings of Pope John Paul II. Since the Second Vatican Council, Mariology has become more and more open to deeper research concerning the identity and mediative role of Mary in the mystery of Christ and the Church. The publishing of *Redemptoris Mater* (Mother of the Redeemer) by John Paul II, the renewed interest in the liturgical celebrations devoted to the Blessed Mother, and the ecumenical dialogues have all been important factors in addressing the question of Mary's mediation.[8] For theologian Angelo Amato, there is an epistemological enrichment that results from the critical approach in method as well as in content to Mariology in Scripture, in the Fathers of the Church, in the Christian traditions of the Orient, in ecumenical dialog, in the contact with human sciences, in the challenge of feminism, in the liturgical dimension, and in living popular Marian devotion. As far as the Mariological content is concerned, John Paul II has reproposed more deeply the Church's understanding of Mary's mediation in *Redemptoris Mater*.[9]

J. Castellano Cervera considers Mary's mediation as "occupying a relevant place in the theology of that Encyclical." For him, the Pope went beyond the terminology of the Council in intensively using the term *mediation*, even though proceeding along a line of continuity with the theology of the Council. Mediation becomes an overall theme of the whole encyclical because meditation, itself, stands in direct relationship with the presence of Mary in the mystery of Christ and of the Church.[10]

At the end of one of his articles, Angelo Amato asked: What distinguishes Mary's mediation from that of her Son, and from that of the angels and the saints? Is it different in its exemplarity? And if it goes beyond the paradigmatic dimension, in what does it consist?[11] Arthur Calkins sees in the term *coredemptrix* a solution to distinguish Mary's maternal mediation from that of angels and human persons.[12]

French theologian René Laurentin has raised the same type of question and sees in the Annunciation one of the fundamental events for justifying Mary's mediation. There, Mary is a woman in solidarity with all human beings and, at the same time, a holy woman cooperating with God's plan of Incarnation and Redemption. When she gave birth to Christ, He became the unique mediator, whereas Mary is still an inter-mediator.[13] Christ's unique mediation is like a bridge that unites the two different parts of a river, and He belongs to the two parts. Christ is God with the Father and the Holy Spirit, and human with humankind; He is not between God and humanity in order to get them to be closer to each other. And where Christ is the bridge that perfectly connects God to humankind, Mary's mediation is like several rocks that stand out of the water to help a person cross the river. Laurentin calls Christ's mediation an *ontological mediation*. If priests, sacraments, and the intercession of saints are instruments of grace, Christ is still the only mediator and Mary is mediatrix only in and through Christ (*Mediatrix in Christo*).[14]

For John Paul II, the basic concept of mediation derives from its biblical foundation. Saint Paul has already confirmed that "we are God's fellow workers,"[15] a fact that makes the Pope maintain the real possibility for people to cooperate with God in the action of Redemption. The collaboration of believers is expressed in the proclamation of the gospel and in their contribution to its taking root in human hearts.[16] From the very beginning of his pontificate, Pope John Paul II confirms that Mary's maternal mediation, despite its complexity and the questions it raises as to its difference from mediation by other creatures,[17] is unique in nature because it is directly related to her motherhood.[18] Salvatore Meo rightly states that the preconciliar expression "universal mediation of all graces" was avoided by Vatican II in order to eliminate pastoral and ecumenical misunderstandings. Pope John Paul II summed up Mary's cooperation in the work of Redemption with the term *mediation* by showing its validity in the theology of the Church.

The Pope introduced in a new concept, however, when he attributed to *mediation* the adjective *maternal*. Such a choice not only clarifies and describes the mediation of Mary but also specifies what type of mediation it is. In the course of analyzing "maternal mediation," one realizes that, as the Mother, Mary cooperates in the history of salvation from the Annunciation to the final glorification of the elect. Therefore, concludes Meo, Mary's mediation is based on her motherhood, both divine and spiritual. Such an approach eliminates many misconceptions and prepares the Church's theology of Mary for further fruitful study of that concept.[19]

Whereas the collaboration by other Christians takes place after the event of the Calvary, Mary cooperated during the event itself and in the role of Mother. Thus her cooperation embraces the whole of Christ's saving work. That cooperation, as one notices in studying the Pope's concept of mediation, assumes different dimensions and is described in various concepts of his Mariology. The common ground is evident, however: when John Paul speaks of mediation in all its forms:

> [H]e always makes it clear that he is referring to her participation in Christ's own action, which is by itself incomparable and sufficient.[20]

Pope John Paul II has based his theological inquiry of the concept of *mediation* on scriptural evidence and draws conclusions in a doctrinal form. This Pope analyzed the mediation of Mary in Scripture (Annunciation, Cana, Calvary) and has produced a traditional foundation for his analysis. He demonstrated how, based on Scripture, the tradition of the

Church has always maintained Mary's mediation as a truth of faith to be celebrated by Christians.[21] Not only the trilogy of Trinitarian encyclicals on the Son (*Redemptor Hominis*), the Father (*Dives in Misericordia*), and the Holy Spirit (*Dominum et Vivificantem*) but also *Mulieris Dignitatem* (On the Dignity and Vocation of Woman, 1988) and *Redemptoris Missio* (The Mission of the Redeemer, 1990) have focused on the Trinitarian dimension of Mariology and consequently on the uniqueness and universality of Christ's mediation. It is in this context that John Paul analyzes the concept of Mary's mediation. His intervention, moreover, has reached not only the doctrinal level of Mariology but also the spiritual level. The maternal mediation of Mary is a pledge of her protection of humankind, a fact that is guaranteed by her constant intervention in the events of the economy of salvation.

MARY AT THE WEDDING OF CANA: MOTHERHOOD AND MEDIATION

The passage of John's Gospel (wedding at Cana) contains a very significant theology as far as the motherhood of Mary is concerned.[22] To that Cana wedding, Jesus and his disciples:

> . . . were invited together with Mary, as if by reason of her presence at the celebration, the Son seems to have been invited because of his Mother.[23]

There, the Lord changed the water into wine when Mary reported to Him that "they have no more wine."

It is significant for John Paul II that the Evangelist John constantly calls Mary "the Mother of Jesus." At the wedding, Mary, as the Mother of Jesus, "in a significant way . . . contributed to that beginning of the signs which reveal the messianic power of her Son."[24] Even though the "hour of Jesus" has not yet come, he still performed the miracle showing that the bond between Him and His Mother must be carefully grasped by those who witness their mutual relationship. It is that mutual relationship between Son–Mother and Mother–Son that constitutes the criterion for considering the presence of Mary in the mystery of Christ and the

Church. Therefore the Pope asks: "What deep understanding existed between Jesus and his Mother? How can we probe the mystery of their intimate union?"[25] The mystery of their intimate union is revealed in a new dimension, a deeper meaning of Mary's motherhood. The performance of the miracle at Cana, despite the blunt statement "my hour has not yet come," is ultimately an event that reveals the real connection between Mary's motherhood and her mediation.[26] As far as the relationship between motherhood and mediation goes, the Pope has already prepared us in his first encyclical, The Redeemer of Man (*Redemptor Hominis*, 22), to understand what he fully develops in *Redemptoris Mater*, 21–22:

> Nobody has been brought into it (the mystery of Redemption) by God himself as Mary has. It is in this that the exceptional character of the grace of the divine motherhood consists. Not only is the dignity of this motherhood unique and unrepeatable in the history of the human race, but Mary's participation, due to this maternity, in God's plan for man's salvation through the mystery of the Redemption is also unique in profundity and range of action.[27]

It will take Pope John Paul II a whole section on the *Maternal Mediation* of Mary in *Redemptoris Mater* to explain what he means by "is also unique in profundity and range of action" in *Redemptor Hominis*, 22.

In the Synoptic Gospels (Matthew, Mark, and Luke), Jesus:

> . . . means above all to contrast the motherhood resulting from the fact of birth with what this "motherhood" (and also "brotherhood") is to be in the dimension of the kingdom of God, in the salvific radius of God's fatherhood.[28]

There emerges the parallel of Mary's motherhood according to the Spirit between the Synoptics and John. In the Synoptics, her motherhood is placed in the context of the Kingdom of God, "in the salvific radius of God's fatherhood." In John, the new dimension of Mary's motherhood has a specific meaning in the "radius of Christ's messianic mission and salvific power."[29] Whereas that contrast remains confined to general terms, in the text of John:

. . . the description of the Cana event outlines what is actually manifested as a new kind of motherhood according to the spirit and not just according to the flesh, that is to say Mary's solicitude for human beings, her coming to them in the wide variety of their wants and needs.[30]

It is of extreme importance that the mediation of Mary in John's text receives its significance from this new dimension of Mary's motherhood, namely her motherhood according to the Spirit. First of all, such a maternal mediation emphasizes the historical aspect of Mary's mediation. As Mary of Nazareth who is the "Mother of Jesus," she intervened for the accomplishment of the "first sign." Historically speaking, Mary's identity in her relationship to Jesus is ultimately connected to her motherhood. Especially in its new dimension, her motherhood is the instrument Mary used in order to intervene on behalf of God's servants. As small as it is, that human need:

. . . has a symbolic value: this coming to the aid of human needs means, at the same time, bringing those needs within the radius of Christ's messianic mission and salvific power.[31]

That whole concept of mediation was discovered by Mary as she lived and advanced in understanding her spiritual motherhood: "She puts herself in the middle, that is to say she acts as a *mediatrix* not as an outsider, but as Mother."[32] The expression "not as an outsider, but as a Mother" means that Mary's motherhood, according to the flesh, constitutes the substance of her spiritual motherhood and, in its part, spiritual motherhood conditions her motherhood according to the flesh. If in God's plan Mary was not meant to be the Mother of the Incarnate Word, the proposal of the angel would not have happened and, therefore, spiritual motherhood would lose its reason of existence (*raison d'être*). To be the Mother according to the flesh carries with it all the privileges that a mother-son relationship has in the natural course of human life. In that natural context, Mary cooperated in manifesting "the messianic power of her Son,"[33] despite the fact that this motherhood according to the flesh was made possible because of Mary's faith and of what spiritual motherhood had contributed to the fulfillment of the Incarnation. Motherhood according to the flesh gives existence and content to spiritual motherhood, and spiritual motherhood, because it is related to Mary's faith and freedom, conditions her motherhood according to the flesh.

If spiritual motherhood was not based on motherhood according to the flesh, Mary would be reduced to anyone else who *spiritually* "conceives" Christ because of obedience of faith. As an immediate consequence of that logic, any person in the history of humanity who had a deep experience of faith could exercise a mediative role just like Mary, a situation which would contradict the concept of her maternal mediation as transmitted by Divine Revelation, the content of the living tradition of the Church, and the magisterium.[34] Laurentin thinks that John Paul calls Mary's mediation a "maternal mediation" in order to specify the particular nature of that mediation and its limits.[35] Unlike any other human being, Mary was the Mother of God because her Son, whom she carried in her womb according to the laws of gestation, was God. The divine maternity becomes the condition of possibility and the key to developing an accurate Marian doctrine of mediation for the Church. The reason that Pope John Paul analyzes maternal mediation in *Redemptoris Mater*, 21–22 is to demonstrate that this type of Marian mediation properly belongs to the deposit of faith as revealed in Scripture (the Gospel of John), confirmed by the tradition of the Church, and soundly interpreted by the magisterium (*Lumen Gentium*, 60, quoted in *Redemptoris Mater*, 22).

Since spiritual motherhood in Mary draws its content from motherhood according to the flesh, her mediation as Mother is based on mediative actions of that historical Mother of God. The maternal mediation of Mary is based on her identity as Mother according to the flesh and, therefore, as the concrete historical Mother of God. As Mary of Nazareth and the Mother of Jesus Christ, she cooperated by her maternal mediation through interventions in the historical developments of the economy of salvation. In that sense, the historical mediation of Mary must, in John Paul II's opinion, constitute the basis for her mediation as extended throughout the entire life of the Church.[36] Also in that sense, the historical event of Cana, in which Mary said to the servants "Do whatever he tells you," becomes a meta-historical measure of her maternal desire to fulfill her Son's wish:

> The Mother of Christ presents herself as the spokeswoman of her
> Son's will, pointing out those things which must be done so that
> the salvific power of the Messiah may be manifested.[37]

The Pope adds: "At Cana Mary appears as believing in Jesus. Her faith
evokes his first sign and helps to kindle the faith of the disciples."[38]
Behind this type of intercession is the relevant element of Mary's identity as the "Mother of Jesus." The whole intercessory mediation of Mary
at Cana[39] draws its content and meaning from the fact that Mary is the
Mother of Jesus. That is the bottom line and the essential cause of such a
mediation to take place. Her faith, which enabled the "first sign" to be
accomplished and "his hour to begin,"[40] is the result of her maternity.

In the thought of the Pope, Mary's motherhood, in its connection
with mediation, also has a meta-historical dimension—meta-historical
in the sense that the historical mediation of Mary, as the Mother of Jesus,
is the foundation for her meta-historical intervention in addressing the
needs of all human beings. The mediation of Mary as analyzed in
Redemptoris Mater, 21 cycles between historicity and meta-historicity,
because the Pope sees an uninterrupted continuity between Mary's
action in history and in heaven.[41] While he was investigating the importance of Mary's motherhood in John's text (the wedding at Cana), he
drew a general concept of mediation that he applies to her presence in the
entire economy of salvation as such:

> Thus there is a mediation: Mary places herself between her Son and
> mankind in the reality of their wants, needs and sufferings. She puts
> herself in the middle, "that is to say she acts as a mediatrix not as an
> outsider, but in her position as Mother. She knows that as such she
> can point out to her Son the needs of mankind, and in fact, she has
> the right to do so. Her mediation is thus in the nature of interces-
> sion: Mary intercedes for mankind. And that is not all. As a Mother
> she also wishes the messianic power of her Son to be manifested,
> that salvific power of his which is meant to help man in his misfor-
> tunes, to free him from the evil which in various forms and degrees
> weighs heavily upon his life.[42]

From his analysis of Mary's presence at Cana, Pope John Paul II
draws a valid principle of mediation in Mariology. The continuity between

Mary's action at Cana and her intervention in the life of the Church becomes possible because of his personalistic approach in theological anthropology.[43] The continuity in her personal identity allows her to continue acting always "in the midst," because her consciousness of who she is, that is, the Mother, did not stop when she was lifted to eternal union with her Son. This shows that her eternal union with God can never contravene her union on earth. Mary's identity and role in the mystery of Christ is naturally extended to the order of grace, because the mystery of Christ is one and the same. Even though the reality of eternal union transcends in its nature the present situation, it is an extension and a perfection of the present situation. If Mary places herself, historically speaking, "between her Son and mankind in the reality of their wants, needs and sufferings," she still places herself between her Son and humankind so that "the messianic power of her Son (will) be manifested."[44]

Mary's consciousness of her maternal role that functioned in the natural context of motherhood continues to work now in a more perfect way in the order of grace. John Paul demonstrates that Mary was conscious of putting herself in the middle, between her Son and God's servants: "She knows that as such she can point out to her Son the needs of mankind, and in fact, she 'has the right' to do so."[45] For John Paul, Mary's earthly consciousness of her role, a fact that was manifested in historical events such as Cana, grows as she proceeds on her pilgrimage of faith. The growth of understanding her motherhood, a motherhood of mediation, will logically reach its climax when Mary fulfills her vocation in cooperating with the mystery of her Son. After her earthly life, the consciousness of the maternal role does not fade away; rather, it becomes perfected and broadened. It is extended to become, so to say, a meta-historical mediation that goes beyond the needs of the servants at Cana in order to reach the needs of humanity of all time. Contributing to the "beginning of signs" at Cana now becomes cooperation in spreading the messianic power in order to deliver people from the oppression of evil. Her intervention in that historical event (the wedding of Cana) now is extended to be an aid for the whole of humanity and the Church. Freeing the servants from the embarrassment of a wine shortage at Cana now becomes the liberation of man "from the evil which in various forms and degrees weighs heavily upon his life."[46]

If the metaphysical situation of a person, in this case Mary, discontinues what the person has fulfilled on earth, the whole idea of consciousness of the human person as a guarantee of continuity in personal identity would disappear. There is no doubt that the transcendence of heaven will bring some discontinuity with our earthly condition as far as categories are concerned according to which the human person exists in heaven. If, however, that discontinuity erases the continuity in personal identity and its resulting consciousness, the whole process of perfecting the being of a person through a series of historically conscious actions loses its value. Actually, the whole idea of earning salvation through cooperation with the free gift of God's grace would become meaningless. What would persons be if, after living an entire life dedicated to God, they would lose their identity and not remain themselves in heaven? The Pope applies this principle to Mary and sees the continuity in her conscious actions as the guarantee of her continued mediation in heaven. That explains the reason for terms related to mediation such as "she knows," she "has the right," "she also wishes."[47] Both the being and the action of the human person are perfected in heaven; otherwise there would be a lack of sincerity on the part of God who promised to give glory according to the degree of perfection that a person reaches in this life. That is the basis for the Church's doctrine concerning the intercession of the saints and especially of Mary, and that is why her mediation, which in line with Vatican II the Pope called maternity "in the order of grace,"[48] is "in the nature of intercession."[49]

For centuries the Catholic Church has based its understanding of Mary's action in the glory of heaven as a continuity of her historical action on earth. Heaven becomes the radicalization and the ultimate perfection and realization of a person's being and action on earth. That is the ground for eternity, resurrection, glory, and the hope of humanity that sees in Mary a renewed humanity in the splendor of the divine grace.[50]

John Paul summons these ideas in *Redemptoris Mater*, 22:

> From the text of John it is evident that it is a mediation which is maternal. As the Council proclaims: Mary became a Mother to us in the order of grace. This motherhood in the order of grace flows from her divine motherhood. Because she was, by the design of

divine providence, the Mother who nourished the divine Redeemer, Mary became an associate of unique nobility, and the Lord's humble handmaid, "who cooperated by her obedience, faith, hope and burning charity in the Savior's work of restoring supernatural life to souls." And this maternity of Mary in the order of grace . . . will last without interruption until the eternal fulfillment of all the elect.[51]

For Pope John Paul II, Mary's maternal mediation in itself necessarily possesses a Christological dimension. Christ who is the *nexus mysteriorum* (the unity and the connection between all the mysteries) joins Mary's motherhood according to the flesh with her spiritual motherhood. Since maternal mediation is based on the Mother-Son relationship in history, the unity of the mystery of Christ gives to the maternal mediation in the order of grace its reason of existence. *Unity of the mystery of Christ* means that, in relationship to Christ, human beings enjoy a continuity in their personal identity, whether they belong to the militant, suffering, or triumphant Church. Christ is the principle for every single action human beings perform in cooperation with the economy of salvation. By reason of her maternity, Mary is the Church member *par excellence* who enjoys a special place in that relationship. Therefore, no relationship to Christ will ever be more Christological than Mary's, a fact that is especially true concerning her maternal mediation. Both Vatican II (*Lumen Gentium*, 60) and John Paul II agree that Mary's mediation "is founded on his (Christ's) mediation, absolutely depends on it, and draws all its efficacy from it."[52]

One should keep in mind that the Christological dimension of Mary's maternal mediation maintains a balance in the theology of Pope John Paul II. This means that the person and action of Mary are not swallowed up by the person and action of Christ. In turn, the person and action of Mary, although authentic and necessary, draw their necessity from the action of the Son, not from themselves. Such a view of Mary's mediation in the plan of salvation puts the thought of the Pope in line with Saint Thomas Aquinas's understanding of the human being in relationship with God. No human being is necessary in the sense of the absolute necessity of God. As authentic as Mary is in her identity and action regarding God's plan, there is an absolute dependency on God. Her mediation, understood as a maternal intercession with her Son, falls into that specific category where, being an authentic human creature, she has an authentic role that is absolutely dependent on God. Christ's mediation, as incomparable and sufficient as it is in itself, does not exclude the cooperation of subordinate mediators. It would seem that Christ could freely associate others with his redemptive action without ceasing to be the full and sufficient cause.[53] In that sense, mediation has in itself a paradoxical dimension that will be recognized only by the logic of those who understand the human being relative to God in the *Thomistic* sense.[54]

MEDIATION OF MARY AT THE FOOT OF THE CROSS

Whereas Chapter VIII of *Lumen Gentium* simply introduced the new idea of the maternity of Mary at the cross, Pope John Paul II has theologically analyzed that concept and searched out its patristic and doctrinal roots. How does he see a mediation in Mary's presence beneath the cross of her Son?[55]

John Paul II's encyclical on the Holy Spirit (*Dominum et Vivificantem*, 16) presents Mary as embracing the cross together with Christ and thereby becoming "associated" with Him.[56] Yet, in a Pneumatological context (context of the Holy Spirit), Mary recognized the reality of that association with Christ's cross as a mean of salvation. It was the Holy Spirit Himself who accomplished in Mary this awareness and made her the associate of Christ at Calvary. Thus, the Pope says this about the Holy Spirit:

> The fullness of the Spirit of God is accompanied by many different gifts, the treasures of salvation, destined in a particular way for the poor and suffering, for all those who open their hearts to these gifts—sometimes through the painful experience of their own existence—but first of all through that interior availability which comes from faith.[57]

Such a statement on the work of the Holy Spirit enables the Pope to look at Mary's cooperation with the Spirit as an instrument of constant search for understanding Christ's mystery. At the foot of the cross, that is, at the climactic point of Christ's mystery, Mary, through the same Spirit that made conception possible at the Annunciation, became aware of salvation through suffering. This is the gift of salvation treasured by the Spirit that took place at Golgotha where Christ embraced the cross "together with his Mother" and she became His "associate."[58]

Also in his encyclical on the Gospel of Life (*Evangelium Vitae*), John Paul continues to explain the nature of Mary's maternal presence and intercession beneath the cross. Here Mary's maternal mediation becomes a sharing of Christ's gift of Himself: "She offers Jesus, gives him over, and begets him to the end for our sake."[59] Such a picture clarifies John Paul's understanding of the deep connection between motherhood and mediation. Mary offers Jesus not only at the Annunciation and at the cross; she continually "begets" Him for the salvation of all. Mediation becomes a necessary dimension that belongs to the very logic of motherhood. In exercising her motherhood, mediation enters as an *automatic* dimension and consequence of Mary's motherly functions:

> The yes spoken on the day of the Annunciation reaches full maturity on the day of the Cross, when the time comes for Mary to receive and beget as her children all those who become disciples, pouring upon them the saving love of her Son.[60]

While in *Evangelium Vitae*, Mary, at the foot of the cross, "offers Jesus, gives him over," in John Paul II's *Redemptionis Donum* (Gift of Redemption) she is described as "obedient even to the point of assenting to the death of her Son, who became obedient unto death!"[61]

The manner of Mary's mediation at the foot of the cross reaches its culminating clarification in John Paul II's *Salvifici Doloris*, 25 (On the Meaning of Christian Suffering). Here Mary is said to have been always at the side of Christ "in the first and most exalted place."[62] According to the gospel and to history, she is there "through the exemplary testimony that she bears by her whole life to this particular Gospel of suffering."[63] And the Pope quickly goes through the life of Mary and shows the suffering that permeated all the stages of her earthly existence next to her Son. The chain of suffering started when Mary heard from the angel at the Annunciation that her mission and destiny as a Mother was to share "in a singular and unrepeatable way, in the very mission of her Son." Not only at the foot of the cross but also throughout her whole life all the suffering Mary endured had a salutary nature in the same sense as spoken of by Saint Paul in the Letter to the Colossians: "In my flesh I complete what is lacking in Christ's afflictions for the sake of his body, that is, the Church."[64]

In several different ways, John Paul II determines the manner of Mary's presence beside her Son. First of all, generally speaking:

[I]n her, the many intense sufferings were amassed in such an inter-connected way that they were not only a proof of her unshakable faith but also a contribution to the Redemption of all.[65]

The concept of *contribution* draws the attention because it points to the manner of Mary's presence at the side of her suffering Son. "Con-tribution" expresses the maximum participation that human beings offer to complete in their flesh "what is lacking in Christ's afflictions for the sake of his body, that is, the Church." Such a "contribution" is explained further as the Pope describes Mary's suffering beside the suffering of Jesus as reaching an intensity which can hardly be imagined from a human point of view but which was mysteriously and supernaturally fruitful for the Redemption of the world.[66]

"Mysteriously and supernaturally fruitful for the Redemption of the world" is the manner of Mary's presence and contribution with her Son at Calvary. "Mysteriously" indicates the mystery of the Mother at the foot of the cross who contributes, as much as it is possible for a human person to be associated in the mystery of Redemption, to the accomplishment of humanity's salvation. "Supernaturally" refers to the redeeming action of Christ who draws His Mother to be present in the mystery of Redemption. Therefore, "contribution" and "mysteriously and supernaturally fruitful" should be understood as a parallel notion to "participation" in Saint Thomas's theology of creation. It is a Redemp-tion executed by the Son attended by the Mother who, on the human level of Redemption, cooperates in the Redemption of all. In that sense, the Pope continues to address the same idea in *Salvifici Doloris* and proposes the concept of "sharing" as the third way of explaining "con-tribution":

> Her ascent of Calvary and her standing at the foot of the cross together with the beloved disciple were a special sort of *sharing* in the redeeming death of her Son.[67]

It is a "special sort of sharing" because every human person is invited to share in the redeeming death of the Lord and complete in one's own body "what is lacking in Christ's affliction." Not that the sufferings of Christ are not sufficient; even as they are sufficient, that does not mean that they are not still open to sharing by others. It is a concept parallel to the Thomistic understanding of creation: even if God is a Self-sufficient Existence in Himself, that does not mean that His Existence cannot be shared by others. Being also self-sufficiently the Redeemer, the act of Redemption is open to be shared by others, too. The gospel of suffering spoken of by Saint Paul "becomes an inexhaustible source for the ever new generations that succeed one another in the history of the Church."[68]

From that point of view, Mary shares with every human person participation with Christ's suffering and becomes "the first and the most exalted of all the redeemed."[69] Yet, because of her call to be the Mother of the Redeemer, Mary's participation is unique in its intensity and quality. Because she gave the Son a human nature and enjoyed all the privileges of Mother-Son relationship, she manifested her motherly sorrow at the foot of the cross in its most concrete and historical dimension of a Mother:

> As a witness to her Son's passion by her presence, and as a sharer in it by her compassion, Mary offered a unique contribution to the Gospel of suffering, by embodying in anticipation the expression of Saint Paul which was quoted above (I complete in my body . . .).[70]

Again in his *Reconciliatio et Paenitentia* (Reconciliation and Penance), John Paul sees Mary enjoying an effective presence in the Redemption accomplished on Calvary for the sake of reconciliation between God and humanity. The grace of the Immaculate Conception enabled Mary to be Mother and, therefore, to be present in a very special way beside her suffering Son. However, her presence is active in humanly causing the Redemption. Redemption is still the exclusive act of Christ while in Mary, being the "mother of Jesus," and:

> ... in whom is effected the reconciliation of God with humanity ..., is accomplished the work of reconciliation, because she has received from God the fullness of grace in virtue of the redemptive sacrifice of Christ. Truly Mary was associated with God, by virtue of her divine motherhood, in the work of reconciliation.[71]

This quote of John Paul is probably one of the strongest concerning the mediation of Mary in reconciling humanity with God. In her "is effected the reconciliation of God with humanity," and "is accomplished the work of reconciliation." John Paul, however, never steps over boundaries and never attributes to Mary a *causality* in that same sense in which Christ directly realizes Redemption. Hers is a direct causality in the sense of a motherly presence that associates her with Christ in the work of Redemption. "Association" will always be a key term in the pontificate of John Paul to describe Mary's manner of active presence at the foot of the cross. And this "association" will assume a universal character, and Mary will be, as "an associate," a constant intercessor so that "humanity may discover and travel the path of penance, the only path that can lead it to full reconciliation."[72]

John Paul II's 1988 Holy Thursday Letter treats the subject of Mary's mediation at the foot of the cross from a totally different angle. Her consent to the immolation of her Son and her suffering together with Him constitute the essential character of Mary's motherly mediation: "Here we reach the high point of Mary's presence in the mystery of Christ and of the Church on earth."[73] For the Pope, then, the maximum degree of Mary's presence in the mystery of Christ and the Church is not Nazareth. The whole pilgrimage of mediative presence started at the Annunciation, but only at the foot of the cross has Mary come to experience the ultimate dimension of her motherhood in the order of grace and its relation to the Church.

In *Redemptoris Mater*, 23, Pope John Paul II further analyzes the maternal mediation of Mary as she stands at the foot of the cross (see John 19:25–27). We are still dealing with Mary's caring motherhood, even though at Calvary John the Evangelist:

> ... confirms this motherhood in the salvific economy of grace at its crowning moment, namely when Christ's sacrifice on the Cross, his Paschal Mystery, is accomplished.[74]

157

Historically speaking, Christ expresses a particular solicitude for His Mother because He is leaving her in such a great sorrow. Such a solicitude is manifested in assigning John to take her to his own home. Yet, beyond the bonds of flesh, there is revealed the ultimate dimension of motherhood of Mary in her relationship to Christ. The Mother-Son relationship is now extended to all human beings of all times. In John Paul II's *Familiaris Consortio*, 86, the extension of Mary's intercession as she stands at the foot of the cross "comfort the sufferings and dry the tears of those in distress."

Although the event of Cana, as shown in *Redemptoris Mater*, 23, already outlined Mary's motherhood of the human race, "now (at the foot of the Cross) it is clearly stated and established"[75] by Christ Himself (parenthetical material added). The connection is not that simple if one notices that, in Cana, Christ has answered the request of His mother and granted the need of the servants. Answering the needs of the servants because the Mother of Jesus has asked for it later becomes a different kind of answer because, at the foot of the cross, Mary stands without any question. If Jesus answered the presence of Mary at Cana by performing the miracle because she is the Mother, at the cross he also answers her presence by responding to the ultimate spiritual dimension of her motherhood, that is, her motherhood of the human race. The logic of the Pope is clear: Jesus does not change his ways with his Mother. At Cana He manifests the power of her mediative intercession; at the foot of the cross He manifests again the power of maternal mediation as the Mother stands at the heart of the mystery of Redemption. The maternal presence of Mary at the foot of the cross is a recorded fact of Scripture.

In *Redemptoris Mater*, 23, at the foot of the cross Christ reveals the whole "truth and reality" of what it means for Mary to be His Mother, as well as the Mother of the human race.[76] The truth and reality of that motherhood is revealed in the context of the paschal mystery, the central event of Jesus' saving activity. If the Redemption accomplished by Christ embraces all humanity, this implies that Mary's involvement in this Redemption should embrace all humanity. But Mary's involvement was expressed in her maternal presence and care at the foot of the cross. Therefore, at the heart of the mystery of Redemption, Mary's motherhood stands in a mysterious relationship with all humanity redeemed by Christ:

> It (Mary's motherhood of the human race) emerges from the
> definitive accomplishment of the Redeemer's Paschal Mystery. The
> Mother of Christ, who stands at the very center of this mys-
> tery—a mystery which embraces each individual and all
> humanity—is given as Mother to every single individual and all
> mankind[77] (parenthetical material added).

If Christ reveals Himself as the Redeemer in His paschal mystery, Mary
is revealed by Him as the Mother of the Redeemer. If Redemption
reaches every person in his or her relationship to the Redeemer, motherhood reaches every person in his or her relationship with the Mother
of the Redeemer. In that sense, Mary is called by Pope John Paul II,
who refers to *Lumen Gentium*, 53 and 54, "the Mother of Christ and
Mother of mankind." The man standing beneath the cross is John the
Evangelist, the disciple whom Jesus loved. Pope John Paul II states in
Redemptoris Mater, 23:

> Following tradition, the Council does not hesitate to call Mary the
> Mother of Christ and Mother of mankind: since she belongs to the
> offspring of Adam she is one with all human beings . . . Indeed she is
> clearly the Mother of the members of Christ . . . since she cooper-
> ated out of love so that there might be born in the Church the faithful.[78]

Redemptoris Mater, 23 also analyzes the word *woman*. In Salvatore
Meo's opinion, the expression *woman* used by Christ is not a sign of
distance that he takes from His Mother. *Woman* appears at the beginning and at the end of the history of salvation, namely in Gen 3:15 and
in Rev 12:1. The Pope's logic is as follows: it is Christ Himself who,
when the hour to fulfill the paschal mystery came, indicates that in the
context of Mary's divine maternity, it is the title *woman* that refers to
her role of cooperation in the work of Redemption. Therefore,
Redemptoris Mater bestows the name "maternal mediation" on that
cooperation.[79]

Ugo Vanni thinks that "offspring" as employed by *Redemptoris
Mater*, 23 contextually refers to Gen 3:15 and Rev 12:1. In fact, the use
of the term "offspring" in Genesis is attributed to Eve and only indirectly to Adam, and it appears at the end of Revelation referring only to
Eve (not to Adam).[80] Analyzing the role of the Virgin Mary, one should
keep in mind from what perspective the Pope is working out his logic.

John Paul's reference to *Lumen Gentium* 53 and 54 presents a universal Redemption of Christ that associates Mary with the offspring of Adam. In that regard, Vatican II has followed the teaching of Saint Thomas Aquinas, for whom every human person should be included in the category of being redeemed. Mary also was redeemed, even though in the theology of Vatican II and John Paul II she was redeemed as the Mother of the members of Christ's body. Mary is at the same time member (the most eminent member as recalled by *Redemptoris Mater*, 7–11) and Mother of the members—"member," because she is redeemed, and "Mother of the members," because she "cooperated out of love so that there might be born in the Church the faithful." The Marian doctrine flowing from the presence of Mary at the foot of the cross enables the Pope to draw the most important conclusion: in the very heart of the mystery of Redemption, Christ Himself reveals the mystery of Mary's motherhood and places her at the center of the body of Christ as the Mother of all those who are to be born into the Church. Being the Mother of the faithful assumes an ecclesiological dimension because the historicity of her motherhood in the Gospel of John receives a meta-historical dimension of being Mother of all who stand with her at the foot of her Son's cross. Thus the conclusion of *Redemptoris Mater*, 23:

> And so this new motherhood of Mary, generated by faith, is the fruit of the new love which came to definitive maturity in her at the foot of the Cross, through her sharing in the redemptive love of her Son.[81]

So far Pope John Paul II has not mentioned the expression *love* in the context of Mary's spiritual motherhood. The notion of *love* introduced into *Redemptoris Mater*, 23 is based on the theological analysis presented in *Redemptoris Mater*, 8. The grace of God in Mary's life has its source in that eternal love among the three Divine Persons. The fruit of that love is the election of Mary to be Mother of Christ and the Mother of the members of Christ's body. Mary's "new motherhood" generated by faith is the direct consequence of that love which sustained Mary in her pilgrimage of faith from Nazareth to Cana and from Cana to the cross. On Golgotha, Mary shares in everything that the Son does as the direct agent of Redemption: He is the Redeemer and she is the Mother of the Redeemer; He redeems because of that eternal love between Him and the Father; she shares in "the redemptive love of her Son."[82] That "sharing" constitutes the essential question of the manner of Mary's presence in the Paschal Mystery. The whole theology of presence is evoked here in order to elucidate the place of Mary in the Redemption accomplished by Christ. This "sharing" is clarified by what the Pope says in *Redemptoris Missio* (Mission of the Redeemer):

> Although participated forms of mediation of different kinds and degrees are not excluded, they acquire meaning and value only from Christ's own mediation, and they cannot be understood as parallel or complementary to his.[83]

The "sharing" spoken of in *Redemptoris Mater*, 23 is explained by the "associate with Him" of *Dominum et Vivificantem* (16), by "offers Jesus, gives him over" of *Evangelium Vitae* (103), by "assenting" of *Redemptionis Donum* (17), and by "contribution to the Redemption of all . . . supernaturally fruitful for the Redemption of the world. Special sort of sharing . . ." of *Salvifici Doloris* (25). That sharing also comes to light as Pope John Paul II draws the parallel between the woman of Gen 3:15 and Mary. In the Protogospel (God's promise of salvation to Eve understood as the first Gospel), the promise that "the seed of the woman . . . will crush the head of the serpent" (cf Gen 3:15) is now fulfilled by the action of Christ on the cross and the presence of His Mother. This text, in the opinion of Ugo Vanni, does not make of Mary the main protagonist, because Christ is the unique direct agent that crushes the head of the serpent. However, the event of the cross as well as the messianic maternity given to Mary in the person of John receive a particular relevance not only because of Mary being a theological personality but also because in *Redemptoris Mater* the "woman" standing beneath the cross joins together, in biblical hermeneutics (interpretation), the "woman" of Gen 3:15 with the "woman" of Rev 12:1.[84]

The *allegorical* (Christ is the key of interpreting Scripture) and the *sensus plenior* (looking at Scripture as a unity inspired by the One God) approach explain the reason behind Jesus' insistence on calling Mary "woman" at Cana and at the foot of the cross. Then the question comes: "How can one doubt that especially now, on Golgotha, this expression goes to the very heart of the mystery of Mary, and indicates the unique place which she occupies in the whole economy of salvation?"[85] The Pope explains the nature of that sharing in the redemptive love of Mary's Son. He does not consider Mary as direct agent of Redemption; rather, she occupies a unique place in the whole economy of salvation. This means that at the foot of the cross Mary, as the *Mother*, was present in a love beyond telling, a love that generated a new dimension in her motherhood. "Sharing" becomes a presence and definitive determination on the part of Mary to orient her whole being and actions toward the same destiny and goals as her Son when He fulfills the Redemption. In that sense, Vatican II teaches that in Mary:

> . . . the exalted Daughter of Sion, and after a long expectation of the promise, the times were at length fulfilled and the new dispensation established.[86]

One should notice that the Second Vatican Council referred to the title "exalted Daughter of Sion" to indicate Mary's messianic maternity in which she culminates the promises of the Old Testament and starts the new economy of salvation leading to fulfillment. Vatican II, therefore, limited the use of the title to the historical reality. Pope John Paul II went one step further and employed the term to designate the definitive condition of Mary in the mystery of eternal glory. In her role as "Queen of the Universe" is identified the union of the Church in pilgrimage with the eschatological reality of the communion of saints.[87]

Pope John Paul II turns back in *Redemptoris Mater*, 24 to analyze the presence of the Apostle John along with Mary at the foot of the cross:

> The words uttered by Jesus from the Cross signify that the motherhood of her who bore Christ finds a new continuation in the Church and through the Church, symbolized and represented by John.[88]

The divine maternity of Mary, which is the essential element of all the dimensions of her motherhood, receives a new reality when Christ on the cross reveals her motherhood of His mystical body, the Church. If the Redemption of Christ transcends the historical realm and includes a universal salvation, so the motherhood of Mary and the sonship of John are extended to all who are redeemed, the Church. John Paul II, because of the infinite value of the actions of the Son of God, gives reason for transferring Jesus' actions into a meta-historical level. Consequently, the Pope universalizes the functions of all the agents involved in the Redemption. Mary becomes the Mother of John and, therefore, of all who stand beneath the cross of the Lord, that is, the believing Church. John becomes the son of Mary and makes all who are "standing" with him receive the sonship of Mary. In that sense John is said to "symbolize" and "represent" the Church.

Mary was introduced into the mystery of Christ as the Immaculate Conception who would give birth to God the Son according to the flesh. Therefore, Mary is present in the mystery of Christ primarily as the "Mother," even though this Mother, as the replacement of Eve, is also the "woman" of Genesis and Apocalypse. The notion of "woman" attributed to Mary has a salvific dimension and places her as the "New" Eve. The notion of "Mother" specifies who this woman is and gives reason for her unique place in the history of salvation. Motherhood according to the flesh, therefore, will always be at the base for developing the Church's doctrine on Mary's motherhood. If Mary has become once and for all the Mother of God according to the flesh, her presence in that mystery will be possible only if Mary continues to be the Mother after the Resurrection of Christ. Through the Church, the mystery of Mary's motherhood is extended throughout history as the "woman." Therefore, since Mary is identified by the Pope as the "woman" of Genesis and Apocalypse, she is present throughout the history of salvation as the Mother of the Church. Her motherhood of the Church, therefore, is what makes Mary accompany the Church throughout all generations as the "woman" of Genesis and Apocalypse. Ugo Vanni points out that the contact between Mary and the Church constitutes, in the theology of Pope John Paul II, the very reason of Mary being the "woman" of Gen 3:15 and Rev 12:1. Through the relevance that Mary receives in the Church, she functions as the New Eve and as the eschatological woman of Revelation clothed with the sun in her final victory.[89] In this sense, Mary's motherhood of the Church is a reflection of her motherhood of the Son of God:

In this way, she who as the one full of grace was brought into the mystery of Christ in order to be his Mother and thus the Holy Mother of God, through the Church remains in that mystery as the woman spoken of by the Book of Genesis (3:15) at the beginning and by the Apocalypse (12:1) at the end of the history of salvation. In accordance with the eternal plan of providence, Mary's divine motherhood is to be poured out upon the Church, as indicated by statements of Tradition, according to which Mary's motherhood of the Church is the reflection and extension of her motherhood of the Son of God.[90]

In the dimension of the Spirit, Mary's motherhood of the Church reflects Pope John Paul's faithfulness to the theology of Vatican II. Mary's "new" motherhood of the Church is symbolized and represented by the presence of John at the foot of the cross. It is confirmed as well by the descent of the Holy Spirit on Mary and the apostles at the time of the birth of the Church.[91] The Council said:

Since it pleased God not to manifest solemnly the mystery of the salvation of the human race until he poured forth the Spirit promised by Christ, we see the Apostles before the day of Pentecost continuing with one mind in prayer with the women and Mary the mother of Jesus, and with his brethren (Acts 1:14). We see Mary prayerfully imploring the gift of the Spirit, who had already overshadowed her in the Annunciation.[92]

The role of the Holy Spirit, the Person-Gift, in the economy of salvation has been already thoroughly explained in my first study on the thought of Pope John Paul II. If, on the level of the Immanent Trinity, the Holy Spirit is that eternal Self-offering of love between Father and Son in space and time, then He is God's Self-offering to creation. The Holy Spirit is the Divine Person who enables God, in His creative or redeeming activity, to come in contact with creation. Therefore, at the beginning of every covenant it is the Holy Spirit who comes down and assures the beginning of that specific economy.[93] Pope John Paul calls "redemptive economy of grace" the action of the Holy Spirit in accomplishing the economy of the New Testament. At the dawn of the New Testament, the Holy Spirit formed the human nature of Christ in the womb of Mary. Through His descent on the apostles and Mary, the Holy Spirit gave birth to the Church:

> And so, in the redemptive economy of grace, brought about through the action of the Holy Spirit, there is a unique correspondence between the moment of the Incarnation of the Word and the moment of the birth of the Church.[94]

Therefore, if on the divine level the Spirit ensures the continuity in the economy of salvation throughout history, then on the human level, "the person who links these two moments is Mary: Mary at Nazareth and Mary in the Upper Room at Jerusalem."[95] Such a contact between the Holy Spirit and Mary in the context of the New Covenant is described in terms of "birth from the Holy Spirit."[96] Mary will always be the authentic human agent that cooperated with this divine agent in order to be present in the mystery of Christ through "birth from the Holy Spirit." It seems that the Spirit refers to a Christological content, even though the contact that first took place with the human agent, Mary, was done through the Holy Spirit. The same Holy Spirit who introduced her into the mystery of Christ by causing the Incarnation at the Annunciation is now introducing her into the mystery of the Church by descending upon her and the apostles on Pentecost. If she was introduced into the mystery of Christ as a Mother, she is also introduced into the mystery of the Church as a Mother. At the foot of the cross, Christ confirmed this when he uttered the words: "Woman, behold your son!"; "Behold, your mother."[97]

From *Redemptoris Mater*, 24, one deduces that the motherhood of Mary has a Christological (her presence in the mystery of Christ) and a Pneumatological dimension (her presence in the mystery of the Church through the Holy Spirit). This approach manifests Pope John Paul II's profound thought about the Marian doctrine of Vatican II. The Christological dimension of the mystery of the Mother focuses on her presence in the economy of the Son, God and man, divine and human. As far as the Pneumatological dimension is concerned, Mary is present in the mystery of the Church, at once a divine and a human institution. In both cases, the Holy Spirit is the *divine* agent that fulfills the contact with Mary; Mary is the *human* agent that cooperates with God's initiative; Christ and the Church are *divine and human*. Both aspects are important because the presence of Mary in the mystery of Christ is the basis for her presence in the mystery of the Church. At the same time, her presence in the mystery of the Church extends, throughout space, time, and history, her presence in the mystery of Christ. The Holy Spirit accomplishes the very reality of that presence.[98]

Pneumatological and Christological studies of Mary's mystery are a sound approach that eliminates false tendencies to exaggerate her independence from the economy of salvation.[99] An overemphasis of her personal privileges without a true knowledge of their connection with the mystery of Christ and the Church results in isolating Mariology from the other theological disciplines. Such an isolation endangers that same enrichment that Vatican II has recovered by incorporating Mary into the overall picture of salvation accomplished by Christ through the Holy Spirit and extended in history by the Church.

An isolation of Mary from the mystery of Christ and the Church could also detach Mary from the historicity of Divine Revelation that occurred through the historical events of Annunciation and Pentecost. When Mary is detached from the historicity of the economy of salvation, one could easily fall into an implicit Gnosticism that overemphasized the spiritual dimension of her reality at the expense of a true, concrete, and historical presence in the mystery of the Incarnation and Pentecost. The notion of "mystery" itself, whether it is the mystery of Christ or the mystery of the Church, emphasizes both the human and the divine dimension of the economy of salvation and eliminates gnostic tendencies.[100] How can one detach Mary from these Redemption mysteries after she has been the human agent who cooperated with the Holy Spirit, the divine agent, in order to accomplish them? In that sense, when John Paul II's *Tertio Millennio Adveniente* describes Mary's presence in the mystery of Christ's Incarnation at the Annunciation, he emphasizes the human dimension of the divine plan. He draws his concept from the Mariology of Saint Bernard of Clairvaux, for whom God Himself was seen to depend on Mary for the fulfillment of His plan: "Never in human history did so much depend, as it did then, upon the consent of human creature."[101]

An isolation of Mary from the mysteries of Christ and the Church could also lead to an idealization of the mystery. It could reduce the mystery to its mere human dimension, allowing thus a rationalistic approach that downsizes the mystery of God to its Marian dimension.

Modern rationalism does not accept the notion of "mystery" because "it attributes to natural reason a knowledge which only the light of faith could confer,"[102] and because it seeks in various ways, at least in its idealistic form:

> . . . to transform faith and its contents, even the mystery of the death and Resurrection of Jesus, into dialectical structures which could be grasped by reason.[103]

If rationalism insisted on a constant claim of understanding the very mystery of God in the natural light of human reason, it would completely ignore the transcendental aspects of the Mother's mystery in its relationship to the mystery of Christ and the Church. That transcendental aspect of Mary's mystery guarantees the development of a sound Mariology against idealistic and rationalistic tendencies.[104] It was not by chance that conciliar and postconciliar Mariology was mainly developed in its relationship with the mystery of Christ and the Church.

UNIQUE MEDIATION OF CHRIST AND MARY'S MEDIATION

Pope John Paul II opens *Redemptoris Mater*, 38 with an emphasis on Saint Paul's teaching that:

> [T]here is only one mediator: For there is one God, and there is one mediator between God and men, the man Christ Jesus, who gave himself as a ransom for all (1 Tim 2:5–6).[105]

The Holy Father refers to the teaching of the Second Vatican Council to show that Mary's mediation is Christological:

> The maternal role of Mary toward people in no way obscures or diminishes the unique mediation of Christ, but rather shows its power: it is mediation in Christ.[106]

In *Tertio Millennio Adveniente*, 43, the Pope uses the same terminology:

> The affirmation of the central place of Christ cannot therefore be separated from the recognition of the role played by his Most Holy

Mother. Veneration of her, when properly understood, can in no way take away from the "dignity and efficacy of Christ the one Mediator."

And, quoting again *Lumen Gentium*, 60, he says:

> The Church knows and teaches that all the saving influences of the Blessed Virgin on mankind originate . . . from the divine pleasure. They flow forth from the superabundance of the merits of Christ, rest on his mediation, depend entirely on it, and draw all their power from it. In no way do they impede the immediate union of the faithful with Christ. Rather, they foster this union.[107]

This text of the Second Vatican Council is of extreme importance for the theology of Pope John Paul II concerning Mary's mediation. He immediately brings into the picture the Pneumatological[108] dimension (the dimension of the Spirit) of Mary's mediation, and he uses it to explain the Christological dimension of that mediation. The Holy Spirit is the only agent that enables the Pope to see a continuity between the saving influence of Mary's divine motherhood and its historical extension expressed in her solicitude for humanity.[109] It is an amazing approach because Vatican II did not introduce Pneumatological elements into the Christological dimension of Mary's mediation. Salvatore Meo considers the observation of the Pope as an enrichment of the approach of the Council.[110]

At the Annunciation the Holy Spirit overshadowed Mary in order to accomplish in her the Incarnation of the Son. This event itself shed light on the meaning of "saving influences." The Holy Spirit coming down on Mary implies that "this saving influence is sustained by the Holy Spirit."[111] The Holy Spirit sustains the saving influence in the sense that He gave Mary the gift to be Mother of God, a gift that will never cease being a source of relationship between Christ and His Mother. The Spirit works for a Christological finality, even though that same Christological finality involves Mary as a Mother and implies a saving influence that depends entirely on Christ. If, in the context of the Incarnation, the Spirit sustains the saving influence of the Blessed Virgin in relationship with her Son, the Spirit will also sustain the saving influence of Mary in relationship with the people who became sons and daughters in the Son. A saving influence acquired because of the Incarnation becomes a solicitude for humanity. In the same way that this saving influence never loses its power because the Holy Spirit sustains Mary in her divine motherhood, the solicitude toward people will also be constant because the same Holy Spirit sustains it in relationship to the divine motherhood. What the Holy Spirit has accomplished in Mary in regard to Christ, He will also accomplish in humanity in regard to the brothers and sisters of Christ:

> This saving influence is sustained by the Holy Spirit, who, just as he overshadowed the Virgin Mary when he began in her the divine motherhood, in a similar way constantly sustains her solicitude for the brothers and sisters of her Son.[112]

Hence the mediation of Mary is *essentially* and *necessarily* maternal.[113]

For Pope John Paul II, if Mary did not receive the saving influence from the divine motherhood, she would not be able to have solicitude toward the brothers and the sisters of the Lord. On the divine level, the Holy Spirit connects the two periods of Mary's activity, that is, with Christ and, after His Resurrection, with the Church. On the human level, Mary extends the same activity as that of Calvary at the side of her Son on earth, to continue to act in the same way in the glory of heaven. Therefore, the mediation of Mary, even though it can be compared to the mediation of other human beings, is unique because it is maternal.[114] Here is the text that quotes *Lumen Gentium*, 62:

> In effect, Mary's mediation is intimately linked with her motherhood. It possesses a specifically maternal character, which distinguishes it from the mediation of the other creatures who in various and always subordinate ways share in the one mediation of Christ, although her own mediation is also a shared mediation. In fact, while it is true that "no creature could ever be classed with the Incarnate Word and Redeemer," at the same time "the unique mediation of the Redeemer does not exclude but rather gives rise among creatures to a manifold cooperation which is but a sharing in this unique source." And thus "the one goodness of God is in reality communicated diversely to his creatures.[115]

The key to understanding the reason for Mary's mediation as such is the last sentence of this text: "And thus the one goodness of God is in reality communicated diversely to his creatures." Here the theology of

Saint Thomas Aquinas is evident. Mediation is based on the mystery of creation and the mystery of Redemption. As far as creation is concerned, God, as absolute as He is in His being and essence, is not in need of any creatures. Yet, the act of creation reveals the divine initiative and the intention of God who wants creatures to *share* in an authentic way in His goodness. That participation in God's goodness, which should be understood in the Thomistic sense, allows creatures to be a part of God's plan without being an absolute necessity. Creation is called "creation" precisely because creatures who are created *ex nihilo* (out of nothing) are invited to participate in the existence of God in a real way. Creatures do really exist. In the order of creation, creatures enjoy different degrees of perfection according to the wisdom of the Creator. In that same context, creatures find themselves in a diversity that belongs to the mystery of creation, not to a concept of partiality in God. This aspect of the mystery of creation in which creatures exist in various degrees of perfection will always be hidden in the very mystery of God. That was the reason Vatican II said that God's goodness "is in reality communicated diversely to his creatures."[116]

If one projects this Thomistic concept of creation to the reality of Redemption, one finds an easier road to understanding why there is mediation and why Mary's mediation is different from the others. Creatures exist and their act of existence, as authentic as it is (they truly exist), shares in the existence of God without adding anything to God's existence. In the same exact way, creatures, in the context of Redemption, are invited to cooperate without adding anything to the Redemption of Christ. John Paul II's *Tertio Millennio Adveniente* stated this reality in simple terms when describing Mary's cooperation with the Incarnation: "Never in human history did so much depend, as it did then, upon the consent of one human creature."[117] Christ's saving act, as sufficient as it is in itself, is shared by creatures, because it is impossible that the principle of creation contradicts the principle of Redemption. In the same way that creatures enjoy different degrees of glory granted to them by God in the mysterious plan of creation, different creatures enjoy different positions of mediation in the mysterious plan of Redemption. This explains the Pope's words in *Redemptoris Missio*, 5:

> Although participated forms of mediation of different kinds and degrees are not excluded, they acquire meaning and value only from Christ's own mediation, and they cannot be understood as parallel or complementary to his.[118]

This theology gives the basis for understanding the mediation of Mary in the context of her divine motherhood. Her role:

> . . . is at the same time special and extraordinary. It flows from her divine motherhood and can be understood and lived in faith only on the basis of the full truth of this motherhood.[119]

In order to explain why the maternal mediation of Mary is *special* and *extraordinary*, Pope John Paul II naturally turns to analyze the event in which Mary actually became Mother—the Annunciation—from the point of view of mediation.

In his search for understanding of Mary's mediation in the context of divine motherhood, John Paul does not hesitate to use philosophy to analyze Scripture. His personalistic approach to the identity and role of Mary in the event of the Annunciation describes her submission to the words of the angel as a conscious act.[120] Mary recognizes in the words of the messenger the will of the Most High and acts accordingly. Her acceptance of God's plan to become the Mother of His Son presents the first step of submission to the mediation of Christ. At the very moment when Mary accepted becoming the Mother, she accepted the incomparable mediation of the Son. She is aware that at the center of all that is happening is the Incarnation:

> The first moment of submission to the one mediation between God and men—the mediation of Jesus Christ—is the Virgin of Nazareth's acceptance of motherhood.[121]

R. Laurentin thinks that, for John Paul II, Mary's *fiat* has founded the physical as well as the mystical body of Christ. That event has introduced her as the first member of the mystical body allowing her to function as a Mother cooperating with the unique mediation of Christ.[122]

In the same way that God made the sovereign decision to grant degrees of perfection to creatures according to His wisdom, He also enjoys an unconditioned freedom to propose to Mary her vocation to motherhood. His decision will influence her whole existence because, through the power of the Holy Spirit, she is invited to become the Mother of the Son. Therefore, the Pope uses expressions such as "Mary consents to God's choice,"[123] in order to describe God's divine initiative to grant Mary not only the highest degree of perfection in her Immaculate Conception but also this special and extraordinary role in the economy of salvation. That role will be extended to her entire existence—on earth and in her eternal union with the Trinity. Hence the Pope says:

> Since by virtue of divine election Mary is the earthly Mother of the Father's consubstantial Son and his generous companion in the work of Redemption, she is a Mother to us in the order of grace.[124]

The acceptance of God's choice by the Mother of His consubstantial Son took place in the context of *virginity*. Pope John Paul II analyzes the concept of virginity first in *Redemptoris Mater*, 39. Virginity and motherhood condition each other because the call to divine motherhood *a priori* gives meaning to Mary's virginity, and her virginity makes it possible to accept and dedicate herself to motherhood. Based on that concept, virginity becomes the ground on which is built her vocation to motherhood:

> It can be said that this consent to motherhood is above all a result of her total self-giving to God in virginity.

For the Pope, virginity is not a negative reality that is geared toward abstinence from sexual relationship. It is a positive choice of consecration, an attitude of the whole being of Mary to belong to God. As a total self-offering of her being to God, Mary's virginity receives a spousal character in its relationship with God:

> She perfectly unites in herself the love proper to virginity and the love characteristic of motherhood, which are joined and, as it were, fused together.[125]

It is a paradoxical union based on and conditioned by total virginity:

> Mary accepted her election as Mother of the Son of God, guided by spousal love, the love which totally consecrates a human being to God. By virtue of this love, Mary wished to be always and in things "given to God," living in virginity.[126]

If one meditates on this concept of virginity in the context of the Annunciation, one realizes that the very motherhood of Mary, even though it gives existence to all other Marian qualifications, took place in the context of virginity and consecration. Virginity becomes the framework in which the divine maternity takes place. If divine maternity is Mary's essential characteristic in the overall picture of salvation, without a framework a picture cannot accomplish its function as a picture. In that sense, virginity conditions her motherhood.

In the fourth century, Saint Gregory of Nyssa seems to be the first Father who proposed Mary's perpetual virginity as a personal vow on the part of Mary.[127] After the Bishop of Nyssa there took place in the Church a very strong tradition concerning the perpetual virginity of Mary understood as a personal vow. More interested in the tradition of the Church and in the *sensus plenior* of the scriptural text than in a critical historical method, Pope John Paul II considers the words of Mary—"Behold, I am the handmaid of the Lord"—as a conscious act of consecration to the divine motherhood through virginity. These words, as the Pope states,

> . . . express the fact that from the outset she accepted and understood as a total gift of self, a gift of her person to the service of the saving plans of the Most High. And to the very end she lived her entire maternal sharing in the life of Jesus Christ, her Son, in a way that matched her vocation to virginity.[128]

Why does Pope John Paul II analyze the maternal mediation of Mary in the context of virginity? Because Mary's motherhood, which "constitutes the first and fundamental dimension of that mediation," is "completely pervaded by her spousal attitude as the 'handmaid of the Lord.'"[129] The motherhood of Mary being accomplished in the context of virginity and her mediation drawing its content from her motherhood lead to the fact that virginity is intimately connected with mediation. The bridge between the two is Mary's motherhood. Her divine maternity is "a result of her total self-giving to God in virginity;" whereas that same motherhood is "the first and fundamental dimension of that mediation."[130]

That Pope John Paul ties the three aspects together is not an arbitrary choice. Before anyone else, it was God, the Eternal Father, "who entrusted himself to the Virgin of Nazareth, giving her his own Son in the mystery of the Incarnation."[131] God's initiative of entrustment preceded Mary's response of consecration through virginity to motherhood. In the context of spousal attitude, Mary cooperated in accomplishing the union between the human and the divine nature in the Person of the Word. That union is and always will be the instrument of our salvation.

From the very beginning of God's contact with Mary, the mechanism of the Incarnation implied her involvement in the salvation of mankind through that ineffable union. Being the Mother of God necessarily places Mary in a soteriological position because she, being the Mother of the Incarnate Word, brought about the union between the two natures in Christ:

> Her election to the supreme office and dignity of Mother of the Son of God refers, on the ontological level, to the very reality of the union of the two natures in the person of the Word (hypostatic union).[132]

Her saving influence on humanity, as authentic as it is, still originates from the union of the two natures in Christ, a union that was possible only through her motherhood. Yet, that motherhood will always take place in the dimension of consecration, a fact that will make the mediation of Mary an instrument of the strength of her virginal relationship with God. *Mediation is based on motherhood; motherhood takes place in the context of virginity; virginity strengthens the spousal character of union with God. From this logic one sees that the mediation of Mary is designed to bring mankind to a stronger union with God.* Mediation, an instrument to promote a tighter union with God, becomes necessary since all of the elements that involve Mary in the economy of salvation were initiated by God Himself. That is really the meaning of the words of the Second Vatican Council quoted above:

> All the saving influences of the Blessed Virgin on Mankind originate from the divine pleasure . . . In no way do they impede the immediate union of the faithful with Christ. Rather, they foster this union.[133]

The Marian doctrine concerning mediation becomes even more meaningful with John Paul's words quoting *Lumen Gentium*, 61, according to which Mary:

> . . . became not only the nursing mother of the Son of Man but also the associate of unique nobility of the Messiah and Redeemer.[134]

"Associate of unique nobility" is an expression that contains two features: the pilgrimage of faith to the foot of the cross and the "maternal cooperation with the Savior's whole mission through her actions and sufferings."[135] Her presence at the foot of the cross is part of a whole journey of faith and, at the same time, a dynamic presence. It is dynamic because it involves cooperation with the mission of the Savior through actions. It is an active presence and, in that sense, is cooperation, specifically maternal mediation. For the Pope, unlike many Mariologists, the presence of Mary beneath the foot of the cross does have a mediative dimension. The nature of that mediation (Mary at the foot of the cross) is directly related to her motherhood which was totally oriented to cooperate with the fulfilling of Christ's saving mission.

The key element for understanding the nature of Mary's mediation in this context is her "burning charity" in accomplishing the work of her Son. Beyond the natural bonds of blood, Mary's motherhood was transformed into an attitude of cooperation and collaboration that brought her pain and suffering. Such an active attitude of "burning charity" manifests Mary's ultimate involvement in the sacrificial offering of Christ on the cross:

> Along the path of this collaboration with the work of her Son, the Redeemer, Mary's motherhood itself underwent a singular transformation, becoming ever more imbued with "burning charity" toward all those to whom Christ's mission was directed. Through this "burning charity," which sought to achieve, in union with Christ, the restoration of "supernatural life to souls," Mary entered, in a way all her own, into the one mediation between God and men which is the mediation of the man Jesus Christ.[136]

This text explains why, for Pope John Paul II, the maternal presence of Mary is a maternal mediation. Actually this is one of the deepest concepts of mediation that he presents in his theology. The motherhood of Mary in its human bonds was the first step into that pilgrimage of faith and spiritual motherhood that made Mary collaborate even to the foot of the cross with the work of Redemption. That same motherhood revealed its intercessory dimension at Cana in Galilee and continued to do that throughout the life of Mary. At the foot of the cross, the intercessory nature of Mary's mediation becomes a mediative presence because Mary's motherhood was transformed, in that specific event, into a burning charity for the salvation of humankind. Her presence beneath the cross is mediative because her intercessory motherhood was totally transformed into burning charity for the salvation of souls. Mary cooperated with the sacrifice of Christ through her burning charity and, in that sense, she became his "associate of unique nobility."[137]

It is of extreme importance to notice how John Paul chose terminology to describe the nature of Mary's mediation:

> Through this "burning charity," which sought to achieve, in union with Christ, the restoration of "supernatural life to souls," Mary entered, in a way all her own, into the one mediation "between God and men" which is the mediation of the man Jesus Christ.[138]

Her cooperation in Christ's work of Redemption has various elements. "Through her burning charity" indicates the manner of her participation in His sacrifice and the content of her maternal presence. "Sought to achieve" shows the dynamic presence of Mary beneath the cross and the convergence of her intention with the Redeemer's saving action. Mary is not a passive agent in the sacrifice of her Son, even though she is not the Redeemer. "In union with Christ"[139] is the essential element for a sound understanding of Mary's mediation at the foot of the cross. Christ is and always will be the exclusive Redeemer of humanity. He is the only agent capable of restoring the supernatural life to souls. If Mary, through her burning charity, sought the restoration of life to souls, she did that only in "union with Christ." With that approach, Pope John Paul II protects Mary from false tendencies that look at her as the agent of Redemption and put her on the level of Christ.

Yet, Mary still entered in a way all her own into the process of Redemption. That entering indicates a true and authentic mediation.

The concept of mediation, as difficult as it is with its various meanings, is a concept that can be applied to Mary in the sense stated above. "In a way all her own" shows that Mary's maternal mediation is different from the mediation of all other creatures. It is a mediation that is specifically maternal and, because it is maternal, it is extraordinary, unique, and unrepeatable. Nobody will ever again be the Mother of Jesus Christ. The Pope faithfully preserves the line of thought of Vatican II's theology since he emphasizes that Mary did enter into the one mediation of Christ. Biblically and in the tradition of the Church, Christ is and always will be the unique mediator between God and human beings.[140] Although Mary entered into the dimension of mediation, she entered into the "one mediation . . . which is the mediation of the man Jesus Christ."[141] Her cooperation is authentic, but it happens within the framework of Christ's unique mediation.

The manner in which that cooperation takes place is elucidated by the Pope when he connects mediation to the event of Annunciation. For him, the fact that Mary is called "full of grace" at the Annunciation is a reality that expresses the consequences of Christ's unique mediation. That "fullness of grace" is the "supernatural life" given to her by Christ who, already then, applies His unique mediation to His Mother. *Lumen Gentium*, 61, which presented Mary as seeking to achieve, in union with Christ, the restoration of "supernatural life to souls," is here applied to Mary who became the first soul to benefit from the supernatural life restored through Christ's unique mediation. It seems that the mediation of Mary is connected to the notion of the Immaculate Conception. As analyzed in the chapter on the Immaculate Conception, Vatican II's theology, according to which Mary is redeemed in "an excellent manner," was developed by the Pope. He considers Mary as a subject of Redemption, even though she entered in a way all her own within the framework of Redemption. Her mediation is, therefore, in the context of Redemption and draws all of its value from the unique mediation of Christ. She is redeemed in a "more excellent manner" states Vatican II in relation to Redemption, which is comparable to John Paul II saying that she:

> . . . entered, in a way all her own, into the one mediation between God and men, which is the mediation of the man Jesus Christ.[142]

If Christ's *exclusive* Redemption is first applied to Mary and she is, therefore, "redeemed in a more excellent manner," His *unique* mediation is also first applied to Mary who, therefore, becomes cooperator in the Redemption. Such a cooperation correctly identifies her mediation as subordinate and understood only in the context of Christ's unique mediation.[143] The event of the Annunciation, in which Mary is proclaimed "full of grace," is a confirmation of the fact that she experienced the "supernatural life" bestowed on souls through the unique mediation of Jesus Christ. John Paul II is the first to apply *Lumen Gentium*, 61, with its notion of restoration of supernatural life to souls, to Mary's fullness of grace. This fullness of grace becomes the condition that enables Mary to cooperate with God's plan of Redemption. So, "fullness of grace" demonstrates that Mary has already experienced this restoration of supernatural life and is the first sign of the unique mediation of Christ. For John Paul II, Mary's experience of supernatural life at the Annunciation is what made her "predisposed to cooperation with Christ, the one Mediator of salvation." Mary's mediation, which is consequently "special and exceptional"[144] since it is in the order of motherhood, becomes mediation in the sense of cooperation. The Pope summarizes these ideas by saying:

> If she was the first to experience within herself the supernatural consequences of this one mediation—in the Annunciation she had been greeted as "full of grace"—then we must say that through this fullness of grace and supernatural life she was especially predisposed to cooperation with Christ, the one Mediator of human salvation. And such cooperation is precisely this mediation subordinate to the mediation of Christ.[145]

MARY'S MEDIATION IN PENTECOST
AND IN ESCHATOLOGY (END OF TIME)

Redemptoris Mater, 40 refers to the titles "Mediatrix," "Advocate," "Auxiliatrix," and "Adjutrix," also used in Vatican II. Before analyzing John Paul's thought, let us take a look at those titles for a moment.

The titles "Advocate" and "Mediatrix" enjoy a long history in the tradition of the Church and were used and accepted by the magisterium as well as by theologians and liturgists. After Pope Pius XII, the Second

Vatican Council did not want to abstain from using those titles despite the proposal of Augustin Cardinal Bea, president and founder of the Secretariat for Unity, which invited the Fathers of the Council to avoid the title *Mediatrix*. His Eminence argued that:

> ... the title was not yet sufficiently clarified in theology to warrant a conciliar pronouncement and that a formal declaration would be ecumenically counterproductive.[146]

Bea's proposal, supported by two other eminent cardinals, Paul Emile Léger and Bernard Alfrink, could not pass because even in the preconciliar preparatory stage, many bishops were in favor of dogmatic definition of Mary's mediation.[147] The unanimity of the Council's Fathers played a stronger role than Bea's appeal and presented the Christological dimension that stands behind the usage in Catholic tradition of "Mediatrix" and other titles such as "Advocate," "Auxiliatrix," and "Adjutrix." Such titles will receive meaning only in their primordial reference to the unique mediation of the Incarnate Word, the unique mediator between God and humankind.[148]

The title *mediatrix* is ancient. It goes back to the fifth century and was used by Basil of Seleucia. In the eighth century its use became common with Andrew of Crete, Germanus of Constantinople, and John Damascene. Medieval saints such as Bernard of Clairvaux, Bonaventure, and Bernardine of Siena frequently referred to that title. Such an employment reached its climax with Saint Louis Marie De Montfort and Saint Alfonsus of Liguori.[149]

Lately, there has been a special emphasis on the title *Mediatrix* in the magisterium of the Church. Leo XIII in 1896, Pius X in 1904, Benedict XV in 1915, Pius XI in 1928: all used the title *Mediatrix*. Pius XII in 1940 abstained from using such a title, even though he urged the faithful to have recourse to Mary. Pius XII, referring to Saint Bernard's, "it is the will of God that we obtain all favors through Mary," makes his statement no less important than all the other Popes quoted above.[150]

In the recent collection of Masses of the Blessed Virgin Mary, she is venerated as "Mediatrix of Grace." Here, Mary's divine maternity stands in direct relation to her maternal mediation in the Church. That mediation is interpreted as "maternal mission of intercession and of forgiveness, of protection and of grace, of reconciliation and of peace." It has its reason of existence in the unique mediation of Christ.[151] In the introduction to that collection, there is given the theological foundation for such a title referring to *Lumen Gentium*, 60:

> But Mary's function as mother of men in no way obscures or diminishes this unique mediation of Christ, but rather shows its power. But the Blessed Virgin's salutary influence on men originates not in any inner necessity but in the disposition of God. It flows forth from the superabundance of the merits of Christ, rests on his mediation, depends entirely on it and draws all its power from it. It does not hinder in any way the immediate union of the faithful with Christ but on the contrary fosters it.[152]

R. Laurentin insists that those who are searching for the proclamation of the title "Mediatrix" as a dogma of faith should be constantly aware of the theological difficulties it raises. For him, such a concept is ambiguous, must always refer to Christ, and should always be implied in the unique mediation of Christ. Although Laurentin acknowledges the attribution of the title to Mary in Vatican II as well as in the magisterial documents, he still prefers not to dogmatize it *ex cathedra*.[153]

The ancient title "Advocate" enjoys a special place in the theology and the devotion of the Catholic Church. Of the proposed titles in Vatican II, "Advocate" is the least burdened with difficulties. It was used in the patristic age by Irenaeus and John Damascene, and in the Middle Ages by Saint Bernard. Mary is implored as "most gracious Advocate" in the *Salve Regina*. Also in the preface of the Feast of the Immaculate Conception she is called "Advocate of Grace." That title adequately expresses the Church's doctrine concerning the function of Mary in the economy of salvation.[154]

After the Second Vatican Council, Orthodox Christians as well as Protestants have shown a certain discomfort vis-à-vis the title "Advocate," because Scripture applies it to the Holy Spirit. In the opinion of Laurentin, two cardinals, Congar and Suenens, shared that discomfort.[155] Avery Dulles does not share Laurentin's opinion, and the fact that "Advocate" is a title applied to the Holy Spirit in the fourth Gospel "can hardly constitute an objection, since Mary's advocacy, as that of a created person, takes place on a different level."[156] Dulles continues his argument by explaining that Mary's advocacy should be understood in the sense of intercession:

> If she is not our advocate, what could her intercession mean? To deny her this title would be in effect to reject the whole doctrine of the intercession of the saints.[157]

In *Redemptoris Mater*, 40, Pope John Paul II analyzes Pentecost from the point of view of mediation. After the Resurrection and the Ascension of the Lord:

> Mary entered the Upper Room together with the Apostles to await Pentecost, and was present there as the Mother of the glorified Lord.[158]

This maternal presence of Mary in the midst of the infant Church plays a major role in relationship to mediation because the Church is the "fruit of the Cross and Resurrection of her Son."[159] In the same way Christ gave Himself as the agent of Redemption to the Church, Mary, "could not but pour out upon the Church, from the very beginning, her maternal self-giving."[160] "Maternal self-giving" is the key expression to understanding the mediation of Mary in Pentecost according to *Redemptoris Mater*, 40. In fact:

> [A]fter her Son's departure, her motherhood remains in the Church as maternal mediation: interceding for all her children, the Mother cooperates in the saving work of her Son, the Redeemer of the world.[161]

John Paul sees the uninterrupted motherhood of Mary reaching from her historical cooperation with her Son's work of salvation to her existence in heaven as she continues to intercede for the Redemption of all. Motherhood is the connecting denominator and the bridge between Mary's action on earth and in heaven. There is a continuity in the identity and role of Mary of Nazareth in the mystery of Christ and the Church, as it was explained in the chapter on motherhood.

Maternal self-giving becomes the action of Mary in the work of her Son and in the Church. It is based on motherhood and, therefore, draws its content from motherhood. Since Mary's motherhood does not cease or change and, since her motherhood in history and in the order of grace maintains its identity and continuity, that same motherhood, therefore, becomes the "condition of possibility" of Mary's maternal mediation in the work of Christ and in the Church. In that sense, the Council teaches that the "motherhood of Mary in the order of grace . . . will last without interruption until the eternal fulfillment of all the elect."[162]

The motherhood of Mary in its mediative function becomes universal because the Redemption of Christ is universal. If the Redemption of Christ is universal, the mediation of Mary, in its subordinate character to Christ's work of salvation, is also universal. Such a parallel confirms John Paul's insistence on the universality of Christ's Redemption and Mary's involvement in it, without compromising the subordinate character of her mediative role. *Redemptoris Mater*, 40 states:

> In this way Mary's motherhood continues unceasingly in the Church as the mediation which intercedes, and the Church expresses her faith in this truth by invoking Mary "under the titles of Advocate, Auxiliatrix, Adjutrix and Mediatrix" (*Lumen Gentium*, 62).[163]

In the light of the role Mary has throughout the history of humanity, the Pope calls her "Advocate of Grace" in *Redemptoris Mater*, 47:

> Thus, the Church throughout her life maintains with the Mother of God a link which embraces, in the saving mystery, the past, the present and the future, and venerates her as the spiritual mother of humanity and the Advocate of grace.[164]

In *Redemptoris Mater*, 41, Pope John Paul II analyzes the mediation of Mary in its eschatological dimension:

> Through her mediation, subordinate to that of the Redeemer, Mary contributes in a special way to the union of the pilgrim Church on earth with the eschatological and heavenly reality of the Communion of Saints, since she has already been assumed into heaven.[165]

The bodily Assumption of Mary into heaven leads Christ's Redemption to its perfection as applied to Mary. Humanity's goal in its relationship with the Redemption of Christ is to benefit in the utmost way from the mediation of Christ and be in union with Him forever in the heavenly glory. For John Paul, the Assumption of Mary has already applied to her all the benefits coming from His unique mediation understood as Redemption:

> By the mystery of the Assumption into heaven there were defini-
> tively accomplished in Mary all the effects of the one mediation of
> Christ the Redeemer of the world and risen Lord.[166]

Everything that the Church, as the fruit of the cross, Resurrection, and
Pentecost, hopes to be is already accomplished in the most perfect way
in Mary's Assumption. The Church, in her pilgrimage toward the kingdom, follows the same way trodden by the Virgin in order to be eternally
united with God. As a consequence of that definitive state of the Church's
being, Christ will subject everything to the Father, so that the communion of saints will be realized in its ultimate and most perfect dimension.
That state is already a reality in the being of the Mother of Christ:

> Thus in her Assumption into heaven, Mary is as it were clothed by
> the whole reality of the Communion of Saints, and her very union
> with the Son in glory is wholly oriented toward the definitive full-
> ness of the kingdom, when God will be all in all.[167]

Assumption is what makes Mary's union with Christ receive its
ultimate dimension. Through her Assumption, Mary "is united by a
close and indissoluble bond" to Christ.[168] As a result of that bond, Mary's
mediation becomes maternal presence in and cooperation with all that
Christ has done for fulfilling the Redemption. Presence and cooperation
enjoy the character of intercession. Since that mediation was revealed as
having an intercessory nature on earth, it will also have an intercessory
nature of heaven. Such an intercession will continue in heaven, where
Mary is united with her Son through the Assumption, that is, as she
awaits the Second Coming. It will also continue when the expectation
of the Second Coming becomes a reality, the final coming. Pope John
Paul II calls "Mediatrix of Mercy"[169] Mary's maternal role of mediation
in the final coming. In that sense, the Church expresses her faith in
Mary, invoking her under the title *Mediatrix*. Both Vatican II and John
Paul II see an uninterrupted continuity in the union between Christ and
Mary that enables her to be called *Mediatrix:*

> For, if as Virgin and Mother she was singularly united with him in
> his first coming, so through her continued collaboration with him
> she will also be united with him in expectation of the second;
> redeemed in an especially sublime manner by reason of her Son,
> she also has that specifically maternal role of mediatrix of mercy at

his final coming, when all those who belong to Christ shall be made alive, when the last enemy to be destroyed is death.[170]

When Pope John Paul II looks at the eschatological state of Mary as being in continuity with her earthly intercessory mediation, he does not forget that eschatology also brings with it a transcendental dimension. He relates the Immaculate Conception as revealed at the Annunciation ("redeemed in especially sublime manner") with the Assumption. The initial coming (Incarnation) is the beginning of the journey toward the final coming; and the final coming is the crowning of the first coming. In both cases Mary is Mediatrix. If, in the eschatology, Mary were to lose her maternal role as Mediatrix of Mercy, heaven would be in a discontinuity with the world's history, a fact that contradicts God's sincerity in His relationship with the world. On the other hand, there is a guaranteed continuity because *Mary's mediation is based on her motherhood:*

> It can be said that motherhood "in the order of grace" preserves the analogy with what "in the order of nature" characterizes the union between mother and child. In the light of this fact it becomes easier to understand why in Christ's testament on Golgotha his Mother's new motherhood is expressed in the singular, in reference to one man: "Behold your son."[171]

Once and for all, motherhood ensures a continual relationship between mother and child, because it involves the totality of the person who generates and the person who is generated. The person of the mother generates the person of the son in human nature. In the case of Mary, the unique relationship established between her and the eternal Word through temporal generation receives a perpetual dimension because generation involves the person. John Paul applies his personalism to Mary:

> Of the essence of motherhood is the fact that it concerns the person. Motherhood always establishes a unique and unrepeatable relationship between two people: between mother and child and between child and mother.[172]

Therefore, the maternal mediation of Mary, as she exercises it now in heaven, will continue to take place in history. The presence of the divine in history through Mary's cooperation in the "fullness of time" (Incarnation) will be extended in every situation in which Mary's intercession in heaven becomes an earthly and historical situation. Throughout her whole being as the Mediatrix in union with Christ her Son, the "fullness of time" will be reproduced until the end of history, that is, when everything will be recapitulated in Christ. Pope John Paul II brings forward the Marian dimension of Saint Irenaeus's theology of recapitulation in which, at the end of time, there will be an inseparable union with Christ. Mary, in that context, remains the subordinate Mediatrix who, as the Mother, cooperates for the fulfillment of that union:

> In this phase too Mary's maternal mediation does not cease to be subordinate to him who is the one Mediator, until the final realization of the "fullness of time," that is to say until "all things are united in Christ" (cf. Eph 1:10).[173]

Notes

CHAPTER ONE

1. See Antoine E. Nachef, *The Mystery of the Trinity in the Theological Thought of Pope John Paul II*, New York: Peter Lang Publishing, 1998.

2. See Johann G. Roten, "La Foi de Marie à la lumière de la théologie actuelle," in *La Foi de Marie Mère du Rédempteur*, Études Mariales, 52e session de la Société Française d'Études Mariales, Josselin, Bretagne, 1995, Paris: Médiaspaul, 1996, 184.

3. See The Congregation for Catholic Education, *The Virgin Mary in Intellectual and Spiritual Formation*, 3. Letter from The Congregation for Catholic Education of March 25, 1988, in *Enchiridion Vaticanum*. EDB, Bologna 1991, vol. 11, 216, no. 285; Emmanuele di Napoli, "Attualità di uno studio sul Vaticano II tra Mariologia e corredenzione," in *Marianum* 151 (1997): 175.

4. Pope John Paul II, *Crossing the Threshold of Hope*, New York: Alfred A. Knopf, 1994, 213. For the presence of Vatican II's Mariology in John Paul II's *Redemptoris Mater*, see Rafael Casasnovas Cortés, "El capítulo octavo de la 'Lumen Gentium' en la carta-encíclica 'Redemptoris Mater.' Análisis metodológico de sus citas y de sus notas," in *Marianum* 139 (1989): 385–407. See also Davide M. Montagna, "Reminiscenze patristiche medioevali nell'enciclica 'Redemptoris Mater,'" in *Marianum* 139 (1989): 379.

5. Avery Dulles, "Mary at the Dawn of the New Millennium," in *America* 178, no. 3 (January 31, 1998): 9.

6. See also Pope John Paul II, *Dominum et Vivificantem*, 66; *Catechesi Tradendae*, 73; *Familiaris Consortio*, 86; Stefano de Fiores, "La Presenza di Maria nella vita della Chiesa alla luce dell'enciclica 'Redemptoris Mater,'" in *Marianum* 139 (1989): 113–114; Mary Smalara Collins, "All Generations Will Call Her Blessed," in *US Catholic* 58 (May 1993): 37–38.

7. See also Davide M. Montagna, "Reminiscenze patristiche medioevali nell'enciclica 'Redemptoris Mater,'" in *Marianum* 139 (1989): 379.

8. Pope John Paul II, *Redemptoris Mater*, 48. See also Pope John Paul II, *Catechesi Tradendae*, 73; *Dominicae Cenae*, 13.

9. The expression "economy of salvation" indicates all that God has done for the salvation of the entire human race.

10. See Johann G. Roten, "La Foi de Marie à la lumière de la théologie actuelle," in *La Foi de Marie Mère du Rédempteur*, Études Mariales, 52e session de la Société Française d'Études Mariales, Josselin, Bretagne, 1995, Paris: Médiaspaul, 1996, 184, 191–193.

11. See Pope John Paul II, *Redemptoris Mater*, 2; Pope Paul VI, *Christi Matri* (September 15, 1966): *AAS* 58 (1966), 745–749; Apostolic Exhortation *Signum Magnum* (May 13, 1967): *AAS* 59 (1967), 465–475; Apostolic Exhortation *Marialis Cultus* (February 2, 1974): *AAS* 66 (1974), 113–168.

12. Pope Paul VI, *Marialis Cultus*, 23–27. See also Pope John Paul II, *Sollicitudo Rei Socialis*, 49.

13. See Pope John Paul II's speech on October 17, 1978; *Crossing the Threshold of Hope*, New York: Alfred A. Knopf, 1994, 212–213; Angel Luis, "La consagración a María en la vida y doctrina de Juan Pablo II," in *Estudios Marianos* 51 (1986): 77.

14. See Pope John Paul II, *Redemptoris Mater*, 48; Alphonse Bossard, "L'encyclique 'Redemptoris Mater' et saint Louis-Marie De Montfort," in *Marianum* 139 (1989): 261; Edward D. O'Connor, "The roots of Pope John Paul II's devotion to Mary," in *Marian Studies* 39 (1988): 85–87.

15. Henri Marie Manteau-Bonamy, "Marie et le Saint Esprit dans l'encyclique 'Redemptoris Mater,'" in *Marianum* 139 (1989): 65–68. One recognizes the presence of De Montfort's style in *Lumen Gentium*'s 52–59, a fact that is affirmed by Mgr. Philips, the author of the Schema that became chapter VIII of *Lumen Gentium*.

16. See Alphonse Bossard, "L'encyclique 'Redemptoris Mater' et saint Louis-Marie De Montfort," in *Marianum* 139 (1989): 263–264; Edward D. O'Connor, "The roots of Pope John Paul II's devotion to Mary," in *Marian Studies* 39 (1988): 85–87.

17. See Pope John Paul II, *Redemptoris Mater*, 48; *Crossing the Threshold of Hope*, New York: Alfred A. Knopf, 1994, 212–213; Carl Bernstein and Marco Politi, *His Holiness John Paul II and the Hidden History of our Time*, New York: Doubleday, 1996, 23.

18. Pope John Paul II, *Redemptor Hominis*, 22. See also Pope John Paul II, *Redemptoris Missio*, 92; *Centesimus Annus*, 62; *Catechesi Tradendae*, 73; *Dominicae Cenae*, 13; *Familiaris Consortio*, 86.

19. Pope John Paul II, *Redemptor Hominis*, 22. See also Pope John Paul II, *Dominum et Vivificantem*, 66; *Redemptoris Missio*, 92; *Evangelium Vitae*, 102; *Catechesi Tradendae*, 73; *Dominicae Cenae*, 13; *Familiaris Consortio*, 22, 86.

20. See Pope John Paul II, *Redemptor Hominis*, 22; *Dominum et Vivificantem*, 51 and 66; *Sollicitudo Rei Socialis*, 49; *Redemptoris Missio*, 92; *Centesimus Annus*, 62; *Veritatis Splendor*, 118, 120; *Evangelium Vitae*, 102; *Fides et Ratio*, 108; *Catechesi Tradendae*, 73; *Dominicae Cenae*, 13; *Familiaris Consortio*, 86; *Redemptionis Donum*, 13; *Salvifici Doloris*, 25; *Reconciliatio et Paenitentia*, 35; *Christifideles Laici*, 58; *Tertio Millennio Adveniente*, 59; *Letter to Families from Pope John Paul II*, 1994, 20.

21. Felipe Gomez, "A New Encyclical Letter: The Mother of the Redeemer," in *East Asian Pastoral Review* 24 (1987): 108; Stefano de Fiores, "La Presenza di Maria nella vita della Chiesa alla luce dell'enciclica 'Redemptoris Mater,'" in *Marianum* 139 (1989): 110–114; Leo Scheffczyk, "Maria und die Kirche in der Enzyklika Redemptoris Mater," in *Marianum* 139 (1989): 85.

22. Cardinal J. Ratzinger, "Il segno della donna," in J. Ratzinger-H. U. von Balthasar, *Maria il sì di Dio all'uomo. Introduzione e commento all'enciclica 'Redemptoris Mater*,' Brescia: Queriniana, 1987, 18.

23. See Jean Galot, "L'itinéraire de foi de Marie selon l'encyclique 'Redemptoris Mater,'" in *Marianum* 139 (1989): 33.

24. A. M. Triacca, "Celebrare' l'anno Mariano: significati e finalità," in *Seminarium* 17 (1987): 590, note 2; Stefano de Fiores, "La Presenza di Maria nella vita della Chiesa alla luce dell'enciclica 'Redemptoris Mater,'" in *Marianum* 139 (1989): 114.

25. Avery Dulles, "Mary at the Dawn of the New Millennium," in *America* 178, no. 3 (January 31, 1998): 15.

26. Jean Galot, "L'itinéraire de foi de Marie selon l'encyclique 'Redemptoris Mater,'" in *Marianum* 139 (1989): 33.

27. Ignace de la Potterie, "Maria, piena di grazia'" (RM 7–11), in *Marianum* 138 (1988): 113.

28. See Luigi Gambero, "La spiritualità Mariana nella vita del cristiano alla luce della 'Redemptoris Mater,'" in *Marianum* 139 (1989): 239.

29. Avery Dulles, "Mary at the Dawn of the New Millennium," in *America* 178, no. 3 (January 31, 1998): 8. See also Thomas H. Stahel, *"Redemptoris Mater*," in *America* 156 (1987): 353.

30. Pope John Paul II, *Redemptoris Mater*, 2. See also Pope John Paul II, *Dominum et Vivificantem*, 66; *Redemptoris Missio*, 92; *Catechesi Tradendae*, 73; *Tertio Millennio Adveniente*, 27, 59; Leo Scheffczyk, "Maria und die Kirche in der Enzyklika 'Redemptoris Mater,'" in *Marianum* 139 (1989): 88.

31. Pope John Paul II, *Tertio Millennio Adveniente*, 27.

32. Pope John Paul II, *Redemptoris Mater*, 51.

33. See also Pope John Paul II, *Centesimus Annus*, 62; *Redemptionis Donum*, 13; *Tertio Millennio Adveniente*, 27, 59; Luigi Sartori, "'Storia della salvezza' e 'Storia dell'umanità' nee'enciclica 'Redemptoris Mater,'" in *Marianum* 139 (1989): 19; Kurt Koch, "Marienenzyklika und Marianisches Jahr," in *Una Sancta* 3 (1987): 223–225.

34. See A. Lobato, "La persona en el pensamiento de Karol Wojtyla," in *Angelicum* 56 (1979): 207f; Carl Bernstein and Marco Politi, *His Holiness John Paul II and the Hidden History of our Time*, New York: Doubleday, 1996, 23; Alejandro Martínez Sierra, "María estrella para el hombre que 'cae' y se levanta,'" in *Marianum* 139 (1989): 235–236.

35. Pope John Paul II, *Crossing the Threshold of Hope*, New York: Alfred A. Knopf, 1994, 212–213.

36. Avery Dulles, "Mary at the Dawn of the New Millennium," in *America* 178, no. 3 (January 31, 1998): 9; Ugo Vanni, "La Donna della Genesi (3,15) e la Donna dell'Apocalisse (12,1) nella 'Redemptoris Mater,'" in *Marianum* 138 (1988): 433.

37. See Johann G. Roten, "La Foi de Marie à la lumière de la théologie actuelle," in *La Foi de Marie Mère du Rédempteur*, Études Mariales, 52e session de la Société Française d'Études Mariales, Josselin, Bretagne, 1995, Paris: Médiaspaul, 1996, 184–193.

38. See Pope John Paul II, *Redemptoris Mater*, 1; *Redemptor Hominis*, 8, 18, 22; *Dominum et Vivificantem*, 16, 21, 66; *Sollicitudo Rei Socialis*, 49; *Redemptoris Missio*, 5, 92; *Centesimus Annus*, 62; *Veritatis Splendor*, 118, 120; *Fides et Ratio*, 108; *Dominicae Cenae*, 13; *Familiaris Consortio*, 22, 86; *Redemptionis Donum*, 13; *Salvifici Doloris*, 25; *Reconciliatio et Paenitentia*, 4, 35; *Redemptoris Custos*, 2; *Tertio Millennio Adveniente*, 2.

39. *L'Osservatore Romano*, January 10, 1996.

40. See Saint Thomas Aquinas, *Summa Theologiae* I, q. 1, a. 3. See also Ugo Vanni, "La Donna della Genesi (3,15) e la Donna dell'Apocalisse (12,1) nella 'Redemptoris Mater,'" in *Marianum* 138 (1988): 433.

41. See Pope John Paul II, *Redemptoris Mater*, 48; *Veritatis Splendor*, 118; *Evangelium Vitae*, 102; *Catechesi Tradendae*, 73; *Familiaris Consortio*, 22; *Redemptoris Custos*, 2; *Tertio Millennio Adveniente*, 2.

42. See Antoine E. Nachef, *The Mystery of the Trinity in the Theological Thought of Pope John Paul II*, New York: Peter Lang Publishing, 1998.

43. Pope John Paul II, *Redemptoris Missio*, 5. See also Pope John Paul II, *Veritatis Splendor*, 118, 120; *Catechesi Tradendae*, 73; *Dominicae Cenae*, 13; *Familiaris Consortio*, 86; *Salvifici Doloris*, 25; *Reconciliatio et Paenitentia*, 12, 34; *Letter to Families from Pope John Paul II*, 1994, 5; Salvatore M. Meo, "La 'mediazione materna' di Maria nell'enciclica 'Redemptoris Mater,'" in *Marianum* 139 (1989): 147; Emmanuele di Napoli, "Attualità di uno studio sul Vaticano II tra Mariologia e corredenzione," in *Marianum* 151 (1997): 169.

44. See Gabriele M. Roschini, *Compendium Mariologiae*, Rome: "Scientia Catholica," 1946, 227–272; *Mariologia* II: Pars Prima, Rome: Bellardetti, 1947, 251–393; *La Madonna secondo la fede e la teologia*, II, Rome: Ferrari, 1953, 311–407; *Maria santissima nella storia della salvezza*, II: 111–198.

45. See S. M. Meo, "La mediazione materna di Maria nell'enciclica '*Redemptoris Mater*,'" in *Marianum* 139 (1989): 145–170.

46. See also Pope John Paul II, *Redemptoris Missio*, 5; *Centesimus Annus*, 62; *Veritatis Splendor*, 118, 120; *Evangelium Vitae*, 102; *Fides et Ratio*, 108; *Catechesi Tradendae*, 73; *Dominicae Cenae*, 13; *Familiaris Consortio*, 22, 86; *Redemptionis Donum*, 13; *Salvifici Doloris*, 25; *Reconciliatio et Paenitentia*, 12, 34; *Letter to Families from Pope John Paul II*, 1994, 5; Arthur Burton Calkins, "Towards Another Marian Dogma? A Response To Father Angelo Amato, S.D.B." in *Marianum* 151 (1997): 163.

47. Brunero Gherardini, La Madre: Maria in una sintesi storico-teologica. Frigento: Casa Mariana Editrice, 1989, 281; Arthur Burton Calkins, "Towards Another Marian Dogma? A Response to Father Angelo Amato, S.D.B." in *Marianum* 151 (1997): 166–167; Emmanuele di Napoli, "Attualità di uno studio sul Vaticano II tra Mariologia e corredenzione," in *Marianum* 151 (1997): 177–178.

48. Pope John Paul II, *Tertio Millennio Adveniente*, 2. See also Pope John Paul II, *Letter to Families from Pope John Paul II*, 1994, 5.

49. The expression *eschatological* points to the end of time and the full and definitive establishment of the Kingdom of God. In the chapter on the Church and Mary it will be explained that in Mary is already realized what the Church hopes to be at the end of time.

50. This method approaches objective reality constantly and from various perspectives.

51. Davide M. Montagna, "Reminiscenze patristiche medioevali nell'enciclica 'Redemptoris Mater,'" in *Marianum* 139 (1989): 383.

52. Jean Galot, "L'itinéraire de foi de Marie selon l'encyclique 'Redemptoris Mater,'" in *Marianum* 139 (1989): 33.

53. See Salvatore M. Meo, "La 'mediazione materna' di Maria nell'enciclica 'Redemptoris Mater,'" in *Marianum* 139 (1989): 158.

CHAPTER TWO

CHAPTER TWO

1. The expressions "divine maternity" or "divine motherhood" mean Mary's true human maternity of the Divine Word. She is authentically and truly the human Mother of the Divine Person of the Son.

2. Pope John Paul II, *Redemptoris Mater*, 1. See also Pope John Paul II, *Redemptor Hominis*, 1; *Centesimus Annus*, 62; *Evangelium Vitae*, 102; *Reconciliatio et Paenitentia*, 35.

3. See March 25, 1987, L'Osservatore Romano 13 (1987): 23; *Acta Apostolicae Sedis* 79 (1987): 361–433; *The Encyclicals of John Paul II.* Edited with Introduction by Michael Miller, Huntington, Indiana: Our Sunday Visitor Publishing Division, 1996, 340.

4. See Jean-Nöel Aletti, "Une lecture de Gal 4, 4–6: Marie et la plénitude du temps," in *Marianum* 138 (1988): 408.

5. See Alphonse Bossard, "L'encyclique 'Redemptoris Mater' et Saint Louis-Marie De Montfort," in *Marianum* 139 (1989): 263–264.

6. Pope John Paul II, *Crossing the Threshold of Hope*, New York: Alfred A. Knopf, 1994, 213.

7. Thomas H. Stahel, "*Redemptoris Mater*," in *America* 156 (1987): 353.

8. See also Pope John Paul II, *Redemptor Hominis*, 22; *Dominum et Vivificantem*, 16, 51; *Sollicitudo Rei Socialis*, 48; *Centesimus Annus*, 62; *Veritatis Splendor*, 118, 120; *Evangelium Vitae*, 102; *Familiaris Consortio*, 22; *Redemptionis Donum*, 13; *Salvifici Doloris*, 26; *Reconciliatio et Paenitentia*, 4; *Tertio Millennio Adveniente*, 43; *Crossing the Threshold of Hope*, New York: Alfred A. Knopf, 1994, 213; Luigi Gambero, "La spiritualità Mariana nella vita del cristiano alla luce della 'Redemptoris Mater,'" in *Marianum* 139 (1989): 239.

9. Avery Dulles, "Mary at the Dawn of the New Millennium," in *America* 178, no. 3 (January 31, 1998): 10. See also Salvatore M. Meo, "La mediazione materna' di Maria nell'enciclica 'Redemptoris Mater,'" in *Marianum* 139 (1989): 148.

10. See Luigi Sartori, "Storia della salvezza' e 'Storia dell'umanità' nell'enciclica 'Redemptoris Mater,'" in *Marianum* 139 (1989): 22.

11. See also Pope John Paul II, *Dominum et Vivificantem*, 16; *Evangelium Vitae*, 102; *Redemptionis Donum*, 13; *Reconciliatio et Paenitentia*, 35; *Crossing the Threshold of Hope*, New York: Alfred A. Knopf, 1994, 213; Ignace de la Potterie, "Maria, piena di grazia'" (RM 7–11), in *Marianum* 138 (1988): 113; Stefano de Fiores, "La Presenza di Maria nella vita della Chiesa alla luce dell'enciclica 'Redemptoris Mater,'" in *Marianum* 139 (1989): 117–118.

12. See also Pope John Paul II, *Salvifici Doloris*, 26; *Redemptoris Custos*, 1; *Pastores Dabo Vobis*, 36; *Tertio Millennio Adveniente*, 43; *Crossing the Threshold of Hope*, New York: Alfred A. Knopf, 1994, 213.

13. Pope John Paul II, *Redemptionis Donum*, 17. See also Pope John Paul II, *Salvifici Doloris*, 26; Holy Thursday Letter of John Paul II, *Behold your Mother*, 1988, 1.

14. Pope John Paul II, *Pastores Dabo Vobis*, 82.

15. Pope John Paul II, *Redemptoris Mater*, 1. See also Pope John Paul II, *Redemptor Hominis*, 1; *Reconciliatio et Paenitentia*, 35; *Redemptoris Custos*, 2.

16. See Pope John Paul II, *Reconciliatio et Paenitentia*, 35; Thomas H. Stahel, "*Redemptoris Mater*," in *America* 156 (1987): 353.

17. See Pope John Paul II, *Dominum et Vivificantem*, 16, 21; *Redemptoris Missio*, 92; *Centesimus Annus*, 62; *Veritatis Splendor*, 118; *Evangelium Vitae*, 102; *Familiaris Consortio*, 22; *Redemptionis Donum*, 13; *Salvifici Doloris*, 26; *Reconciliatio et Paenitentia*, 35; Holy Thursday Letter of John Paul II, *Behold your Mother*, 1988, 1; *Crossing the Threshold of Hope*, New York: Alfred A. Knopf, 1994, 213; Avery Dulles, "Mary at the Dawn of the New Millennium," in *America* 178, no. 3 (January 31, 1998): 10; Antoine E. Nachef, *The Mystery of the Trinity in the Theological Thought of Pope John Paul II*, New York: Peter Lang Publishing, 1998.

18. The term "soteriological" means salvific. "Soteriological function" or "soteriological dimension" indicates a dimension that pertains to salvation.

19. See *Lumen Gentium*, 52 and the whole Chapter VIII, entitled "The Role of the Blessed Virgin Mary, Mother of God, in the Mystery of Christ and the Church." See also Pope John Paul II, *Redemptor Hominis*, 1, 22; *Redemptoris Missio*, 92; *Centesimus Annus*, 62; *Evangelium Vitae*, 102; *Redemptionis Donum*, 13; *Crossing the Threshold of Hope*, New York: Alfred A. Knopf, 1994, 213.

20. See Pope John Paul II, *Redemptoris Mater*, 1. See also Pope John Paul II, *Redemptor Hominis*, 22; *Redemptoris Missio*, 92; *Evangelium Vitae*, 102; *Redemptionis Donum*, 13.

21. See Pope John Paul II, *Redemptor Hominis*, 22; *Evangelium Vitae*, 102; *Salvifici Doloris*, 26; *Crossing the Threshold of Hope*, New York: Alfred A. Knopf, 1994, 213.

22. John 1:14: "And the Word became flesh and dwelt among us." John 3:16: "For God so loved the world that he gave his only Son, that whoever believes in him should not perish but have eternal life." See also Pope John Paul II, *Redemptoris Mater*, 1; *Redemptor Hominis*, 1; *Crossing the Threshold of Hope*, New York: Alfred A. Knopf, 1994, 213.

23. Pope John Paul II quotes John 1:14 and John 3:16 at the beginning of both encyclicals, *Redemptor Hominis* and *Redemptoris Mater*.

24. See footnote 2 in Pope John Paul II, *Redemptoris Mater*, 1. See also Pope John Paul II, *Evangelium Vitae*, 102; Holy Thursday Letter of John Paul II, *Behold your Mother*, 1988, 1; *Redemptoris Custos*, 15; *Crossing the Threshold of Hope*, New York: Alfred A. Knopf, 1994, 213.

25. See Luigi Sartori, "'Storia della salvezza' e Storia dell'umanità' nell'enciclica 'Redemptoris Mater,'" in *Marianum* 139 (1989): 21.

26. Pope John Paul II, *Redemptoris Mater*, 1. See also Pope John Paul II, *Redemptor Hominis*, 1; *Evangelium Vitae*, 102; Ignace de la Potterie, "Maria, 'piena di grazia'" (RM 7–11), in *Marianum* 138 (1988): 113; Jean-Nöel Aletti, "Une lecture de Ga 4, 4–6: Marie et la plénitude du temps," in *Marianum* 138 (1988): 410–411.

27. The *sensus plenior* looks at the whole Bible as inspired by the One God. All the texts are, therefore, interrelated and should be explained in the light of one another.

28. *Exegesis* is the science of interpreting Scripture. Often it is also called *biblical hermeneutic*.

29. Especially significant as far as John Paul's usage of the *sensus plenior* is *Redemptoris Custos*, 2–3; Jean-Nöel Aletti, "Une lecture de Ga 4, 4–6: Marie et la

plénitude du temps," in *Marianum* 138 (1988): 410–411; Luigi Sartori, "'Storia della salvezza' e 'Storia dell'umanità' nell'enciclica 'Redemptoris Mater,'" in *Marianum* 139 (1989): 22.

30. Ignace de la Potterie, "Maria, 'piena di grazia'" (RM 7–11), in *Marianum* 138 (1988): 113.

31. As I explained before, *eschatology* is the end of time, the last things. See Pope John Paul II, *Redemptoris Mater*, 1, note 2.

32. See Jean-Nöel Aletti, "Une lecture de Ga 4, 4–6: Marie et la plénitude du temps," in *Marianum* 138 (1988): 411–414.

33. See A. Vanhoye, "La Mère de Dieu selon Ga. 4, 4," in *Marianum* 40 (1978): 237–247.

34. See S. M. Meo, "La mediazione materna di Maria nell'enciclica 'Redemptoris Mater,'" in *Marianum* 139 (1989): 158.

35. *Fiat* designates Mary's "yes" to the angel at the Annunciation.

36. Pope John Paul II, *Reconciliatio et Paenitentia*, 35.

37. Pope John Paul II, *Christifideles Laici*, 50.

38. Pope John Paul II, *Christifideles Laici*, 50.

39. Pope John Paul II, *Redemptoris Mater*, 3, 48. See also Pope John Paul II, *Dominum et Vivificantem*, 66; *Sollicitudo Rei Socialis*, 49; *Redemptoris Missio*, 92; *Centesimus Annus*, 62; *Redemptionis Donum*, 17; *Tertio Millennio Adveniente*, 43, 59; Leo Scheffczyk, "Maria und die Kirche in der Enzyklika 'Redemptoris Mater,'" in *Marianum* 139 (1989): 88.

40. Pope John Paul II, *Redemptoris Mater*, 3; *Redemptor Hominis*, 18; *Redemptoris Missio*, 92; *Redemptionis Donum*, 13; Davide M. Montagna, "Reminiscenze patristiche medioevali nell'enciclica 'Redemptoris Mater,'" in *Marianum* 139 (1989): 380; Alejandro Martínez Sierra, "María estrella para el hombre que 'cae' y se 'levanta,'" in *Marianum* 139 (1989): 231.

41. See also Pope John Paul II, *Reconciliatio et Paenitentia*, 35.

42. This was the letter that Pope Pius IX used to proclaim Mary as the Immaculate Conception in 1854.

43. Pope John Paul II, *Redemptoris Mater*, 3; Saint John Damascene, *Homilia in Dormitionem*, I, 8–9: *SCH* 80, 103–107; Pope Pius IX, Apostolic Letter *Ineffabilis Deus* (December 8, 1854): *Pii IX P. M. Acta*, I, 597–599; The Congregation for Catholic Education, *The Virgin Mary in Intellectual and Spiritual Formation*, 3, Letter from The Congregation for Catholic Education of March 25, 1988, in *Enchiridion Vaticanum*. EDB, Bologna 1991, vol. 11, 216, no. 285.

44. Pope John Paul II, *Redemptoris Mater*, 3. See also Pope John Paul II, *Dominum et Vivificantem*, 66; *Sollicitudo Rei Socialis*, 49.

45. Pope John Paul II, *Redemptoris Mater*, 3. See also Pope John Paul II, *Redemptor Hominis*, 18; *Dominum et Vivificantem*, 16; *Redemptoris Missio*, 92; *Redemptionis Donum*, 13; *Reconciliatio et Paenitentia*, 35.

46. See also Pope John Paul II, *Redemptor Hominis*, 18, 22; *Dominum et Vivificantem*, 51; *Redemptionis Donum*, 13, 17; *Reconciliatio et Paenitentia*, 35.

47. See Henri Marie Manteau-Bonamy, "Marie et le Saint Esprit dans l'encyclique 'Redemptoris Mater,'" in *Marianum* 139 (1989): 56.

48. *Gaudium et Spes* is Vatican II's document concerning The Church in the Modern World. See also Pope John Paul II, *Redemptoris Mater*, 4. See also Pope John Paul II, *Redemptor Hominis*, 8, 18; *Crossing the Threshold of Hope*, New York: Alfred A. Knopf, 1994, 213; Alphonse Bossard, "L'encyclique 'Redemptoris Mater' et saint Louis-Marie De Montfort," in *Marianum* 139 (1989): 265–267.

49. Pope John Paul II, *Redemptoris Mater*, 4. See also Pope John Paul II, *Evangelium Vitae*, 102; *Crossing the Threshold of Hope*, New York: Alfred A. Knopf, 1994, 213.

50. Pope John Paul II, *Redemptoris Mater*, 1, 4; *Crossing the Threshold of Hope*, New York: Alfred A. Knopf, 1994, 213.

51. Pope John Paul II, *Redemptoris Mater*, 4. See also Pope John Paul II, *Familiaris Consortio*, 22; *Crossing the Threshold of Hope*, New York: Alfred A. Knopf, 1994, 213.

52. See also Pope John Paul II, *Redemptoris Missio*, 5; *Evangelium Vitae*, 102; *Salvifici Doloris*, 26; Holy Thursday Letter of John Paul II, *Behold your Mother*, 1988, 1; *Crossing the Threshold of Hope*, New York: Alfred A. Knopf, 1994, 213.

53. Pope John Paul II, *Redemptoris Mater*, 4. See also Pope John Paul II, *Redemptor Hominis*, 22; *Dominum et Vivificantem*, 51; *Crossing the Threshold of Hope*, New York: Alfred A. Knopf, 1994, 213.

54. Pope John Paul II, *Redemptoris Mater*, 4. See also Pope John Paul II, *Redemptor Hominis*, 1, 8, 18; *Sollicitudo Rei Socialis*, 48; *Veritatis Splendor*, 118; *Evangelium Vitae*, 102; *Familiaris Consortio*, 22; *Christifideles Laici*, 14; Holy Thursday Letter of John Paul II, *Behold your Mother*, 1988, 1; *Tertio Millennio Adveniente*, 7; *Crossing the Threshold of Hope*, New York: Alfred A. Knopf, 1994, 213.

55. See Pope John Paul II, *Redemptor Hominis*, 22. See also Pope John Paul II, *Dominum et Vivificantem*, 16, 21, 51; *Sollicitudo Rei Socialis*, 48; *Redemptoris Missio*, 92; *Evangelium Vitae*, 102; *Dominicae Cenae*, 13; *Redemptionis Donum*, 17; *Salvifici Doloris*, 26; Holy Thursday Letter of John Paul II, *Behold your Mother*, 1988, 1; *Redemptoris Custos*, 1; *Tertio Millennio Adveniente*, 43; *Crossing the Threshold of Hope*, New York: Alfred A. Knopf, 1994, 213; Ignace de la Potterie, "Maria, piena di grazia'" (RM 7–11), in *Marianum* 138 (1988): 113.

56. For the theology on the Holy Spirit as the Divine Person-Uncreated Gift, see Antoine E. Nachef, *The Mystery of the Trinity in the Theological Thought of Pope John Paul II*, New York: Peter Lang Publishing, 1998, 227–232.

57. Pope John Paul II, *Dominum et Vivificantem*, 51. See also Pope John Paul II, *Sollicitudo Rei Socialis*, 48; *Redemptoris Missio*, 92; *Veritatis Splendor*, 120; *Dominicae Cenae*, 13; *Redemptionis Donum*, 17; *Salvifici Doloris*, 26; *Tertio Millennio Adveniente*, 43; Paul Peeters, "*Dominum et Vivificantem*: The Conscience and the Heart," in *Communio* 15 (1988): 152.

58. See Henri Marie Manteau-Bonamy, "Marie et le Saint Esprit dans l'encyclique 'Redemptoris Mater,'" in *Marianum* 139 (1989): 57. Also in *Dominum et Vivificantem*, 49, John Paul II emphasizes the personal coming of the Holy Spirit on Mary during the Annunciation.

59. Nazarius, *Commentaria et controversiae in IIIam partem*, Bologna, in q. 25 a. 5, 305.

60. Henri Marie Manteau-Bonamy, "Marie et le Saint Esprit dans l'encyclique 'Redemptoris Mater,'" in *Marianum* 139 (1989): 59

61. See Henri Marie Manteau-Bonamy, "Marie et le Saint Esprit dans l'encyclique 'Redemptoris Mater,'" in *Marianum* 139 (1989): 59, 60; Ibid., *Maternité divine et Incarnation*. Étude historique et doctrinale, de S. Thomas à nos jours (Bibliothèque Thomiste XXVII), Vrin, 1949, 60, 163, 187–190.

62. See the chapters on Mary's divine maternity in Saint Basil, Saint Gregory Nazianzen, and Saint Gregory of Nyssa in Antoine Nachef, "Mary: Virgin Mother in the Theological Thought of the Cappadocian Fathers," Dayton, Ohio: Diss. International Marian Research Institute, University of Dayton, 1997.

63. See Henri Marie Manteau-Bonamy, "Marie et le Saint Esprit dans l'encyclique 'Redemptoris Mater,'" in *Marianum* 139 (1989): 62–68.

64. For the concept of "divine maternity," see Henri Marie Manteau-Bonamy, "Marie et le Saint Esprit dans l'encyclique 'Redemptoris Mater,'" in *Marianum* 139 (1989): 56–84.

65. See Saint Thomas Aquinas, Contra Gentiles, livre 4, XI.

66. Pope John Paul II, *Redemptoris Mater*, 7; *Familiaris Consortio*, 22. The relationship between creation and salvation in the theology of Pope John Paul II was developed at length in my first volume, *The Mystery of the Trinity in the Theological Thought of Pope John Paul II*. [Also cf. Stefano de Fiores, "La Presenza di Maria nella vita della Chiesa alla luce dell'enciclica 'Redemptoris Mater,'" in *Marianum* 139 (1989): 117–118].

67. Pope John Paul II, *Redemptoris Mater*, 7. See also Pope John Paul II, *Crossing the Threshold of Hope*, New York: Alfred A. Knopf, 1994, 213.

68. Pope John Paul II, *Redemptoris Mater*, 7. See also Pope John Paul II, *Evangelium Vitae*, 102; *Familiaris Consortio*, 22; *Crossing the Threshold of Hope*, New York: Alfred A. Knopf, 1994, 213.

69. Pope John Paul II, *Redemptoris Mater*, 7. See also Pope John Paul II, *Familiaris Consortio*, 22; *Crossing the Threshold of Hope*, New York: Alfred A. Knopf, 1994, 213; Ugo Vanni, "La Donna della Genesi (3,15) e la Donna dell'Apocalisse (12,1) nella 'Redemptoris Mater,'" in *Marianum* 138 (1988): 422–435; Stefano de Fiores, "La Presenza di Maria nella vita della Chiesa alla luce dell'enciclica 'Redemptoris Mater,'" in *Marianum* 139 (1989): 117–118; Leo Scheffczyk, "Maria und die Kirche in der Enzyklika 'Redemptoris Mater,'" in *Marianum* 139 (1989): 90.

70. Ugo Vanni, "La Donna della Genesi (3,15) e la Donna dell'Apocalisse (12,1) nella 'Redemptoris Mater,'" in *Marianum* 138 (1988): 427–428; P. J. Kearney, "Gen 3:15 and Johannine Theology," in *Marian Studies* 27 (1976): 99–109; S. Virgulin, "La madre dei viventi," in *PSV* 6 (1982): 11–24; Ibid., "Ricerche su Genesi 3,15 dal 1970 al 1977," in *Marianum* 40 (1978): 13–30; M. Gorg, "Das Wort zur Schlange (Gen 3:14f). Gedanken zum Sogenannten Protoevangelium," in *Biblische Notizen* 20 (1983): 121–139.

71. Ugo Vanni, "La Donna della Genesi (3,15) e la Donna dell'Apocalisse (12,1) nella 'Redemptoris Mater,'" in *Marianum* 138 (1988): 423.

72. Ugo Vanni, "La Donna della Genesi (3,15) e la Donna dell'Apocalisse (12,1) nella 'Redemptoris Mater,'" in *Marianum* 138 (1988): 424.

73. The LXX is the Greek-inspired text of the Old Testament. See also Ugo Vanni, "La Donna della Genesi (3,15) e la Donna dell'Apocalisse (12,1) nella 'Redemptoris Mater,'" in *Marianum* 138 (1988): 429.

74. S. Virgulin, "Ricerche su Genesi 3,15 dal 1970 al 1977," in *Marianum* 40 (1978): 15–20; Ugo Vanni, "La Donna della Genesi (3,15) e la Donna dell'Apocalisse (12,1) nella 'Redemptoris Mater,'" in *Marianum* 138 (1988): 430–431.

75. S. Virgulin, "Ricerche su Genesi 3,15 dal 1970 al 1977," in *Marianum* 40 (1978): 20–22; Ugo Vanni, "La Donna della Genesi (3,15) e la Donna dell'Apocalisse (12,1) nella 'Redemptoris Mater,'" in *Marianum* 138 (1988): 430–431.

76. S. Virgulin, "Ricerche su Genesi 3,15 dal 1970 al 1977," in *Marianum* 40 (1978): 22–27; Ugo Vanni, "La Donna della Genesi (3,15) e la Donna dell'Apocalisse (12,1) nella 'Redemptoris Mater,'" in *Marianum* 138 (1988): 430–431.

77. Ugo Vanni, "La Donna della Genesi (3,15) e la Donna dell'Apocalisse (12,1) nella 'Redemptoris Mater,'" in *Marianum* 138 (1988): 430–431.

78. See Pope John Paul II, *Redemptoris Mater*, 4; *Familiaris Consortio*, 22; *Crossing the Threshold of Hope*, New York: Alfred A. Knopf, 1994, 213; Leo Scheffczyk, "Maria und die Kirche in der Enzyklika 'Redemptoris Mater,'" in *Marianum* 139 (1989): 90.

79. Pope John Paul II, *Redemptoris Mater*, 7. See also Pope John Paul II, *Crossing the Threshold of Hope*, New York: Alfred A. Knopf, 1994, 213.

80. Pope John Paul II, *Redemptoris Mater*, 37. See also Pope John Paul II, *Familiaris Consortio*, 22; Johann G. Roten, "La Foi de Marie à la lumière de la théologie actuelle," in *La Foi de Marie Mère du Rédempteur*, Études Mariales, 52e session de la Société Française d'Études Mariales, Josselin, Bretagne, 1995, Paris: Médiaspaul, 1996, 185.

81 See also Pope John Paul II, *Evangelium Vitae*, 102; *Familiaris Consortio*, 22.

82. *Ontological* is an expression that relates to the very metaphysical being.

83. Ugo Vanni, "La Donna della Genesi (3,15) e la Donna dell'Apocalisse (12,1) nella 'Redemptoris Mater,'" in *Marianum* 138 (1988): 425.

84. Pope John Paul II, *Redemptoris Mater*, 37; *Evangelium Vitae*, 102; *Familiaris Consortio*, 22; Johann G. Roten, "La Foi de Marie à la lumière de la théologie actuelle," in *La Foi de Marie Mère du Rédempteur*, Études Mariales, 52e session de la Société Française d'Études Mariales, Josselin, Bretagne, 1995, Paris: Médiaspaul, 1996, 184–185.

85. Pope John Paul II, *Redemptoris Mater*, 37; Johann G. Roten, "La Foi de Marie à la lumière de la théologie actuelle," in *La Foi de Marie Mère du Rédempteur*, Études Mariales, 52e session de la Société Française d'Études Mariales, Josselin, Bretagne, 1995, Paris: Médiaspaul, 1996, 184–185.

86. Allegorical exegesis interprets the whole Scripture in the light of Jesus Christ. He is the key of explaining the Old as well as the New Testament.

87. Saint Gregory of Nyssa, *In Canticum Canticorum*, Hom. 13; PG 44: 1053. See also Carlos Ignacio González, *María en los Padres griegos*, México, D.F.: Conferencia del Episcopado Mexicano, 1993, 98, 101; A. Meredith, "Allegory in Porphyry and Gregory of Nyssa," in *Studia Patristica XVI*, part II, Berlin: Akademie-Verlag, 1985, 425; G. Söll, "Die Mariologie der Kappadozier im Licht der Dogmengeschichte," in *Theologische Quartalschrift* 131 (1951): 297, 298; Antoine E. Nachef, *Mary: Virgin Mother in the Theological Thought of Saint Basil the Great, Saint Gregory Nazianzen,*

and Saint Gregory of Nyssa, Dayton, Ohio: Diss. International Marian Research Institute, Fairview Park: Anderson Print & Copy, 1997, 178.

88. Pope John Paul II, *Evangelium Vitae*, 102.

89. Pope John Paul II, *Evangelium Vitae*, 102.

90. Pope John Paul II, *Evangelium Vitae*, 102.

91. Pope John Paul II, *Evangelium Vitae*, 102.

92. *Predestination* tends to believe that what happens in the world is exclusively God's will and what He predestined His creatures to be. It denies the intervention of free human beings who could do what does not belong to God's original plan of salvation.

93. Saint John Damascene, *Homilia in Dormitionem*, I, 3: *SCh* 80, 85; Pope John Paul II, *Redemptoris Mater*, 7; *Crossing the Threshold of Hope*, New York: Alfred A. Knopf, 1994, 213.

94. *Lumen Gentium*, 55; Pope John Paul II, *Redemptoris Mater*, 7; *Crossing the Threshold of Hope*, New York: Alfred A. Knopf, 1994, 213.

95. See Antoine E. Nachef, *The Mystery of the Trinity in the Theological Thought of Pope John Paul II*, New York: Peter Lang Publishing, 1998, 119–122.

96. In that sense, Pope John Paul II, confirming what he has already said in *Tertio Millennio Adveniente*, 10, says in his encyclical letter *Fides et Ratio*: "God's Revelation is therefore immersed in time and history. Jesus Christ took flesh in the 'fullness of time' (Gal 4:4); and two thousand years later, I feel bound to restate forcefully that 'in Christianity time has a fundamental importance.'" (Pope John Paul II, *Fides et Ratio*, 11) See also Pope John Paul II, *Redemptor Hominis*, 22; *Centesimus Annus*, 62; *Evangelium Vitae*, 102; *Redemptionis Donum*, 13; *Salvifici Doloris*, 26; *Crossing the Threshold of Hope*, New York: Alfred A. Knopf, 1994, 213.

97. Pope John Paul II, *Letter to Families from Pope John Paul II*, 1994, 20; Ignace de la Potterie, "Maria, 'piena di grazia'" (RM 7–11), in *Marianum* 138 (1988): 115–117; Leo Scheffczyk, "Maria und die Kirche in der Enzyklika 'Redemptoris Mater,'" in *Marianum* 139 (1989): 91.

98. Pope John Paul II, *Fides et Ratio*, 15. See also Pope John Paul II, *Redemptionis Donum*, 13.

99. Pope John Paul II, *Redemptoris Mater*, 7.

100. See also Pope John Paul II, *Redemptoris Mater*, 8; *Redemptoris Custos*, 2.

101. Pope John Paul II, *Redemptoris Mater*, 20.

102. Pope John Paul II, *Redemptoris Mater*, 20.

103. See Richard J. Taylor, "*Redemptoris Mater*: Pope John Paul's Encyclical for the Marian Year: Some reflections," in *Priest & People* 2 (1988): 133.

104. Stefano de Fiores, "La Presenza di Maria nella vita della Chiesa alla luce dell'enciclica 'Redemptoris Mater,'" in *Marianum* 139 (1989): 119.

105. Pope John Paul II, *Redemptoris Mater*, 20.

106. Pope John Paul II, *Redemptoris Mater*, 20. See also Pope John Paul II, *Dominum et Vivificantem*, 16, 21; *Redemptoris Missio*, 92; *Evangelium Vitae*, 102; *Letter of the Pope to Children in the Year of the Family*, Boston: Pauline Books & Media, 1994, 12.

107. Pope John Paul II, *Redemptoris Mater*, 20. See also *Dominum et Vivificantem*, 51; *Evangelium Vitae*, 102; *Catechesi Tradendae*, 73; *Redemptionis Donum*, 17; Luigi Gambero, "La spiritualità Mariana nella vita del cristiano alla luce della 'Redemptoris Mater,'" in *Marianum* 139 (1989): 241.

108. See also Pope John Paul II, *Redemptionis Donum*, 17.

109. Pope John Paul II, *Redemptoris Mater*, 20. See also Pope John Paul II, *Catechesi Tradendae*, 73; *Letter of the Pope to Children in the Year of the Family*, Boston: Pauline Books & Media, 1994, 9.

110. Pope John Paul II, *Redemptoris Mater*, 20. See also Pope John Paul II, *Redemptor Hominis*, 22; *Letter of the Pope to Children in the Year of the Family*, Boston: Pauline Books & Media, 1994, 12; Luigi Gambero, "La spiritualità Mariana nella vita del cristiano alla luce della 'Redemptoris Mater,'" in *Marianum* 139 (1989): 241.

111. Pope John Paul II, *Redemptoris Mater*, 20. See also Pope John Paul II, *Redemptoris Missio*, 92; *Letter of the Pope to Children in the Year of the Family*, Boston: Pauline Books & Media, 1994, 12.

112. See also Pope John Paul II, *Redemptor Hominis*, 22; *Redemptoris Missio*, 92; *Redemptionis Donum*, 13; *Salvifici Doloris*, 26; *Letter of the Pope to Children in the Year of the Family*, Boston: Pauline Books & Media, 1994, 12; Luigi Gambero, "La spiritualità Mariana nella vita del cristiano alla luce della 'Redemptoris Mater,'" in *Marianum* 139 (1989): 241.

113. Pope John Paul II, *Redemptoris Mater*, 20. See also Pope John Paul II, *Redemptor Hominis*, 22; *Redemptoris Missio*, 92; *Evangelium Vitae*, 102; *Redemptionis Donum*, 13, 17; *Letter of the Pope to Children in the Year of the Family*, Boston: Pauline Books & Media, 1994, 12.

114. Pope John Paul II, *Redemptoris Mater*, 20. See also Pope John Paul II, *Redemptor Hominis*, 22; *Redemptoris Missio*, 92; *Evangelium Vitae*, 102; *Redemptoris Custos*, 2; *Letter of the Pope to Children in the Year of the Family*, Boston: Pauline Books & Media, 1994, 12.

115. See Pope Paul VI, *Lumen Ecclesiae*, 8; Pope John Paul II, *Fides et Ratio*, 43; *Salvifici Doloris*, 26; Holy Thursday Letter of John Paul II, *Behold your Mother*, 1988, 3; *Letter of the Pope to Children in the Year of the Family*, Boston: Pauline Books & Media, 1994, 12.

116. Pope John Paul II, *Redemptoris Mater*, 20.

117. Pope John Paul II, *Redemptoris Mater*, 20. See also Pope John Paul II, *Redemptor Hominis*, 22; *Dominum et Vivificantem*, 51; *Redemptionis Donum*, 17; *Salvifici Doloris*, 26; Holy Thursday Letter of John Paul II, *Behold your Mother*, 1988, 3; *Redemptoris Custos*, 2.

118. Pope John Paul II, *Redemptoris Mater*, 20. See also *Dominum et Vivificantem*, 51; *Redemptoris Custos*, 2.

119. Pope John Paul II, *Redemptoris Mater*, 20. See also Pope John Paul II, *Redemptor Hominis*, 22; *Redemptoris Custos*, 2; *Letter of the Pope to Children in the Year of the Family*, Boston: Pauline Books & Media, 1994, 12.

120. Pope John Paul II, *Redemptoris Mater*, 20; *Redemptoris Custos*, 2.

121. Pope John Paul II, *Redemptoris Mater*, 20. See also Pope John Paul II, *Redemptor Hominis*, 22; *Dominum et Vivificantem*, 51; *Salvifici Doloris*, 26. A parallel

document summarizes in a powerful yet concise way the theology of the Pope: "Her spousal love reached its height in the divine Motherhood through the power of the Holy Spirit" (Pope John Paul II, *Redemptionis Donum*, 17).

122. Pope John Paul II, *Redemptoris Mater*, 20. See also Pope John Paul II, *Redemptor Hominis*, 22; *Dominum et Vivificantem*, 51; *Redemptoris Missio*, 92; *Pastores Dabo Vobis*, 82.

123. Pope John Paul II, *Catechesi Tradendae*, 73. See also Pope John Paul II, *Pastores Dabo Vobis*, 82.

124. Pope John Paul II, *Catechesi Tradendae*, 73. See also Pope John Paul II, *Pastores Dabo Vobis*, 82.

125. Pope John Paul II, *Redemptionis Donum*, 17. See also Pope John Paul II, *Pastores Dabo Vobis*, 82.

126. Pope John Paul II, *Dives in Misericordia*, 9. See also Pope John Paul II, *Dives in Misericordia*, 15.

127. See Johann G. Roten, "La Foi de Marie à la lumière de la théologie actuelle," in *La Foi de Marie Mère du Rédempteur*, Études Mariales, 52e session de la Société Française d'Études Mariales, Josselin, Bretagne, 1995, Paris: Médiaspaul, 1996, 191–193.

128. Pope John Paul II, *Dives in Misericordia*, 9. See also Pope John Paul II, *Dives in Misericordia*, 15; *Dominum et Vivificantem*, 16; *Redemptoris Missio*, 92; *Veritatis Splendor*, 118.

129. See also Pope John Paul II, *Dominum et Vivificantem*, 16.

130. Pope John Paul II, *Dives in Misericordia*, 9. See also Pope John Paul II, *Dives in Misericordia*, 15; *Dominum et Vivificantem*, 16. The same term "Mother of Mercy" occurs again in *Veritatis Splendor*, 118.

131. See Johann G. Roten, "La Foi de Marie à la lumière de la théologie actuelle," in *La Foi de Marie Mère du Rédempteur*, Études Mariales, 52e session de la Société Française d'Études Mariales, Josselin, Bretagne, 1995, Paris: Médiaspaul, 1996, 193–199.

132. Pope John Paul II, *Dives in Misericordia*, 9. See also Pope John Paul II, *Dives in Misericordia*, 15; *Dominum et Vivificantem*, 16.

133. See Johann G. Roten, "La Foi de Marie à la lumière de la théologie actuelle," in *La Foi de Marie Mère du Rédempteur*, Études Mariales, 52e session de la Société Française d'Études Mariales, Josselin, Bretagne, 1995, Paris: Médiaspaul, 1996, 191–193.

134. Pope John Paul II, *Dives in Misericordia*, 9. See also Pope John Paul II, *Dives in Misericordia*, 15.

135. Pope John Paul II, *Dives in Misericordia*, 9. See also Pope John Paul II, *Dives in Misericordia*, 15; *Veritatis Splendor*, 118; *Redemptoris Custos*, 1. In *Dominum et Vivificantem*, 16, the Pope continues to emphasize the personalistic approach of Mary's involvement in the history of salvation. The coming of the Holy Spirit took place at the expense of the departure of Christ through the cross, "which he would have to embrace together with his Mother. The Virgin Mary, who 'had conceived by the Holy Spirit,' sensed this even more clearly, when she pondered in her heart the 'mysteries' of the Messiah, with whom she was associated."

136. See also Pope John Paul II, *Dominum et Vivificantem*, 16; *Redemptoris Missio*, 92.

137. Pope John Paul II, *Dives in Misericordia*, 9. Later on and in the same line of thought, the Pope calls her "spiritual mother of mankind" (*Dives in Misericordia*, 15). See also Pope John Paul II, *Redemptoris Missio*, 92.

138. Pope John Paul II, *Salvifici Doloris*, 26.

139. Pope John Paul II, *Veritatis Splendor*, 118.

140. John Paul quotes the Missale: "O inaestimabilis dilectio caritatis: ut servum redimeres, Filium tradisti!" (Pope John Paul II, *Veritatis Splendor*, 118).

141. Pope John Paul II, *Veritatis Splendor*, 118.

142. Pope John Paul II, *Veritatis Splendor*, 118. See also Pope John Paul II, *Dominicae Cenae*, 13.

143. See Pope John Paul II, *Veritatis Splendor*, 120.

144. See Johann G. Roten, "La Foi de Marie à la lumière de la théologie actuelle," in *La Foi de Marie Mère du Rédempteur*, Études Mariales, 52e session de la Société Française d'Études Mariales, Josselin, Bretagne, 1995, Paris: Médiaspaul, 1996, 193–199.

CHAPTER THREE

1. See Antoine E. Nachef, *The Mystery of the Trinity in the Theological Thought of Pope John Paul II*, New York: Peter Lang Publishing, 1998.

2. See also Pope John Paul II, *Redemptor Hominis*, 22.

3. Pope John Paul II, *Redemptoris Mater*, 1. See also Pope John Paul II, *Redemptor Hominis*, 8, 18, 22; Luigi Sartori, "Storia della salvezza' e Storia dell'umanità' nell'enciclica 'Redemptoris Mater,'" in *Marianum* 139 (1989): 21–24; Felipe Gomez, "A New Encyclical Letter: The Mother of the Redeemer," in *East Asian Pastoral Review* 24 (1987): 109–110.

4. See Pope Pius IX, *Acta*, I, 609; Pope John Paul II, *Redemptoris Mater*, 1.

5. Pope John Paul II, *Redemptoris Mater*, 1. See also *Dominum et Vivificantem*, 51; *Veritatis Splendor*, 120; *Familiaris Consortio*, 22; *Reconciliatio et Paenitentia*, 35.

6. See Henri Marie Manteau-Bonamy, "Marie et le Saint Esprit dans l'encyclique 'Redemptoris Mater,'" in *Marianum* 139 (1989): 76.

7. Ignace de la Potterie, "Maria, piena di grazia'" (RM 7–11), in *Marianum* 138 (1988): 113; Luigi Sartori, "Storia della salvezza' e Storia dell'umanità' nell'enciclica 'Redemptoris Mater,'" in *Marianum* 139 (1989): 25.

8. See Henri Marie Manteau-Bonamy, "Marie et le Saint Esprit dans l'encyclique Redemptoris Mater,'",@ in *Marianum* 139 (1989): 68–81; Antoine E. Nachef, *The Mystery of The Trinity in the Theological Thought of Pope John Paul II*, New York: Peter Lang Publishing, 1998.

9. Pope John Paul II, *Dominum et Vivificantem*, 51. See also Pope John Paul II, *Veritatis Splendor*, 120; *Reconciliatio et Paenitentia*, 35.

10. Pope John Paul II, *Reconciliatio et Paenitentia*, 35; General Audience Address of December 7, 1983, 2; General Audience Address of January 4, 1984: *Insegnamenti*, VII, 1 (1984): 16–18.

11. Davide M. Montagna, "Reminiscenze patristiche medioevali nell'enciclica 'Redemptoris Mater,'" in *Marianum* 139 (1989): 382.

12. Pope John Paul II, *Redemptoris Mater*, 1. See also Pope John Paul II, *Familiaris Consortio*, 22; *Letter of His Holiness John Paul II to the Bishops of the United States* (April 3, 1983), 4; *Redemptionis Donum*, 17; *Reconciliatio et Paenitentia*, 12; Ignace de la Potterie, "Maria, piena di grazia'" (RM 7–11), in *Marianum* 138 (1988): 113.

13. Pope John Paul II, *Redemptoris Mater*, 8.

14. Pope John Paul II, *Redemptoris Mater*, 8. See also Pope John Paul II, *Redemptor Hominis*, 22; *Veritatis Splendor*, 120; Ignace de la Potterie, "Maria, piena di grazia'" (RM 7–11), in *Marianum* 138 (1988): 118.

15. See also Leo Scheffczyk, "Maria und die Kirche in der Enzyklika 'Redemptoris Mater,'" in *Marianum* 139 (1989): 94.

16. Ignace de la Potterie, "Κεχαριτωμενη en Lc 1, 28. Étude philologique," in *Biblica* 68 (1987): 357–382.

17. Pope John Paul II, *Redemptoris Mater*, 8; Ignace de la Potterie, "Maria, piena di grazia'" (RM 7–11), in *Marianum* 138 (1988): 115; Stefano de Fiores, "La Presenza di Maria nella vita della Chiesa alla luce dell'enciclica 'Redemptoris Mater,'" in *Marianum* 139 (1989): 117–118; Luigi Gambero, "La spiritualità Mariana nella vita del cristiano alla luce della 'Redemptoris Mater,'" in *Marianum* 139 (1989): 241.

18. Pope John Paul II, *Redemptoris Mater*, 8.

19. Pope John Paul II, *Redemptoris Mater*, 8. See also Pope John Paul II, *Redemptor Hominis*, 22; *Dominum et Vivificantem*, 51; *Reconciliatio et Paenitentia*, 12.

20. See also Pope John Paul II, *Reconciliatio et Paenitentia*, 12.

21. Pope John Paul II, *Redemptoris Mater*, 8; Luigi Gambero, "La spiritualità Mariana nella vita del cristiano alla luce della 'Redemptoris Mater,'" in *Marianum* 139 (1989): 241; Henri Marie Manteau–Bonamy, "Marie et le Saint Esprit dans l'encyclique 'Redemptoris Mater,'" in *Marianum* 139 (1989): 75–76.

22. Pope John Paul II, *Redemptoris Mater*, 8; Ignace de la Potterie, "Maria, piena di grazia'" (RM 7–11), in *Marianum* 138 (1988): 115–117.

23. See Pius IX, *Acta*, I, 609; B. Prete, "I fondamenti biblici del dogma dell'Immacolata," in *Sapienza* 7 (1954): 431–469.

24. See *Acta Apostolicae Sedis* 45 (1953): 579.

25. See Luigi Gambero, "La spiritualità Mariana nella vita del cristiano alla luce della 'Redemptoris Mater,'" in *Marianum* 139 (1989): 242–243.

26. See J. Fitzmyer, *The Gospel according to Luke I–IX*, New York: 1981, 346; R. Brown, La nascita del Messia, Cittadella, 1981, 438; G. Miegge, *La vergine Maria*, Torino, 1982, 27; G. Barbaglio, *Maria, nostra sorella*, a cura della Federazione delle Chiese evangeliche in Italia, Roma, 1988, 45; Ignace de la Potterie, "Maria, piena di grazia'" (RM 7–11), in *Marianum* 138 (1988): 121–122.

27. M. Jugie, L'Immaculée Conception dans l'Écriture Sainte et dans la Tradition orientale, Rome, 1952, 47–48; Ignace de la Potterie, "Maria, piena di grazia'" (RM 7–11), in *Marianum* 138 (1988): 122; Chr. Mohrmann, "Ave gratificata," in *Rivista della Storia della Chiesa in Italia* 5 (1951): 189–191; Fr. Stummer, "Lc 1, 28 nelle versioni latine," in *ZAW* 62 (1949): 152–167; S. Zedda, *Vangelo secondo Luca,* in *La Bibbia parola di Dio,* III, Marietti, 1980, 231; E. Delebecque, "Sur la salutation de Gabriel à Marie (Lc 1,28)," in *Biblica* 65 (1984): 352–354.

28. See F. Marchisano, L'interpretazione di κεχαριτωμενη (Lc 1,28) fino alla metà del secolo XIII. Contributo alla mariologia biblica. Dissertation ad lauream Pont. Univ. Gregoriana, Roma, 1957, 17.

29. *Vulgata* is the Latin translation of the Greek Bible.

30. Pope John Paul II, *Redemptoris Mater*, 8; Alejandro Martínez Sierra, "María estrella para el hombre que 'cae' y 'se levanta,'" in *Marianum* 139 (1989): 232.

31. Pope John Paul II, *Redemptoris Mater*, 8; Leo Scheffczyk, "Maria und die Kirche in der Enzyklika 'Redemptoris Mater,'" in *Marianum* 139 (1989): 90; Alejandro Martínez Sierra, "María estrella para el hombre que 'cae' y 'se levanta,'" in *Marianum* 139 (1989): 232.

32. Ignace de la Potterie, "Maria, piena di grazia'" (RM 7–11), in *Marianum* 138 (1988): 114–115.

33. S. Lyonnet, "Χαιρε, κεχαριτωμενη," in *Biblica* 20 (1939): 131–141; Ignace de la Potterie, "La 'figlia di Sion.' Lo sfondo biblico della mariologia dopo il Concilio," in *Civiltà Cattolica* 139 (1988 I): 535–549; Leo Scheffczyk, "Maria und die Kirche in der Enzyklika 'Redemptoris Mater,'" in *Marianum* 139 (1989): 90.

34. Ignace de la Potterie, "Maria, piena di grazia'" (RM 7–11), in *Marianum* 138 (1988): 114–116; J. A. De Aldama, "El tema Mariano 'La Hija de Sion' en la liturgia visigótica," in *La Ciudad de Dios* 181 (1968): 863–881.

35. See N. Lemmo, *'Figlia di Sion' a partire da Lc 1, 26–38. Bilancio esegetico dal 1939 al 1982* (Excerpt from a Thesis in Sacred Theology, Marianum, 37), Roma 1985; Ignace de la Potterie, *Maria nel mistero dell'Alleanza*, Genova, 1988, 18–32.

36. Pope John Paul II, *Redemptoris Mater*, 8. See also Pope John Paul II, *Redemptor Hominis*, 22; *Veritatis Splendor*, 120; Stefano de Fiores, "La Presenza di Maria nella vita della Chiesa alla luce dell'enciclica 'Redemptoris Mater,'" in *Marianum* 139 (1989): 117–118.

37. Pope John Paul II, *Redemptoris Mater*, 8. See also Pope John Paul II, *Dominum et Vivificantem*, 51; Henri Marie Manteau-Bonamy, "Marie et le Saint Esprit dans l'encyclique 'Redemptoris Mater,'" in *Marianum* 139 (1989): 75–76.

38. See Antoine E. Nachef, *The Mystery of the Trinity in the Theological Thought of Pope John Paul II,* New York: Peter Lang Publishing, 1998.

39. Pope John Paul II, *Redemptoris Mater*, 8; Pope John Paul II, *Dominum et Vivificantem*, 51.

40. Pope John Paul II, *Redemptoris Mater*, 8. See also Pope John Paul II, *Dominum et Vivificantem*, 51; Emmanuele di Napoli, "Attualità di uno studio sul Vaticano II tra Mariologia e corredenzione," in *Marianum* 151 (1997): 177–178.

41. Pope John Paul II, *Redemptoris Mater*, 8. See also Pope John Paul II, *Dominum et Vivificantem*, 51; Luigi Gambero, "La spiritualità Mariana nella vita del cristiano alla luce della 'Redemptoris Mater,'" in *Marianum* 139 (1989): 242–243.

42. Pope John Paul II, *Redemptoris Mater*, 8. See also Pope John Paul II, *Dominum et Vivificantem*, 51; *Familiaris Consortio*, 22.

43. See Jean Galot, "L'itinéraire de foi de Marie selon l'encyclique 'Redemptoris Mater,'" in *Marianum* 139 (1989): 36.

44. See also Pope John Paul II, *Veritatis Splendor*, 120; Jean Galot, "L'itinéraire de foi de Marie selon l'encyclique 'Redemptoris Mater,'" in *Marianum* 139 (1989): 36.

45. Pope John Paul II, *Veritatis Splendor*, 120. See also Pope John Paul II, *Pastores Dabo Vobis*, 36; Emmanuele di Napoli, "Attualità di uno studio sul Vaticano II tra Mariologia e corredenzione," in *Marianum* 151 (1997): 177–178.

46. Pope John Paul II, *Veritatis Splendor*, 120. See also Pope John Paul II, *Pastores Dabo Vobis*, 36; Damian P. Fedoryka, "The Gift of *Veritatis Splendor*," *Social Justice Review* 85 (1994): 146; William E. May, "*Veritatis Splendor*: An Overview of the Encyclical," in *Communio* 21 (1994): 251.

47. Pope John Paul II, *Veritatis Splendor*, 120. See also Pope John Paul II, *Redemptoris Custos, 17*; *Pastores Dabo Vobis*, 36; William E. May, "*Veritatis Splendor*: An Overview of the Encyclical," in *Communio* 21 (1994): 251 Damian P. Fedoryka, "The Gift of *Veritatis Splendor*," *Social Justice Review* 85 (1994): 146.

48. Pope John Paul II, *Veritatis Splendor*, 120; *Fides et Ratio*, 108.

49. Pope John Paul II, *Veritatis Splendor*, 120; *Pastores Dabo Vobis*, 36.

50. Pope John Paul II, *Veritatis Splendor*, 120.

51. See also Pope John Paul II, *Pastores Dabo Vobis*, 36.

52. Pope John Paul II, *Veritatis Splendor*, 120; *Pastores Dabo Vobis*, 82.

53. Pope John Paul II, *Veritatis Splendor*, 120. See also Ignace de la Potterie, "Maria, piena di grazia'" (RM 7–11), in *Marianum* 138 (1988): 113; William E. May, "*Veritatis Splendor*: An Overview of the Encyclical," in *Communio* 21 (1994): 251.

54. Pope John Paul II, *Veritatis Splendor*, 120.

55. Pope John Paul II, *Veritatis Splendor*, 120. See also William E. May, "*Veritatis Splendor*: An Overview of the Encyclical," in *Communio* 21 (1994): 251.

56. Pope John Paul II, *Veritatis Splendor*, 120. See also William E. May, "*Veritatis Splendor*: An Overview of the Encyclical," in *Communio* 21 (1994): 251.

57. See Saint Augustine, *Tracts on John* 17, 8: PL 35, 1532; Francis X. Martin, "The Integrity of Christian Moral Activity: The First Letter of John and *Veritatis Splendor*," in *Communio* 21 (1994): 284.

58. Pope John Paul II, *Fides et Ratio*, 108.

59. See also Pope John Paul II, *Pastores Dabo Vobis*, 82; Emmanuele di Napoli, "Attualità di uno studio sul Vaticano II tra Mariologia e corredenzione," in *Marianum* 151 (1997): 177–178.

60. Pope John Paul II, *Fides et Ratio*, 108; *Pastores Dabo Vobis*, 36, 82.

61. Pope John Paul II, *Fides et Ratio*, 108.

62. *Fideism* ignores the capacities of the human reason's natural light given by God to every human person.

63. *Pelagianism* is a tendency to attribute to the human person capacities that enable him or her to reach the good without the help of God.

64. Pseudo-Epiphanius, *Homily in praise of Holy Mary Mother of God*: PG 43, 493; Pope John Paul II, *Fides et Ratio*, 108.

65. Pope John Paul II, *Redemptoris Mater*, 9; *Veritatis Splendor*, 120; Stefano de Fiores, "La Presenza di Maria nella vita della Chiesa alla luce dell'enciclica 'Redemptoris Mater,'" in *Marianum* 139 (1989): 117–118.

66. See Pope John Paul II, *Fides et Ratio*, 42; *Veritatis Splendor*, 120; *Fides et Ratio*, 108; *Pastores Dabo Vobis*, 36; Emmanuele di Napoli, "Attualità di uno studio sul Vaticano II tra Mariologia e corredenzione," in *Marianum* 151 (1997): 177–178.

67. See also Pope John Paul II, *Veritatis Splendor*, 120; *Familiaris Consortio*, 22; *Pastores Dabo Vobis*, 36.

68. Pope John Paul II, *Letter of His Holiness John Paul II to the Bishops of the United States* (April 3, 1983), 4; *Pastores Dabo Vobis*, 36.

69. Pope John Paul II, *Redemptoris Mater*, 9. See also Pope John Paul II, *Veritatis Splendor*, 120; Stefano de Fiores, "La Presenza di Maria nella vita della Chiesa alla luce dell'enciclica 'Redemptoris Mater,'" in *Marianum* 139 (1989): 117–118.

70. See Antoine E. Nachef, *The Mystery of the Trinity in the Theological Thought of Pope John Paul II*, New York: Peter Lang Publishing, 1998; Alejandro Martínez Sierra, "María estrella para el hombre que 'cae' y 'se levanta,'" in *Marianum* 139 (1989): 232.

71. Pope John Paul II, *Redemptoris Mater*, 9. See also Pope John Paul II, *Redemptor Hominis*, 22; *Veritatis Splendor*, 120; *Familiaris Consortio*, 22; *Reconciliatio et Paenitentia*, 12.

72. Pope John Paul II, *Redemptoris Mater*, 9. See also Pope John Paul II, *Redemptor Hominis*, 8, 18, 22; *Familiaris Consortio*, 22.

73. See also Pope John Paul II, *Redemptor Hominis*, 22; *Veritatis Splendor*, 120; *Familiaris Consortio*, 22; *Reconciliatio et Paenitentia*, 12.

74. Manteau-Bonamy thinks that in *Redemptoris Mater*, 10, there is an evident influence of Saint Maximilien M. Kolbe's understanding of Mary's Immaculate Conception (see Henri Marie Manteau-Bonamy, "Marie et le Saint Esprit dans l'encyclique 'Redemptoris Mater,'" in *Marianum* 139 (1989): 76–77).

75. Pope John Paul II, *Redemptoris Mater*, 10; *Familiaris Consortio*, 22; *Reconciliatio et Paenitentia*, 12; Pius IX, Apostolic Letter *Ineffabilis Deus* (December 8, 1854): *Pii IX P.M. Acta*, I, 616; *Lumen Gentium*, 53.

76. See Pope John Paul II, *Veritatis Splendor*, 120; *Familiaris Consortio*, 22; *Reconciliatio et Paenitentia*, 12; Angelo Amato, "Verso un altro dogma Mariano," *Marianum* 149 (1996): 230.

77. See also Davide M. Montagna, "Reminiscenze patristiche medioevali nell'enciclica 'Redemptoris Mater,'" in *Marianum* 139 (1989): 380.

78. Pope John Paul II, *Redemptoris Mater*, 10. See also Pope John Paul II, *Veritatis Splendor*, 120; *Familiaris Consortio*, 22; Saint Germanus of Constantinople, *In Annuntiationem Sanctissimae Deiparae Homilia*: PG 98, 327–328; Saint Andrew of Crete, *Canon in Beatae Mariae Natalem*, 4: PG 97, 1321–1322; *In Nativitatem Beatae Mariae*, I: PG 97: 811–812; *Homilia in Dormitionem Sanctae Mariae*, I: Patrologia Graeca 97, 1067–1068.

79. See Antoine E. Nachef, *Mary: Virgin Mother in the Theological Thought of*

Saint Basil the Great, Saint Gregory Nazianzen, and Saint Gregory of Nyssa, Dayton, Ohio: Diss. International Marian Research Institute, Fairview Park: Anderson Print & Copy, 1997, 27–31.

80. Pope John Paul II, *Redemptoris Mater*, 10; Liturgy of the Hours of August 15, Assumption of the Blessed Virgin Mary, Hymn at First and Second Vespers; Saint Peter Damian, *Carmina et Preces*, XLVII: Patrologia Latina 145, 934; Dante Alighieri, *The Divine Comedy*, Paradise, XXXIII, 1.

81. L. Bouyer, *Le Trône de la Sagesse*, Paris, 1957, 76–77; Ignace de la Potterie, "Maria, 'piena di grazia'" (RM 7–11), in *Marianum* 138 (1988): 115.

82. Pope John Paul II, *Redemptoris Mater*, 10. See also Pope John Paul II, *Reconciliatio et Paenitentia*, 12.

83. See Pope John Paul II, *Redemptoris Mater*, 10.

84. See Pope John Paul II, *Dominum et Vivificantem*, 51; Antoine E. Nachef, *The Mystery of the Trinity in the Theological Thought of Pope John Paul II*, New York: Peter Lang Publishing, 1998.

85. See Pope John Paul II, *Redemptoris Mater*, 11; Luigi Gambero, "La spiritualità Mariana nella vita del cristiano alla luce della 'Redemptoris Mater,'" in *Marianum* 139 (1989): 244; Stefano de Fiores, "La Presenza di Maria nella vita della Chiesa alla luce dell'enciclica 'Redemptoris Mater,'" in *Marianum* 139 (1989): 117–118; Alejandro Martínez Sierra, "María estrella para el hombre que 'cae' y 'se levanta,'" in *Marianum* 139 (1989): 232.

86. See Pope John Paul II, *Redemptoris Mater*, 11.

87. See Pope John Paul II, *Redemptoris Mater*, 11; *Veritatis Splendor*, 120; Luigi Gambero, "La spiritualità Mariana nella vita del cristiano alla luce della 'Redemptoris Mater,'" in *Marianum* 139 (1989): 244.

88. Ugo Vanni, "La Donna della Genesi (3,15) e la Donna dell'Apocalisse (12,1) nella 'Redemptoris Mater,'" in *Marianum* 138 (1988): 433.

89. See Pope John Paul II, *Redemptoris Mater*, 11; *Veritatis Splendor*, 120; Ugo Vanni, "La Donna della Genesi (3,15) e la Donna dell'Apocalisse (12,1) nella 'Redemptoris Mater,'" in *Marianum* 138 (1988): 433.

90. Louis–Marie Grignion De Montfort, *Traité de la vraie dévotion à la Sainte Vierge*, No. 2, in *Oeuvres complètes*, Paris: Seuil, 1966, 488. As far as that same concept is concerned, Saint Louis was influenced by Bérulle (see *Vie de Jésus* 6, 2)

91. See also Pope John Paul II, *Veritatis Splendor*, 120.

92. See Pope John Paul II, *Redemptoris Mater*, 11.

93. Pope John Paul II, *Fides et Ratio*, 17.

CHAPTER FOUR

1. See Johann G. Roten, "La Foi de Marie à la lumière de la théologie actuelle," in *La Foi de Marie Mère du Rédempteur*, Études Mariales, 52e session de la Société Française d'Études Mariales, Josselin, Bretagne, 1995, Paris: Médiaspaul, 1996, 186.

2. *Ecclesiology* is the study of the Church.

3. Pope John Paul II, *Redemptoris Mater*, 47. See also Pope John Paul II, *Redemptoris Missio*, 92; *Evangelium Vitae*, 102; *Redemptoris Custos*, 1; *Crossing the Threshold of Hope*, New York: Alfred A. Knopf, 1994, 213.

4. See also Pope John Paul II, *Redemptoris Missio*, 92; *Centesimus Annus*, 62; *Evangelium Vitae*, 102; *Redemptoris Custos*, 1; *Crossing the Threshold of Hope*, New York: Alfred A. Knopf, 1994, 213; Leo Scheffczyk, "Maria und die Kirche in der Enzyklika 'Redemptoris Mater,'" in *Marianum* 139 (1989): 85; Salvador Muñoz Iglesias, "La fe de María y la fe de Abraham," in *Marianum* 138 (1988): 179.

5. See Johann G. Roten, "La Foi de Marie à la lumière de la théologie actuelle," in *La Foi de Marie Mère du Rédempteur*, Études Mariales, 52e session de la Société Française d'Études Mariales, Josselin, Bretagne, 1995, Paris: Médiaspaul, 1996, 191–193.

6. Pope Paul VI, Address at the Closing of the Third Session of the Second Vatican Ecumenical Council (November 21, 1964): *AAS* 56 (1964), 1015; Pope John Paul II, *Redemptoris Mater*, 47.

7. Pope John Paul II, *Redemptor Hominis*, 22. See also Pope John Paul II, *Dominum et Vivificantem*, 66; *Redemptoris Missio*, 92; *Evangelium Vitae*, 102, 103; *Reconciliatio et Paenitentia*, 4; *Crossing the Threshold of Hope*, New York: Alfred A. Knopf, 1994, 213.

8. Pope John Paul II, *Redemptor Hominis*, 22. See also Pope John Paul II, *Dominum et Vivificantem*, 66; *Redemptoris Missio*, 92; *Evangelium Vitae*, 102; *Dominicae Cenae*, 13; *Redemptionis Donum*, 17; *Reconciliatio et Paenitentia*, 12; *Crossing the Threshold of Hope*, New York: Alfred A. Knopf, 1994, 213; Jean Galot, "L'itinéraire de foi de Marie selon l'encyclique 'Redemptoris Mater,'" in *Marianum* 139 (1989): 33; James Kroeger, "Rekindling Mission Enthusiasm," in *The Priest* 48 (January, 1992): 36.

9. Pope John Paul II, *Redemptoris Mater*, 1. See also Pope John Paul II, *Redemptoris Missio*, 92; *Evangelium Vitae*, 102; *Dominicae Cenae*, 13; *Reconciliatio et Paenitentia*, 12; *Crossing the Threshold of Hope*, New York: Alfred A. Knopf, 1994, 213; *Redemptoris Custos*, 1; Stefano de Fiores, "La Presenza di Maria nella vita della Chiesa alla luce dell'enciclica 'Redemptoris Mater,'" in *Marianum* 139 (1989): 112; Leo Scheffczyk, "Maria und die Kirche in der Enzyklika 'Redemptoris Mater,'" in *Marianum* 139 (1989): 88; Timothy O'Donnell, "The Crisis of Faith and the Theology of Mission: A Reflection on *Redemptoris Missio*," in *Faith and Reason* 18:3 (1992): 13.

10. See Pope John Paul II, *Redemptoris Mater*, 28, 33.

11. See Pope John Paul II, *Redemptoris Mater*, 28, 32, 44.

12. See Pope John Paul II, *Redemptoris Mater*, 45.

13. Pope John Paul II, *Discorso ai pescatori della diocesi di Termoli-Larino* (March 25, 1987), in *L'Osservatore Romano* of March 26, 1987, 10.

14. See Stefano de Fiores, "La Presenza di Maria nella vita della Chiesa alla luce dell'nciclica 'Redemptoris Mater,'" in *Marianum* 139 (1989): 110.

15. See "Presente," "Presenza," and "Ubicazione" in *Dizionario delle idee* (a cura del centro di studi filosofici di Gallarate), Sansoni, Firenze 1977, 914–915, 1212; R. Troisfontaines, *La notion de présence chez Gabriel Marcel*, in *Existentialisme chrétien*, Paris, 1947.

16. See R. Busa, *La terminologia tomista dell'interiorità. Saggi di metodo per un'interpretazione della metafisica della presenza*, Milano, 1949; T. Turi, *Maria 'oggi'=*

La presenza attuale di Maria nella vita della Chiesa e dell'umanità secondo la 'Redemptoris Mater,'" in AA. VV., *Con Maria per un cammino di Chiesa,* Edizioni La Scala, Noci 1988, 215–219.

17. Saint Thomas Aquinas, *Summa Theologiae,* I, q. 8, a. 3.

18. Saint John Damascene, *De fide orthodoxa,* 1, 13, Patrologia Graeca 94: 851 B.

19. See J. H. Leuba, *La psicologia del misticismo religioso,* Feltrinelli, Milano, 1960, 300–301; S. Lyonnet, "Presenza di Cristo e del suo Spirito nell'uomo," in *Concilium* 5 (1969) 10: 113 and 125; J. Murphy-O'Connor, "La presenza di Dio attraverso Cristo nella Chiesa e nel mondo," in *Concilium* 5 (1969) 10: 133, 138; F. Neirynck, "La dottrina di Paolo su Cristo in noi'–'noi in Cristo,'" in *Concilium* 5 (1969) 10: 165–178.

20. Stefano de Fiores, "La Presenza di Maria nella vita della Chiesa alla luce dell'enciclica 'Redemptoris Mater,'" in *Marianum* 139 (1989): 112.

21. *Osservatore Romano,* Dec. 12–13, 1988, 4. See also A. Ambrosanio, *La presenza di Maria nella Chiesa, in AA. VV. Una luce sul cammino dell'uomo. Per una lettura della 'Redemptoris Mater.'* Libreria Editrice Vaticana, 1987, 91.

22. Stefano de Fiores, "La Presenza di Maria nella vita della Chiesa alla luce dell'enciclica 'Redemptoris Mater,'" in *Marianum* 139 (1989): 113; Leo Scheffczyk, "Maria und die Kirche in der Enzyklika 'Redemptoris Mater,'" in *Marianum* 139 (1989): 88.

23. See R. Laurentin, *Un anno di grazia con Maria. La sua storia, il dogma, la sua presenza,* Queriniana, Brescia, 1987, 176.

24. B. Billet, *Un thème centrale de l'encyclique 'Redemptoris Mater': la présence de Marie,* in *Esprit et Vie* 16. 7. (1987): 428.

25. I. Scinella, "La presenza tipica' di Maria nel mistero di Cristo," in *Rassegna di Teologia* 29 (1988): 460.

26. See Stefano de Fiores, "La Presenza di Maria nella vita della Chiesa alla luce dell'enciclica 'Redemptoris Mater,'" in *Marianum* 139 (1989): 123–127.

27. See also Pope John Paul II, *Redemptor Hominis,* 22; *Dominum et Vivificantem,* 66; *Redemptoris Missio,* 92; *Centesimus Annus,* 62; *Evangelium Vitae,* 102; *Catechesi Tradendae,* 73; *Dominicae Cenae,* 13; *Pastores Dabo Vobis,* 38.

28. Pope John Paul II, *Redemptoris Mater,* 1. See also Pope John Paul II, *Redemptor Hominis,* 22; *Dominum et Vivificantem,* 66; *Redemptoris Missio,* 92; *Catechesi Tradendae,* 73.

29. See also Pope John Paul II, *Redemptor Hominis,* 22; *Evangelium Vitae,* 103.

30. See Stefano de Fiores, "La Presenza di Maria nella vita della Chiesa alla luce dell'enciclica 'Redemptoris Mater,'" in *Marianum* 139 (1989): 121–122.

31. Pope John Paul II, *Evangelium Vitae,* 103.

32. Pope John Paul II, *Evangelium Vitae,* 103. In that sense also the Pope calls Mary the Church's "first model" in *Redemptionis Donum,* 17 and "exemplar and model" in *Redemptoris Custos,* 1.

33. See also Pope John Paul II, *Redemptoris Custos,* 1; Ignace de la Potterie, "Maria, 'piena di grazia'" (RM 7–11), in *Marianum* 138 (1988): 113; Avery Dulles, "Mary at the Dawn of the New Millennium," in *America* 178, no. 3 (January 31, 1998): 18.

34. Pope John Paul II, *Evangelium Vitae*, 103; Avery Dulles, "Mary at the Dawn of the New Millennium," in *America* 178, no. 3 (January 31, 1998): 18–19.

35. See Ignace de la Potterie, "Maria, 'piena di grazia'" (RM 7–11), in *Marianum* 138 (1988): 114; R. Laurentin, Structure et théologie de Luc I–II, Paris 1957, 148–163: "Marie Fille de Sion et tabernacle eschatologique;" L. Bouyer, "Le culte de la Mère de Dieu dans l'Église catholique," in *Irénikon* 22 (1949): 139–159.

36. See also Pope John Paul II, *Dominum et Vivificantem*, 66; *Redemptoris Missio*, 92; *Crossing the Threshold of Hope*, New York: Alfred A. Knopf, 1994, 213; Avery Dulles, "Mary at the Dawn of the New Millennium," in *America* 178, no. 3 (January 31, 1998): 9.

37. Pope John Paul II, *Redemptoris Mater*, 1; R. Laurentin, "Pétitions internationales pour une définition dogmatique de la médiation et la corédemption," in *Marianum* 150 (1996): 433.

38. Pope John Paul II, *Redemptoris Mater*, 4.

39. Pope John Paul II, *Redemptoris Mater*, 4.

40. See Karol Wojtyla, *The Acting Person*, D. Reidel Publishing Company, Analecta Husserliana X, 1979, 261–299; "The Person: Subject and Community," in *The Review of Metaphysics* 33 (1979): 288–308.

41. See Karol Wojtyla, "The Person: Subject and Community," in *The Review of Metaphysics* 33 (1979): 288; "Subjectivity and the Irreducible in Man," in *Analecta Husserliana* 7 (1979): 109; Rocco Buttiglione, *Karol Wojtyla: The Thought of the Man who Became Pope John Paul II*, trans. Paolo Guietti and Francesca Murphy, Grand Rapids/Cambridge: William B. Eerdmans Publishing Company, 1997, 74–75.

42. See Karol Wojtyla, "The Person: Subject and Community," in *The Review of Metaphysics* 33 (1979): 288; "The Task of Christian Philosophy Today," in *Proceedings of the American Catholic Philosophical Association* 53 (1979): 3.

43. *Intoduction to Saint Thomas Aquinas*, edited with an Introduction by Anton C. Pegis, New York: The Modern Library, 1948, xix. See also T. B. Strong, "The history of the theological term 'substance': Part I," in *The Journal of Theological Studies* 2 (1901): 226–233.

44. Karol Wojtyla, "The Person: Subject and Community," in *The Review of Metaphysics* 33 (1979): 288.

45. Karol Wojtyla, "The Person: Subject and Community," in *The Review of Metaphysics* 33 (1979): 288. See also Pope John Paul II, *Dominum et Vivificantem*, 16.

46. Pope John Paul II, *Christifideles Laici*, 37.

47. Pope John Paul II, *Redemptoris Mater*, 1. See also Pope John Paul II, *Redemptor Hominis*, 22; *Redemptoris Missio*, 92; *Centesimus Annus*, 62; *Evangelium Vitae*, 102; *Christifideles Laici*, 14.

48. See also Pope John Paul II, *Dominum et Vivificantem*, 16; *Evangelium Vitae*, 102; *Christifideles Laici*, 37.

49. Pope John Paul II, *Redemptoris Mater*, 1. See also Pope John Paul II, *Redemptoris Missio*, 92; *Centesimus Annus*, 62; *Evangelium Vitae*, 102; *Catechesi Tradendae*, 73; *Christifideles Laici*, 37.

50. Pope John Paul II, *Redemptoris Mater*, 1. See also Pope John Paul II, *Dominum et Vivificantem*, 16; *Veritatis Splendor*, 120; *Evangelium Vitae*, 102; *Catechesi Tradendae*, 73.

51. Pope John Paul II, *Redemptoris Mater*, 1. See also Pope John Paul II, *Redemptor Hominis*, 22; *Dominum et Vivificantem*, 66; *Redemptoris Missio*, 92; *Evangelium Vitae*, 102; *Catechesi Tradendae*, 73; *Dominicae Cenae*, 13.

52. See also Pope John Paul II, *Dominum et Vivificantem*, 66; *Redemptoris Missio*, 92; *Centesimus Annus*, 62; *Evangelium Vitae*, 102, 103; *Catechesi Tradendae*, 73; *Dominicae Cenae*, 13.

53. Pope John Paul II, *Dives in Misericordia*, 15. See also Pope John Paul II, *Dives in Misericordia*, 9; *Dominum et Vivificantem*, 66; *Redemptoris Missio*, 92; *Centesimus Annus*, 62; *Evangelium Vitae*, 102; *Catechesi Tradendae*, 73; *Dominicae Cenae*, 13.

54. See also Pope John Paul II, *Dominum et Vivificantem*, 16, 66; *Redemptoris Missio*, 92; *Centesimus Annus*, 62; *Evangelium Vitae*, 102; *Catechesi Tradendae*, 73; *Dominicae Cenae*, 13.

55. Pope John Paul II, *Redemptoris Mater*, 5. See also Pope John Paul II, *Dominum et Vivificantem*, 66; *Redemptoris Missio*, 92; *Evangelium Vitae*, 102; Leo Scheffczyk, "Maria und die Kirche in der Enzyklika 'Redemptoris Mater,'" in *Marianum* 139 (1989): 88.

56. Pope John Paul II, *Redemptoris Mater*, 5; *Redemptoris Missio*, 92; *Centesimus Annus*, 62; R. Laurentin, "Pétitions internationales pour une définition dogmatique de la médiation et la corédemption," in *Marianum* 150 (1996): 433.

57. Pope John Paul II, *Redemptoris Mater*, 5. See also Pope John Paul II, *Dominum et Vivificantem*, 66; *Redemptoris Missio*, 92; *Evangelium Vitae*, 102.

58. Pope John Paul II, *Redemptoris Mater*, 5. See also Pope John Paul II, *Dominum et Vivificantem*, 66; *Redemptoris Missio*, 92; *Centesimus Annus*, 62; *Evangelium Vitae*, 102.

59. Saint Augustine, De Civitate Dei, XVIII, 51: CCL 48, 650; *Lumen Gentium*, 8. See also Pope John Paul II, *Centesimus Annus*, 62; *Evangelium Vitae*, 103; *Reconciliatio et Paenitentia*, 12.

60. Pope John Paul II, *Redemptoris Mater*, 25.

61. *Lumen Gentium*, 9; Pope John Paul II, *Redemptoris Mater*, 25.

62. *Lumen Gentium*, 9; Pope John Paul II, *Redemptoris Mater*, 25.

63. Pope John Paul II, *Redemptoris Mater*, 25. See also Pope John Paul II, *Redemptoris Missio*, 92; *Centesimus Annus*, 62; *Reconciliatio et Paenitentia*, 12.

64. Pope John Paul II, *Redemptoris Mater*, 25. See also Pope John Paul II, *Dominicae Cenae*, 13.

65. See also Pope John Paul II, *Dominum et Vivificantem*, 66; *Redemptoris Missio*, 92; *Evangelium Vitae*, 102.

66. *Lumen Gentium*, 9; Pope John Paul II, *Redemptoris Mater*, 25. See also Pope John Paul II, *Centesimus Annus*, 62; *Evangelium Vitae*, 102, 103; *Reconciliatio et Paenitentia*, 12.

67. See also Pope John Paul II, *Redemptoris Missio*, 92; *Centesimus Annus*, 62; *Evangelium Vitae*, 102, 103; *Reconciliatio et Paenitentia*, 12 Timothy O'Donnell, "The Crisis of Faith and the Theology of Mission: A Reflection on *Redemptoris Missio*," in *Faith and Reason* 18:3 (1992): 13.

68. Pope John Paul II, *Redemptoris Mater*, 25. See also Pope John Paul II, *Centesimus Annus*, 62; *Reconciliatio et Paenitentia*, 12.

69. Pope John Paul II, *Redemptoris Mater*, 25.

70. See also Pope John Paul II, *Dominum et Vivificantem*, 25, 30; *Redemptoris Missio*, 92; *Evangelium Vitae*, 102, 103; Rinaldo Fabris, "La presenza della Vergine nel Cenacolo (At 1, 14): l'interpretazione di Giovanni Paolo II," in *Marianum* 138 (1988): 398.

71. Pope John Paul II, *Redemptoris Mater*, 26. The Pope refers to the same theology in *Centesimus Annus*, 62, where Mary "goes before the Church on the pilgrimage of faith." See also Pope John Paul II., *Catechesi Tradendae*, 73.

72. Pope John Paul II, *Redemptoris Mater*, 26. For the expression "spouse of the Holy Spirit," see also Pope John Paul II, *Dominicae Cenae*, 13; Avery Dulles, "Mary at the Dawn of the New Millennium," in *America* 178, no. 3 (January 31, 1998): 16.

73. Pope John Paul II, *Redemptoris Mater*, 26. See also Pope John Paul II, *Redemptoris Missio*, 92; *Centesimus Annus*, 62; Rinaldo Fabris, "La presenza della Vergine nel Cenacolo (At 1, 14): l'interpretazione di Giovanni Paolo II," in *Marianum* 138 (1988): 398.

74. Pope John Paul II, *Redemptoris Mater*, 26; Henri Marie Manteau-Bonamy, "Marie et le Saint Esprit dans l'encyclique 'Redemptoris Mater,'" in *Marianum* 139 (1989): 68–69.

75. See also Pope John Paul II, *Dominum et Vivificantem*, 66; *Redemptoris Missio*, 92; *Redemptoris Custos*, 1.

76. See Saint Thomas Aquinas, *I Sent.*, dist. 16, q. 1, a. 2, ad 4.

77. *Lumen Gentium*, 59.

78. See Henri Marie Manteau-Bonamy, "Marie et le Saint Esprit dans l'encyclique 'Redemptoris Mater,'" in *Marianum* 139 (1989): 69–71.

79. Pope John Paul II, *Redemptoris Mater*, 26. See also Pope John Paul II, *Dominum et Vivificantem*, 25 and 30; *Redemptoris Missio*, 92.

80. Pope John Paul II, *Redemptoris Mater*, 26. See also Pope John Paul II, *Redemptoris Missio*, 92.

81. Pope John Paul II, *Redemptoris Mater*, 26. See also Pope John Paul II, *Dominum et Vivificantem*, 25, 30.

82. Pope John Paul II, *Redemptoris Mater*, 26.

83. Rinaldo Fabris, "La presenza della Vergine nel Cenacolo (At 1, 14): l'interpretazione di Giovanni Paolo II," in *Marianum* 138 (1988): 402.

84. See Arthur Burton Calkins, "'Towards another Marian Dogma?' A Response to Father Angelo Amato, S.D.B.," in *Marianum* 151 (1997): 164. See also Pope John Paul II, *Catechesi Tradendae*, 73.

85. See also Pope John Paul II, *Dominum et Vivificantem*, 16; *Evangelium Vitae*, 102, 103; *Catechesi Tradendae*, 73; *Redemptionis Donum*, 17; Johann G. Roten, "La Foi de Marie à la lumière de la théologie actuelle," in *La Foi de Marie Mère du Rédempteur*, Études Mariales, 52e session de la Société Française d'Études Mariales, Josselin, Bretagne, 1995, Paris: Médiaspaul, 1996, 193–199.

86. Pope John Paul II, *Redemptoris Mater*, 26. See also Pope John Paul II, *Dominum et Vivificantem*, 16; *Catechesi Tradendae*, 73.

87. Pope John Paul II, *Redemptoris Mater*, 26. See also Pope John Paul II, *Dominum et Vivificantem*, 16; *Catechesi Tradendae*, 73.

88. Pope John Paul II, *Redemptoris Mater*, 27.See also Pope John Paul II, *Redemptor Hominis*, 22; *Dominum et Vivificantem*, 25, 30; Rinaldo Fabris, "La presenza della Vergine nel Cenacolo (At 1, 14): l'interpretazione di Giovanni Paolo II," in *Marianum* 138 (1988): 401.

89. Pope John Paul II, *Redemptoris Mater*, 27.

90. Pope John Paul II, *Redemptoris Mater*, 27. See also Pope John Paul II, *Dominum et Vivificantem*, 66; *Pastores Dabo Vobis*, 38.

91. See also Johann G. Roten, "La Foi de Marie à la lumière de la théologie actuelle," in *La Foi de Marie Mère du Rédempteur*, Études Mariales, 52e session de la Société Française d'Études Mariales, Josselin, Bretagne, 1995, Paris: Médiaspaul, 1996, 193-199.

92. Pope John Paul II, *Redemptoris Mater*, 27. See also Pope John Paul II, *Redemptor Hominis*, 22; *Redemptoris Missio*, 92; *Centesimus Annus*, 62; *Catechesi Tradendae*, 73; *Redemptoris Custos*, 1; Stefano de Fiores, "La Presenza di Maria nella vita della Chiesa alla luce dell'enciclica 'Redemptoris Mater,'" in *Marianum* 139 (1989): 121-122.

93. *Lumen Gentium*, 65; Pope John Paul II, *Redemptoris Mater*, 28. See also Pope John Paul II, *Dominum et Vivificantem*, 16.

94. Pope John Paul II, *Redemptoris Mater*, 28. See also Pope John Paul II, *Redemptor Hominis*, 22; *Centesimus Annus*, 62; *Catechesi Tradendae*, 73; *Reconciliatio et Paenitentia*, 12.

95. Pope John Paul II, *Redemptoris Mater*, 28. See also Pope John Paul II, *Reconciliatio et Paenitentia*, 12.

96. Pope John Paul II, *Redemptoris Mater*, 28. See also Pope John Paul II, *Redemptor Hominis*, 22; *Dominum et Vivificantem*, 21, 66; *Redemptoris Missio*, 92; *Evangelium Vitae*, 102.

97. *Lumen Gentium*, 13; Pope John Paul II, *Redemptoris Mater*, 28; *Dominum et Vivificantem*, 66.

98. Pope John Paul II, *Redemptoris Mater*, 28. See also Pope John Paul II, *Redemptoris Missio*, 92.

99. See also Pope John Paul II, *Dominum et Vivificantem*, 66; *Redemptoris Missio*, 92.

100. Pope John Paul II, *Salvifici Doloris*; Antoine E. Nachef, *The Mystery of the Trinity in the Theological Thought of Pope John Paul II*, New York: Peter Lang Publishing, 1998, chapter on Redemption.

101. Pope John Paul II, *Redemptoris Mater*, 28.

102. Pope John Paul II, *Redemptoris Mater*, 28.

103. Pope John Paul II, *Redemptoris Mater*, 36. See also Pope John Paul II, *Tertio Millennio Adveniente*, 54.

104. Pope John Paul II, *Redemptoris Mater*, 36. See also Pope John Paul II, *Dominum et Vivificantem*, 16; *Tertio Millennio Adveniente*, 54; Johann G. Roten,

"La Foi de Marie à la lumière de la théologie actuelle," in *La Foi de Marie Mère du Rédempteur*, Études Mariales, 52e session de la Société Française d'Études Mariales, Josselin, Bretagne, 1995, Paris: Médiaspaul, 1996, 193–199.

105. Pope John Paul II, *Redemptoris Mater*, 36. See also Pope John Paul II, *Tertio Millennio Adveniente*, 54; Avery Dulles, "Mary at the Dawn of the New Millennium," in *America* 178, no. 3 (January 31, 1998): 18.

106. Pope John Paul II, *Redemptoris Mater*, 36. See also Pope John Paul II, *Tertio Millennio Adveniente*, 54; Avery Dulles, "Mary at the Dawn of the New Millennium," in *America* 178, no. 3 (January 31, 1998): 18.

107. Pope John Paul II, *Redemptoris Mater*, 36. See also Pope John Paul II, *Tertio Millennio Adveniente*, 54.

108. See Antoine E. Nachef, *The Mystery of the Trinity in the Theological Thought of Pope John Paul II*, New York: Peter Lang Publishing, 1998.

109. Pope John Paul II, *Redemptoris Mater*, 36. See also Pope John Paul II, *Tertio Millennio Adveniente*, 54.

110. Pope John Paul II, *Redemptoris Mater*, 36. See also Pope John Paul II, *Tertio Millennio Adveniente*, 54.

111. Pope John Paul II, *Redemptoris Mater*, 36. See also Pope John Paul II, *Tertio Millennio Adveniente*, 54; Avery Dulles, "Mary at the Dawn of the New Millennium," in *America* 178, no. 3 (January 31, 1998): 18.

112. Pope John Paul II, *Redemptor Hominis*, 22. See also Pope John Paul II, *Dominum et Vivificantem*, 66; *Redemptoris Missio*, 92.

113. Pope John Paul II, *Redemptor Hominis*, 22. See also Pope John Paul II, *Dominum et Vivificantem*, 66; *Redemptoris Missio*, 92; *Evangelium Vitae*, 102, 103; *Familiaris Consortio*, 86.

114. Pope Paul VI, Address at the Closing of the Third Session of the Second Vatican Ecumenical Council (November 21, 1964): *AAS* 56 (1964): 1015; Pope John Paul II, *Redemptor Hominis*, 22.

115. Pope John Paul II, *Redemptor Hominis*, 22. See also Pope John Paul II, *Slavorum Apostoli*, 32; *Redemptoris Missio*, 92; *Dominicae Cenae*, 13; *Familiaris Consortio*, 86; *Reconciliatio et Paenitentia*, 12; *Fidei Depositum*, 4; *Crossing the Threshold of Hope*, New York: Alfred A. Knopf, 1994, 213

116. See Pope John Paul II, *Redemptor Hominis*, 22. See also Pope John Paul II, *Dominum et Vivificantem*, 66; *Redemptoris Missio*, 92; *Dominicae Cenae*, 13; *Reconciliatio et Paenitentia*, 12.

117. *Distinctiones monasticae*, Editions Pitra, in *Spicilegium Solesmense* 3, 130–131; R. Laurentin, "Pétitions internationales pour une définition dogmatique de la médiation et la corédemption," in *Marianum* 150 (1996): 441; Luigi Gambero, "La spiritualità Mariana nella vita del cristiano alla luce della 'Redemptoris Mater,'" in *Marianum* 139 (1989): 240.

118. *Lumen Gentium*, 53; Avery Dulles, "Mary at the Dawn of the New Millennium," in *America* 178, no. 3 (January 31, 1998): 9.

119. Pope Paul VI, Address at the Closing of the Third Session of the Second Vatican Ecumenical Council (November 21, 1964): *AAS* 56 (1964): 1015; Pope John Paul II, *Redemptor Hominis*, 22.

120. See Pope Paul VI, *Christi Matri* (September 15, 1966): *AAS* 58 (1966), 745-749; Apostolic Exhortation *Signum Magnum* (May 13, 1967): *AAS* 59 (1967), 465–475; Apostolic Exhortation *Marialis Cultus* (February 2, 1974): *AAS* 66 (1974), 113–168; Pope John Paul II, *Redemptoris Mater*, 2; *Evangelium Vitae*, 102; *Reconciliatio et Paenitentia*, 12.

121. See Pope John Paul II, *Redemptor Hominis*, 22; *Redemptoris Missio*, 92; *Evangelium Vitae*, 102; *Dominicae Cenae*, 13; *Reconciliatio et Paenitentia*, 12; *Fidei Depositum*, 4; *Crossing the Threshold of Hope*, New York: Alfred A. Knopf, 1994, 213; *Ordinatio Sacerdotalis*, 3.

122. *L'Osservatore Romano*, weekly English edition, Oct. 22, 1997; Avery Dulles, "Mary at the Dawn of the New Millennium," in *America* 178, no. 3 (January 31, 1998): 10

123. Pope John Paul II, *Redemptoris Mater*, 2; Felipe Gomez, "A New Encyclical Letter: The Mother of the Redeemer," in *East Asian Pastoral Review* 24 (1987): 109.

124. Pope John Paul II, *Redemptoris Mater*, 42. See also Pope John Paul II, *Dominum et Vivificantem*, 66; *Evangelium Vitae*, 102, 103.

125. Pope John Paul II, *Redemptoris Mater*, 42. See also Pope John Paul II, *Dominum et Vivificantem*, 66; *Evangelium Vitae*, 102, 103; *Redemptoris Custos*, 1.

126. See Pope John Paul II, *Redemptionis Donum*, 17; *Redemptoris Custos*, 1.

127. Pope John Paul II, *Redemptoris Mater*, 42. See also Pope John Paul II, *Dominum et Vivificantem*, 66; *Evangelium Vitae*, 102; *Familiaris Consortio*, 16; *Redemptoris Custos*, 1; *Pastores Dabo Vobis*, 82.

128. *Lumen Gentium*, 64; Pope John Paul II, *Redemptoris Mater*, 43. See also Pope John Paul II, *Dominum et Vivificantem*, 66; *Redemptoris Missio*, 92; *Evangelium Vitae*, 102; *Pastores Dabo Vobis*, 82.

129. Pope John Paul II, *Redemptoris Mater*, 43. See also Pope John Paul II, *Evangelium Vitae*, 102; *Pastores Dabo Vobis*, 82.

130. Pope John Paul II, *Redemptoris Mater*, 43. See also Pope John Paul II, *Dominum et Vivificantem*, 66; *Redemptoris Missio*, 92; *Evangelium Vitae*, 102; *Pastores Dabo Vobis*, 82.

131. Pope John Paul II, *Redemptoris Mater*, 43; *Pastores Dabo Vobis*, 82.

132. Pope John Paul II, *Redemptoris Mater*, 43. See also Pope John Paul II, *Evangelium Vitae*, 102; *Pastores Dabo Vobis*, 82.

133. See Johann G. Roten, "La Foi de Marie à la lumière de la théologie actuelle," in *La Foi de Marie Mère du Rédempteur*, Études Mariales, 52e session de la Société Française d'Études Mariales, Josselin, Bretagne, 1995, Paris: Médiaspaul, 1996, 191–193.

134. Pope John Paul II, *Redemptoris Mater*, 43. See also Pope John Paul II, *Redemptor Hominis*, 22; *Dominum et Vivificantem*, 66; *Redemptoris Missio*, 92; *Evangelium Vitae*, 102; *Redemptionis Donum*, 17; *Redemptoris Custos*, 1.

135. Pope John Paul II, *Redemptoris Mater*, 43. See also Pope John Paul II, *Dominum et Vivificantem*, 66; *Redemptoris Missio*, 92; *Evangelium Vitae*, 102.

136. Pope John Paul II, *Evangelium Vitae*, 103. See also Terence Curley, "*Evangelium Vitae* and Our Culture," in *The Priest* 51 (October 1995): 20; Daniel Callam, "The Gospel of Life," in *The Canadian Catholic Review* 13 (June 1995): 3.

137. Pope John Paul II, *Evangelium Vitae*, 103.

138. Pope John Paul II, *Evangelium Vitae*, 103. See also Pope John Paul II, *Familiaris Consortio*, 22; *Redemptionis Donum*, 17; *Redemptoris Custos*, 1; Terence Curley, "*Evangelium Vitae* and Our Culture," in *The Priest* 51 (October 1995): 20; Daniel Callam, "The Gospel of Life," in *The Canadian Catholic Review* 13 (June 1995): 3.

139. Pope John Paul II, *Evangelium Vitae*, 103.

140. Pope John Paul II, *Evangelium Vitae*, 104.

141. Pope John Paul II, *Evangelium Vitae*, 104.

142. Pope John Paul II, *Redemptoris Mater*, 43; *Lumen Gentium*, 64. See also Pope John Paul II, *Dominum et Vivificantem*, 66; *Familiaris Consortio*, 37.

143. Pope John Paul II, *Redemptoris Mater*, 43. See also Pope John Paul II, *Dominum et Vivificantem*, 66; *Familiaris Consortio*, 37.

144. Pope John Paul II, *Redemptoris Mater*, 43. See also Pope John Paul II, *Dominum et Vivificantem*, 16 and 66; *Evangelium Vitae*, 102; *Familiaris Consortio*, 37.

145. Pope John Paul II, *Redemptoris Mater*, 43; *Lumen Gentium*, 64. See also Pope John Paul II, *Redemptor Hominis*, 22; *Dominum et Vivificantem*, 16, 66; *Evangelium Vitae*, 102.

146. Pope John Paul II, *Redemptoris Mater*, 43. See also Pope John Paul II, *Dominum et Vivificantem*, 66; *Redemptoris Missio*, 92; *Evangelium Vitae*, 102.

147. Pope John Paul II, *Redemptoris Mater*, 43. See also Pope John Paul II, *Dominum et Vivificantem*, 16.

148. Pope John Paul II, *Redemptoris Mater*, 44; *Lumen Gentium*, 63. See also Pope John Paul II, *Dominum et Vivificantem*, 66; *Redemptoris Missio*, 92; *Evangelium Vitae*, 102, 103.

149. See also Pope John Paul II, *Redemptor Hominis*, 22; *Dominum et Vivificantem*, 16.

150. Pope John Paul II, *Redemptoris Mater*, 47. See also Pope John Paul II, *Dominum et Vivificantem*, 66; *Redemptoris Missio*, 92; *Evangelium Vitae*, 103.

151. Pope John Paul II, *Redemptoris Mater*, 47. See also Pope John Paul II, *Dominum et Vivificantem*, 66; *Redemptoris Missio*, 92; *Evangelium Vitae*, 103.

152. Pope John Paul II, *Redemptoris Mater*, 47; Pope Paul VI, Address at the Closing of the Third Session of the Second Vatican Ecumenical Council (November 21, 1964): *AAS* 56 (1964): 1016. See also Pope John Paul II, *Dominum et Vivificantem*, 66; *Evangelium Vitae*, 102, 103; *Redemptoris Custos*, 1.

CHAPTER FIVE

1. See Johann G. Roten, "La Foi de Marie à la lumière de la théologie actuelle," in *La Foi de Marie Mère du Rédempteur*, Études Mariales, 52e session de la Société Française d'Études Mariales, Josselin, Bretagne, 1995, Paris: Médiaspaul, 1996, 185.

2. See Luigi Gambero, "La spiritualità Mariana nella vita del cristiano alla luce della 'Redemptoris Mater,'" in *Marianum* 139 (1989): 245; U. Betti, *La Madonna nella*

Chiesa in cammino, in AA. VV (various authors). *Una luce sul cammino dell'uomo. Per una lettura della 'Redemptoris Mater,'* Libreria Editrice Vaticana, 1987, 28.

3. See Gianfranco Ravasi, "'Beata colei che ha creduto' (Lc 1:45)," in *Marianum* 138 (1988): 159.

4. S. M. Meo, "Una enciclica sulla B. V. Maria ed un anno Mariano, per la Chiesa in cammino verso l'anno 2000," in *Seminarium* 17 (1987): 408; Stefano de Fiores, "La Presenza di Maria nella vita della Chiesa alla luce dell'nciclica 'Redemptoris Mater,'" in *Marianum* 139 (1989): 114.

5. See Salvador Muñoz Iglesias, "La fe de María y la fe de Abraham," in *Marianum* 138 (1988): 176, 187.

6. See A. Amato, "L'enciclica Mariana 'Redemptoris Mater' di Giovanni Paolo II. Problemi e interpretazioni," in *Salesianum* 49 (1987): 820.

7. Leo Scheffczyk, "Maria und die Kirche in der Enzyklika 'Redemptoris Mater,'" in *Marianum* 139 (1989): 86, 95.

8. See also Johann G. Roten, "La Foi de Marie à la lumière de la théologie actuelle," in *La Foi de Marie Mère du Rédempteur*, Études Mariales, 52e session de la Société Française d'Études Mariales, Josselin, Bretagne, 1995, Paris: Médiaspaul, 1996, 185.

9. Jean Galot, "L'itinéraire de foi de Marie selon l'encyclique 'Redemptoris Mater,'" in *Marianum* 139 (1989): 33, 35. See also D. Arancic, *La dottrina mariologica negli scritti di Carlo Balic*, Roma: Pont. Univ. Lateranense 1980, 89–144.

10. Luigi Gambero, "La spiritualità Mariana nella vita del cristiano alla luce della 'Redemptoris Mater,'" in *Marianum* 139 (1989): 247.

11. Pope John Paul II, *Redemptoris Mater*, 2; *Lumen Gentium*, 58. See also Pope John Paul II, *Dives in Misericordia*, 9; *Catechesi Tradendae*, 73; Holy Thursday Letter of John Paul II, *Behold your Mother*, 1988, 2.

12. Pope John Paul II, *Redemptoris Mater*, 2. See also Pope John Paul II, *Dives in Misericordia*, 9; *Catechesi Tradendae*, 73; *Familiaris Consortio*, 86; Holy Thursday Letter of John Paul II, *Behold your Mother*, 1988, 2; *Tertio Millennio Adveniente*, 43; Luigi Sartori, "'Storia della salvezza' e Storia dell'umanità' nell'enciclica 'Redemptoris Mater,'" in *Marianum* 139 (1989): 28.

13. Pope John Paul II, *Redemptoris Mater*, 5. See also Pope John Paul II, *Catechesi Tradendae*, 73; *Familiaris Consortio*, 86; Holy Thursday Letter of John Paul II, *Behold your Mother*, 1988, 2; *Redemptoris Custos*, 4; Luigi Gambero, "La spiritualità Mariana nella vita del cristiano alla luce della 'Redemptoris Mater,'" in *Marianum* 139 (1989): 249–250.

14. See Gianfranco Ravasi, "'Beata colei che ha creduto' (Lc 1:45)," in *Marianum* 138 (1988): 174.

15. Pope John Paul II, *Redemptoris Mater*, 5. See also Pope John Paul II, *Catechesi Tradendae*, 73; *Familiaris Consortio*, 86; Holy Thursday Letter of John Paul II, *Behold your Mother*, 1988, 2; *Redemptoris Custos*, 4; *Tertio Millennio Adveniente*, 43.

16. Pope John Paul II, *Redemptoris Mater*, 5. See also Pope John Paul II, *Dives in Misericordia*, 9; *Catechesi Tradendae*, 73; *Familiaris Consortio*, 86; Holy Thursday Letter of John Paul II, *Behold your Mother*, 1988, 2; *Redemptoris Custos*, 4; *Tertio Millennio Adveniente*, 43.

17. Pope John Paul II, *Redemptoris Mater*, 5. See also Pope John Paul II, *Catechesi Tradendae*, 73; *Familiaris Consortio*, 86; Holy Thursday Letter of John Paul II, *Behold your Mother*, 1988, 2; *Redemptoris Custos*, 4; *Tertio Millennio Adveniente*, 43; Gianfranco Ravasi, "'Beata colei che ha creduto' (Lc 1:45)," in *Marianum* 138 (1988): 174.

18. Pope John Paul II, *Redemptoris Mater*, 5. See also Pope John Paul II, *Catechesi Tradendae*, 73; *Familiaris Consortio*, 86; Holy Thursday Letter of John Paul II, *Behold your Mother*, 1988, 2; *Redemptoris Custos*, 4; *Tertio Millennio Adveniente*, 43.

19. Pope John Paul II, *Redemptoris Mater*, 5; *Tertio Millennio Adveniente*, 43; Jean Galot, "L'itinéraire de foi de Marie selon l'encyclique 'Redemptoris Mater,'" in *Marianum* 139 (1989): 34–35.

20. See Johann G. Roten, "La Foi de Marie à la lumière de la théologie actuelle," in *La Foi de Marie Mère du Rédempteur*, Études Mariales, 52e session de la Société Française d'Études Mariales, Josselin, Bretagne, 1995, Paris: Médiaspaul, 1996, 191–193.

21. See Johann G. Roten, "La Foi de Marie à la lumière de la théologie actuelle," in *La Foi de Marie Mère du Rédempteur*, Études Mariales, 52e session de la Société Française d'Études Mariales, Josselin, Bretagne, 1995, Paris: Médiaspaul, 1996, 193–199.

22. Pope John Paul II, *Redemptoris Mater*, 5; *Lumen Gentium*, 64. See also Pope John Paul II, *Dominum et Vivificantem*, 16.

23. Pope John Paul II, *Redemptoris Mater*, 6. See also Pope John Paul II, *Catechesi Tradendae*, 73; *Familiaris Consortio*, 86; Holy Thursday Letter of John Paul II, *Behold your Mother*, 1988, 2.

24. Pope John Paul II, *Redemptoris Mater*, 6. See also Pope John Paul II, *Catechesi Tradendae*, 73; *Familiaris Consortio*, 86; Holy Thursday Letter of John Paul II, *Behold your Mother*, 1988, 2.

25. Pope John Paul II, *Redemptoris Mater*, 6. See also Pope John Paul II, *Dives in Misericordia*, 9; *Catechesi Tradendae*, 73; Holy Thursday Letter of John Paul II, *Behold your Mother*, 1988, 2.

26. See *Oeuvres de piété*, 77, in *Oeuvres du card. De Bérulle*, Migne 1856, col. 1052–1053, 1058–1059; G. Moioli, *La perdurante presenza dei misteri di Cristo nel pensiero del card. De Bérulle*, in *La scuola cattolica* 90 (1962): 115–132; Saint Louis De Montfort, *Méthodes pour réciter le rosaire*, in *Oeuvres complètes*, 393–405; *True Devotion*, no. 214.

27. Pope John Paul II, *Redemptoris Mater*, 6; *Lumen Gentium*, 65; *Tertio Millennio Adveniente*, 43; Felipe Gomez, "A New Encyclical Letter: The Mother of the Redeemer," in *East Asian Pastoral Review* 24 (1987): 109.

28. Pope John Paul II, *Redemptoris Mater*, 6.

29. Pope John Paul II, *Redemptoris Mater*, 6; *Lumen Gentium*, 65; *Tertio Millennio Adveniente*, 43; Felipe Gomez, "A New Encyclical Letter: The Mother of the Redeemer," in *East Asian Pastoral Review* 24 (1987): 109.

30. Pope John Paul II, *Redemptoris Mater*, 6; Saint Bernard, *In Nativitate Beatae Mariae Sermo, De Aquaeductu*, 6: *Sancti Bernardi Opera*, V, 1968, 279; Jean Galot, "L'itinéraire de foi de Marie selon l'encyclique 'Redemptoris Mater,'" in *Marianum* 139 (1989): 36.

31. Pope John Paul II, *Redemptoris Mater*, 6; *Lumen Gentium*, 63; *Familiaris Consortio*, 86; Jean Galot, "L'itinéraire de foi de Marie selon l'encyclique 'Redemptoris Mater,'" in *Marianum* 139 (1989): 36.

32. For John Paul II's analysis of the encounter between Mary and Elizabeth, see Mario Masini, "Il saluto di Elisabetta a Maria (Lc 1,42)," in *Marianum* 138 (1988): 138–158.

33. Pope John Paul II, *Redemptoris Mater*, 12. See also Pope John Paul II, *Dominum et Vivificantem*, 51; *Redemptoris Custos*, 4; Avery Dulles, "Mary at the Dawn of the New Millennium," in *America* 178, no. 3 (January 31, 1998): 18.

34. Gianfranco Ravasi, "'Beata colei che ha creduto' (Lc 1:45)," in *Marianum* 138 (1988): 161; B. Corsani, "Pneuma' nell'Evangelo di Luca," in *RstLetRel* 5 (1963): 229–255.

35. Pope John Paul II, *Redemptoris Mater*, 12. See also Pope John Paul II, *Dominum et Vivificantem*, 51; *Familiaris Consortio*, 86; *Redemptoris Custos*, 4.

36. Pope John Paul II, *Redemptoris Mater*, 12. See also Pope John Paul II, *Dominum et Vivificantem*, 51; *Familiaris Consortio*, 86; *Redemptoris Custos*, 4.

37. Pope John Paul II, *Redemptoris Mater*, 12. See also Pope John Paul II, *Familiaris Consortio*, 86; *Redemptoris Custos*, 4.

38. Pope John Paul II, *Dominum et Vivificantem*, 51. See also Pope John Paul II, *Familiaris Consortio*, 86; *Redemptoris Custos*, 4.

39. See also Pope John Paul II, *Redemptoris Custos*, 4; Paul Peeters, "*Dominum et Vivificantem*: The Conscience and the Heart," in *Communio* 15 (1988): 152; Jean Galot, "L'itinéraire de foi de Marie selon l'encyclique 'Redemptoris Mater,'" in *Marianum* 139 (1989): 39; Avery Dulles, "Mary at the Dawn of the New Millennium," in *America* 178, no. 3 (January 31, 1998): 18.

40. See also Pope John Paul II, *Redemptoris Custos*, 4; Johann G. Roten, "La Foi de Marie à la lumière de la théologie actuelle," in *La Foi de Marie Mère du Rédempteur*, Études Mariales, 52e session de la Société Française d'Études Mariales, Josselin, Bretagne, 1995, Paris: Médiaspaul, 1996, 196–199.

41. Pope John Paul II, *Redemptoris Mater*, 13. See also Pope John Paul II, *Fides et Ratio*, 108; *Familiaris Consortio*, 86.

42. Pope John Paul II, *Redemptoris Mater*, 13. See also Pope John Paul II, *Dominum et Vivificantem*, 51; *Fides et Ratio*, 108; *Catechesi Tradendae*, 73. The Pope exclaims in *Redemptionis Donum*, 17: "How obedient she [Mary] was at the moment of the Annunciation."

43. B. Buby, *Mary of Galilee*, Vol. III, New York: Alba House, 19. See also Avery Dulles, "Mary at the Dawn of the New Millennium," in *America* 178, no. 3 (January 31, 1998): 18.

44. See Gianfranco Ravasi, "'Beata colei che ha creduto' (Lc 1:45)," in *Marianum* 138 (1988): 172.

45. St. Irenaeus, *Expositio Doctrinae Apostolicae*, 33: Sch 62, 83–86; Pope John Paul II, *Redemptoris Mater*, 13, footnote 30; *Fides et Ratio*, 108; *Catechesi Tradendae*, 73; *Familiaris Consortio*, 22; Gianfranco Ravasi, "'Beata colei che ha creduto' (Lc 1:45)," in *Marianum* 138 (1988): 173.

46. One senses that Saint Irenaeus indirectly refers to the infancy narratives of Saint Matthew, whereas the Pope strictly stays with the beginning of Luke's Gospel.

47. Pope John Paul II, *Redemptoris Mater*, 13. See also Pope John Paul II, *Dominum et Vivificantem*, 51; *Fides et Ratio*, 108; *Familiaris Consortio*, 86.

48. Saint Thomas Aquinas, *Summa Theologiae*, II–II, 2, 9; Vatican I: DS, 3010; Pope John Paul II, *Redemptoris Mater*, 13. See also Pope John Paul II, *Dominum et Vivificantem*, 51; *Fides et Ratio*, 108; *Familiaris Consortio*, 86; Alejandro Martínez Sierra, "María estrella para el hombre que 'cae' y 'se levanta,'" in *Marianum* 139 (1989): 236.

49. Pope John Paul II, *Redemptoris Mater*, 13; *Lumen Gentium*, 56. See also Pope John Paul II, *Dominum et Vivificantem*, 51; *Fides et Ratio*, 108; *Catechesi Tradendae*, 73; *Familaris Consortio*, 86.

50. Pope John Paul II, *Redemptoris Mater*, 13; *Lumen Gentium*, 56; Luigi Gambero, "La spiritualità Mariana nella vita del cristiano alla luce della 'Redemptoris Mater,'" in *Marianum* 139 (1989): 246.

51. See also Pope John Paul II, *Dominum et Vivificantem*, 51; *Fides et Ratio*, 108; *Catechesi Tradendae*, 73.

52. Pope John Paul II, *Redemptoris Mater*, 13. See also Pope John Paul II, *Dominum et Vivificantem*, 51; *Fides et Ratio*, 108; *Catechesi Tradendae*, 73.

53. Pope John Paul II, *Redemptoris Mater*, 13; Heb 10:5–7; Luigi Gambero, "La spiritualità Mariana nella vita del cristiano alla luce della 'Redemptoris Mater,'" in *Marianum* 139 (1989): 247.

54. Pope John Paul II, *Redemptoris Mater*, 13. See also Pope John Paul II, *Fides et Ratio*, 108; *Catechesi Tradendae*, 73; Alejandro Martínez Sierra, "María estrella para el hombre que 'cae' y 'se levanta,'" in *Marianum* 139 (1989): 236.

55. Pope John Paul II, *Redemptoris Mater*, 13. See also Pope John Paul II, *Dominum et Vivificantem*, 51.

56. Pope John Paul II, *Redemptoris Mater*, 13; *Lumen Gentium*, 56. See also Pope John Paul II, *Dives in Misericordia*, 9; *Dominum et Vivificantem*, 51; *Fides et Ratio*, 108; *Catechesi Tradendae*, 73.

57. Pope John Paul II, *Redemptoris Mater*, 13. See also Pope John Paul II, *Dominum et Vivificantem*, 51; *Fides et Ratio*, 108; *Catechesi Tradendae*, 73.

58. Pope John Paul II, *Redemptoris Mater*, 13. See also Pope John Paul II, *Dominum et Vivificantem*, 51; Luigi Gambero, "La spiritualità Mariana nella vita del cristiano alla luce della 'Redemptoris Mater,'" in *Marianum* 139 (1989): 246.

59. Pope John Paul II, *Redemptoris Mater*, 13. See also Pope John Paul II, *Fides et Ratio*, 108.

60. Luigi Gambero, "La spiritualità Mariana nella vita del cristiano alla luce della 'Redemptoris Mater,'" in *Marianum* 139 (1989): 247; Ibid., "Itinerario di fede della Madre del Signore," in *Seminarium* 38 (1987): 501–502.

61. See Antoine E. Nachef, *The Mystery of the Trinity in the Theological Thought of Pope John Paul II*, New York: Peter Lang Publishing, 1998.

62. Pope John Paul II, *Redemptoris Mater*, 14. See also Pope John Paul II, *Tertio Millennio Adveniente*, 48; Johann G. Roten, "La Foi de Marie à la lumière de la théologie actuelle," in *La Foi de Marie Mère du Rédempteur*, Études Mariales, 52e

session de la Société Française d'Études Mariales, Josselin, Bretagne, 1995, Paris: Médiaspaul, 1996, 196–199.

63. For the relationship between Mary's faith and the New Covenant, see John McHugh, "Mary's Fiat as the Commencement of the New Covenant," in *Marianum* 138 (1988): 133–137.

64. Pope John Paul II, *Redemptoris Mater*, 14. See also Pope John Paul II, *Tertio Millennio Adveniente*, 48.

65. Pope John Paul II, *Redemptoris Mater*, 14. See also Pope John Paul II, *Tertio Millennio Adveniente*, 48; Avery Dulles, "Mary at the Dawn of the New Millennium," in *America* 178, no. 3 (January 31, 1998): 18.

66. See also Pope John Paul II, *Redemptoris Mater*, 1, footnote 2; *Catechesi Tradendae*, 73; *Tertio Millennio Adveniente*, 48.

67. Pope John Paul II, *Redemptoris Mater*, 14. See also Pope John Paul II, *Tertio Millennio Adveniente*, 48.

68. See Salvador Muñoz Iglesias, "La fe de María y la fe de Abraham," in *Marianum* 138 (1988): 178, 180.

69. Pope John Paul II, *Redemptoris Mater*, 14. See also Pope John Paul II, *Dominum et Vivificantem*, 51; *Fides et Ratio*, 108; *Catechesi Tradendae*, 73; *Tertio Millennio Adveniente*, 48.

70. Pope John Paul II, *Redemptoris Mater*, 14. See also Pope John Paul II, *Tertio Millennio Adveniente*, 48.

71. Pope John Paul II, *Redemptoris Mater*, 14; The First Vatican Ecumenical Council, Session III (24 April 1870). Dogmatic Constitution *De Fide Catholica*, chapter 3. See also Pope John Paul II, *Dominum et Vivificantem*, 51; *Fides et Ratio*, 108; *Catechesi Tradendae*, 73; *Tertio Millennio Adveniente*, 48.

72. Pope John Paul II, *Redemptoris Mater*, 14. See also Pope John Paul II, *Fides et Ratio*, 108; *Catechesi Tradendae*, 73; *Tertio Millennio Adveniente*, 48; Luigi Gambero, "La spiritualità Mariana nella vita del cristiano alla luce della 'Redemptoris Mater,'" in *Marianum* 139 (1989): 248.

73. Pope John Paul II, *Redemptoris Mater*, 15; Lk 1:32–33; Salvador Muñoz Iglesias, "La fe de María y la fe de Abraham," in *Marianum* 138 (1988): 178; Avery Dulles, "Mary at the Dawn of the New Millennium," in *America* 178, no. 3 (January 31, 1998): 18.

74. Pope John Paul II, *Redemptoris Mater*, 8; Salvador Muñoz Iglesias, "La fe de María y la fe de Abraham," in *Marianum* 138 (1988): 178; Avery Dulles, "Mary at the Dawn of the New Millennium," in *America* 178, no. 3 (January 31, 1998): 18.

75. Pope John Paul II, *Redemptoris Mater*, 15; Salvador Muñoz Iglesias, "La fe de María y la fe de Abraham," in *Marianum* 138 (1988): 178; Avery Dulles, "Mary at the Dawn of the New Millennium," in *America* 178, no. 3 (January 31, 1998): 18.

76. Pope John Paul II, *Redemptoris Mater*, 15.

77. For John Paul II's theology on Jesus' presentation to the Temple see Alberto Valentini, "Il secondo annuncio a Maria" (RM 16), in *Marianum* 138 (1988): 290–322.

78. See also Pope John Paul II, *Evangelium Vitae*, 103; *Letter of the Pope to Children in the Year of the Family*, Boston: Pauline Books & Media, 1994, 6–7.

79. Pope John Paul II, *Redemptoris Mater*, 16; *Evangelium Vitae*, 103; Holy Thursday Letter of John Paul II, *Behold your Mother*, 1988, 2; *Letter of the Pope to Children in the Year of the Family*, Boston: Pauline Books & Media, 1994, 6–7.

80. See Pope John Paul II, *Redemptoris Mater*, 16; *Evangelium Vitae*, 103; Holy Thursday Letter of John Paul II, *Behold your Mother*, 1988, 2; *Letter of the Pope to Children in the Year of the Family*, Boston: Pauline Books & Media, 1994, 6–7; Henri Marie Manteau-Bonamy, "Marie et le Saint Esprit dans l'encyclique 'Redemptoris Mater,'" in *Marianum* 139 (1989): 68–81.

81. See Antoine E. Nachef, *The Mystery of the Trinity in the Theological Thought of Pope John Paul II*, New York: Peter Lang Publishing, 1998.

82. Pope John Paul II, *Redemptoris Mater*, 16. See also Pope John Paul II, *Evangelium Vitae*, 103; Holy Thursday Letter of John Paul II, *Behold your Mother*, 1988, 2.

83. Pope John Paul II, *Redemptoris Mater*, 16. See also Pope John Paul II, *Evangelium Vitae*, 103; Holy Thursday Letter of John Paul II, *Behold your Mother*, 1988, 2; *Letter of the Pope to Children in the Year of the Family*, Boston: Pauline Books & Media, 1994, 6–7.

84. Pope John Paul II, *Redemptoris Mater*, 16.

85. Pope John Paul II, *Redemptoris Mater*, 14. See also Pope John Paul II, *Evangelium Vitae*, 103; Holy Thursday Letter of John Paul II, *Behold your Mother*, 1988, 2; *Letter of the Pope to Children in the Year of the Family*, Boston: Pauline Books & Media, 1994, 6–7.

86. Pope John Paul II, *Redemptoris Mater*, 16. See also Pope John Paul II, *Evangelium Vitae*, 103; Holy Thursday Letter of John Paul II, *Behold your Mother*, 1988, 2; *Letter of the Pope to Children in the Year of the Family*, Boston: Pauline Books & Media, 1994, 6–7.

87. Pope John Paul II, *Redemptoris Mater*, 16; Holy Thursday Letter of John Paul II, *Behold your Mother*, 1988, 2; Salvador Muñoz Iglesias, "La fe de María y la fe de Abraham," in *Marianum* 138 (1988): 178.

88. See Saint Basil the Great, *Epist.* 260:9; Patrologia Graeca 32: 968 A; Antoine Nachef, Mary: "Virgin Mother in the Theological Thought of Saint Basil the Great, Saint Gregory Nazianzen, and Saint Gregory of Nyssa," Dayton, Ohio: Diss. International Marian Research Institute, Fairview Park: Anderson Print & Copy, 1997, 54–55.

89. See Johann G. Roten, "La Foi de Marie à la lumière de la théologie actuelle," in *La Foi de Marie Mère du Rédempteur*, Études Mariales, 52e session de la Société Française d'Études Mariales, Josselin, Bretagne, 1995, Paris: Médiaspaul, 1996, 196–199.

90. Pope John Paul II, *Redemptoris Mater*, 14. See also Pope John Paul II, *Dominum et Vivificantem*, 16; *Evangelium Vitae*, 103; *Letter of the Pope to Children in the Year of the Family*, Boston: Pauline Books & Media, 1994, 6–7.

91. See also Pope John Paul II, *Dominum et Vivificantem*, 16; *Evangelium Vitae*, 103; Holy Thursday Letter of John Paul II, *Behold your Mother*, 1988, 2; *Letter of the Pope to Children in the Year of the Family*, Boston: Pauline Books & Media, 1994, 6–7.

92. Pope John Paul II, *Redemptoris Mater*, 17. See also Pope John Paul II, *Dominum et Vivificantem*, 16; *Catechesi Tradendae*, 73; *Letter to Families from Pope John Paul II*, 2; Luigi Gambero, "La spiritualità Mariana nella vita del cristiano alla luce della 'Redemptoris Mater,'" in *Marianum* 139 (1989): 248–249.

93. Gianfranco Ravasi, "'Beata colei che ha creduto' (Lc 1:45)," in *Marianum* 138 (1988): 175. See also Luigi Sartori, "'Storia della salvezza' e 'Storia dell'umanità' nell'enciclica 'Redemptoris Mater,'" in *Marianum* 139 (1989): 28.

94. Pope John Paul II, *Redemptoris Mater*, 17. See also Pope John Paul II, *Catechesi Tradendae*, 73; *Letter to Families from Pope John Paul II*, 1994, 2; Jean Galot, "L'itinéraire de foi de Marie selon l'encyclique 'Redemptoris Mater,'" in *Marianum* 139 (1989): 37.

95. Pope John Paul II, *Redemptoris Mater*, 17. See also Pope John Paul II, *Dominum et Vivificantem*, 51; *Letter to Families from Pope John Paul II*, 1994, 2.

96. Pope John Paul II, *Redemptoris Mater*, 17. See also Pope John Paul II, *Catechesi Tradendae*, 73; *Letter to Families from Pope John Paul II*, 1994, 2.

97. See also Pope John Paul II, *Dominum et Vivificantem*, 16; *Catechesi Tradendae*, 73.

98. See Antoine E. Nachef, *The Mystery of the Trinity in the Theological Thought of Pope John Paul II*. New York: Peter Lang Publishing, 1998, chapter 1.

99. See Jean Galot, "L'itinéraire de foi de Marie selon l'encyclique 'Redemptoris Mater,'" in *Marianum* 139 (1989): 36–37.

100. Pope John Paul II, *Redemptoris Mater*, 17. See also Pope John Paul II, *Catechesi Tradendae*, 73; *Letter to Families from Pope John Paul II*, 1994, 2.

101. Pope John Paul II, *Redemptoris Mater*, 17. See also Pope John Paul II, *Dominum et Vivificantem*, 51; *Catechesi Tradendae*, 73; *Letter to Families from Pope John Paul II*, 1994, 2.

102. See also Johann G. Roten, "La Foi de Marie à la lumière de la théologie actuelle," in *La Foi de Marie Mère du Rédempteur*, Études Mariales, 52e session de la Société Française d'Études Mariales, Josselin, Bretagne, 1995, Paris: Médiaspaul, 1996, 193–199.

103. Pope John Paul II, *Redemptoris Mater*, 17. See also Pope John Paul II, *Dominum et Vivificantem*, 16 and 51; *Catechesi Tradendae*, 73; *Letter to Families from Pope John Paul II*, 1994, 2.

104. Pope John Paul II, *Redemptoris Mater*, 17. See also Pope John Paul II, *Dominum et Vivificantem*, 16; *Catechesi Tradendae*, 73; *Letter to Families from Pope John Paul II*, 1994, 2.

105. Pope John Paul II, *Redemptoris Mater*, 17. See also Pope John Paul II, *Dominum et Vivificantem*, 16; *Letter to Families from Pope John Paul II*, 1994, 2.

106. Pope John Paul II, *Redemptoris Mater*, 17. See also Pope John Paul II, *Dominum et Vivificantem*, 16; *Catechesi Tradendae*, 73; *Letter to Families from Pope John Paul II*, 1994, 2.

107. Pope John Paul II, *Redemptoris Mater*, 17. See also Pope John Paul II, *Dominum et Vivificantem*, 51; *Catechesi Tradendae*, 73; *Letter to Families from Pope John Paul II*, 1994, 2.

108. Pope John Paul II, *Redemptoris Mater*, 17. See also Pope John Paul II, *Catechesi Tradendae*, 73; *Letter to Families from Pope John Paul II*, 1994, 2.

109. Pope John Paul II, *Redemptoris Mater*, 17. See also Pope John Paul II, *Dominum et Vivificantem*, 51; *Catechesi Tradendae*, 73; *Letter to Families from Pope John Paul II*, 1994, 2; Salvador Muñoz Iglesias, "La fe de María y la fe de Abraham," in *Marianum* 138 (1988): 178.

110. See also Johann G. Roten, "La Foi de Marie à la lumière de la théologie actuelle," in *La Foi de Marie Mère du Rédempteur*, Études Mariales, 52e session de la Société Française d'Études Mariales, Josselin, Bretagne, 1995, Paris: Médiaspaul, 1996, 193–199.

111. See Pope John Paul II, *Fides et Ratio*, 49–51.

112. Pope John Paul II, *Fides et Ratio*, 51.

113. Pope John Paul II, *Fides et Ratio*, 50.

114. Pope John Paul II, *Fides et Ratio*, 52.

115. Pope John Paul II, *Fides et Ratio*, 52; Alejandro Martínez Sierra, "María estrella para el hombre que 'cae' y 'se levanta,'" in *Marianum* 139 (1989): 234.

116. Vatican I, *Dei Filius*, IV: *DS* 3015; Vatican II, *Gaudium et Spes*, 59; Pope John Paul II, *Fides et Ratio*, 53.

117. Vatican I, *Dei Filius*, IV, *DS* 3017; Pope John Paul II, *Fides et Ratio*, 53.

118. Pope John Paul II, *Fides et Ratio*, 49.

119. Pope John Paul II, *Redemptoris Mater*, 17. See also Pope John Paul II, *Dominum et Vivificantem*, 51; *Fides et Ratio*, 108; *Catechesi Tradendae*, 73; Paul Peeters, "*Dominum et Vivificantem*: The Conscience and the Heart," in *Communio* 15 (1988): 152; Alejandro Martínez Sierra, "María estrella para el hombre que 'cae' y 'se levanta,'" in *Marianum* 139 (1989): 234.

120. Pope John Paul II, *Redemptoris Mater*, 17. See also Pope John Paul II, *Dominum et Vivificantem*, 16 and 51; *Fides et Ratio*, 108; *Catechesi Tradendae*, 73.

121. See Pope John Paul II, *Fides et Ratio*, 46. See also Pope John Paul II, *Dominum et Vivificantem*, 51.

122. See also Pope John Paul II, *Dominum et Vivificantem*, 16; *Fides et Ratio*, 108; *Catechesi Tradendae*, 73; Paul Peeters, "*Dominum et Vivificantem*: The Conscience and the Heart," in *Communio* 15 (1988): 152.

123. Pope John Paul II, *Redemptoris Mater*, 17. See also Pope John Paul II, *Dominum et Vivificantem*, 16; *Fides et Ratio*, 108; *Catechesi Tradendae*, 73.

124. Pope John Paul II, *Redemptoris Mater*, 17. See also Pope John Paul II, *Dominum et Vivificantem*, 51; *Fides et Ratio*, 108; *Catechesi Tradendae*, 73.

125. Pope John Paul II, *Redemptoris Mater*, 17; Saint John of the Cross, *The Ascent of Mount Carmel*, Book II, Chapter 3, 4–6. See also Pope John Paul II, *Dominum et Vivificantem*, 51; *Fides et Ratio*, 108; *Catechesi Tradendae*, 73.

126. See also Pope John Paul II, *Dominum et Vivificantem*, 16; *Fides et Ratio*, 108; *Catechesi Tradendae*, 73.

127. Pope John Paul II, *Redemptoris Mater*, 17; Lk 2:48–50.

128. Pope John Paul II, *Redemptoris Mater*, 17; *Lumen Gentium*, 58. See also *Fides et Ratio*, 108; *Catechesi Tradendae*, 73; Holy Thursday Letter of John Paul II, *Behold your Mother*, 1988, 2; Luigi Gambero, "La spiritualità Mariana nella vita del cristiano alla luce della 'Redemptoris Mater,'" in *Marianum* 139 (1989): 248–249.

129. Salvador Muñoz Iglesias, "La fe de María y la fe de Abraham," in *Marianum* 138 (1988): 179; Alejandro Martínez Sierra, "María estrella para el hombre que 'cae' y 'se levanta,'" in *Marianum* 139 (1989): 237.

130. Pope John Paul II, *Redemptoris Mater*, 18. See also Pope John Paul II, *Dominum et Vivificantem*, 16; Holy Thursday Letter of John Paul II, *Behold your Mother*, 1988, 2.

131. Pope John Paul II, *Redemptoris Mater*, 18; Holy Thursday Letter of John Paul II, *Behold your Mother*, 1988, 2; *Tertio Millennio Adveniente*, 54.

132. Pope John Paul II, *Redemptoris Mater*, 18; *Lumen Gentium*, 58; *Dives in Misericordia*, 9; *Dominum et Vivificantem*, 16; Holy Thursday Letter of John Paul II, *Behold your Mother*, 1988, 2; *Tertio Millennio Adveniente*, 54; Gianfranco Ravasi, "'Beata colei che ha creduto' (Lc 1:45)," in *Marianum* 138 (1988): 175.

133. Pope John Paul II, *Redemptoris Mater*, 18. See also Pope John Paul II, *Dives in Misericordia*, 9; Holy Thursday Letter of John Paul II, *Behold your Mother*, 1988, 2; *Tertio Millennio Adveniente*, 54.

134. Pope John Paul II, *Redemptoris Mater*, 18; *Dei Verbum*, 5. See also Pope John Paul II, *Dives in Misericordia*, 9; Holy Thursday Letter of John Paul II, *Behold your Mother*, 1988, 2; *Tertio Millennio Adveniente*, 54.

135. Pope John Paul II, *Redemptoris Mater*, 18. See also Pope John Paul II, *Dominum et Vivificantem*, 16; Holy Thursday Letter of John Paul II, *Behold your Mother*, 1988, 2; *Tertio Millennio Adveniente*, 54.

136. See Antoine E. Nachef, *The Mystery of the Trinity in the Theological Thought of Pope John Paul II*, New York: Peter Lang Publishing, 1998.

137. Pope John Paul II, *Redemptoris Mater*, 18; *Lumen Gentium*, 58; Holy Thursday Letter of John Paul II, *Behold your Mother*, 1988, 2; *Tertio Millennio Adveniente*, 54.

138. See Henri Marie Manteau-Bonamy, "Marie et le Saint Esprit dans l'encyclique 'Redemptoris Mater,'" in *Marianum* 139 (1989): 68–81.

139. Pope John Paul II, *Redemptoris Mater*, 18; Phil 2:5–8. See also Pope John Paul II, *Dives in Misericordia*, 9; Holy Thursday Letter of John Paul II, *Behold your Mother*, 1988, 2; *Tertio Millennio Adveniente*, 54.

140. Pope John Paul II, *Redemptoris Mater*, 18. See also Pope John Paul II, *Dominum et Vivificantem*, 16; Holy Thursday Letter of John Paul II, *Behold your Mother*, 1988, 2; *Tertio Millennio Adveniente*, 54.

141. Pope John Paul II, *Redemptoris Mater*, 18. See also Pope John Paul II, *Dives in Misericordia*, 9; Holy Thursday Letter of John Paul II, *Behold your Mother*, 1988, 2; *Tertio Millennio Adveniente*, 54.

142. See Luis Díez Merino, "María junto a la Cruz (Jn 19, 25-27). Relectura evangélica de Juan Pablo II en la 'Redemptoris Mater,'" in *Marianum* 138 (1988): 366–396.

143. *Lumen Gentium*, 56; Pope John Paul II, *Redemptoris Mater*, 19; Holy Thursday Letter of John Paul II, *Behold your Mother*, 1988, 2; *Tertio Millennio Adveniente*, 54.

144. *Lumen Gentium*, 56; Holy Thursday Letter of John Paul II, *Behold your Mother*, 1988, 2; *Tertio Millennio Adveniente*, 54.

145. Pope John Paul II, *Redemptoris Mater*, 19. See also Pope John Paul II, *Dives in Misericordia*, 9; Holy Thursday Letter of John Paul II, *Behold your Mother*, 1988, 2; *Tertio Millennio Adveniente*, 54.

146. See Johann G. Roten, "La Foi de Marie à la lumière de la théologie actuelle," in *La Foi de Marie Mère du Rédempteur*, Études Mariales, 52e session de la Société Française d'Études Mariales, Josselin, Bretagne, 1995, Paris: Médiaspaul, 1996, 193–199.

147. Pope John Paul II, *Redemptoris Mater*, 19.

148. See Johann G. Roten, "La Foi de Marie à la lumière de la théologie actuelle," in *La Foi de Marie Mère du Rédempteur*, Études Mariales, 52e session de la Société Française d'Études Mariales, Josselin, Bretagne, 1995, Paris: Médiaspaul, 1996, 193–199.

149. Saint Irenaeus, *Adversus Haereses* III, 22, 4: Sch 211, 438–444; *Lumen Gentium*, 56; Pope John Paul II, *Redemptoris Mater*, 19.

150. See Saint Irenaeus, Ibid.; B. Buby, *Mary of Galilee*, Vol. III, New York: Alba House, 1997, 18–27.

151. See also Pope John Paul II, *Dominum et Vivificantem*, 51; Holy Thursday Letter of John Paul II, *Behold your Mother*, 1988, 2; Stefano de Fiores, "La Presenza di Maria nella vita della Chiesa alla luce dell'enciclica 'Redemptoris Mater,'" in *Marianum* 139 (1989): 114.

152. Pope John Paul II, *Redemptoris Mater*, 19. See also Pope John Paul II, *Dominum et Vivificantem*, 51; Holy Thursday Letter of John Paul II, *Behold your Mother*, 1988, 2; Stefano de Fiores, "La Presenza di Maria nella vita della Chiesa alla luce dell'enciclica 'Redemptoris Mater,'" in *Marianum* 139 (1989): 114–115.

153. Pope John Paul II, *Redemptoris Mater*, 19.

CHAPTER SIX

1. See Jn 14:6; 1 Tm 2:5-6; Heb 8:6; G. M. Roschini, *Maria santissima nella storia della salvezza*, II: *Le singolari funzioni di Maria*, Isola del Liri: Tipografia Editrice M. Pisani, 1969, 111-252.

2. See Salvatore M. Meo, "La mediazione materna' di Maria nell'enciclica Redemptoris Mater'," in *Marianum* 139 (1989): 145.

3. See S. M. Perrella, *I vota' e i consilia' dei Vescovi italiani sulla mariologia e sulla corredenzione nella fase antipreparatoria del Concilio Vaticano II*. Scripta Pontificiae Facultatis Theologicae Marianum', no. 47. Ed. Marianum, Roma, 1994, VII-XII, 238.

4. G. Iammarone, *Redenzione*. La Liberazione dell'uomo nel cristianesimo e nelle religioni universali. Cinisello Balsamo: Ed. San Paolo, 1995, 113-304; Salvatore M. Meo, "La mediazione materna' di Maria nell'enciclica Redemptoris Mater,'" in *Marianum* 139 (1989): 148; Emmanuele di Napoli, AAttualità di uno studio sul Vaticano II tra Mariologia e corredenzione," in *Marianum* 151 (1997): 169.

5. See S. M. Perrella, *I vota' e i consilia' dei Vescovi italiani sulla mariologia e sulla corredenzione nella fase antipreparatoria del Concilio Vaticano II*. Scripta Pontificiae Facultatis Theologicae Marianum', no. 47. Ed. Marianum, Roma, 1994, VII-XII, 223; Avery Dulles, "Mary at the Dawn of the New Millennium," in *America* 178, no. 3 (January 31, 1998): 13.

6. See M. O'Carroll, *Mary's Mediation: Vatican II and John Paul II*, in *Virgo Liber Verbi*. Miscellanea in onore di P. Giuseppe M. Besutti, O.S.M. A cura di Ignazio

M. Calabuig. Edizioni Marianum, Roma, 1991, 543-559; R. Laurentin, *Le problème de la mediation de Marie dnas son développement historique et son incidence aujourd'hui*, in AA. VV. *Il ruolo di Maria nell'oggi della Chiesa e del mondo*. Edizioni Marianum, Roma, 1979, 9-33.

7. See Salvatore M. Meo, "La mediazione materna' di Maria nell'enciclica Redemptoris Mater,'" in *Marianum* 139 (1989): 148.

8. See I. M. Calabuig, *Il culto alla beata Vergine: fondamenti teologici e collocazione nell'ambito del culto cristiano*, in AA.VV. *Aspetti della presenza di Maria nella chiesa in cammino verso il Duemila*. Ed. Marianum, Roma, 1989, 190-242.

9. See Angelo Amato, "Verso un altro dogma Mariano," in *Marianum* 149 (1996): 229-230; Avery Dulles, "Mary at the Dawn of the New Millennium," in *America* 178, no. 3 (January 31, 1998): 13.

10. J. Castellano Cervera, *La mediazione materna di Maria e il suo influsso sulla vita consacrata*, in AA. VV., *I religiosi sulle orme di Maria*, Libreria Editrice Vaticana, Città del Vaticano, 1987, 57.

11. Angelo Amato, "Verso un altro dogma Mariano," in *Marianum* 149 (1996): 232.

12. Arthur Burton Calkins, "Towards Another Marian Dogma? A Response to Father Angelo Amato, S.D.B." in *Marianum* 151 (1997): 166-167.

13. R. Laurentin, "Pétitions internationales pour une définition dogmatique de la médiation et la corédemption," in *Marianum* 150 (1996): 430-431.

14. R. Laurentin, "Pétitions internationales pour une définition dogmatique de la médiation et la corédemption," in *Marianum* 150 (1996): 432-433.

15. 1 Cor 3:9.

16. Avery Dulles, "Mary at the Dawn of the New Millennium," in *America* 178, no. 3 (January 31, 1998): 15.

17. See Pope John Paul II, *Redemptoris Missio*, 5; *Veritatis Splendor*, 120; R. Laurentin, "Pétitions internationales pour une définition dogmatique de la médiation et la corédemption," in *Marianum* 150 (1996): 429-438 and 440; Angelo Amato, "Verso un altro dogma Mariano," in *Marianum* 149 (1996): 232.

18. See Pope John Paul II, *Redemptor Hominis*, 22; *Dives in Misericordia*, 9 and 15; *Sollicitudo Rei Socialis*, 49; *Redemptoris Missio*, 5; *Centesimus Annus*, 62; *Veritatis Splendor*, 120; *Evangelium Vitae*, 103; *Fides et Ratio*, 108; *Dominicae Cenae*, 13; *Familiaris Consortio*, 86; *Letter of His Holiness John Paul II to the Bishops of the United States* (April 3, 1983), 4; *Salvifici Doloris*, 25; *Reconciliatio et Paenitentia*, 12; *Christifideles Laici*, 58; *Tertio Millennio Adveniente*, 43; *Letter to Families from Pope John Paul II*, 1994, 5.

19. See Salvatore M. Meo, "La mediazione materna' di Maria nell'enciclica Redemptoris Mater,'" in *Marianum* 139 (1989): 155-156.

20. Avery Dulles, "Mary at the Dawn of the New Millennium," in *America* 178, no. 3 (January 31, 1998): 15. See also Stefano de Fiores, "La Presenza di Maria nella vita della Chiesa alla luce dell'enciclica Redemptoris Mater,'" in *Marianum* 139 (1989): 130.

21. See Angelo Amato, "Verso un altro dogma Mariano," in *Marianum* 149 (1996): 231; Avery Dulles, "Mary at the Dawn of the New Millennium," in *America* 178, no. 3 (January 31, 1998): 13.

22. For the presence and role of Mary at Cana see Giorgio Zevini, "Presenza e ruolo di Maria alle nozze messianiche di Cana (Gv 2, 1-12) nella lettura di Giovanni Paolo II," in *Marianum*138 (1988): 347-365.

23. Pope John Paul II, *Redemptoris Mater*, 21. See also Pope John Paul II, *Sollicitudo Rei Socialis*, 49; *Letter to Families from Pope John Paul II*, 1994, 5; Salvatore M. Meo, "La mediazione materna' di Maria nell'enciclica Redemptoris Mater,'" in *Marianum* 139 (1989): 150-151.

24. Pope John Paul II, *Redemptoris Mater*, 21. See also Pope John Paul II, *Sollicitudo Rei Socialis*, 49; *Redemptoris Missio*, 92; *Veritatis Splendor*, 120; *Letter to Families from Pope John Paul II*, 1994, 5; Jean Galot, "L'itinéraire de foi de Marie selon l'encyclique Redemptoris Mater,'" in *Marianum* 139 (1989): 37.

25. Pope John Paul II, *Redemptoris Mater*, 21. See also Pope John Paul II, *Veritatis Splendor*, 120; *Fides et Ratio*, 108; *Salvifici Doloris*, 25; *Christifideles Laici*, 58; *Tertio Millennio Adveniente*, 43; *Letter to Families from Pope John Paul II*, 1994, 5; R. Laurentin, "Pétitions internationales pour une définition dogmatique de la médiation et la corédemption," in *Marianum* 150 (1996): 434.

26. See also Pope John Paul II, *Redemptoris Mater*, 38; *Sollicitudo Rei Socialis*, 49; *Redemptoris Missio*, 92; *Veritatis Splendor*, 120; *Evangelium Vitae*, 103; *Fides et Ratio*, 108; *Salvifici Doloris*, 25; *Christifideles Laici*, 58; *Tertio Millennio Adveniente*, 43; *Letter to Families from Pope John Paul II*, 1994, 5; Angelo Amato, "Verso un altro dogma Mariano," in *Marianum* 149 (1996): 231.

27. See also Pope John Paul II, *Redemptor Hominis*, 22; *Sollicitudo Rei Socialis*, 49; *Redemptoris Missio*, 92; *Centesimus Annus*, 62; *Veritatis Splendor*, 120; *Evangelium Vitae*, 103; *Fides et Ratio*, 108; *Letter of His Holiness John Paul II to the Bishops of the United States* (April 3, 1983), 4; *Salvifici Doloris*, 25; *Christifideles Laici*, 58; *Tertio Millennio Adveniente*, 43; *Letter to Families from Pope John Paul II*, 1994, 5; Angelo Amato, "Verso un altro dogma Mariano," in *Marianum* 149 (1996): 231.

28. Pope John Paul II, *Redemptoris Mater*, 21; Salvatore M. Meo, "La mediazione materna' di Maria nell'enciclica Redemptoris Mater,'" in *Marianum* 139 (1989): 150-151.

29. Pope John Paul II, *Redemptoris Mater*, 21. See also Pope John Paul II, *Sollicitudo Rei Socialis*, 49; *Veritatis Splendor*, 120.

30. Pope John Paul II, *Redemptoris Mater*, 21. See also Pope John Paul II, *Dives in Misericordia*, 15; *Sollicitudo Rei Socialis*, 49; *Redemptoris Missio*, 92; *Centesimus Annus*, 62; *Veritatis Splendor*, 120; *Christifideles Laici*, 58; *Tertio Millennio Adveniente*, 43; R. Laurentin, "Pétitions internationales pour une définition dogmatique de la médiation et la corédemption," in *Marianum* 150 (1996): 434.

31. Pope John Paul II, *Redemptoris Mater*, 21. See also Pope John Paul II, *Sollicitudo Rei Socialis*, 49; *Redemptoris Missio*, 92; *Veritatis Splendor*, 120; *Christifideles Laici*, 58; *Letter to Families from Pope John Paul II*, 1994, 5.

32. Pope John Paul II, *Redemptoris Mater*, 21. See also Pope John Paul II, *Dives in Misericordia*, 15; *Sollicitudo Rei Socialis*, 49; *Veritatis Splendor*, 120; *Christifideles Laici*, 58; *Tertio Millennio Adveniente*, 43; *Letter to Families from Pope John Paul II*, 1994, 5.

33. Pope John Paul II, *Redemptoris Mater*, 21. See also Pope John Paul II, *Sollicitudo Rei Socialis*, 49; *Redemptoris Missio*, 92; *Veritatis Splendor*, 120; *Evangelium Vitae*, 103; *Christifideles Laici*, 58; *Letter to Families from Pope John Paul II*, 1994, 5.

34. See also Pope John Paul II, *Centesimus Annus*, 62; *Veritatis Splendor*, 120; *Evangelium Vitae*, 103; *Fides et Ratio*, 108; *Christifideles Laici*, 58; *Tertio Millennio Adveniente*, 43; *Letter to Families from Pope John Paul II*, 1994, 5.

35. R. Laurentin, "Pétitions internationales pour une définition dogmatique de la médiation et la corédemption," in *Marianum* 150 (1996): 433.

36. In *Sollicitudo Rei Socialis*, 49, Pope John Paul II refers to Pope Paul VI who has already considered the "maternal concern" of Mary as a dimension that, being based on her maternal intervention in the historical ministry of Jesus, "extends to the personal and social aspects of people's life on earth." (Paul VI, *Marialis Cultus*, 37; Pope John Paul II, Homily at the Shrine of Our Lady of Zapopan, Mexico (January 30, 1979), 4: *AAS* 71 (1979), 230; *Centesimus Annus*, 62; *Veritatis Splendor*, 120; *Evangelium Vitae*, 103; *Salvifici Doloris*, 25; *Christifideles Laici*, 58; *Tertio Millennio Adveniente*, 43; *Letter to Families from Pope John Paul II*, 1994, 5.

37. Pope John Paul II, *Redemptoris Mater*, 21. See also Pope John Paul II, *Dives in Misericordia*, 15; *Sollicitudo Rei Socialis*, 49; *Redemptoris Missio*, 92; *Veritatis Splendor*, 120; *Christifideles Laici*, 58; *Letter to Families from Pope John Paul II*, 1994, 5.

38. Pope John Paul II, *Redemptoris Mater*, 21; *Christifideles Laici*, 58; *Letter to Families from Pope John Paul II*, 1994, 5.

39. See also Pope John Paul II, *Sollicitudo Rei Socialis*, 49; *Veritatis Splendor*, 120; *Christifideles Laici*, 58; *Letter to Families from Pope John Paul II*, 1994, 5.

40. Pope John Paul II, *Redemptoris Mater*, 21; *Veritatis Splendor*, 120; *Letter to Families from Pope John Paul II*, 1994, 5.

41. See also Pope John Paul II, *Dives in Misericordia*, 15; *Sollicitudo Rei Socialis*, 49; *Centesimus Annus*, 62; *Veritatis Splendor*, 120; *Evangelium Vitae*, 103; *Fides et Ratio*, 108; *Salvifici Doloris*, 25; *Christifideles Laici*, 58; *Tertio Millennio Adveniente*, 43; *Letter to Families from Pope John Paul II*, 1994, 5; Stefano de Fiores, "La Presenza di Maria nella vita della Chiesa alla luce dell'enciclica Redemptoris Mater,'" in *Marianum* 139 (1989): 130.

42. Pope John Paul II, *Redemptoris Mater*, 21. See also Pope John Paul II, *Dives in Misericordia*, 15; *Sollicitudo Rei Socialis*, 49; *Redemptoris Missio*, 92; *Centesimus Annus*, 62; *Veritatis Splendor*, 120; *Evangelium Vitae*, 103; *Fides et Ratio*, 108; *Salvifici Doloris*, 25; *Christifideles Laici*, 58; *Tertio Millennio Adveniente*, 43; *Letter to Families from Pope John Paul II*, 1994, 5.

43. See Johann G. Roten, "La Foi de Marie à la lumière de la théologie actuelle," in *La Foi de Marie Mère du Rédempteur*, Études Mariales, 52e session de la Société Française d'Études Mariales, Josselin, Bretagne, 1995, Paris: Médiaspaul, 1996, 193-199.

44. Pope John Paul II, *Redemptoris Mater*, 21. See also Pope John Paul II, *Dives in Misericordia*, 15; *Dominum et Vivificantem*, 16; *Sollicitudo Rei Socialis*, 49; *Centesimus Annus*, 62; *Veritatis Splendor*, 120; *Christifideles Laici*, 58; *Letter to Families from Pope John Paul II*, 1994, 5; Salvatore M. Meo, "La mediazione materna' di Maria nell'enciclica Redemptoris Mater,'" in *Marianum* 139 (1989): 150-151.

45. Pope John Paul II, *Redemptoris Mater*, 21. See also Pope John Paul II, *Centesimus Annus*, 62; *Veritatis Splendor*, 120; *Christifideles Laici*, 58; *Tertio Millennio Adveniente*, 43; *Letter to Families from Pope John Paul II*, 1994, 5.

46. Pope John Paul II, *Redemptoris Mater*, 21. See also Pope John Paul II, *Sollicitudo Rei Socialis*, 49; *Centesimus Annus*, 62; *Veritatis Splendor*, 120; *Evangelium Vitae*, 103; *Fides et Ratio*, 108; *Salvifici Doloris*, 25; *Christifideles Laici*, 58; *Tertio Millennio Adveniente*, 43; *Letter to Families from Pope John Paul II*, 1994, 5; Avery Dulles, "Mary at the Dawn of the New Millennium," in *America* 178, no. 3 (January 31, 1998): 13.

47. Pope John Paul II, *Redemptoris Mater*, 21. See also Pope John Paul II, *Dives in Misericordia*, 9 and 15; *Dominum et Vivificantem*, 16; *Veritatis Splendor*, 120; *Tertio Millennio Adveniente*, 43; *Letter to Families from Pope John Paul II*, 1994, 5.

48. Pope John Paul II, *Redemptoris Mater*, 22; *Lumen Gentium*, 61. See also Pope John Paul II, *Sollicitudo Rei Socialis*, 49; *Veritatis Splendor*, 120; *Evangelium Vitae*, 103; *Fides et Ratio*, 108; *Salvifici Doloris*, 25; *Christifideles Laici*, 58; *Tertio Millennio Adveniente*, 43; *Letter to Families from Pope John Paul II*, 1994, 5.

49. Pope John Paul II, *Redemptoris Mater*, 21. See also Pope John Paul II, *Centesimus Annus*, 62; *Veritatis Splendor*, 120; *Evangelium Vitae*, 103; *Fides et Ratio*, 108; *Salvifici Doloris*, 25; *Christifideles Laici*, 58; *Tertio Millennio Adveniente*, 43; *Letter to Families from Pope John Paul II*, 1994, 5.

50. See Angelo Amato, "Verso un altro dogma Mariano," in *Marianum* LVIII (1996): 232. See also Pope John Paul II, *Veritatis Splendor*, 120; *Evangelium Vitae*, 103; *Fides et Ratio*, 108; *Tertio Millennio Adveniente*, 43; *Letter to Families from Pope John Paul II*, 1994, 5.

51. Pope John Paul II, *Redemptoris Mater*, 22. See also Pope John Paul II, *Sollicitudo Rei Socialis*, 49; *Redemptoris Missio*, 92; *Veritatis Splendor*, 120; *Evangelium Vitae*, 103; *Fides et Ratio*, 108; *Salvifici Doloris*, 25; *Christifideles Laici*, 58; *Tertio Millennio Adveniente*, 43.

52. Pope John Paul II, *Redemptoris Mater*, 22. See also Pope John Paul II, *Dives in Misericordia*, 15; *Redemptoris Missio*, 92; *Veritatis Splendor*, 120; *Evangelium Vitae*, 103; *Fides et Ratio*, 108; *Salvifici Doloris*, 25; *Tertio Millennio Adveniente*, 43.

53. See also Pope John Paul II, *Dives in Misericordia*, 9 and 15; *Sollicitudo Rei Socialis*, 49; *Redemptoris Missio*, 5; *Veritatis Splendor*, 120; *Evangelium Vitae*, 103; *Tertio Millennio Adveniente*, 43.

54. See also Pope John Paul II, *Redemptoris Missio*, 5; *Veritatis Splendor*, 120; *Evangelium Vitae*, 103; *Fides et Ratio*, 108; *Tertio Millennio Adveniente*, 43.

55. See Luis Díez Merino, "María junto a la Cruz (Jn 19, 25-27). Relectura evangílica de Juan Pablo II en la Redemptoris Mater,'" in *Marianum* 138 (1988): 366-396.

56. See Pope John Paul II, *Dominum et Vivificantem*, 16; *Redemptoris Missio*, 5; *Centesimus Annus*, 62; *Familiaris Consortio*, 86; Holy Thursday Letter of John Paul II, *Behold your Mother*, 1988, 2; *Tertio Millennio Adveniente*, 43.

57. Pope John Paul II, *Dominum et Vivificantem*, 16. See also Pope John Paul II, *Familiaris Consortio*, 86; Holy Thursday Letter of John Paul II, *Behold your Mother*, 1988, 3; Jean Galot, "L'itinéraire de foi de Marie selon l'encyclique Redemptoris Mater,'" in *Marianum* 139 (1989): 37.

58. Pope John Paul II, *Dominum et Vivificantem*, 16. See also Pope John Paul II, *Familiaris Consortio*, 86; Holy Thursday Letter of John Paul II, *Behold your Mother*, 1988, 2.

59. Pope John Paul II, *Evangelium Vitae*, 103; Holy Thursday Letter of John Paul II, *Behold your Mother*, 1988, 3.

60. Pope John Paul II, *Evangelium Vitae*, 103; Holy Thursday Letter of John Paul II, *Behold your Mother*, 1988, 3; Jean Galot, "L'itinéraire de foi de Marie selon l'encyclique Redemptoris Mater,'" in *Marianum* 139 (1989): 37.

61. Pope John Paul II, *Redemptionis Donum*, 17; Holy Thursday Letter of John Paul II, *Behold your Mother*, 1988, 3.

62. Pope John Paul II, *Salvifici Doloris*, 25; Holy Thursday Letter of John Paul II, *Behold your Mother*, 1988, 2; Jean Galot, "L'itinéraire de foi de Marie selon l'encyclique Redemptoris Mater,'" in *Marianum* 139 (1989): 37.

63. Pope John Paul II, *Salvifici Doloris*, 25; Holy Thursday Letter of John Paul II, *Behold your Mother*, 1988, 2.

64. Col 1:24; Pope John Paul II, *Salvifici Doloris*, 25; Holy Thursday Letter of John Paul II, *Behold your Mother*, 1988, 3.

65. Pope John Paul II, *Salvifici Doloris*, 25; Holy Thursday Letter of John Paul II, *Behold your Mother*, 1988, 2.

66. Pope John Paul II, *Salvifici Doloris*, 25; Holy Thursday Letter of John Paul II, *Behold your Mother*, 1988, 2.

67. Pope John Paul II, *Salvifici Doloris*, 25; Holy Thursday Letter of John Paul II, *Behold your Mother*, 1988, 2; Jean Galot, "L'itinéraire de foi de Marie selon l'encyclique Redemptoris Mater,'" in *Marianum* 139 (1989): 37.

68. Pope John Paul II, *Salvifici Doloris*, 25; Holy Thursday Letter of John Paul II, *Behold your Mother*, 1988, 3.

69. Pope John Paul II, *Salvifici Doloris*, 26; Holy Thursday Letter of John Paul II, *Behold your Mother*, 1988, 3.

70. Pope John Paul II, *Salvifici Doloris*, 25; Holy Thursday Letter of John Paul II, *Behold your Mother*, 1988, 3.

71. Pope John Paul II, *Reconciliatio et Paenitentia*, 35; General Audience Address of December 7, 1983, 2; General Audience Address of January 4, 1984: *Insegnamenti*, VII, 1 (1984): 16–18.

72. Pope John Paul II, *Reconciliatio et Paenitentia*, 35.

73. Pope John Paul II, Holy Thursday Letter of John Paul II, *Behold your Mother*, 1988, 2.

74. Pope John Paul II, *Redemptoris Mater*, 23. See also Pope John Paul II, *Dives in Misericordia*, 9 and 15; *Evangelium Vitae*, 103; *Familiaris Consortio*, 86; Holy Thursday Letter of John Paul II, *Behold your Mother*, 1988, 2.

75. Pope John Paul II, *Redemptoris Mater*, 23; *Evangelium Vitae*, 103; Holy Thursday Letter of John Paul II, *Behold your Mother*, 1988, 3; Salvatore M. Meo, "La mediazione materna' di Maria nell'enciclica Redemptoris Mater,'" in *Marianum* 139 (1989): 150-151.

76. See Salvatore M. Meo, "La mediazione materna' di Maria nell'enciclica Redemptoris Mater,'" in *Marianum* 139 (1989): 151-152.

77. Pope John Paul II, *Redemptoris Mater*, 23. See also Pope John Paul II, *Dives in Misericordia*, 9 and 15; *Evangelium Vitae*, 103; Holy Thursday Letter of John Paul II, *Behold your Mother*, 1988, 3.

78. Pope John Paul II, *Redemptoris Mater*, 23. See also Pope John Paul II, *Dives in Misericordia*, 9 and 15; *Evangelium Vitae*, 103; Holy Thursday Letter of John Paul II, *Behold your Mother*, 1988, 3; Ugo Vanni, "La Donna della Genesi (3,15) e la Donna dell'Apocalisse (12,1) nella Redemptoris Mater,'" in *Marianum* 138 (1988): 425; Leo Scheffczyk, "Maria und die Kirche in der Enzyklika Redemptoris Mater,'" in *Marianum* 139 (1989): 90.

79. Salvatore M. Meo, "La mediazione materna' di Maria nell'enciclica Redemptoris Mater,'" in *Marianum* 139 (1989): 152.

80. Ugo Vanni, "La Donna della Genesi (3,15) e la Donna dell'Apocalisse (12,1) nella Redemptoris Mater,'" in *Marianum* 138 (1988): 425.

81. Pope John Paul II, *Redemptoris Mater*, 23. See also Pope John Paul II, *Dives in Misericordia*, 9and 15; *Evangelium Vitae*, 103; Holy Thursday Letter of John Paul II, *Behold your Mother*, 1988, 2.

82. Pope John Paul II, *Redemptoris Mater*, 23. See also Pope John Paul II, *Evangelium Vitae*, 103; Holy Thursday Letter of John Paul II, *Behold your Mother*, 1988, 2.

83. Pope John Paul II, *Redemptoris Missio*, 5. See also Pope John Paul II, *Evangelium Vitae*, 103; Holy Thursday Letter of John Paul II, *Behold your Mother*, 1988, 3.

84. Ugo Vanni, "La Donna della Genesi (3,15) e la Donna dell'Apocalisse (12,1) nella Redemptoris Mater,'" in *Marianum* 138 (1988): 426.

85. Pope John Paul II, *Redemptoris Mater*, 23; *Evangelium Vitae*, 103; Holy Thursday Letter of John Paul II, *Behold your Mother*, 1988, 2.

86. *Lumen Gentium*, 55; Pope John Paul II, *Redemptoris Mater*, 24. See also Pope John Paul II, *Evangelium Vitae*, 103; Holy Thursday Letter of John Paul II, *Behold your Mother*, 1988, 2; Ugo Vanni, "La Donna della Genesi (3,15) e la Donna dell'Apocalisse (12,1) nella Redemptoris Mater,'" in *Marianum* 138 (1988): 426.

87. See Salvatore M. Meo, "La mediazione materna' di Maria nell'enciclica Redemptoris Mater,'" in *Marianum* 139 (1989): 157-158.

88. Pope John Paul II, *Redemptoris Mater*, 24. See also Pope John Paul II, *Evangelium Vitae*, 103; Holy Thursday Letter of John Paul II, *Behold your Mother*, 1988, 3; Luigi Gambero, "La spiritualità Mariana nella vita del cristiano alla luce della Redemptoris Mater,'" in *Marianum* 139 (1989): 245; Ugo Vanni, ALa Donna della Genesi (3,15) e la Donna dell'Apocalisse (12,1) nella Redemptoris Mater,'" in *Marianum* 138 (1988): 426.

89. Ugo Vanni, "La Donna della Genesi (3,15) e la Donna dell'Apocalisse (12,1) nella Redemptoris Mater,'" in *Marianum* 138 (1988): 426.

90. Pope John Paul II, *Redemptoris Mater*, 24. See also Pope John Paul II, *Evangelium Vitae*, 103; Ugo Vanni, "La Donna della Genesi (3,15) e la Donna dell'Apocalisse (12,1) nella Redemptoris Mater,'" in *Marianum* 138 (1988): 426.

91. Rinaldo Fabris, "La presenza della Vergine nel Cenacolo (At 1, 14): l'interpretazione di Giovanni Paolo II," in *Marianum* 138 (1988): 398.

92. *Lumen Gentium*, 59; Pope John Paul II, *Redemptoris Mater*, 24. See also Pope John Paul II, *Dominum et Vivificantem*, 25 and 30.

93. See Pope John Paul II, *Dominum et Vivificantem*, 16, 25 and 30; Antoine E. Nachef, *The Mystery of the Trinity in the Theological Thought of Pope John Paul II*, New York: Peter Lang Publishing, 1998; Henri Marie Manteau-Bonamy, "Marie et le Saint Esprit dans l'encyclique Redemptoris Mater,'" in *Marianum* 139 (1989): 68-81.

94. Pope John Paul II, *Redemptoris Mater*, 24. See also Pope John Paul II, *Dominum et Vivificantem*, 25 and 30 ; Henri Marie Manteau-Bonamy, "Marie et le Saint Esprit dans l'encyclique Redemptoris Mater,'" in *Marianum* 139 (1989): 68-81.

95. Pope John Paul II, *Redemptoris Mater*, 24. See also Pope John Paul II, *Dominum et Vivificantem*, 25 and 30.

96. Pope John Paul II, *Redemptoris Mater*, 24.

97. Pope John Paul II, *Redemptoris Mater*, 24. See also Pope John Paul II, *Evangelium Vitae*, 103; Holy Thursday Letter of John Paul II, *Behold your Mother*, 1988, 2 and 3.

98. See also Pope John Paul II, *Dominum et Vivificantem*, 16, 25, and 30.

99. See also Pope John Paul II, *Redemptoris Missio*, 5; *Evangelium Vitae*, 103.

100. See also Pope John Paul II, *Redemptor Hominis*, 22; *Dominum et Vivificantem*, 25 and 30; *Sollicitudo Rei Socialis*, 49; *Redemptoris Missio*, 5; *Evangelium Vitae*, 103.

101. Pope John Paul II, *Tertio Millennio Adveniente*, 2; Saint Bernard; *In Laudibus Virginis Matris*, *Homilia* IV, 8, *Opera omnia*, Edit. Cisterc. (1966): 53; Davide M. Montagna, "Reminiscenze patristiche medioevali nell'enciclica Redemptoris Mater,'" in *Marianum* 139 (1989): 382.

102. Pope John Paul II, *Fides et Ratio*, 52. See also Pope John Paul II, *Tertio Millennio Adveniente*, 2.

103. Pope John Paul II, *Fides et Ratio*, 46. See also Pope John Paul II, *Tertio Millennio Adveniente*, 2.

104. See also Pope John Paul II, *Sollicitudo Rei Socialis*, 49; *Redemptoris Missio*, 5; *Evangelium Vitae*, 103; *Tertio Millennio Adveniente*, 2.

105. Pope John Paul II, *Redemptoris Mater*, 38. See also Pope John Paul II, *Redemptoris Missio*, 5; *Evangelium Vitae*, 103; R. Laurentin, "Pétitions internationales pour une définition dogmatique de la médiation et la corédemption," in *Marianum* 150 (1996): 432-433.

106. *Lumen Gentium*, 60; Pope John Paul II, *Redemptoris Mater*, 38. See also Pope John Paul II, *Sollicitudo Rei Socialis*, 49; *Redemptoris Missio*, 5; *Veritatis Splendor*, 120; *Evangelium Vitae*, 103. In *Tertio Millennio Adveniente*, 43, the Pope uses the same terminology: "The affirmation of the central place of Christ cannot therefore be separated from the recognition of the role played by his Most Holy Mother. Veneration of her, when properly understood, can in no way take away from the dignity and efficacy of Christ the one Mediator."

107. Pope John Paul II, *Redemptoris Mater*, 38. See also Pope John Paul II, *Sollicitudo Rei Socialis*, 49; *Veritatis Splendor*, 120; *Evangelium Vitae*, 103; *Tertio Millennio Adveniente*, 43.

108. See Salvatore M. Meo, "La mediazione materna' di Maria nell'enciclica Redemptoris Mater,'" in *Marianum* 139 (1989): 147.

109. See also Pope John Paul II, *Dominum et Vivificantem*, 25 and 30; *Sollicitudo Rei Socialis*, 49; *Evangelium Vitae*, 103.

110. See Salvatore M. Meo, "La mediazione materna' di Maria nell'enciclica Redemptoris Mater,'" in *Marianum* 139 (1989): 147.

111. Pope John Paul II, *Redemptoris Mater*, 38. See also Pope John Paul II, *Dominum et Vivificantem*, 16; *Tertio Millennio Adveniente*, 43; Salvatore M. Meo, "La mediazione materna' di Maria nell'enciclica Redemptoris Mater,'" in *Marianum* 139 (1989): 147.

112. Pope John Paul II, *Redemptoris Mater*, 38. See also Pope John Paul II, *Dominum et Vivificantem*, 16; *Sollicitudo Rei Socialis*, 49; *Tertio Millennio Adveniente*, 43.

113. See Salvatore M. Meo, "La mediazione materna' di Maria nell'enciclica Redemptoris Mater,'" in *Marianum* 139 (1989): 147-148.

114. See also Pope John Paul II, *Sollicitudo Rei Socialis*, 49; *Veritatis Splendor*, 120; *Tertio Millennio Adveniente*, 43.

115. Pope John Paul II, *Redemptoris Mater*, 38. See also Pope John Paul II, *Sollicitudo Rei Socialis*, 49; *Redemptoris Missio*, 5; *Centesimus Annus*, 62; *Veritatis Splendor*, 120; *Evangelium Vitae*, 103; *Tertio Millennio Adveniente*, 43.

116. Pope John Paul II, *Redemptoris Mater*, 38; *Veritatis Splendor*, 120; *Evangelium Vitae*, 103; *Tertio Millennio Adveniente*, 43; R. Laurentin, "Pétitions internationales pour une définition dogmatique de la médiation et la corédemption," in *Marianum* 150 (1996): 432-433.

117. Pope John Paul II, *Tertio Millennio Adveniente*, 2; R. Laurentin, "Pétitions internationales pour une définition dogmatique de la médiation et la corédemption," in *Marianum* 150 (1996): 432-433; Avery Dulles, "Mary at the Dawn of the New Millennium," in *America* 178, no. 3 (January 31, 1998): 13.

118. See also Pope John Paul II, *Veritatis Splendor*, 120; *Evangelium Vitae*, 103; R. Laurentin, "Pétitions internationales pour une définition dogmatique de la médiation et la corédemption," in *Marianum* 150 (1996): 432-433.

119. Pope John Paul II, *Redemptoris Mater*, 38. See also Pope John Paul II, *Veritatis Splendor*, 120; *Evangelium Vitae*, 103.

120. See Johann G. Roten, "La Foi de Marie à la lumière de la théologie actuelle," in *La Foi de Marie Mère du Rédempteur*, Études Mariales, 52e session de la Société Française d'Études Mariales, Josselin, Bretagne, 1995, Paris: Médiaspaul, 1996, 193-199.

121. Pope John Paul II, *Redemptoris Mater*, 39. See also Pope John Paul II, *Dominum et Vivificantem*, 16; R. Laurentin, "Pétitions internationales pour une définition dogmatique de la médiation et la corédemption," in *Marianum* 150 (1996): 432-433.

122. R. Laurentin, "Pétitions internationales pour une définition dogmatique de la médiation et la corédemption," in *Marianum* 150 (1996): 433.

123. Pope John Paul II, *Redemptoris Mater*, 39 ; Salvatore M. Meo, "La mediazione materna' di Maria nell'enciclica Redemptoris Mater,'" in *Marianum* 139 (1989): 149. In a parallel context, *Dominum et Vivificantem*, 16, reports the expression "(Mary) sensed this (the coming of the Holy Spirit as a result of Christ's cross) even more clearly, when she pondered in her heart the mysteries of the Messiah, with whom she was associated." See also *Veritatis Splendor*, 120.

124. Pope John Paul II, *Redemptoris Mater*, 38 ; Salvatore M. Meo, "La mediazione materna' di Maria nell'enciclica Redemptoris Mater,'" in *Marianum* 139 (1989): 149.

125. Pope John Paul II, *Redemptoris Mater*, 39. See also Pope John Paul II, *Dominum et Vivificantem*, 66 ; Salvatore M. Meo, "La mediazione materna' di Maria nell'enciclica Redemptoris Mater,'" in *Marianum* 139 (1989): 149.

126. Pope John Paul II, *Redemptoris Mater*, 39. See also Pope John Paul II, *Dominum et Vivificantem*, 66 ; Salvatore M. Meo, "La mediazione materna' di Maria nell'enciclica Redemptoris Mater,'" in *Marianum* 139 (1989): 149.

127. See T. Koehler, "Maria nei Primi Secoli," in *Fons Signatus* 10. Centro Mariano Chaminade, 1971, 62; Antoine E. Nachef, *Mary: Virgin Mother in the Theological Thought of Saint Basil the Great, Saint Gregory Nazianzen, and Saint Gregory of Nyssa*, diss. International Marian Research Institute, Dayton, Ohio, Fairview Park: Anderson Print & Copy, 1997, 167-168.

128. Pope John Paul II, *Redemptoris Mater*, 39. See also Pope John Paul II, *Dominum et Vivificantem*, 66; *Centesimus Annus*, 62.

129. Pope John Paul II, *Redemptoris Mater*, 39.

130. Pope John Paul II, *Redemptoris Mater*, 39. See also Pope John Paul II, *Dominum et Vivificantem*, 66; Salvatore M. Meo, "La mediazione materna' di Maria nell'enciclica Redemptoris Mater,'" in *Marianum* 139 (1989): 149.

131. Pope John Paul II, *Redemptoris Mater*, 39.

132. Pope John Paul II, *Redemptoris Mater*, 39. See also Pope John Paul II, *Sollicitudo Rei Socialis*, 48.

133. *Lumen Gentium*, 60; Pope John Paul II, *Redemptoris Mater*, 38. See also Pope John Paul II, *Sollicitudo Rei Socialis*, 49; *Veritatis Splendor*, 120.

134. Pope John Paul II, *Redemptoris Mater*, 39. See also Pope John Paul II, *Veritatis Splendor*, 120.

135. Pope John Paul II, *Redemptoris Mater*, 39. See also Pope John Paul II, *Sollicitudo Rei Socialis*, 49; *Evangelium Vitae*, 103.

136. Pope John Paul II, *Redemptoris Mater*, 39. See also Pope John Paul II, *Sollicitudo Rei Socialis*, 49; *Veritatis Splendor*, 120; *Evangelium Vitae*, 103.

137. Also *Dominum et Vivificantem*, 16, refers to the same terminology. Christ embraces the cross "together with his Mother," and Mary becomes the constant companion of Christ "with whom she was associated." See also Pope John Paul II, *Evangelium Vitae*, 103; Avery Dulles, "Mary at the Dawn of the New Millennium," in *America* 178, no. 3 (January 31, 1998): 10-13.

138. Pope John Paul II, *Redemptoris Mater*, 39. See also Pope John Paul II, *Sollicitudo Rei Socialis*, 49; *Evangelium Vitae*, 103; Avery Dulles, "Mary at the Dawn of the New Millennium," in *America* 178, no. 3 (January 31, 1998): 10-13.

139. See also Pope John Paul II, *Dominum et Vivificantem*, 16; *Evangelium Vitae*, 103; Avery Dulles, "Mary at the Dawn of the New Millennium," in *America* 178, no. 3 (January 31, 1998): 10-13.

140. Pope John Paul II, *Redemptoris Mater*, 39. See also Pope John Paul II, *Evangelium Vitae*, 103.

141. Pope John Paul II, *Redemptoris Mater*, 39. See also Pope John Paul II, *Evangelium Vitae*, 103; Avery Dulles, "Mary at the Dawn of the New Millennium," in *America* 178, no. 3 (January 31, 1998): 10-13.

142. Pope John Paul II, *Redemptoris Mater*, 39; Avery Dulles, "Mary at the Dawn of the New Millennium," in *America* 178, no. 3 (January 31, 1998): 10-13.

143. "Subordinate mediation" in reference to Christ is, in the opinion of Salvatore Meo, a new terminology. (See Salvatore M. Meo, "La mediazione materna' di Maria nell'enciclica Redemptoris Mater'," in *Marianum* 139 (1989): 149.)

144. Pope John Paul II, *Redemptoris Mater*, 39. See also Pope John Paul II, *Dominum et Vivificantem*, 16.

145. Pope John Paul II, *Redemptoris Mater*, 39. See also Pope John Paul II, *Veritatis Splendor*, 120; *Evangelium Vitae*, 103.

146. Avery Dulles, "Mary at the Dawn of the New Millennium," in *America* 178, no. 3 (January 31, 1998): 12.

147. See Emmanuele di Napoli, "Attualità di uno studio sul Vaticano II tra Mariologia e corredenzione," in *Marianum* 151 (1997): 170.

148. See R. Laurentin, "Pétitions internationales pour une définition dogmatique de la médiation et la corédemption," in *Marianum* 150 (1996): 437; Avery Dulles, "Mary at the Dawn of the New Millennium," in *America* 178, no. 3 (January 31, 1998): 12.

149. Avery Dulles, "Mary at the Dawn of the New Millennium," in *America* 178, no. 3 (January 31, 1998): 12.

150. Avery Dulles, "Mary at the Dawn of the New Millennium," in *America* 178, no. 3 (January 31, 1998): 12-13.

151. See Angelo Amato, "Verso un altro dogma Mariano," in *Marianum* 149 (1996): 230.

152. See also Pope John Paul II, *Sollicitudo Rei Socialis*, 49; *Redemptoris Missio*, 5 and 92; *Veritatis Splendor*, 120; *Salvifici Doloris*, 25; *Reconciliatio et Paenitentia*, 12; *Tertio Millennio Adveniente*, 43; *Letter to Families from Pope John Paul II*, 1994, 5.

153. R. Laurentin, "Pétitions internationales pour une définition dogmatique de la médiation et la corédemption," in *Marianum* 150 (1996): 435-436.

154. See Angelo Amato, "Verso un altro dogma Mariano," in *Marianum* 149 (1996): 230.

155. R. Laurentin, "Pétitions internationales pour une définition dogmatique de la médiation et la corédemption," in *Marianum* 150 (1996): 440; Ibid., "Esprit Saint et théologie mariale," in *Nouvelle Revue Théologique* 89 (1967): 26-30.

156. Avery Dulles, "Mary at the Dawn of the New Millennium," in *America* 178, no. 3 (January 31, 1998): 12.

157. Avery Dulles, "Mary at the Dawn of the New Millennium," in *America* 178, no. 3 (January 31, 1998): 12.

158. Pope John Paul II, *Redemptoris Mater*, 40; Salvatore M. Meo, "La mediazione materna' di Maria nell'enciclica Redemptoris Mater,'" in *Marianum* 139 (1989): 152-153.

159. Pope John Paul II, *Redemptoris Mater*, 40.

160. Pope John Paul II, *Redemptoris Mater*, 39; Salvatore M. Meo, "La mediazione materna' di Maria nell'enciclica Redemptoris Mater,'" in *Marianum* 139 (1989): 152-153.

161. Pope John Paul II, *Redemptoris Mater*, 39. See also Pope John Paul II, *Sollicitudo Rei Socialis*, 49; *Veritatis Splendor*, 120.

162. *Lumen Gentium*, 62; Pope John Paul II, *Redemptoris Mater*, 39. See also Pope John Paul II, *Sollicitudo Rei Socialis*, 49; *Veritatis Splendor*, 120.

163. Pope John Paul II, *Redemptoris Mater*, 40; Salvatore M. Meo, "La mediazione materna' di Maria nell'enciclica Redemptoris Mater.'" in *Marianum* 139 (1989): 152-153.

164. See also Pope John Paul II, *Veritatis Splendor*, 120.

165. Pope John Paul II, *Redemptoris Mater*, 41.

166. Pope John Paul II, *Redemptoris Mater*, 41. See also Pope John Paul II, *Sollicitudo Rei Socialis*, 49.

167. Pope John Paul II, *Redemptoris Mater*, 41.

168. Pope John Paul II, *Redemptoris Mater*, 41; *Lumen Gentium*, 53.

169. See also Pope John Paul II, *Sollicitudo Rei Socialis*, 49; Salvatore M. Meo, "La mediazione materna' di Maria nell'enciclica Redemptoris Mater,'" in *Marianum* 139 (1989): 153-154.

170. Pope John Paul II, *Redemptoris Mater*, 41; *Lumen Gentium*, 53. See also Pope John Paul II, *Sollicitudo Rei Socialis*, 49.

171. Pope John Paul II, *Redemptoris Mater*, 45; *Letter to Families from Pope John Paul II*, 1994, 5.

172. Pope John Paul II, *Redemptoris Mater*, 45. See also Pope John Paul II, *Dominum et Vivificantem*, 16; *Letter to Families from Pope John Paul II*, 1994, 5.

173. Pope John Paul II, *Redemptoris Mater*, 41. See also Pope John Paul II, *Sollicitudo Rei Socialis*, 49.

Bibliography

KAROL WOJTYLA

Wojtyla, Karol. *Abe Chrystus sie Nami Postugiwal*. Kraków: Wydawnictwo Znak, 1979.

———. *The Acting Person*. Trans. Andrzej Potocki. Holland: R. Reidel Publishing Company, 1979.

———. *Amore e Responsabilità*. Milan: Marietti, 1978.

———. *La Bottega Dell'orefice*. Vatican City: Libreria Editrice Vaticana, 1979.

———. *Collected Poems*. Trans. J. Peterkiewicz. New York: Random House, 1979.

———. *The Collected Plays and Writings on Theatre*. Berkely: University California Press, 1987.

———. *Czlowiek Droga Koscióla*. Rome: Fundacja Jana Pawla II-Osrodek Dokumentacji Pontyficatu, 1992.

———. *Czlowiek w Polu Odpowiedzialnosci*. Rzym-Lublin, Poland: Instytut Jana Pawla II, KUL, 1991.

———. *Easter Vigil and Other Poems*. Trans. Jerzy Peterkiewicz. London: Hutchinson and New York: Random House, 1979.

———. *Faith According to Saint John of the Cross*. San Francisco: Ignatius Press, 1981.

———. *La Fede della Chiesa*. Milano: Editzioni Ares, 1978.

———. *Fruitful and Responsible Love*. New York: Seabury, 1979.

———. *The Jeweler's Shop*. New York: Random House, 1980.

———. *Kazania: 1962–1978*. Kraków: Wydawnictwo Znak, 1979.

———. *Milosc i Odpowiedzialnosc*. Lublin, Poland: Wydawnictwo Towarzystwa Naukowego Katolickiego Uniwersytetu Lubelskiego, 1985.

———. *Obecnosc: Karol Wojtyla w Katolickim Uniwersytecie Lubleskim*. Lublin, Poland: Redakcja Wydawnictwo, KUL, 1989.

———. *Opere Letterarie: Poesie e Drammi*. Vatican City: Libreria Editrice Vaticana, 1993.

———. *Pietra di luce: Poesie*. Vatican City: Libreria Editrice Vaticana, 1979.

———. *Persona e atto*. Rome: Libreria Editrice Vaticana, 1982.

———. *Person: Subjekt und Gemeinschaft*. Der Streit um den Menschen. Kevelær: Butzon and Bercker, 1970.

———. "The Person: Subject and Community." *Review of Metaphysics* 33 (1979): 273–308.

————. *Poezje i Dramaty.* Kraków: Wydawnictwo Znak, 1987.

————. *Przemówienia i Wywiady w Radio Watykanskim.* Rome: Fundacja Jana Pawla II-Osrodek Dokumentacji Pontyficatu.

————. *Questio de Fide apud S. Johannem a Cruce* (1948). San Francisco: Ignatius Press, 1981.

————. *Segno di contraddizione.* Milan: Vita e Pensiero, 1977.

————. *Sign of Contradiction.* New York: Seabury Press, 1979.

————. "Slowo konkowe." *Analecta Cracoviesia* n. 5–6, (1973–1974): 243–263.

————. *Sources of Renewal: The Implementation of the Second Vatican Council.* San Francisco: Harper and Row, 1980.

————. "The Task of Christian Philosophy Today." *Proceedings of the American Catholic Philosophical Association* 53 (1979): 3–4.

————. *Wyklady Lubelski: Czlowiek i Moralnosc.* Lublin, Poland: Wydawnictwo Towarzystwa Naukowego Katolickiego Uniwersytetu Lubelskiego, 1986.

————. *Zagadnienie Wiary w Dzielach Sw. Jana od Krzyza.* Kraków: Wydawnictwo O. O. Karmelitów Bosych, 1990.

POPE JOHN PAUL II

John Paul II. *Address to Presidents of Catholic Colleges and Universities* (at Catholic University). (October 7, 1979): 163–167.

————. *Address to the General Assembly of the United Nations,* October 2,1980, 16–30.

————. *Address to the Youth of Paris.* (June 1, 1980), *L'Osservatore Romano* (English Edition), (June 16, 1980): 13.

————. *Affido a Te, O Maria.* Ed. Sergio Trassati and Arturo Mari. Bergamo: Editrice Velar, 1982.

————. *Africa: Apostolic Pilgrimage.* Boston: Saint Paul Editions, 1980.

————. *Africa: Land of Promise, Land of Hope.* Boston: Saint Paul Editions, 1982.

————. *Amantissima Providentia,* Apostolic Letter, 1980.

————. *The Apostles of the Slavs (Commemorating Saints Cyril and Methodius): Fourth Encyclical Letter, June 2, 1985.* Washington D.C.: Office for Publishing and Promotion Services. United States Catholic Conference, 1985.

————. *Augustinum Hipponensem.* August 28, 1986. Boston: Saint Paul Editions, 1986.

————. *Behold your Mother.* Holy Thursday Letter of John Paul II. Boston: Saint Paul Editions, 1988.

————. *Brazil: Journey in the Light of the Eucharist.* Boston: Saint Paul Editions, 1980.

————. Il Buon Pastore: *Scritti, Disorsi e Lettere Pastorali.* Trans. Elzbieta Cywiak and Renzo Panzone. Rome Edizioni Logos, 1978.

————. *Catechesi Tradendae. On Catechesis in Our Time.* Boston: Saint Paul Editions, 1979.

———. *Centesimus Annus (Commemorating the Centenary of Rerum Novarum by Leo XIII): Ninth Encyclical Letter, May 1, 1991.* Washington D.C.: Office for Publishing and Promotion Services, United States Catholic Conference, 1991.

———. "Charter of the Rights of the Family." *The Wanderer.* Vol. 116, no 52 (December 29, 1983): 6.

———. *Chiamati all'Amore: Itinerari di Santità.* Trans. Aldo Cantarini. Rome: Edizioni Logos, 1980.

———. "Congedo dall'*Anno Mariano.*" *Marianum* 50, no. 138 (1988): 108–109.

———. *Crossing the Threshold of Hope.* New York: Alfred A. Knopf, 1994.

———. *Dilecti Amici*, Apostolic Letter, 1985.

———. "A Discipline That Ennobles Human Love." *L'Osservatore Romano* (English Edition) Vol. 17, no. 36 (September 3, 1984): 1–6.

———. *Dives in Misericordia. On the Mercy of God.* Boston: Saint Paul Editions, 1980.

———. *Divini Amoris Scientia.* Apostolic Letter, 1997.

———. *Divinus Perfectionis Magister.* Apostolic Constitution, 1983.

———. *Dominum et Vivificantem. On the Holy Spirit in the Life of the Church and the World.* Boston: Saint Paul Editions, 1986.

———. *Dominicae Cenae.* The Mystery and Worship of the Eucharist. Boston, Daughters of Saint Paul, 1980.

———. *Ecclesia in Africa.* Apostolic Exhortation, 1995.

———. *Ecclesia in Urbe.* Apostolic Constitutions, 1998.

———. *Egreggiae Virtutis.* Apostolic Letter, 1980.

———. *The Encyclicals of John Paul II.* Edited with Introductions by Michael Miller, Indiana: Our Sunday Visitor, Inc., 1996.

———. *Euntes in Mundum.* Apostolic Letter, 1988.

———. *Evangelium Vitae.* Encyclical Letter, 1995.

———. *Ex Corde Ecclesiae.* Apostolic Constitution, 1990.

———. *Familiaris Consortio.* Apostolic Exhortation. *The Role of the Christian Family in the Modern World.* Boston: Daughters of Saint Paul, 1981.

———. *The Far East: Journey of Peace and Brotherhood.* Boston: Saint Paul Editions, 1981.

———. *Fidei Depositum.* Apostolic Constitution, 1992.

———. *Fifth Centenary of Evangelization of the New World.* Apostolic Letter, 1990.

———. *Fiftieth Anniversary of the Beginning of World War II.* Apostolic Letter, 1989.

———. *For the 1600th Anniversary of the First Council of Constantinople and the 1550th Anniversary of the Council of Ephesus.* Boston: Saint Paul Editions, 1981.

———. *Fourth Centenary of the Union of Brest.* Apostolic Letter, 1995.

———. *France: Message of Peace, Trust, Love and Faith.* Boston: Saint Paul Editions, 1980.

———. *The Freedom of Conscience and of Religion.* Boston: Saint Paul Editions, 1980.

———. *Germany: Pilgrimage of Unity and Peace.* Boston, Saint Paul Editions, 1981.

———. *Gift and Mystery. On the Fiftieth Anniversary of My Priestly Ordination.* Doubleday: New York, December, 1996.

———. *Insegnamenti di Giovanni Paolo II* (1978). Vatican City: Libreria Editrice Vaticana, 1979.

———. *Ireland "In the Footsteps of Saint Patrick."* Boston: Saint Paul Editions, 1979.

———. "Jesus Christ, Living Peace and Living Justice." (Homily of His Holiness at Mass in Yankee Stadium on October 2, 1979). *The Pope in America.* Saint Paul: Wanderer Press, 1979, 25–27.

———. *John Paul II in America: Talks Given on the Papal Tour, September 1987.* Compiled and Indexed by the Daughters of Saint Paul. Boston: Saint Paul Editions, 1987.

———. *John Paul II, Pilgrimage of Faith: The First Year of the New Pope and the Story of His Visit to the United States.* Edited and Illustrated by National Catholic News Service. New York: Seabury Press, 1979.

———. *Laborem Exercens. On Human Work.* Boston: Saint Paul Editions, 1981.

———. *Laborem Exercens. On Human Work. L'Osservatore Romano* (English Edition) Vol. 14, no. 38 (September 21, 1981): 1–13.

———. *Laetamur Magnopere.* Apostolic Letter, 1997.

———. *Les Grands Mystères.* Apostolic Letter, 1984.

———. *Letter of His Holiness John Paul II to the Bishops of the United States.* Boston: Saint Paul Editions, 1983.

———. *Letter of Pope John Paul II to Women.* Boston: Saint Paul Editions, 1995.

———. *Letter of the Pope to Children in the Year of the Family.* Boston: Saint Paul Editions, 1994.

———. *Letter to Families from Pope John Paul II.* 1994 Year of the Family. Boston: Saint Paul Editions, 1994.

———. "Letter to German Episcopal Conference, May 15, 1980." *L'Osservatore Romano* (June 30, 1980): 8–9.

———. *Love and Responsibility.* Trans. H. T. Willetts. New York: Farrar, Straus, Giroux, 1981.

———. *Magnum Matrimonii Sacramentum.* Apostolic Constitution, 1982.

———. *Maria: Omelie.* Preface by Stefan Cardinal Wyszynski. Trans. Janina Korzeniewska. Vatican City: Libreria Editrice Vaticana, 1982.

———. *Maximilian Kolbe, Patron de notre siècle difficile.* Paris: Lethielleux, 1982.

———. *Messages of John Paul II: Servant of Truth.* Boston: Saint Paul Editions, 1979.

———. *Message for World Peace Day.* London: Catholic Truth Society, 1979.

———. "Messagio al convegno di studio sull'enciclica *Redemptoris Mater.*" *Marianum* 50, no. 138 (1988): 63–66.

———. *Na Dalekim Wschodzie: Homilie i Przemówienia: 2 V 1984–11 V 1984.* Warsaw: Instytut Wydawniczy Pax, 1988.

———. *Negotiation: the Only Realistic Solution to the Continuing Threat of War. An Address to Men of Science.* Boston: Saint Paul Editions, 1982.

———. "Oratio pro Anno Mariali." *Marianum* 48, no. 136 (1986): 541–542.

———. *On the Christian Meaning of Human Suffering* [Salvifici Doloris]. Washington, D.C. Office of Publishing Services, 1984.

———. *On the Dignity and Vocation of Women* [Mulieris Dignitatem]. Boston: Saint Paul Editions, 1988.

———. *On the Dignity and Vocation of Women: Apostolic Letter, August 15, 1988.* Washington D.C.: Office for Publishing and Promotion Services. United States Catholic Conference, 1988.

———. *On the Holy Spirit in the Life of the Church and the World: Fifth Encyclical Letter, May 18, 1986.* Washington D.C.: Office for Publishing and Promotion Services. United States Catholic Conference, 1986.

———. *On Human Work: Third Encyclical Letter, September 14, 1981.* Washington D.C.: Office for Publishing and Promotion Services. United States Catholic Conference, 1981.

———. *On the Mercy of God: Second Encyclical Letter, November 30, 1980.* Washington D.C.: Office for Publishing and Promotion Services. United States Catholic Conference, 1980.

———. *On the Mystery and Worship of the Eucharist* [Dominicae Cenae]. Boston: Saint Paul Editions, 1980.

———. *On the Occasion of the Marian Year.* Letter May 22, 1988. Washington D.C.: Office of Publishing and Promotion Services, United States Catholic Conference, 1988.

———. *On the Permanent Validity of the Church's Missionary Mandate: Eighth Encyclical Letter, January 22, 1991.* Washington D.C.: Office of Publishing and Promotion Services, United States Catholic Conference, 1991.

———. *On the Role of Mary in the Mystery of Christ: Sixth Encyclical Letter, March 25, 1987.* Washington D.C.: Office of Publishing and Promotion Services, United States Catholic Conference, 1987.

———. *On Social Concerns: Seventh Encyclical Letter, December 30, 1987.* Washington D.C.: Office of Publishing and Promotion Services, United States Catholic Conference, 1987.

———. *Operosam Diem.* Apostolic Letter, 1996.

———. *Orientale Lumen, The Light of the East.* Apostolic Letter. Boston: Saint Paul Editions, 1995.

———. *Ordinatio Sacerdotalis. On Preserving Priestly Ordination to Men Alone.* Boston: Saint Paul Editions, 1994.

———. *L'Osservatore Romano,* weekly edition in English.

———. *Pastor Bonus.* Apostolic Constitution, 1988.

———. *Pastores Dabo Vobis. I Will Give You Shepherds.* Post-Synodal Apostolic Exhortation of John Paul II. Boston: Saint Paul Editions, 1992.

———. *Patres Ecclesiae.* Apostolic Letter, 1980.

———. "Peace Through Truth and Justice." (Address of His Holiness to the United Nations on October 2, 1979). *The Pope in America.* Saint Paul: Wanderer Press, 1979, 11–18.

———. *Per il Centenario dell'Opera di S. Pietro Apostolo.* Apostolic Letter, 1989.

———. *Per la Pace nel Golfo.* Vatican City: Libreria Editrice Vaticana, 1991.

———. *Pilgrim of Peace.* Washington D.C.: Office of Publishing and Promotion Services, United States Catholic Conference, 1979.

———. *Pilgrim to Poland.* Boston: Saint Paul Editions, 1979.

———. *Pope John Paul II in Argentina.* Boston: Saint Paul Editions, 1983.

———. *Pope John Paul II's Journey to America* [sound recording]. Cupertino, CA: Journey to America, 1979.

———. *Portugal: Message of Fatima.* Boston: Saint Paul Editions, 1983.

———. *Prayer of the Holy Father John Paul II on the Occasion of Holy Thursday, To All the Priests of the Church.* Boston: Saint Paul Editions, 1982.

———. *Predigten und Ansprachen von Papst Johannes Paul II bei seinem Pastoralbesuch in Deutschland sowie Begrüssungsworte und Reden, die an den Heiligen Vater gerichtet wurden.* Bonn: Sekretariat der Deutschen Bischofskonferenz, 1980.

———. *Pzemówienia, Homilie: Polska 2 VI 1979–10 VI 1979.* Kraków: Wydawnictwo Znak, 1979.

———. *Pzemówienia, Homilie 9 VI 1987–14 VI 1987.* Kraków: Wydawnictwo Znak, 1987.

———. *Pzemówienia, Homilie 16 VI 1983–22 VI 1983.* Kraków: Wydawnictwo Znak, 1984.

———. *Reconciliatio et Penitentia.* Boston: Saint Paul Editions, 1984.

———. *Redeemer of Man: First Encyclical Letter, March 4, 1979.* Washington D. C.: Office of Publishing and Promotion Services, United States Catholic Conference, 1979.

———. *The Redeemer of Man (Redemptor Hominis).* Boston: Saint Paul Editions, 1979.

———. *Redemptionis Donum (To Men and Women Religious on Their Consecration in the Light of the Mystery of the Redemption).* Boston: Saint Paul Editions, 1984.

———. *Redemptor Hominis (The Redeemer of Man).* L'Osservatore Romano (English Edition) Vol. 12, no. 12 (March 19, 1979): 3–14.

———. *Redemptoris Custos (On the Person and Mission of Saint Joseph in the Life of Christ and of the Church).* Boston: Saint Paul Editions, 1989.

———. *Redemptoris Mater (Mary: God's Yes to Man).* Introduction by Joseph Cardinal Ratzinger. Commentary by Hans Urs von Balthasar. San Francisco: Ignatius Press, 1988.

———. *Redemptoris Missio.* Encyclical Letter, 1990.

———. "Remain Faithful to the Universal Magisterium." (Address of His Holiness Delivered in Chicago to a Plenary Assembly of the Bishops of the United States on October 5, 1979). *The Pope in America.* Saint Paul: Wanderer Press, 1979, 53–58.

———. *Rutilans Agmen.* Apostolic Letter, 1979.

———. *Sacrae Disciplinae Leges (Apostolic Constitution for the Promulgation of the New Code of Canon Law).* Boston: Saint Paul Editions, 1983.

————. *Salvifici Doloris (The Christian Meaning of Human Suffering)*. *Origins* Vol. 13, no. 37 (February 23, 1984): 609, 610–624.

————. *Sanctorum Altrix*. Apostolic Letter, 1980.

————. *Sapientia Christiana* (April 15, 1979). English Text. Washington D.C.: Office of Publishing and Promotion Services, United States Catholic Conference, 1979.

————. *Sescentesima Anniversaria*. Apostolic Letter, 1987.

————. *Situation in Lebanon*. Apostolic Letter, 1989.

————. *Slavorum Apostoli (In Commemoration of the Eleventh Centenary of the Evangelizing Work of Saints Cyril and Methodius)*. Boston: Saint Paul Editions, 1985.

————. *The Splendor of Truth (Veritatis Splendor)*. Boston: Saint Paul Editions, 1993.

————. *Sollicitudo Rei Socialis*. Boston: Saint Paul Editions, 1987.

————. *Sources of Renewal: The Implementation of the Second Vatican Council*. Trans. P. S. Falla. San Francisco: Harper & Row, 1980.

————. *Talks of John Paul II*. Boston: Saint Paul Editions, 1979.

————. *Tertio Millennio Adveniente (Apostolic Letter on Preparation for the Jubilee of the Year 2000, November 10, 1994)*. Vatican City: Libreria Editrice Vaticana, 1994.

————. *Theology of the Body* (A series of sixty-three addresses at the Wednesday audiences.) *L'Osservatore Romano*. (English Edition). Vol. 12, nos. 37–40, 42, 44–48, 51–53, (September 10, 17, 24; October 1, 15, 29; November 5, 12, 19, 26; December 17, 24, 1979). Vol. 13, nos. 1–3, 5–8, 10–11, 13–14, 16–18, 20, 22–23, 25–26, 30–46, 49–50, 52, (January 7, 14, 21; February 4, 11, 18, 25; March 10, 17, 31; April 8, 21, 28; May 5, 19; June 2, 9, 23, 30; July 28; August 4, 11, 25; September 1, 8, 15, 22, 29; October 6, 13, 20, 27; November 3, 10, 17; December 9, 15, 29, 1980). Vol. 14, nos. 2–3, 5–7, 12, 14–19 (January 12, 19; February 2, 9, 16; March 23; April 6, 13, 21, 27; May 4, 11, 1981). This series can also be found in the two-volume series: *Original Unity of Man and Woman: Catechesis on the Book of Genesis* and *Blessed Are the Pure of Heart: Catechesis on the Sermon on the Mount and Writings of Saint Paul*. Boston: Saint Paul Editions, 1981, 1983.

————. *To the Youth of the World*. Boston: Saint Paul Editions, 1985.

————. *Three Hundred Fifty Years of Union of Uzhorod*. Apostolic Letter, 1996.

————. *Truth's Splendor: Tenth Encyclical Letter, August 6, 1993*. Washington D.C.: Office for Publishing and Promotion Services, United States Catholic Conference, 1993.

————. *Turkey–Ecumenical Pilgrimage*. Boston: Saint Paul Editions, 1980.

————. *Unity in the Work of Service: On the Occasion of His Second Pastoral Visit to the United States*. Washington D.C.: National Catholic Conference of Catholic Bishops, United States Catholic Conference, 1987.

————. *Universi Dominici Gregis*. Apostolic Constitution, 1996.

————. *U.S.A.–The Message of Justice, Peace and Love*. Boston: Saint Paul Editions, 1979.

————. *Ut Unum Sint*. Encyclical Letter, 1995.

————. *The Word Made Flesh: The Meaning of the Christmas Season.* Trans. Leslie Wearne, San Francisco: Harper & Row, 1985.

————. *Veritatis Splendor.* Encyclical Letter, 1993.

————. *Vicesimus Quintus Annus.* Apostolic Letter, 1988.

————. *Vita Consecrata (Consecrated Life).* Post-Synodal Apostolic Exhortation of the Holy Father John Paul II, Boston: Saint Paul Editions, 1996.

————. *Words of Certitude: Excerpts from His Talks and Writings as Bishop and Pope.* New York: Paulist Press, 1980.

————. *W Polsce: Przemówienia i Homilie 1979, 1983, 1987.* Warsaw: Instytut Wydawniczy Pax, 1991.

————. *W Indiach: Homilie i Przemówienia: 31–11 II 1986.* Warsaw: Instytut Wydawniczy Pax, 1990.

————. *W Weilkiej Brytanii 28 V 1982–2 VI 1982 i Argentynie 11 VI 1982–12 Vi 1982: Homilie i Przemówienia.* Warsaw: Instytut Wydawniczy Pax, 1989.

TRINITARIAN THEOLOGY

Biffi, Giacomo. "The Action of the Holy Spirit in the Church and the World," in *JohnPaul II: A Panorama of His Teachings.* Preface by Joseph Bernardin. New York: New York City Press, 1989, 38–47.

"Encyclical: *Dives in Misericordia.*" Editorial. *The Tablet* 234 (1980): 1210.

Every, George. "*Slavorum Apostoli*: A Note." *One in Christ* 21 (1985): 271–273.

Ferraro, Giuseppe. "The Pneumatological Dimension." *L'Osservatore Romano* 37 (1981): 5.

Galichon, Alain. "The First Encyclical." *L'Osservatore Romano* 33 (1979): 6–7.

Hamer, Jerome. "Presentation at the Press Conference for the Publication of *Dominum et Vivificantem.*" *L'Osservatore Romano* 23 (1986): 16–17.

Lapide, Pinchas. "*Dives in Misericordia*: An Encyclical for Christians and Jews." *Journal of Ecumenical Studies* 18 (1981): 140–142.

Martin, Ralph. "Rich in Mercy." *New Covenant* 11 (July 1981): 20–22.

McDermott, John M., Ed. *The Thought of Pope John Paul II.* Rome: Gregorian University, 1993.

Mondin, Battista. "A Monumental Comment on *Dives in Misericodia.*" *L'Osservatore Romano* 36 (1981): 5.

Morneau, Robert F. "*Dives in Misericordia*: Themes and Theses." *Review for Religious* 40 (1981): 670–683.

————. *Themes and Theses of Six Recent Papal Documents: A Commentary.* New York: Alba House, 1985, 111–135.

O'Carroll, Michael. "*Dominum et Vivificantem.*" in *Veni Creator Spiritus: A Theological Encyclopedia of the Holy Spirit.* Collegeville: Liturgical Press, 1990, 70–72.

O'Hare, Joseph. "Mercy Appears." *America* 143 (1980): 402.

Peeters, Paul L. "*Dominum et Vivificantem:* The Conscience and the Heart." *Communio: International Catholic Review* 15 (1988): 148–155.

Scola, Angelo. "'Claim' of Christ, 'Claim' of the World: On the Trinitarian Encyclicals of John Paul II." *Communio* 18 (1991): 331–332.

Various Authors. *John Paul II: A Panorama of His Teachings.* New York: New York City Press, 1989.

CHRISTOLOGY

"All Ways Lead to Man." Editorial. *America* 140 (1979): 249.

Baum, Gregory. "The First Papal Encyclical." *The Ecumenist* 17 (1979): 55–59.

Buttiglione, Rocco. *Il Pensiero Di Karol Wojtyla.* Milano: Editoriale Jaca Book, 1982.

———. *Karol Wojtyla: The Thought of the Man Who Became Pope John Paul II.* Grand Rapids: William B. Eerdmans Publishing Company, 1997.

Galichon, Alain. "The First Encyclical." *L'Osservatore Romano* 33 (1979): 6–7.

Gawronski, Raymond T. *"Redemptor Hominis"* in *The Thought of Pope John Paul II.* Edited by John M. McDermott. Rome: Gregorian University Press, 1993.

Honoré, Jean. "Christ the Redeemer, Core of John Paul II's Teaching," in *John Paul II: A Panorama of His Teachings.* Preface by Joseph Bernardin. New York: New York City Press, 1989.

McCabe, Herbert. "Manuals and Rule Books." *The Tablet* 247 (1993): 1583–1585.

———. *"Redemptor Hominis."* *New Blackfriars* 60 (1979): 146–147.

McDermott, John M., Ed. *The Thought of Pope John Paul II.* Rome: Gregorian University, 1993.

McDonagh, Edna. "*Redemptor Hominis* and Ireland." *The Furrow* 30 (1979): 624–640.

Morneau, Robert F. "*Redemptor Hominis*: Themes and Theses." *Review for Religious* 390 (1980): 247–262.

———. *Themes and Theses of Six Recent Papal Documents: A Commentary.* New York: Alba House, 1985, 111–135.

Richards, Michael. "Mankind Redeemed." *Clergy Review* 64 (1979): 194–195.

Saward, John. *Christ is the Answer: The Christ-Centered Teaching of Pope John Paul II.* Edinburgh: T & T Clark, 1995.

Schall, James. "*Redemptor Hominis*: The Amazement of God." *Homiletic and Pastoral Review* 80 (October 1979): 11–19.

Stevens, M. "*Redemptor Hominis*," in *The New Dictionary of Catholic Social Thought.* Edited by Judith A. Dwyer. Collegeville: Liturgical Press, 1994, 817–822.

Various Authors. *John Paul II: A Panorama of His Teachings.* New York: New York City Press, 1989.

Williams, George Huntston. *The Mind of John Paul II: Origins of His Thought and Action.* New York: Seabury Press, 1981.

MARIOLOGY

Aletti, Jean-Noel, S.J. "Une lecture de Ga 4, 4–6: Marie et la plénitude du temps." *Marianum* 50, no. 138 (1988): 408–421.

Allchin, Arthur MacDonal. "*Redemptoris Mater*: An Anglican Response." *One in Christ* 23 (1988): 324–329.

Amato, Angelo, S.D.B. "Verso Un Altro Dogma Mariano?" *Marianum* 58, no. 149 (1996): 229–232.

Aristide, Serra, O.S.M. "Le fonte bibliche della Redemptoris Mater,'" in *Redemptoris Mater: Contenuti e Prospettive Dottrinali e Pastorali*, 71–78. Rome: Pontificia Accademia Mariana Internazionale, 1988.

Beigel, George. *Faith and Social Justice in the Teaching of Pope John Paul II.* New York: Peter Lang Publishing, 1997.

Bertetto, Domenico, S.D.B., Ed. *Maria nel Magistero di Giovanni Paolo II; Primo Anno di Pontificato, 16 ottobre 1978–21 ottobre 1979.* Rome: Libreria Ateneo Salesiano, 1980.

———. *Maria nel Magistero di Giovanni Paolo II; Secondo Anno di Pontificato, 22 ottobre 1979–21 ottobre 1980.* Rome: Libreria Ateneo Salesiano, 1981.

———. *Maria nel Magistero di Giovanni Paolo II; Terzo Anno di Pontificato, 22 ottobre 1980–21 ottobre 1981.* Rome: Libreria Ateneo Salesiano, 1983.

———. *Maria nel Magistero di Giovanni Paolo II; Quarto Anno di Pontificato, 22 ottobre 1981–21 ottobre 1982.* Rome: Libreria Ateneo Salesiano, 1984.

———. *Maria nel Magistero di Giovanni Paolo II; Quinto Anno di Pontificato, 22 ottobre 1982–21 ottobre 1983.* Rome: Libreria Ateneo Salesiano, 1986.

———. *Maria nel Magistero di Giovanni Paolo II; Sesto Anno di Pontificato, 22 ottobre 1983–21 ottobre 1984.* Rome: Libreria Ateneo Salesiano, 1986.

Besutti, Guiseppe M., O.S.M. "La mediazione di Maria secondo gli studi di due Commissioni instituite da Pio XI." *Marianum* 47, no. 133 (1985): 37–41.

Bossard, Alphonse, S.M.M. "L'encyclique *Redemptoris Mater* et Saint Louis-Marie de Montfort." *Marianum* 51, no. 139 (1989): 261–268.

Calabuig, Ignazio M. O.S.M. "La Beata Vergine e la Vita Consacrata." *Marianum* 47, no. 133 (1985): 503–512.

———. "Un Dossier Inedito: gli studi di due Commissioni Pontificie sulla definibilità della Mediazione Universale di Maria." *Marianum* 47, no. 133 (1985): 7–11.

Calkins, Arthur Burton. "John Paul II's Consecration to the Immaculate Heart of Mary: Christological Foundation." *Miles Immaculatae 23* (1987): 88–116, 364–417.

———. "Towards Another Marian Dogma? A Response to Father Angelo Amato S.D.B." *Marianum* 59, no. 151 (1997): 159–167.

Catanese, Alfonso M., O.S.M. "L'antifona *Alma Redemptoris Mater* Il commento di Giovanni Paolo II." *Marianum* 51, no. 139 (1989): 359–378.

Collins, Mary Smalara. "All Generations Will Call Her Blessed." *U.S. Catholic* 58 (May 1993): 37–40.

"Conferencia Episcopal Española. Carta sobre el año mariano." *Marianum* 49, no. 137 (1987): 32–39.

Cortés, Rafael Casasnovas, S.D.B. "El capítulo octavo de la *Lumen gentium* en la carta-encíclica *Redemptoris Mater.*" *Marianum* 51, no. 139 (1989): 385–407.

Dadaglio, Luigi Cardinal and Mariano de Nicolo. "Consilium Primarium Anno Mariali Celebrando." *Marianum* 48, no. 136 (1986): 475–481.

———. "Consilium Primarium Anno Mariali Celebrando: Seconda lettera circolare ai Vescovi." *Marianum* 49, no. 137 (1987): 13–23.

———. "Consilium Primarium Anno Mariali Celebrando: Terza lettera circolare ai Vescovi." *Marianum* 49, no. 137 (1987): 24–31.

de Fiores, Stefano, S.M.M. "La presenza di Maria nella vita della Chiesa alla luce dell'enciclica *Redemptoris Mater.*" *Marianum* 51, no. 139 (1989): 110–144.

———. "La 'Redemptoris Mater' e la spiritualità mariana," in *Redemptoris Mater: Contenuti e Prospettive Dottrinali e Pastorali*, 55–70. Rome: Ponteficia Accademia Mariana Internazionale, 1988.

de la Potterie, Ignace, S.J. "*Maria piena di grazia* (RM7–11)." *Marianum* 50, no. 138 (1988): 113–132.

de Sainte-Marie, Joseph, O.C.D. "Réflexions sur un acte de consécration: Fatima, 13 mai 1982." *Marianum* 44, no. 128 (1982): 88–142.

di Napoli, Emmanuele. "Attualità di uno studio sul Vaticano II tra Mariologia e Corredenzione." *Marianum* 59, no. 151 (1997): 169–181.

"*Divini Scientia Amoris:* Apostolic Letter of Pope John Paul II." *Carmelite Digest* 13, no. 2 (Spring 1998): 4–23.

Donders, Joseph G., Ed. *John Paul II: The Encyclicals in Everyday Language.* Maryknoll, NY: Orbis, 1996.

Fabris, Rinaldo. "La presenza della Vergine nel Cenacolo (AT 1, 14): l'interpretazione di Giovanni Paolo II." *Marianum* 50, no. 138 (1988): 397–407.

Fehlner, Peter Damian, O.F.M. "Mulieris Dignitatem." *Miles Immaculatae* 25 (1989): 6–9.

Galot, Jean, S.I. "L'itinéraire de foi de Marie selon l'encyclique *Redemptoris Mater.*" *Marianum* 51, no. 139 (1989): 33–55.

———. "Prospettive Metodologiche e Dottrinali dell' Enciclica 'Redemptoris Mater,'" in *Redemptoris Mater: Contenuti e Prospettive Dottrinali e Pastorali*, 37–52. Rome: Ponteficia Accademia Mariana Internazionale, 1988.

Gambero, Luigi, S.M. "La spiritualità mariana nella vita del cristiano alla luce della *Redemptoris Mater.*" *Marianum* 51, no. 139 (1989): 239–260.

Gomez, Felipe. "A New Encyclical Letter: The Mother of the Redeemer." *East Asian Pastoral Review* 24 (1987): 108–118.

Heft, James L. "*Redemptoris Mater:* Mary's Journey of Faith." *Catechist* 21 (September 1987): 4–5.

Iglesias, Salvador Muñoz. "La fe de Maria y la fe de Abraham." *Marianum* 50, no. 138 (1988): 176–192.

Koehler, T. S.M. "Paul VI and Marian Devotion: An Ecclesial Renewal." *Marianum* 41, no. 123 (1979): 445–460.

Laurentin, René. "Pétitions internationales pour une définition dogmatique de la médiation et la corédemption." *Marianum* 58, no. 150 (1996): 429–446.

Little, Joyce A. "*Redemptoris Mater*: The Significance of Mary for Women." *Marian Studies 39* (1988): 136–158.

Llamas, E., O.C.D. "El primer principio de la mariología conciliar. El ayer y el hoy de este problema." *Marianum* 41, no. 123 (1979): 333–372.

López, Beteta P. *La missión del Espiritu Santo explicada por Juan Pablo II*. Madrid: Palabra, 1997.

Lourdusamy, D. Simon, Cardinal, and Miroslav S. Marusyn. "Congregatio pro Ecclesiis Orientalibus." *Marianum* 48, no. 136 (1986): 543–553.

Luis, Angel, C.SS.R. "La consegración a Maria en la vida y doctrina de Juan Pablo II." *Estudios Marianos 51* (1986): 77–112.

Luneau, René. *Le rêve de Compostelle*. Paris: Centurion, 1989.

Manteau-Bonamy, Henri-Marie, O.P. "Marie et la Saint Esprit dans l'encyclique *Redemptoris Mater*." *Marianum* 51, no. 139 (1989): 56–84.

Mayer, Paul Augustin Cardinal O.S.B. and Virgilio Noè. "Congregazione per il Culto Divino." *Marianum* 48, no. 136 (1986): 483–536.

McBrien, Richard P. *Lives of the Popes: The Pontiffs from Saint Peter to John Paul II*. New York: Harper San Francisco, 1997.

McDermott, John M., Ed. *The Thought of Pope John Paul II*. Rome: Gregorian University, 1993.

McHugh, John. "Mary's Fiat as the Commencement of the New Covenant." *Marianum* 50, no. 138 (1988): 133–137.

Meo, Salvatore, O.S.M. "La 'Mediazione materna' di Maria nella Enciclica '*Redemptoris Mater*,'" in *Redemptoris Mater: Contenuti e Prospettive Dottrinali e Pastorali*, 131–157. Rome: Pontificia Accademia Mariana Internazionale, 1988.

———. "La *mediazione materna* di Maria nell'enciclica *Redemptoris Mater*." *Marianum* 51, no. 139 (1989): 145–170.

Merino, Luis Diez. "María junto a la Cruz (Jn 19, 25–27): Relectura evangélica de Juan Pablo II en la *Redemptoris Mater*." *Marianum* 50, no. 138 (1988): 366–396.

Montagna, Davide M., O.S.M. "Reminiscenze patristiche medioevali" nell'enciclica *Redemptoris Mater*." *Marianum* 51, no. 139 (1989): 379–384.

Moralejo, G. Calvo, O.F.M. "XLVIII Semana de Estudios Marianos del la Sociedad Mariológica Española sobre *La Redemptoris Mater de Juan Pablo II. Análisis y perspectivas*." *Marianum* 56, no. 146 (1994): 466–472.

O'Connor, Edward D., C.S.C. "The Roots of Pope John Paul II's Devotion to Mary." *Marian Studies 39* (1988): 78–114.

Ossanna, Tullio F. "Maria e la Famiglia Nella Esortazione Apostolica *Familiaris Consorto*." *Marianum* 46, no. 128 (1982): 162–170.

Peretto, E. O.S.M. "Una ricerca storica sull'Ordine dei Servi di Maria dal 1233 al 1304." *Marianum* 41, no. 123 (1979): 541–587.

Perrella, Salvatore M., O.S.M. "Il parto verginale di Maria nel dibattito teologico contemporaneo (1962–1994)." *Marianum* 56, no. 146 (1994): 95–213.

"Premessa al Dossier di Documenti sull'Anno Mariano." *Marianum* 48, no. 136 (1986).

Ratzinger, Joseph Cardinal. Presentation at the Press Conference for the Publication of *Redemptoris Mater*. *L'Osservatore Romano* 13 (1987): 21, 23.

Ravasi, Gianfranco. "*Beata colei che ha creduto (LC 1, 45)*." *Marianum* 50, no. 138 (1988): 159–175.

Russo, G. *Evangelium vitae. Commento all'enciclica sulla bioetica.* Leumann: Editrice Elle Do Ci, 1995.

Sartori, Luigi. "*Storia della salvezza e storia dell'umanita* nell'enciclica *Redemptoris Mater.*" *Marianum* 51, no. 139 (1989): 19–32.

Scheffczyk, Leo. "Maria und die Kirche in der Enzyklika *Redemptoris Mater.*" *Marianum* 51, no. 139 (1989): 85–109.

Sierra, Alejandro Martínez, S.I. "María estrella para el hombre que *cae* y *se levanta.*" *Marianum* 51, no. 139 (1989): 171–187.

Solesmes, Benedictine Monks of., Eds. *Our Lady's Papal Teachings.* Trans. Daughters of Saint Paul. Boston: Saint Paul Editions, 1961.

Stahel, Thomas H. "*Redemptoris Mater.*" *America* 156 (1987): 353–354.

Suro, Roberto. "The Writing of *Sollicitudo Rei Socialis*: A Behind-the-Scenes Account." *Critic* 6 (May 1988): 13–18.

"Symposium on *Redemptoris Mater.* Report on the 1988 Convention." *Marian Studies* 39 (1988): 34–162.

Synder, Patrick. *La femme selon Jean-Paul II.* Fides, 1999.

Taylor, Richard J. "*Redemptoris Mater.* Pope John Paul II's Encyclical for the Marian Year: Some Reflections." *Priest & People* 2 (1988): 133–136.

Valentini, Alberto, S.M.M. "Il secondo annuncio a Maria (RM 16)." *Marianum* 50, no. 138 (1988): 290–322.

Vanni, Ugo, S.I. "La Donna della Genesi (3,15) e la Donna dell'Apocalisse (12, 1) nella *Redemptoris Mater.*" *Marianum* 50, no. 138 (1988): 422–435.

Winowska, Maria. "Le Culte Mariale en Poplogne," in *Maria: Études sur la Sainte Vierge*, Ed. Hubert du Manoir, S.J., 4: 684–709. Paris: Beauchesne et Ses Fils, 1956.

Zalecki, Marian, O.S.P. *Theology of a Marian Shrine: Our Lady of Czestochowa.* Marian Library Studies, no. 8. Dayton, OH: University of Dayton, 1976.

Zevini, Giorgio, S.D.B. "Presenza e ruolo di Maria alle nozze messianiche di Cana (GV 2, 1–12) nella lettura di Giovanni Paolo II." *Marianum* 50, no. 138.

ECCLESIOLOGY

Casaroli, Agostino. *Nella Chiesa per il Mondo: Omelie e Discorsi.* Milan: Rusconi Libri, 1987.

Del Rio, Domenico. *Memoria del Concilio.* Rome: Borla, 1985.

Dionne, Robert J. *The Papacy and the Church.* New York: Philosophical Library, 1987.

Dunn, Joseph. *No Lions in the Hierarchy.* Dublin: Columbia Press, 1994.

Evangelisti, David. *Joannes Paulus II: Light in the Church.* Vatican City: Libreria Editrice Vaticana, 1980.

Faulhaber, Robert William. "The Church and Culture—John Paul II's 'On Human Work.'" *Listening* 18 (1983): 103–118.

Guasco, Maurilo, Elio Guerriero and Francesco Traianiello. *La chiesa del Vaticano II.* Milan: San Paolo, 1994.

Kelly, George A. *Keeping the Church Catholic with John Paul II.* San Francisco: Ignatius Press, 1993.

Kilmartin, Edward J., *Church, Eucharist and Priesthood: A Theological Commentary on "The Mystery and Worship of the Most Holy Eucharist."* New York: Paulist Press, 1981.

McDermott, John M., Ed. *The Thought of Pope John Paul II.* Rome: Gregorian University, 1993.

Williams, George Huntston. *The Mind of John Paul II: Origins of His Thought and Action.* New York: Seabury Press, 1981.

MISSIOLOGY/EVANGELIZATION

Alazraki, Valentina. *Juan Pablo II El Viajero De Dios.* Mexico: Editorial Diana, 1990.

Balducci, Ernesto. *L'uomo planetario.* Milan: Camunia, 1985.

Bland, Joan, Ed. *The Pastoral Vision of John Paul II.* Chicago: Franciscan Herald Press, 1982.

Boyaxhiu, Mother Theresa. "Charity: The Soul of Missionary Activity." *L'Osservatore Romano* 14 (1991): 5.

Braaten, Carl E. "A Papal Letter on the Church's Missionary Mandate." *Dialog* 30 (1991): 182–183.

Burrows, William R., Ed. *Redemption and Dialogue: Reading "Redemptoris Missio" and Dialogue and Proclamation.* Maryknoll, NY: Orbis, 1993.

Caggiano, Pietro, Hilary Ngweno and M. Amin. *John Paul II in Kenya: Karibu Kenya Babe Mtakatifu.* Nairobi: Kenya Catholic Secretariat: Catholic Bookshop, 1980.

Colombo, Domenico. "Mission and the Kingdom." *L'Osservatore Romano* 17 (1991): 6.

De Montclos, Christine. *Les voyages de Jean Paul II.* Paris: Centurion, 1990.

Del Rio, Domenico. *Wojtyla: Un Pontificato Itinerante.* Bologne: Edizioni Dehoniane, 1994.

Del Rio, Domenico and Luigi Accatoli. *Wojtyla, The New Moses.* Milan: Mondadori, 1988.

———. *Wojtyla: Il nuovo Mosè.* Milan: Mondadori, 1988.

Dominic, A. Paul. "Mission before Mission: God's Mission Within Us." *Review for Religious* 52 (1992): 119–130.

Dorr, Donal. *"Redemptoris Missio:* Reflections on the Encyclical." *The Furrow* 42 (1991): 339–347.

D'Souza, Henry Sebastian. "Pope John Paul's New Challenge to Asia." *L'Osservatore Romano* 14 (1991): 6.

Every, George. *"Slavorum Apostoli:* A Note." *One in Christ* 21 (1985): 271–273.

Gheddo, Piero. "Gospel and Development." *L'Osservatore Romano* 11 (1991): 5.

Giardini, F. "Trinitarian Communion and Christian Mission in *Redemptoris Missio*." *Euntes* 47 (1994): 151–166.

John Paul II and the New Evangelization. Laurence J, McGulley Lecture by Avery Dulles, S. J. New York: Fordham University, 1991.

Kaiser, Philip M. *Journeying Far and Wide: A Political and Diplomatic Memoir*. New York: Charles Scribner and Sons, 1992.

Kalvoda, Josef. "The Cyrilo-Methodian Idea." *The Priest* 42 (February 1986): 18–19.

Kroeger, James H. "Rekindling Mission Enthusiasm." *The Priest* 48 (January 1992): 32–36.

Lopez-Gay, Jesus. "Spirit, Salvation and Mission." *L'Osservatore Romano* 9 (1991): 6.

Loya, Joseph A. "John Paul II's Encyclical *Slavorum Apostoli*: An Ecumenical Assessment." *Ecumenical Trends* 14 (1985): 167–168.

Major Addresses of Pope John Paul II on His Pastoral Visits to Various Countries. Boston: Daughters of Saint Paul.

McDermott, John M., Ed. *The Thought of Pope John Paul II*. Rome: Gregorian University, 1993.

Montclos, Christine de. *Les Voyages de Jean-Paul II*. Paris: Centurion, 1990.

Morneau, Robert F. *Themes and Theses of Six Recent Papal Documents: A Commentary*. New York: Alba House, 1985, 111–135.

Murphy, Francis Xavier. *The Pilgrim Pope, A Man for All People: John Paul II's Visits to the U.S.A., Mexico, Poland and Ireland*. South Hackensack, N J: Shepherd Press, 1979.

Neuhaus, Richard John. "Reviving the Missionary Mandate." *First Things* 16 (1991): 61–64.

O'Donnell, Timothy. "The Crisis of Faith and the Theology of Mission: A Reflection on *Redemptoris Missio*." *Faith and Reason* 18:3 (1992): 5–13.

Offredo, Jean. *Jean Paul II: L'aventurier de Dieu*. Paris: Carrere-Michel Lafon, 1986.

Saint John-Stevas, Norman. *Pope John Paul II: His Travels and Mission*. London, Boston: Faber and Faber, 1982.

Stransky, Thomas F. "From Vatican II to *Redemptoris Missio*: A Development in the Theology of Mission," in *The Good News of the Kingdom: Mission Theology for the Third Millennium*. Edited by Charles Van Engen, Dean S. Gillilan, and Paul E. Pierson. Maryknoll, NY: Orbis, 1993, 137–147.

Teissier, Henri. "Ours Is Not a Silent Witness to Muslims." *L'Osservatore Romano* 38 (1992): 7.

Tomko, Josef. Presentation at the Press Conference for the Publication of *Redemptoris Missio*. *L'Osservatore Romano* 4 (1991): 1, 21.

Ureña, Manuel. "The Missionary Impulse in the Church According to *Redemptoris Missio*." *Communio* 19 (1992): 94–102.

Zago, Marcello. "Church's Mission: Is It One or Many?" *L'Osservatore Romano* 9 (1991): 7, 9.

PHILOSOPHICAL ANTHROPOLOGY/MORALITY

Albacete, Lorenzo. "The Pope against Moralism and Legalism." *Anthropos* 10 (1994): 81–86.

Allsopp, Michael E. and John J. O'Keefe, Eds. *Veritatis Splendor: American Responses.* Kansas City: Sheed & Ward, 1995.

Anderson, Carl A. "*Veritatis Splendor* and the New Evangelization." *Anthropos* 10 (1994): 61–74.

———. "Gospel Offers Man the Opportunity to Regain His Authentic Personhood." *L'Osservatore Romano* 26 (1995): 10.

Basso, Domingo. "Encyclical is Meant Vigorously to Arouse the Conscience of Society." *L'Osservatore Romano* 36 (1995): 6.

Bennet, J. "Whatever the Consequences." *Analysis* 26 (1996): 83–102.

Bergonzoni, Luciano. *Sessualità E Amore: Catechesi di Papa Wojtyla Sulla Teologia Del Corpo.* Padova: Edizioni Messaggero Padova, 1981.

Bernardin, Joseph. *Consistent Ethic of Life.* Kansas City: Sheed & Ward, 1988.

Brugués, Jean-Louis. "Man Comes from Beyond Himself Since He Is Created in God's Image." *L'Osservatore Romano* 15 (1994): 10–11.

Buttiglione, Rocco. *Il Pensiero Di Karol Wojtyla.* Milano: Editoriale Jaca Book, 1982.

———. *Karol Wojtyla: The Thought of the Man Who Became Pope John Paul II.* Grand Rapids: William B. Eerdmans Publishing Company, 1997.

Caffarra, Carlo. "Death of God's Only Son Revealed Dignity and Value of All Human Life." *L'Osservatore Romano* 21 (1995): 10.

Cahill, Lisa Sowle. "The Lasting Contribution of *Veritatis Splendor.*" *Commonweal* 120 (1993): 15–16.

Callam, Daniel. "The Gospel of Life." *The Canadian Catholic Review* 13 (June 1995): 2–3.

Carrasco de Paula, Ignacio. "Church's Moral Teaching Shows Man the Way to Eternal Salvation." *L'Osservatore Romano* 32/33 (1995): 6.

Casini, Carlo. "When Sense of God Is Lost, There Is Tendency to Lose Sense of Man." *L'Osservatore Romano* 18 (1995): 6.

Cessario, Romanus. "Moral Absolutes in the Civilization of Love." *Crisis* 13 (May 1995): 18–23.

Chappelle, A. "Les enjeux de 'Veritatis Splendor.'" *Nouvelle Revue Theologique* (November-December 1993): 801–817.

———. "Encyclical's Clarifications Develop Catechism's Treatment of Morality." *L'Osservatore Romano* 18 (1994): 21–22.

Ciccione, Lino. "Acceptance of Contraception Leads to Promotion of Abortion." *L'Osservatore Romano* 24 (1995): 10.

Clément, Oliver. "Some Orthodox Reflections on Recent Papal Encyclicals." *One in Christ* 31 (1995): 237–280.

Cole, Basil. "The New Sins against Faith and *Evangelium Vitae.*" *Angelicum* 73 (1996): 3–19.

Colombo, Roberto. "Discoveries of Science Support Prohibition of Killing Human Embryo." *L'Osservatore Romano* 42 (1995): 10–11.

Cottier, Georges. "Distorted Concept of Subjectivity Contradicts Dignity of the Person." *L'Osservatore Romano* 43 (1995): 10.

———. "Morality of a Human Act Depends Primarily on Object Chosen by Will." *L'Osservatore Romano* 6 (1994): 11.

"A Coup for the Pope." Editorial. *The Tablet* 247 (1993): 1251–1252.

Curley, Terence P. "*Evangelium Vitae* and Our Culture." *The Priest* 51 (October 1995): 18–20.

Curran, Charles E. *The Living Tradition of Catholic Moral Theology.* Notre Dame, IN: University of Notre Dame Press, 1992.

Curran, Charles and Richard A. McCormick, S.J., Eds. *Readings in Moral Theology No. 5: Official Catholic Social Teachings.* New York: Paulist Press, 1986.

Devaux, Michaël. "The Truth of Love, The Lie of Death." *Communio* 23 (1996): 110–121.

Drane, J. F. "The Philosophical Roots of John Paul II." *America* (May 26, 1975): 426–429.

Dulles, Avery. "John Paul II and the Truth about Freedom." *First Things* 55 (1995): 36–41.

Durkin, Mary G. *Feast of Love: Pope John Paul II on Human Intimacy.* Chicago: Loyola University Press, 1983.

Ernst, Wilhelm. "Theology Is Essentially an Ecclesiastical Science That Must Serve the Church." *L'Osservatore Romano* 16 (1994): 6.

Fedoryka, Damian P. "The Gift of '*Veritatis Splendor.*'" *Social Justice Review* 85 (1994): 140–150.

Figueiredo, Fernando A. "Human Beings Are Merely Stewards and Not Lords Who Can Dispose of Life at Will." *L'Osservatore Romano* 46 (1995): 10.

Finnis, J. *Natural Law and Natural Rights.* Oxford: Oxford University Press, 1980.

Finnis, John. "Beyond the Encyclical." *The Tablet* 248 (1994): 9–10.

———. "Goods Are Meant for Everyone." *L'Osservatore Romano* 12 (1988): 11.

Finnis, John and Germain Grisez. "Negative Moral Precepts Protect the Dignity of the Human Person." *L'Osservatore Romano* 8 (1994): 6–7.

Ford, John C. and Germain Grisez. "Contraception and the Infallibility of the Ordinary Magisterium." *Theological Studies* Vol. 39, no. 2 (June 1978): 258–312.

Fraling, Bernhard. "Freedom Is Not Abolished by God's Law, But Is Protected and Promoted." *L'Osservatore Romano* 3 (1994): 9–10.

Fuchs, Joseph. "Good Acts and Good Persons." *The Tablet* 247 (1993): 1444–1445.

Greeley, Andrew M. *The Young Catholic Family: Religious Images and Marriage Fulfillment.* Chicago: Thomas More Press, 1980.

Grisez, G. "Against Consequentialism." *American Journal of Jurisprudence* 23 (1978).

———. *Contraception and the Natural Law.* Milwaukee: Bruce, 1964.

Grisez, G. and J. Boyle. *Life and Death with Liberty and Justice.* Notre Dame, IN: University of Notre Dame Press, 1979.

Grisez, Germain. "*Veritatis Splendor:* Revealed Truth Versus Dissent." *Homiletic and Pastoral Review* 94 (March 1994): 8–17.

Grootaers, Jan and Joseph A. Selling. *The 1980 Synod of Bishops on the Role of the Family.* Louvain: Leuven University Press, 1983.

Guggenheim, Antoine. "Liberté et verité selon K. Wojtyla." *Nouvelle Revue Theologique* 115 (March/April 1993): 194–210.

Haas, John. "'The Gospel of Life' and the Death of Penalty." *Crisis* 13 (July/August 1995): 20–23.

Hamlon, John S., *A Call to Families: Study Guide and Commentary for Familaris Consortio.* Foreword by Archbishop Edourd Gagnon. Collegeville: Human Life Center, Saint John's University, 1984.

Hauerwas, Stanley Martin. "*Veritatis Splendor* Is Unique." *Commonweal* 120 (1993): 16–18.

Hausman, Noëlle. "Moral Theologians Are Obliged to Teach Authentic Church Doctrine." *L'Osservatore Romano* 12 (1994): 8–17.

Healy, Jack. "*Veritatis Splendor* and the Human Person." *The Linacre Quarterly* 61 (November 1994): 16–36.

Hellman, John. "John Paul II and the Personalist Movement." *Cross Currents* XXX, 4 (1981).

Herranz, Gonzalo. "The Respect and Care of All Human Beings Is Part of Doctor's Charism." *L'Osservatore Romano* 30 (1995): 10.

Herranz, Julián. "Conversion of the Offender Is Goal of Canonical Sanction for Abortion." *L'Osservatore Romano* 25 (1995): 10.

Hickey, James A. "The Path to Spiritual Healing after Abortion Is through Reconciliation." *L'Osservatore Romano* 40 (1995): 6.

Hittinger, Russell. "Law and Liberty in *Veritatis Splendor.*" *Crisis* 13 (May 1995): 13–17.

———. "The Pope and the Theorists: The Oneness of Truth." *Crisis* 11 (December 1993): 31–36.

Hogan, Richard. "A Commentary on 'Familiaris Consortio.'" *The Wanderer.* Vol. 115, no. 10 (March 11, 1982): Supplement, 1–3.

———. "A Theology of the Body: A Commentary on the Audiences of Pope John Paul II from September 5, 1979 to May 6, 1981." *Fidelity* Vol. 1, no. 1 (December, 1981): 10–15, 24–27.

Hogan, Richard M. and John M. LeVoir. *Covenant of Love, Pope John Paul II on Sexuality, Marriage, and Family in the Modern World.* San Francisco: Ignatius Press, 1985.

Horkhiemer, M. "Materialismo e morale." *Teoria critica* Vol. I, 75.

Hume, Basil. "Introducing the Encyclical *Evangelium Vitae.*" *Briefing* 25 (April 1995): 3–8.

Janssens, Louis and Joseph A. Selling. "Theology and Proportionality: Thoughts about the Encyclical *Veritatis Splendor.*" *Bijdragen* 55 (1994): 118–132.

Johnstone, Brian V. "The Catholic Moral Tradition and *Veritatis Splendor.*" *Studia Moralia* 31 (1993): 283–306.

———. "The Encyclical *Veritatis Splendor.*" *The Ecumenical Review* 48 (1994): 345–350.

———. "Life in a Culture of Death." *Priests & People* 9 (November 1995): 409–413.

———. "Sin Is Healed by Grace, But Church Must Help Sinner Acknowledge Guilt." *L'Osservatore Romano* 5 (1994): 10.

Keating, James. "An Ethic of Prayerful Listening: *Veritatis Splendor.*" *Emmanuel* 100 (1994): 345–350.

Kennedy, Terrence. "'Fundamental Option' Can Radically Change as Result of Popular Acts." *L'Osservatore Romano* 5 (1994): 10.

Kiely, Bartholomew. "Humble Admission of Limitations Allows Person to Grow in Freedom." *L'Osservatore Romano* 4 (1994): 11.

Kmiec, Douglas W. "Behind the 'Empty Cloud' of Autonomous Reason–Or Why It Doesn't Matter if Natural Law of *Veritatis Splendor* Is Real Law.'" *The American Journal of Jurisprudence* 39 (1995): 37–46.

Krapiec, Mieczylaw. *I–Man.* Trans. Marie Lescoe, Andrew Woznicki, Theresa Sandok, et al. New Britain, CT.: Marial Publications, 1983.

Lake, Frank. *With Respect: A Doctor's Response to a Healing Pope.* London: Darton, Longman and Todd, 1982.

Lauer, Q. Review of *The Acting Person. America* 140 (1979) 337.

Law, Bernard Cardinal. *Christian Marriage–A Covenant of Love and Life.* Boston: Daughters of Saint Paul, 1998.

Lawler, Ronald D., O.F.M., Cap. *The Christian Personalism of John Paul II.* Chicago: Franciscan Herald Press. 1982

Lecomte, Bernard. *La Verité l'emportera toujours sur le mensonge.* Paris: J. C. Lattes, 1991.

Lescoe, F. *Philosophy Serving Contemporary Needs of the Church.* New Britain, CT: Marial Publications, 1979.

Letter to the Bishops of the Catholic Church on the Pastoral Care of Homosexual Persons. Vatican City: Congregation for the Doctrine of the Faith, 1986.

Lobato, Abelardo. "Technological Man Has Neglected Moral Sense That Underlies Culture." *L'Osservatore Romano* 20 (1995): 10–11.

López Trujillo, Alfonso. "Church Believes That Human Life, However Weak, Is Gift from God." *L'Osservatore Romano* 17 (1995): 9–10.

MacIntyre, Alsadair. "How Can We Learn What *Veritatis Splendor* Has To Teach?" *The Thomist* 58 (1994): 171–195.

Maestri, William F. *A Guide for the Study of "Veritatis Splendor."* Boston: Saint Paul Books and Media, 1993.

Marthaler, Berard L. "The Gospel of Life." *Living Light* 32 (Fall 1995): 6–45.

Martin, Francis X. "The Integrity of Christian Moral Activity: The First Letter of John and *Veritatis Splendor.*" *Communio* 21 (1994): 265–285.

Martini, Marco. "Gospel Is Basis for Action." *L'Osservatore Romano* 29 (1991): 9.

Maritain, J. "The End of Machiavellianism" *The Range of Reason.* London: G. Bles, 1953.

———. "Truth and Tolerance." *Commonweal* 66 (1957): 631–633.

May, William. *Sex, Marriage and Chastity: Reflection of a Catholic Layman, Spouse and Parent.* Chicago: Franciscan Herald Press, 1981.

———. "Evangelium Vitae." *Linacre Quarterly* (February 1995): 87–96.

———. "Moral Theologians and *Veritatis Splendor.*" *Homiletic and Pastoral Review* 95 (December 1994): 7–16.

———. "The Splendor of Accuracy: How Accurate?" *Anthropos* 10 (1994): 465–483.

———. "Theologians and Theologies in the Encyclical." *Anthropos* 10 (1994): 39–60.

McCartney, James J. *Unborn Persons: Pope John Paul II and the Abortion Debate.* New York: Peter Lang Publishing, 1987.

McCormick, Richard A. "Some Early Reactions to *Veritatis Splendor.*" *Theological Studies* 55 (1994): 481–506. Reply by John Neuhaus. "Moral Theology and Its Pique." *First Things* 49 (1985): 88–92.

———. "*Veritatis Splendor* and Moral Theology." *America* 169 (October 30, 1993): 8–11.

McDermott, John M., Ed. *The Thought of Pope John Paul II.* Rome: Gregorian University, 1993.

McHugh, James T. "Bishops Must See that the Church's Moral Doctrine Is Faithfully Taught." *L'Osservatore Romano* 17 (1994): 22.

McInerny, Ralph. "Locating Right and Wrong: *Veritatis Splendor* Versus Muddled Moralizing." *Crisis* 11 (December 1993): 37–40.

McQuillen, Michael P. "The Tarnished Splendor of Autonomy." *Linacre Quarterly* 62 (Fall 1995): 49–51.

Medina Estévez, Jorge. "Communion with God Gives Truth and Joy to Every Expression of Life." *L'Osservatore Romano* 23 (1995): 10–11.

Melady, Thomas. "Public Catholicism and *Evangelium Vitae.*" *Crisis* 13 (June 1995): 16.

Melina, Livio. "Conscience Witnesses to a Truth that Precedes It and Surpasses It." *L'Osservatore Romano* 2 (1994): 10–11.

———. "Lack of Objective Moral Anchor Leads to Abuse of Political Power." *L'Osservatore Romano* 19 (1995): 10–11.

Merecki, Jaroslaw and Tadeusz Styczen. "Denying Legal Protection to Weakest Undermines the State Itself." *L'Osservatore Romano* 44 (1995): 10.

———. "The Splendor of Human Freedom Must Be Seen in Relation to Truth." *L'Osservatore Romano* 49 (1993): 10–11.

Moynihan, Robert. "Truth Is Ecumenical, Says Ratzinger: Letter from Rome." *Crisis* 11 (November 1993): 25–27.

Mudge, Lewis S. "*Veritatis Splendor* and Today's Ecumenical Conversation." *The Ecumenical Review* 48 (1996): 158–163.

Mumford, Stephen D. *The Pope and the New Apocalypse: The Holy War Against Family Planning.* North Carolina: Center for Research on Population and Security, 1986.

Nash, Nicholas. "Teaching in Crisis." *The Tablet* 247 (1993): 1480–1482.

Negri, L. *L'uomo e la cultura nel magistero di Giovanni Paolo II*. Bologna: CSEO, 1983.

Neuhaus, Richard John. "The Prophetic Humanism of *Evangelium Vitae*." *Crisis* 14 (May 1996): 22–24.

———. "The Splendor of Truth: A Symposium." *First Things* 39 (1994): 14–29.

"The New Encyclical." Editorial. *America* 169 (October 23, 1993): 3.

Novak, Michael. "The Gospel of Life." *Crisis* 13 (June 1995): 6–7.

———. "The Hope of Splendor." *Crisis* 11 (December 1993): 4–5.

———. "The Pope Strikes Again." *Crisis* 11 (November 1993): 5–7.

O'Connor, John J. "Holy Father Warns Us That We Face an Objective Conspiracy Against Life.'" *L'Osservatore Romano* 27 (1995): 10.

Petrà, B. "God's Laws Are Not Impossible, for Divine Grace Enables Man to Obey." *L'Osservatore Romano* 11 (1994): 10–11.

Pinckaers, Servais. "The Use of Scripture and the Renewal of Moral Theology: The Catechism and *Veritatis Splendor*." *The Thomist* 59 (1995): 1–19.

———. "We Are Capable of Living Christ's Love by Saving Grace of His Spirit." *L'Osservatore Romano* 47 (1993): 11.

Porter, Jean. "Moral Reasoning, Authority and Community in *Veritatis Splendor*." *Anuual of the Society of Christian Ethics* 15 (1995): 201–209.

Potterie, Ignace de la. "Believers Should Live and Act in Light of Christ's Life and Example." *L'Osservatore Romano* 46 (1993): 10.

Propati, Giuseppe. "L'affermazione dei valori umani negli studi di Karol Wojtyla." *Rassegna di Teologia* (January/February 1979): 6–18.

Ratzinger, Joseph Cardinal. "Christian Faith as 'the Way': An Introduction to *Veritatis Splendor*." *Communio* 21 (1994): 109–207.

———. "Glaube als Weg Hinführung zur Enzyklika des Papstes über die Grundlagen der Moral." *Internationale Katholische Zeitschrift* 6/93 (November 1993): 564–570.

———. Presentation at the Press Conference for the Publication of *Evangelium Vitae*. *L'Osservatore Romano* 14 (1995): 1–2.

"The Resplendence of Truth." Editorial, *The Tablet* 247 (1993): 999–1000.

Rhonheimer, Martin. "Given His Creaturely Status, Man's Autonomy Is Essentially Theonomy." *L'Osservatore Romano* 51/52 (1993): 8–9.

———. "Intrinsically Evil Acts and the Moral Viewpoint: Clarifying a Central Teaching of *Veritatis Splendor*." *The Thomist* 58 (1994): 1–39.

Rodriquez Luño, Angel. "Decisions Contrary to the Law of God Are Not Justified by 'Good Intention.'" *L'Osservatore Romano* 7 (1994): 10–11.

Roth, Gottfried. "Life Must Awaken in the Physician a Reverential Awe of the Lord's Gift." *L'Osservatore Romano* 37 (1995): 6.

"The Sacredness of Human Life." Editorial. *The Tablet* 249 (1995): 411.

Schindler, David I. "Christological Aesthetics and *Evangelium Vitae*." *Communio* 22 (1995): 193–224.

Schmitz, Kenneth L. *At the Center of the Human Drama: The Philosophical Anthropology of Karol Wojtyla/Pope John Paul II*. Washington D.C.: Catholic University of America Press, 1993.

Schooyans, Michel. "Man Can Misuse His Will, Claiming a Sovereignty That Is Not His Own." *L'Osservatore Romano* 10 (1994): 10–11.

Scola, Angelo. "Following Christ: On John Paul II's Encyclical *Veritatis Splendor*." *Communio* 20 (1993): 724–727.

———. "In Christ Man Learns That Freedom and Moral Law Are Not Opposed." *L'Osservatore Romano* 44 (1993): 10.

Segalla, Giuseppe. "In His Life and Teaching Jesus Fulfills the Law and Reveals the Will of God." *L'Osservatore Romano* 48 (1993): 10–11.

Seifert, Josef. "Karol Cardinal Wojtyla (Pope John Paul II) as Philosopher and the Cracow/Lublin School of Philosophy." *Aletheia* Vol. 2 (1981): 130–199.

Selling, Joseph A. and Jan Jans, Eds. *The Splendor of Accuracy: An Examination of the Assertions Made by Veritatis Splendor*." Grand Rapids: William B. Eerdmans Publishing Company, 1994.

Sgreccia, Elio. "New Connection Emerges between Safeguarding Life and Environment." *L'Osservatore Romano* 29 (1995): 10–11.

Shaw, R. "Contraception, Infallibility and the Ordinary Magisterium." *Homiletic and Pastoral Review* 78 (July 1978): 9–19.

Smith, Janet. "Natural Law Is a Guide to Morality for Christians and Non-Christians." *L'Osservatore Romano* 1 (1994): 10.

Smith, Russell E. "*Veritatis Splendor* Teaches the Splendor of Truth." *Faith & Reason* 21 (1995): 55–75.

Smith, William. "The Role of the Christian Family, Articles 28–35." *Pope John Paul and the Family*. Edited by Michael J. Wrenn. Chicago: Franciscan Herald Press, 1983, 73–107.

Smith, William B. "*Veritatis Splendor* Is a Moral Masterpiece: No Truth, No Freedom." *Crisis* 11 (November 1993): 28–31.

Spaemann, Robert. "Even the Best of Intentions Does Not Justify the Use of Evil Means." *L'Osservatore Romano* 50 (1993): 11.

Stafford, Jame Francis. "Reflections on *Veritatis Splendor*." *Communio* 21 (1994): 363–366.

Stravopoulos, Alexandre M. "*Veritatis Splendor*: An Orthodox Reaction." *The Ecumenical Review* 48 (1996): 155–157.

Sullivan, Francis A. "The Doctrinal Weight of *Evangelium Vitae*." *Theological Studies* 56 (1995): 560–565.

Suro, Roberto. "The Writing of *Sollicitudo Rei Socialis*: A Behind-the-Scenes Account." *Critic* 6 (May 1988): 13–18.

"Symposium on *Evangelium Vitae*." *The Human Life Review* 21 (Summer 1995): 25–72.

Szostek, Andrzej. "Man's Fundamental Option Can Be Radically Altered by Individual Acts." *L'Osservatore Romano* 16 (1994): 14.

"Teen Fertility Awareness/Billings Method Study." *Fellowship of Catholic Scholars Newsletter* Vol. 7, no. 2 (March, 1984): 11, 15.

Tettamanzi, Dionigi. "The Call to Freedom Lived in Truth Is Heart of the New Evangelization." *L'Osservatore Romano* 13 (1994): 9–10.

Torre, Joseph M. de la. "John Paul's Stubborn Humanism." *Homiletic and Pastoral Review* 92 (February 1992): 56–59.

Tremblay, Réal. "Grace of Christ's Presence Heals and Transforms the Human Heart." *L'Osservatore Romano* 45 (1993): 10.

Tuck, Mary. "A Message in Season." *The Tablet* 247 (1993): 1583–1585.

Tymieniecka, Anna-Teresa. "The Origins of the Philosophy of John Paul II." *Proceedings of The American Catholic Philosophical Association Meeting.* (1979). Washington, D.C.: Catholic University, 1979, 16–27.

Various Authors. *La Filosofia Di Karol Wojtyla.* Bologna, Italy: Centro Studi Europa Orientale, 1983.

"The Vatican's Summary of *Evangelium Vitae.*" *Origins* 24 (1995): 728–730.

Vial Correra, Juan de Dios. "Objective Forms of Evil Aimed at Weakest Have No Justification." *L'Osservatore Romano* 31 (1995): 6.

Vree, Dale. "The Splendor of Truth and the Squalor of Sin." *New Oxford Review* 60 (December 1993): 2–8.

Wilkins, John, Ed. *Considering Veritatis Splendor.* Cleveland: The Pilgrims Press, 1994.

Williams, B. *Consequentialism: For and Against.* Cambridge: Cambridge University Press, 1973.

Williams, George Huntston. *The Mind of John Paul II: Origins of His Thought and Action.* New York: Seabury Press, 1981.

Woznicki, Andrew A. *A Christian Humanism: Karol Wojtyla's Existential Personalism.* New Britain, CT, Marial Publications, 1980.

———. "Dialogistic Thomism and Dialectical Marxism." *The New Scholasticism* 52 (1978): 214–35.

———. "The Influence of Maritain in Poland." Lecture at the International Maritain Congress, Niagra University, May 28, 1937.

Wren, Michael, Ed. *Pope John Paul II and the Family.* Chicago: Franciscan Herald Press, 1983.

———. "Wyszynski, Wojtyla and the Woman: A True Love Story." *Mater Fidei Et Fidelium* 17–23: 445–452. Collected Essays to Honor Theodore Koehler on his 80th Birthday. Marian Library Studies, Dayton, OH: University of Dayton, 1985–1991.

Zieba, Maciej. "Truth and Freedom in the Thought of Pope John Paul." *The Tablet* 247 (1993): 1510–1512.

SOCIAL TEACHING

Acts of the United Nations Seminar on *Centesimus Annus*: John Paul's Latest Social Encyclical. *L'Osservatore Romano* 47 (1991): Supplement, i–xii.

After 1991: Capitalism and Ethics. A Colloquium in the Vatican 1992. Vatican City: Pontifical Council for Justice and Peace, 1992.

Andrè-Vincent, I. (Phillipe). *Les Droits de L'Homme Dans L'Enseignement de Jean Paul II.* Paris: Librairie Générale de Droit et de Jurisprudence, 1983.

Aristide, Jean-Bertrand. *Théologie et Politique.* Montréal: Les Éditions du CIDIHCA, 1992.

Aubert, Robert, et al. *The Christian Centuries, vol. 5: The Church in a Secularized Society.* New York: Paulist Press, and London: Darton, Longman and Todd, 1978.

Barta, Russel. "Work: In Search of New Meanings." *Chicago Studies* 23 (August 1984): 155–168.

Baum, Gregory. "The Anti-Cold War Encyclical." *The Ecumenist* 26 (1988): 65–74.

———. "Capitalism *ex cathedra.*" *Health Progress* 73 (April 1992): 44–48.

———. "*Laborem Exercens.*" In *The New Dictionary of Catholic Social Thought.* Edited by Judith A. Dwyer. Collegeville: Liturgical Press, 1994, 527–535.

———. *The Priority of Labor: A Commentary on Laborem Exercens: Encyclical Letter of Pope John Paul II.* New York: Paulist Press, 1982.

Baum, Gregory and Robert Ellsberg, Eds. *The Logic of Solidarity: Commentaries on Pope John Paul II's Encyclical on Social Concern.* Maryknoll, NY: Orbis Books, 1990.

Bayer, Richard C. "Christian Personalism and Democratic Capitalism." *Horizons* 21 (1994): 313–331.

Bedoyere, Quentin de la. "Man and His Work." *The Tablet* 235 (1981): 1192–1194.

Bianchi, Eugene C. and Rosemary Radford Reuther, Eds. *A Democratic Catholic Church and the Reconstruction of Roman Catholicism.* New York: Crossroad, 1992.

Boff, Leonardo. *Church, Charism and Power.* London: SCM Press, 1985.

———. *Liberation Theology: From Confrontation to Dialogue.* New York: Harper & Row, 1986.

Bowe, Paul. "*Centesimus Annus.*" *Doctrine and Life* 41 (1991): 312–318, 324–331.

———. "*Sollicitudo Rei Socialis*: A Commentary on the Encyclical." *Doctrine and Life* 38 (1988): 227–233.

Brovedani, E. "Giovanni Paolo II e la scienza." *Aggiornamenti sociali* 24 (1984): 9–10.

Brown, Lester R. *Our Democratically Divided World.* Washington, D.C.: Worldwatch Institute, 1986.

Brzezínski, Zbigniew. *Power and Principle.* New York: Farrar, Straus and Giroux, 1983.

Burns, Gene. *The Frontiers of Catholicism.* Berkeley: University of California Press, 1992.

Buttiglione, Rocco. "Behind *Centesimus Annus.*" *Crisis* 9 (June 1991): 8–9.

———. "Christian Economics 101." *Crisis* (July-August 1991): 8–9.

Byron, William J. "Solidarity, Path to Development and Peace." *America* 158 (1988): 445–446.

Caldecott, Stratford. "Cosmology, Eschatology, Ecology: Some Reflections on *Sollicitudo Rei Socialis.*" *Cummunio* 15 (1988): 305–318.

Calvez, Jean-Yves. "*Sollicitudo Rei Socialis,*" in *The New Dictionary of Catholic Social Thought.* Edited by Judith A. Dwyer. Collegeville: Liturgical Press, 1994, 912–917.

Carrier, Hervé, S. J. *The Social Doctrine of the Church Revisited.* Vatican City: Vatican Polyglot Press, 1990.

Cassin, R. *Religions et Droits de l'Homme. Amicorum discipulorumque Liber.* (1972): 97.

———. "Le Droits de l'Homme." *RCADI* 140 (1974): 330.

Charrier, Fernando. "Labor and Capital." *L'Osservatore Romano* 42 (1981): 8.

Cox, Harvey. *The Secular City.* New York: Collier Books, MacMillan, 1990.

———. *The Silencing of Leonardo Boff.* Oak Park, IL: Meyer-Stone Books, 1988.

D'Amato, Al. *Power, Pasta and Politics.* New York: Hyperion, 1995.

de La Chappelle, P. *La Déclaration Universelle des Droits de l'Homme et le Catholicisme.* Paris: L.G.D.J., 1967.

de Laubier, Patrick. *La Pensée Sociale de L'Église Catholique: Un Idéal Historique de Léon XIII à Jean Paul II.* Paris: Éditions Albatros, 1980.

Desto, Robert A. "*Laborem Exercens.*" in *A Century of Catholic Social Thought.* Edited by George Weigel and Robert Royal. Lanham: University Press of America 1991. 145–161.

Donahue, Thomas R. *Trade Union Perspective of Laborem Exercens.* Washington: American Federation of Labor and Congress of Industrial Organizations, 1982.

D'Onorio, J. B., Ed. *Le Saint-Siège dans les relations internationales.* Paris: Cerf, 1989.

Dorr, Donal. "The New Social Encyclical." *The Furrow* 32 (1981): 700–712.

Duncan, Roger. "On Reading *Laborem Exercens.*" *Homiletic and Pastoral Review* 86 (July 1986): 11–19.

Etchegary, Roger. "Presentation at the Press Conference for the Presentation of *Centesimus Annus.*" *L'Osservatore Romano* 18 (1991): 1, 4.

———. "Presentation at the Press Conference for the Publication of *Sollicitudo Rei Socialis.*" *L'Osservatore Romano* 9 (1988): 14.

Ethical and Pastoral Dimensions of Population Trends. Vatican City: Pontifical Council for the Family, Libreria Editrice Vaticana, 1994.

Faley, Roland James. "Pope as Prophet: The New Social Encyclical." *America* 158 (1988): 447–450.

Fantoli, Annibale. *Galileo: per il Copernicanesimo e per la Chiesa.* Vatican City: Libreria Editrice Vaticana, 1993.

"Fasting and Solidarity": Pontifical Messages for Lent. Vatican City: Pontifical Council Cor Unum. 1991.

Faulhaber, Robert William. "The Church and Culture–John Paul II's 'On Human Work.'" *Listening* 18 (1983): 103–118.

Filibeck, Giorgio. *Les Droits de l'Homme dans l'Enseignement de l'Église: De Jean XXIII à Jean-Paul II.* Vatican City: Libreria Editrice Vaticana, 1992.

————. *The Social Teaching of John Paul II: Human Rights.* Vatican City Press, 1980.

Fiore, Benjamin. "*Laborem Exercens.*" In *The Thought of John Paul II: A Collection of Essays and Studies.* Edited by John M. McDermott. Rome: Gregorian University Press, 1983, 231–236.

Fonseca, Aloysius J. "Reflections on the Encyclical Letter *Sollicitudo Rei Socialis.*" *Gregorianum* 70 (1989): 5–24.

Fortin, Ernest L. "Free Markets Have Their Limits: Three Cheers for Capitalism." *Crisis* 10 (November 1992): 20–25.

Gargantini, Mario. *I Papi E La Scienza: Antologia del magistero della Chiesa sulla questione scientifica da Leone XIII a Giovanni Paolo II.* Milano: Jaca Book, 1985.

Gini, Al. "Meaningful Work and the Rights of the Worker: A Commentary on *Rerum Novarum* and *Laborem Exercens.*" *Thought* 67 (1992): 225–239.

Ginsburg, Helen. "Teachings of John Paul II on Work and Rights of Workers." *Social Thought* 13 (Spring/Summer 1987): 46–59.

Glemp, Jozef. "Human Work in the Teaching of Our Holy Father John Paul II." in *John Paul II: A Panorama of His Teachings.* Preface by Joseph Bernardin. New York: New City Press, 1989, 144–160.

Guttierrez, Gustavo. *The Pope and Revolution: John Paul II Confronts Liberation Theology.* Washington, D.C.: Ethics and Public Policy Center, 1982.

Guttierrez, Gustavo, Francis McDonagh, Cândido Padin, O.S.B. and John Sobrino, S.J. *Santo Domingo and After: The Challenges for the Latin American Church.* London: Catholic Institute for International Relations, 1993.

Haas, Richard: "The Market Place." *Living Prayer* 27 (July/August 1994): 10–11.

Habiger, Matthew. *Papal Teaching on Private Property 1891–1981.* Lanham: University Press of America, 1990.

————. "Reflections on *Centesimus Annus.*" *Social Justice Review* 82 (1991): 139–142.

————. "Situating *Sollicitudo Rei Socialis* in Catholic Social Teaching." *Social Justice Review* 79 (1988): 138–144.

Hanson, Eric O. *The Catholic Church in World Politics.* Princeton, NJ: Princeton University Press, 1987.

Hauerwas, Stanley. "In Praise of *Centesimus Annus.*" in *To Do Justice and Right Upon Earth.* Edited by Mary E. Stamps. Collegeville: Liturgical Press, 1993. 63–83.

Hebblethwaite, Margaret. *Basic Is Beautiful: Base Ecclesial Communities from Third World to First World.* London: Harper Collins, 1993.

Heckel, Roger. *The Social Teaching of John Paul II: Basis for Motivations and Ways of the Church's Intervention on Socio-Political Issues.* Rome: Vatican City Press, 1981.

————. "Continuity and Renewal." *L'Osservatore Romano* 40 (1981): 4–5.

————. *The Social Teaching of John Paul II: General Aspects of the Social Catechesis of John Paul II–The Use of the Expression "Social Doctrine" of the Church.* Rome: Vatican City Press, 1980.

————. *The Social Teaching of John Paul II: The Human Person and Social Structures.* Rome: Vatican City Press, 1980.

———. *The Social Teaching of John Paul II: Religious Freedom.* Rome: Vatican City Press, 1980.

———. *The Social Teaching of John Paul II: The Theme of Liberation.* Rome: Vatican City Press, 1980.

———. *The Struggle Against Racism: Some Contributions of the Church.* Rome: Vatican City Press, 1979.

Hehir, J. Bryan. "Challenge to a Tradition." *Commonweal* 108 (1981): 522.

———. "Reordering the World." *Commonweal* (June 14, 1991): 393–394.

———. "Taking on the Super-Rivals: Reactions to the Pope's Latest Encyclical." *Commonweal* 115 (1988): 169–170.

Hennelly, Alfred T. "Pope John Paul's Spirituality of Work." *America* 146 (1982): 31–33.

Higgins, George G. with William Bole. *Organized Labor and the Church.* Mahweh, NJ: Paulist Press, 1993.

Hittinger, Russell. "The Pope and the Liberal State." *First Things* 28 (1992): 33–41.

Hoffe, Otfried. *Jean Paul II et les Droits de l'Homme.* Fribourg: Édition Saint-Paul, 1980.

Hollenbach, David. "Christian Social Ethics After the Cold War." *Theological Studies* 53 (1992): 75–95.

———. "The Pope and Capitalism." *America* 164 (1991): 590–591.

Holy See at the Service of Peace: Pope John Paul II's Addresses to the Diplomatic Corps (1978–1988). Vatican City: Pontifical Council for Justice and Peace, 1988.

Houck, John W. and Oliver F. Williams, eds. *Co-creation and Capitalism: John Paul II's Laborem Exercens.* Washington D.C.: University Press of America, 1983.

Human Rights and the Church: Historical and Theological Reflections. Vatican City: Pontifical Council for Justice and Peace, 1990.

International Economics: Interdependence and Dialogue. Vatican City: Pontifical Council for Justice and Peace, 1984.

Joblin, Joseph, S.J. "Doctrine et Action Sociale: Reflexion Sur l'Évolution du Movement Social Chrétien Avant et Après *Rerum Novarum.*" *Rerum Novarum Laborem Exercens 2000: Symposium* (1982): 89–114.

Johnson, Paul. *Pope John Paul II and the Catholic Restoration.* New York: Saint Martin's Press, 1981.

Kaiser, R. B. *The Politics of Sex and Religion.* Kansas City, MO: Leaven Press, 1985.

Kelley, John J. "The Silence about Subsidiarity." *America* 145 (1981): 382–383.

Kennedy, Robert G. *Dignity of Work: John Paul II Speaks to Managers and Workers.* Lanham, MD: University Press of America, 1994.

Keston College. *Religion in Communist Lands*, Vol. 9 nos. 1–2.

Kiliroor, Matthew. "Social Doctrine in *Sollicitudo Rei Socialis.*" *The Month* 21 (1988): 711–714.

Krys, Roman. "Collective Political Human Rights According to Pope John Paul II." *Revue Belge de Droit International* (1981).

———. "Individual Human Rights According to Pope John Paul II." *Revue de Droit International des Sciences Diplomatiques et Politiques* 3.

Kuzcynski, Janusz. "To Elevate the World: The Potential of Pope John Paul II's Pontificate." *Dialectics and Humanism. The Polish Philosophical Quarterly*, Vol. 6 (1979): 3–27.

Lader, Lawrence. *Politics, Power and the Church: The Catholic Crisis and Its Challenge to American Pluralism.* New York: MacMillan, 1987.

Langan, Thomas. "The Strained Theology of Gregory Baum." *This World* 6 (Fall 1983): 71–84.

Lawler, Philip F., Ed. *Papal Economics.* Washington: Heritage Foundation, 1981.

Loades, Anne L., Ed. "On *Centesimus Annus.*" *Theology* 95 (1992): 405–432.

Lopinski, Maciej, Marcin Moskit and Mariusz Wilk. *Konspira: Solidarity Underground.* Berkeley: University of Berkeley Press, 1990.

Lynn, Thomas D. "Of Politics, Catholics and the Social Doctrine." *Social Justice Review* 84 (1993): 18–21.

Mahoney, Roger M. "Perspectives for Viewing the Social Concerns Encyclical." *Origins* 18 (1988): 69–72.

McCormick, Patrick. "*Centesimus Annus,*" in *The New Dictionary of Catholic Social Thought.* Edited by Judith A. Dwyer. Collegeville: Liturgical Press, 1994. 132–143.

———. "That They May Converse: Voices of Catholic Social Thought." *Cross Currents* 42 (Winter 1992): 521–527.

McDermott, John M., Ed. *The Thought of Pope John Paul II.* Rome: Gregorian University, 1993.

McGurn, William. "*Sollicitudo Rei Socialis,*" in *A Century of Catholic Social Thought.* Edited by George Weigel and Robert Royal. Lanham: University Press of America, 1991, 163–176.

Morneau, Robert F. "The Church's Social Concerns: Ten Lessons." *Emmanuel* 95 (1989): 70–73.

———. *Themes and Theses of Six Recent Papal Documents: A Commentary.* New York: Alba House, 1985, 111–135.

Mourgeon, J. *Les Droits de l'Homme.* Paris: PUF, 1978.

Murphy, William, Msgr. *The Social Teaching of John Paul II: The Person, the Nation and the State.* Vatican City Press, 1980.

Myers, Kenneth A., Ed. *Aspiring to Freedom: Commentaries on John Paul II's Encyclical "The Social Concerns of the Church."* Grand Rapids: William B. Eerdmans Publishing Company, 1988.

Naughton, Michael J. "The Virtuous Manager and *Centesimus Annus.*" *Social Justice Review* 85 (1994): 150–152.

Nell-Breuning, Oswald V. *Soziallehre der Kirche: Erläuterungen der lehramtlichen Dokumente.* Zurich: Eropaverlag, 1983.

———. *Arbeit vor Kapital: Kommentar zur Enzyklika Laborem Exercens von Johannes Paul II.* Zürich: Europaverlag, 1983.

Neuhaus, Richard John. *Doing Well and Doing Good: The Challenge to the Christian Capitalist.* New York: Doubleday, 1992.

————. "John Paul's 'Second Thoughts' on Capitalism." *First Things* 41 (1994): 65–67.

Novak, Michael. *The Catholic Ethic and the Spirit of Capitalism.* New York: The Free Press, 1993.

————. *Catholic Social Thought and Liberal Institutions.* New Brunswick, NJ: Transaction Publishers, 2nd.

————. *The Spirit of Democratic Capitalism.* New York: Simon and Schuster, 1992.

Preston R. H. "*Centesimus Annus*: An Appraisal." *Theology* 95 (1992): 405–416.

Preston, Ronald. "Twenty Years After *Populorum Progressio*: An Appraisal of Pope John Paul's Commemorative Encyclical." *Theology* 92 (1989): 519–525.

Preston, Ronald H. "Pope John Paul II on Work." *Theology* 86 (January 1983): 19–24.

Przetacznik, Frank. *The Catholic Concept of Genuine and Just Peace as a Basic Collective Human Right.* Lewiston, NY: The Edwin Mellen Press, 1991.

Quade, Quentin, ed. *The Pope and the Revolution: John Paul II Confronts Liberation Theology.* Washington, D.C.: Ethics and Public Policy Center, 1982.

Rauscher, Anton. "Laborem Exercens Within the Context of the Church's Commitment to the Work of Peace and Justice." *Rerum Novarum Laborem Exercens 2000: Symposium* (1982): 179.

Refugees: A Challenge to Solidarity. Vatican City: Pontifical Council for the Care of Migrants and Itinerant People, Libraria Editrice Vaticana, 1992.

Romero, Oscar Archbishop. "La Liberación Integral en América Latina." *Opiniones Latinoamericanas* (June 1979).

Roos, Lothar. "On Theology and Ethics of Work." *Communio* 11 (1984): 136–144.

Rossi, Romano, Msgr. *The Social Teaching of John Paul II: Human Labor.* Rome: Vatican City Press, 1981.

Schall, James. "The Teaching of *Centesimus Annus*." *Gregorianum* 74 (1993): 17–43.

Schall, James V., S.J., Ed. "Capitalism, Business and Human Priorities," in J. W. Houck and O. F. Williams, eds. *The Judeo-Christian Vision of the Modern Corporation.* Notre Dame, IN: University of Notre Dame Press, 1982.

————. *The Church, the State and Society in the Thought of John Paul II.* Chicago: Franciscan Herald Press, 1982.

————. *Sacred in All its Forms.* Boston: Saint Paul Editions, 1984.

————. "The Unexpected Encyclical." *Social Justice Review* (September/October 1991): 143–147.

Schambeck, Herbert. "State Cannot Create Human Values but Only Respect and Promote Them." *L'Osservatore Romano* 35 (1995): 6.

Schotte, Jan. "The Social Teaching of the Church: *Laborem Exercens*, A New Challenge." *Review of Social Economy* 40 (1982): 340–357.

Schotte, Jan, C.I.C.M. and the Pontificia Commissio Justitia et Pax, Eds. *Rerum Novarum Laborem Exercens 2000: Symposium.* Rome: Instituto Pio XI, 1982.

Selling, Joseph A. "The Theological Presuppositions of *Centesimus Annus*." *Louvain Studies* 17 (Spring 1192): 35–47.

Seminar on Pope John Paul II's Encyclical *Sollicitudo Rei Socialis. L'Osservatore Romano* 45 (1988): Supplement, i–viii.

Six, Jean-François. *Church and Human Rights.* United Kingdom: Saint Paul Publications, 1992.

"Socialism and Antheism." *Dialectics and Humanism, The Polish Philosophical Quarterly* (January 1987).

"The Solidarity Encyclical." Editorial. *America* 158 (1988): 251.

"*Sollicitudo Rei Socialis.*" Editorial. *Commonweal* 115 (1988): 131–132.

Sorge, Bartolome. "*Laborem Exercens*: Toward a New Solidarity," in *Official Catholic Social Teaching: Readings in Moral Theology.* Edited by Charles Curran and Richard McCormick. Vol. 5. New York: Paulist Press, 1986, 241–246.

Spasowski, Romuald. *The Liberation of One.* Orlando, FL: Harcourt Brace Jovanovich, 1986.

Spiazzi, Raimondo. *I documenti sociali della Chiesa. Da Pio IX a Giovanni Paolo II (1864–1982).* Milan: Massimo, 1983.

———. "Gospel of Work and Dignity of Man." *L'Osservatore Romano* 41 (1981): 9–10.

Suro, Roberto. "The Writing of *Sollicitudo Rei Socialis*: A Behind-the-Scenes Account." *Critic* 6 (May 1988): 13–18.

"Symposium on *Centesimus Annus.*" *The Pope Speaks* 37 (1992): 80–82.

Traffas, John R. "The Spirit of Community and the Spirituality of Work: A Note on *Laborem Exercens.*" *Communio* 10 (1983): 407–411.

Tucker, Jeffrey A. "Papal Economics 101: The Catholic Ethic and the Spirit of Capitalism." *Crisis* 9 (June 1991): 16–21.

Turner, Frank. "John Paul II's Social Analysis." *The Month* 24 (1991): 344–349.

Utz, Arthur F. "*Centesimus Annus* Gives Us a Profoundly Ethical View of Social and Economic Politics." *L'Osservatore Romano* 28 (1991): 8, 10.

Vasak, K. *Les Dimensions Internationales des Droits de l'Homme.* UNESCO, 1978.

Villey, M. *Philosophie du Droit.* Paris: Dalloz, 1979.

Volf, Miroslav. "On Human Work: An Evaluation of the Key Ideas of the Encyclical *Laborem Exercens.*" *Scottish Journal of Theology* 37 (1984): 65–67.

Walsh, Michael and Brian Davies, Eds. *Proclaiming Justice and Peace.* Mystic CT: Twenty-Third Publications, 1991.

Weigel, George, Ed. *A New Worldly Order: John Paul II and Human Freedom.* Washington, D.C.: Ethics and Public Policy Center, 1991.

White, Robert Edward. "Blaming the Villains, Not the Victim: John Paul II and the Superpowers." *Commonweal* 115 (1988): 555–559.

Williams, George Huntston. *The Contours of the Church and State in the Thought of John Paul II.* Waco, TX: Baylor University Press, 1983.

———. *The Law of Nations and the Book of Nature.* Collegeville: Saint John's University Press, 1984.

———. *The Mind of John Paul II: Origins of His Thought and Action.* New York: Seabury Press, 1981.

Williams, Oliver F. and John W. Houck, Eds. *The Making of an Economic Vision: John Paul II's "On Social Concern."* Lanham: University Press of America, 1991.

Williams, Paul L., Ed. *Catholic Social Thought and the Teaching of John Paul II.* Scranton, PA: Northeast Books, 1983.

Wood, Jr., James E. and Derek Davis, Eds. *The Role of Religion in the Making of Public Policy.* Waco, TX: Baylor University Press, 1991.

Woodrow, Alain. "The Pope's Challenge to Western Democracy." *The Tablet* 249 (1995): 448–449.

Wright, Clive. "Work, Life-style and Gospel." *The Way* 34 (April 1994): 126–137.

History/Biography/Spirituality

Accattoli, Luigi. *Io ho Avuto Paura a Ricevere Questa Nomina.* Torino: Società Editrice Internazionale, 1993.

Actes et Documents du Saint Siège relatifs à la seconde guerre mondiale. II, La Sainte Siège et la situation religieuse en Polonge et dans les pays baltes. 2 Vols. Rome: Vatican Press, 1967.

Andreotti, Giulio. *Ad ogni morte di Papa.* Milan: Rizzoli, 1980.

Andrews, T. *The Polish National Catholic Church in America and Poland.* London: SPCK, 1953.

Annuario Pontifico 1994. Vatican City: Libreria Editrice Vaticana, 1994.

Arias, Juan. *El Enigma Wojtyla.* Madrid: Ediciones El Pais, 1985.

———. *L'enigma Wojtyla.* Rome: Borla, 1986.

Ash, Timothy Garton. *Polish Revolution: Solidarity.* New York: Scribner and Sons, 1983.

———. *The Magic Lantern.* New York: Random House, 1990.

———. *The Uses of Adversity.* New York: Vintage, 1990.

———. *We the People.* Cambridge: Granta Books, 1990.

Ascherson, Neal. *The Struggles for Poland.* London: M. Joseph, 1987.

———. *The Polish August: The Self-Limiting Revolution.* New York: Viking Press, 1982.

Baker, K., "John Paul II in the United States of America." *Homiletic and Pastoral Review* 80 (January 1980): 21–27.

Bergonzoni, Luciano. *Emilia Kaczorowska in Wojtyla.* Edizioni Carroccio, Vigodarzere, 1998.

———. *Edmondo Wojtyla.* Padova: Centro Editoriale Cattolico Carroccio, 1992.

Bernstein, Carl and Marco Politi. *His Holiness.* New York: Doubleday, 1996.

Blazynski, George. *John Paul II: A Man From Krakow.* London: Weidenfeld & Nicolson, 1979.

———. *Pope John Paul II: A Biography.* London: Weidenfeld & Nicolson, and New York: William Morrow, 1979.

Briggs, Kenneth. *Holy Siege: The Year That Shook Catholic America.* San Francisco: Harper San Francisco, 1992.

Brumberg, Abraham, Ed. *Poland: Genesis of a Revolution.* New York: Random House, 1983.

Cannon, Lou. *President Reagan: The Role of a Lifetime.* New York: Simon and Schuster, 1991.

Chelini, Jean. *La vita quotidiana in Vaticano sotto Giovanni Paolo II.* Milan: Rizzoli, 1986.

Comas, José. *Polonia y Solidaridad.* Madrid: Ediciones El País, 1985.

Conway, Ronald. "Papal Obsessions." *World Press Review* (December 1993): 45.

Cooney, John. *The American Pope: The Life and Times of Francis Cardinal Spellman.* New York: Times Books, 1984.

Craig, Mary. *The Crystal Spirit.* London: Hodder & Stoughton, 1986.

———. *Man from a Far Country: A Portrait of Pope John Paul II.* New York: William Morrow, 1979.

Davies, Norman. *God's Playground: A History of Poland.* Vols. 1 and 2. New York: Columbia University Press, 1982.

Davis, Raymond, Trans., Ed. *The Book of Pontiffs* (*Liber Pontificalis*). Liverpool: Liverpool University Press, 1989.

Della Rocca, Fernando. *Papi di Questo Secolo.* Padova, Italy: Cedam, 1981.

Dobrowski, Tadeusz. *Polish Painting from the Enlightenment to Recent Times.* Warsaw: Ossolineum, 1981.

Finke, Roger and Rodney Stark. *The Churching of America: 1776–1990.* New Brunswick, NJ: Rutgers University Press, 1992.

Fisher, Loren, Ed. *Pope John Paul II. An American Celebration.* Somerville, NJ: Elf Publishing, 1995.

Frossard, André. *"Be Not Afraid!": Pope John Paul II Speaks Out on His Life, His Beliefs, and His Inspiring Vision for Humanity.* Trans. J. R. Foster. New York: Saint Martin's Press, 1984.

———. *Diálogo con Juan Pablo II.* Milan: Rusconi, 1983.

———. *Portrait de Jean-Paul II.* Paris: Éditions Robert Laffont, 1988.

———. *Portrait of John Paul II.* San Francisco: Ignatius Press, 1988.

———. *Portret Jan Pawla II.* Kraków: Wydawnictwo Znak, 1988.

Gawronski, Jas. *Il Mondo di Giovanni Paolo II.* Milan: Mondadori, 1994.

Gelmi, Josef. *Die Päpste in Lebensbildern.* Vienna: Verlag Styria, 1989.

Ginsborg, Paul. *A History of Contemporary Italy.* New York: Penguin, 1990.

Gligora, Francesco and Biagia Catanzaro. *Storia dei Papi e degli Antipapi da San Pietro a Giovanni Paolo II,* 2 Vols. Rome: Panda Edizioni, 1989.

Gorbachev, Mikhail. *Erinnerungen.* Berlin: Siedler Verlag, 1995.

———. *Perestroika: New Thinking for Our Country and the World.* New York: Harper & Row, 1987.

Greeley, Andrew M. *A Catholic Myth: The Behavior and Beliefs of American Catholics.* New York: Collier Books, MacMillan, 1990.

————. *The Making of the Popes.* London: Futura, 1979.

————. *The Making of the Popes 1978: The Politics of Intrigue in the Vatican.* Kansas City, KS: Andrews and McMeel, 1979.

Grygiel, Stanislaw. *L'uomo vista della Vistola.* Bologna: CSEO, 1978.

Haig, Alexander. *Caveat: Realism, Reagan and Foreign Policy.* New York: MacMillan, 1984.

Hebblethwaite, Peter. *In The Vatican.* New York: Oxford University Press, 1987.

————. *The Papal Year.* London: Cassell, Ltd., 1981.

————. *Paul VI.* London: Harper Collins, 1993.

————. *Paul VI: The First Modern Pope.* New York: Paulist Press, 1993.

————. "Pope John Paul II as Philosopher and Poet." *The Heythrop Journal* XXI (1980).

————. *Synod Extraordinary.* London: Darton, Longman and Todd, 1985.

————. *The Year of Three Popes.* Cleveland: William Collins, 1979.

Hebblethwaite, Peter and Ludwig Kaufmann. *John Paul II: A Pictorial Biography.* Maidenhead, England: McGraw-Hill Book Company, 1979.

Herman, Edward S. and Frank Brodhead. *The Rise and Fall of the Bulgarian Connection.* New York: Sheridan Square Publications, 1986.

Hitchcock, James. *Pope John Paul II & American Catholicism.* New York: The National Committee of Catholic Laymen, Inc.

Honea, Charles H., Ed. *A Reader's Companion to Crossing the Threshold of Hope.* Brewster, MA: Paraclete Press, 1996.

Jaruzelski, Wojciech. *Erinnerungen.* München: Piper, 1993.

Jennings, Peter and Eamonn McCabe. *The Pope in Britain: Pope John Paul II's British Visit, 1982.* London: Bodley Head, 1982.

Johnson Paul. *Pope John Paul II.* London, 1982.

Karolek, Tadeusz. *John Paul II: The Pope from Poland.* Trans. David Evans. Warsaw: Interpress Publishers, 1979.

Kreutz, Andej. *Vatican Policy on the Palestinian-Israeli Conflict.* New York: Greenwood Press, 1990.

"La biographie du nouveau pape." *Documentation Catholique* 75 (November 5, 1978): 906–907.

Lapide, P. *The Last Three Popes and the Jews.* London, 1967.

Le Corre, Dominique and Mark Sabotka. *John Paul II in Poland: 2–10 June 1979.* Bagnolet, France: Le Corre, 1979.

Lernoux, Penny. *People of God: The Struggle for World Catholicism.* New York: Viking Press, 1989.

Levillain, Phillipe and Francois-Charles Uginet. *Il Vaticano o le frontiere della grazia.* Milan: Rizzoli, 1985.

Libanio, Christo and Carlos Alberto. *Diaro di Puebla.* Brescia: Ed. Queriniana, 1979.

Licheri, Gianni. *Quel conclave e poi Wojtyla jet.* Brescia: Queriniana, 1979.

Longford, Lord. *Pope John Paul II: An Authorized Biography.* New York: William Morrow, 1982.

Macciocchi, M. A. *Di là dalle Porte di Bronzo*. Milan: Mondadori, 1987.

MacDowell, Bart. *Inside the Vatican*. Washington: National Geographic Society, 1991.

MacEoin, Gary. *The Inner Elite*. Kansas City: Sheed, Andrews and McMeel, 1978.

Maffeo, Sabino, S.J. *In the Service of Nine Popes: 100 Years of the Vatican Observatory*. Vatican City: The Vatican Observatory and the Pontifical Academy of Sciences, 1991.

Malinski, Mieczyslaw. *Il mio vecchio amico Karol*. Rome: Ed. Paoline, 1980.

———. *The Life of Karol Wojtyla*. Trans. P. S. Falla. New York: Doubleday, 1979.

———. *Pontyfikat Jana Pawla II: 1983–1988*. Poznan, Poland: Ksiegarnia Sw. Wojciecha, 1991.

———. *Pope John Paul II: The Life of My Friend Karol Wojtyla*. London: Burns and Oats and New York: Seabury Press, 1979.

———. *Pope John Paul II: The Life of Karol Wojtyla*. Trans. P. S. Falla. New York: Seabury Press, 1979.

———. *Le radici di Papa Wojtyla*. Rome: Borla, 1980.

———. *Las raices del Papa Wojtyla*. Rome: Ediciones Borla, 1980.

———. *Wezwano Mnie z Dalekiego Kraju*. Poznan, Poland: Pallottimun, 1987.

Mariotti, Piergiorgi. *Karol Wojtyla. Perfil crítico del Papa polaco*. Rome: Ediciones Napoleone, 1983.

Marton, Kati. "The Paradoxical Pope." *Atlantic Monthly* (May 1980): 41–49.

May, William W., Ed. *Vatican Authority and American Catholic Dissent*. New York: Crossroad, 1987.

McBrien, Richard P. *Lives of the Popes. The Pontiffs from Saint Peter to John Paul II*. San Francisco: Harper San Francisco, 1997.

McDermott, John M., Ed. *The Thought of Pope John Paul II*. Rome: Gregorian University, 1993.

Melady, Thomas Patrick. *The Ambassador's Story: The United States and the Vatican in World Affairs*. Huntington, IN: Our Sunday Visitor Publishing Division, 1994.

Messori, Vittorio. *La Sfida della Fede*. Torino: Edizioni San Paolo, 1993.

———. *Rapporto sulla fede*. Milan: Edizioni Paolina, 1985.

———. *Varcare la soglia della speranza*. Milan: Mondadori, 1994.

Micewski, Anrzej. *Cardinal Wyszynski: A Biography*. Orlando, FL: Harcourt Brace Jovanovich, 1984.

Michel, Patrick. *Politics and Religion in Eastern Europe*. Oxford: Polity Press, 1991.

Michnik, Adam. *The Church and the Left*. Chicago: University of Chicago Press, 1993.

———. *Letters from Prison and Other Essays*. Berkeley: University of California Press, 1985.

Murphey, Francis X. *The Papacy Today*. London: Weidenfeld and Nicolson, 1981.

National Catholic News Service. *Nights of Sorrow, Days of Joy: Papal Transition, Paul VI, John Paul I, John Paul II*. Washington, D.C.: The Service, 1978.

Naughton, Michael. *The Good Stewards*. Lanham, MD: University Press of America, 1992.

Nemic, L. *John Paul II. A Festive Profile*. New York: Catholic Book Publishing Company, 1979.

Nichols, Bruce. *The Uneasy Alliance: Religion, Refugee Work and U. S. Foreign Policy*. New York: Oxford University Press, 1988.

O'Brien, Darcy. *The Hidden Pope*. New York: DayBreak Books, 1998.

O'Byrne, Seamus, ed. *Challenge or Crisis?: Texts by Pope John Paull II on Religious Life*. Dublin, Ireland: Veritas Publications, 1987.

O'Carroll, Michael. *Poland and John Paul II*. Dublin: Veritas Publications, 1979.

Ockrent, Christine and Alexandre De Marenches. *Dans le secret des princes*. Paris: Edition Stock, 1986.

Oram, James. *The People's Pope*. Sydney: Bay Books.

Parker, Michael. *Priest of the World's Destiny: John Paul II*. Milford, OH: Faith Publishing Company, 1995.

Perea, Francisco J. *El Papa en México*. México: Editorial Diana, 1979.

Persico, Joseph E. *Casey*. New York: Viking, 1990.

Piekarski, Adam. *The Church in Poland*. Warsaw: Interpress Publishers, 1978.

Pope John Paul II on Jews and Judaism: 1979–1986. Washington, D.C.: Office for Publishing and Promotion Services, United States Catholic Conference, 1987.

Priesthood In the Third Millennium: Adresses of Pope John Paul II–1993. Compiled by Rev. James P. Socias. New Jersey: Scepter Publishers, 1994.

Quinn, J. "An Open Moment for Faith." *Origins* 9 (November 22, 1979): 365.

Ramet, Pedro, Ed. *Catholicism and Politics in Communist Societies*. Durham, NC: Duke University Press, 1990.

Reese, Thomas J., S. J. *Archbishop: Inside the Power Structure of the American Catholic Church*. New York: Harper and Row, 1989.

———. *A Flock of Shepherds: The National Conference of Catholic Bishops*. Kansas City: Sheed & Ward, 1992.

Rendina, Claudio. *I Papi*. Rome: Newton Compton Editori, 1983.

Rhynne, Xavier. *John Paul's Extraordinary Synod*. Wilmington, DE.: Michael Glazier, 1986.

Ricciardi, Andrea E. *Il Potere del Papa: da Pio XII a Giovanni-Paolo II*. Rome: Editori Laterza, 1993.

———. *Il Vaticano e Mosca 1940–1990*. Rome: Editori Laterza, 1993.

Richard, Lucien, O.M.I., Daniel Harrington, S.J. and John W. O'Malley, S.J., Eds. *Vatican II: The Unfinished Agenda: A Look to the Future*. Mahweh, NJ: Paulist Press, 1987.

Roeck, Jeff. *Juan Pablo II: El Hombre Que Vino de Polonia*. Averbode, Belgium: Verlag Altiora, 1978.

Romero, Oscar Archbishop. *A Shepherd's Diary*. Cincinnati: Saint Anthony Messenger Press, 1986.

Rosenberg, Tina. *The Haunted Land*. New York: Random House, 1995.

Ruiz, José María González. *Memoria del Concilio*. Rome: Borla, 1985.

Rynne, Catherine. *Knock 1879–1979*. Dublin: Veritas, 1979.

Schopflin, George. *Politics in Eastern Europe 1945–92*. Oxford: Blackwell, 1993.

Svidercoschi, Gianfranco. *Lettera a un amico ebreo*. Milan: Mondadori, 1993.

————. *Letter to a Jewish Friend*. New York: Crossroad, 1994.

Synod of 1985. Extraordinary. Boston: Saint Paul Editions, 1986.

Synodus Extraordinaria. Relatio Finalis. L'Osservatore Romano (December 10, 1985): Supplement.

Szajkowski, Bogdan. *Next to God . . . Poland: Politics and Religion in Contemporary Poland*. New York: Saint Martin's, 1983.

Szoldrski, O. W., C.S.S.R., *Martyrologium Cleri Polonici Sub Occupatione Germanica, 1939–1945*. Rome, 1965.

Szostak. John M. and Frances Spatz Leighton. *In the Footsteps of Pope John Paul II: An Intimate Personal Portrait*. Englewood Cliffs, NJ: Prentice Hall, 1980.

Szulc, Tad. *Pope John Paul II: The Biography*. New York: Scribner and Sons, 1995.

Tajne Dokumenty, Panstwo Kosciól: 1980–1989. London: Aneks Publishers, 1993.

Talks of John Paul II. Boston: Daughters of Saint Paul, 1979.

Thatcher, Margaret. *The Downing Street Years*. London: Harper Collins, 1993.

Thomas, Gordon and Max Morgan-Witts. *Averting Armageddon*. New York: Doubleday, 1984.

————. *Pontiff*. Garden City, NJ: Doubleday, 1983.

Tulat, Jean. *Le Pape Contre la Guerre du Golfe*. Paris: Oeil, 1991.

Uboldi, Rafaello. *Vita di Papa Wojtyla*. Milan: Rizzoli, 1983.

Vree, Dale. *Un Chemin d'Espoir: Autobiographie*. Paris: Fayard, 1987.

————. *A Way of Hope: An Autobiography*. New York: Henry Holt, 1987.

Vircondelet, Alain. *Jean-Paul II: Biographie*. Paris: Édition Juilliard, 1994.

Von Rauch, Georg. *A History of Soviet Russia*. Trans. Peter and Annette Jacobsohn. New York: Frederick A. Praeger.

Walesa, Lech. *The Struggle and The Triumph: An Autobiography*. New York: Arcade, 1992.

Walsh, Michael. *John Paul II*. London: Harper Collins, 1994.

Weigel, George. *Witness To Hope: The Biography of Pope John Paul II*. New York: Cliff Street Books, 1999.

Weschler, Lawrence. *The Passion of Poland*. New York: Pantheon Books, 1984.

Whale, John, Ed. *The Pope from Poland: An Assessment*. London: Collins, 1980.

Whale John, ed. and Peter Hebblethwaite. *The Man Who Leads the Church: An Assessment of Pope John Paul II*. San Francisco: Harper & Row, 1980.

Will, George. "A Pope with Authority." *Newsweek* (June 23, 1980): 92.

Willebrands, Johannes Cardinal. *The Church and Jewish People: New Considerations*. Mahweh, NJ: Paulist Press, 1992.

Willey, David. *God's Politician: Pope John Paul II, the Catholic Church and the New World Order*. New York: Saint Martin's Press, 1992.

Wills, Garry. *Under God: Religion and American Politics*. New York: Simon and Schuster, 1990.

Winn, Wilton. *Keepers of the Keys: John XXIII, Paul VI and John Paul II: Three Who Changed the Church*. New York: Random House, 1988.

Woodward, Bob. *Veil*. New York: Simon and Schuster, 1987.

Wynn, Wilton. *Keeper of the Keys*. New York: Random House, 1988.

Zizola, Giancarlo. *Il Conclave: storia i segreti. L'elezione papale da San Pietro a Giovanni Paolo II*. Rome: Newtown Compton Editori, 1993.

———. *Le restaurazioni di papa Wojtyla*. Bari: Laterza, 1985.

———. *Le successeur*. Paris: Desclée de Brouwer, 1995.

ECUMENISM

"An Offer from the Pope." *The Tablet* 249 (1995): 694–695.

"Applause for the Pope's Unity Call—with Reservations." *The Tablet* 249 (1995): 714.

Bouboutsis, E. K. "Toward Unity with Diversity and Equality." *Ecumenical Trends* 25 (1996): 10–12.

Cassidy, Edward Idris. "*Ut Unum Sint* and the Great Jubilee Year 2000." *Bulletin* [Centro Pro Unione] 49 (Spring 1996): 3–8.

Cassidy, Edward Idris and Eleuterio F. Fortino. "Comment on the Encyclical Letter *Ut Unum Sint* of the Holy Father Pope John Paul II on Commitment to Ecumenism." *Information Service* [Pontifical Council for Promoting Christian Unity] 89 (1995): 83–87.

Crow, P. A. "One of the Most Powerful Witnesses in Recent Time." *Inside the Oikoumene* 9 (1995): 6–8.

Directory for the Application of Principles and Norms on Ecumenism. Vatican City: Pontifical Council for Christian Unity, 1993.

McDermott, John M., Ed. *The Thought of Pope John Paul II*. Rome: Gregorian University, 1993.

McFarlane, R. "An Anglican Response to the Encyclical *Ut Unum Sint*." *Ecumenical Trends* 25 (1996): 12–14.

Neuhaus, Richard John. "'That They May All Be One': The Pope's Twelfth Encyclical." *Crisis* 13 (September 1995): 25–27.

Nilson, J. "The Challenges of *Ut Unum Sint*." *Ecumenical Trends* 25 (1996): 8–10.

"Reactions to *Ut Unum Sint* from Protestant Churches Around the World." *Catholic International* 6 (1995): 397–398.

Reardon, Ruth. "'A Source of Joy': *Ut Unum Sint* and Interchurch Families." *One in Christ* 31 (1995): 397–398.

Stron, R. "An Anglican Response to the Papal Encyclical *Ut Unum Sint*." *Unity Digest* 13 (1995): 7–12.

Suenens, Léon Joseph Cardinal. *Ecumenism and Charismatic Renewal.* London: Darton, Longman and Todd, 1978.

Zago, Marcello. "The Missionary Importance of the Encyclical *Ut Unum Sint.*" *Omnis Terra* 29 (1995): 488–494.

INDISPENSABLE BIBLIOGRAPHY FOR UNDERSTANDING POPE JOHN PAUL II

Acta Apostolicae Sedis (1909–).

Acta Sanctae Sedis (1865–1908).

Acta Synodalia Sacrosancti Concilii Oecumenici Vaticana Secundi. Vatican Press, 1970.

Aquinas, Thomas. *In Librum Aristotelis de caelo et mundo commentarium.* I, 1.22 (Parma edition, 1865, t. XIX, 58).

———. *Summa Theologica.* New York: Benziger Brothers, Inc., 1947.

Augustine, Saint. *The Confessions.* New York: Collier Books, 1961.

———. *Contra Academicos (Against the Sceptics). Fathers of the Church: Writings of Saint Augustine* (Vol. 1). New York: Gima, 1948.

Bertetto, Domenico, S.D.B., ed. *La Madonna nella Parola di Paolo VI.* 2nd Edition. Rome: Libreria Ateneo Salesiano, 1980.

Bokenknotter, Thomas. *A Concise History of the Catholic Church.* New York: Doubleday, 1990.

Borghi, C. "Mentalità scientifica e religione." *Cristiani e società* (1980).

Bosco, Father Teresio. *Saint Maximilian Kolbe.* Melbourne: A.C.T.S. Publications.

Caprile, Giovanni. *Il Concilio Vaticano II.* Rome: La Civiltà Cattolica.

———. *Il sinodo straordinario, 1985.* Rome: La Civiltà Cattolica, 1986.

Catechism of the Catholic Church. English Translation. United States Catholic Conference, Libreria Editrice Vaticana, Mahwah, NJ: Paulist Press, 1994.

Catholic Almanac. Huntington, IN: Our Sunday Visitor Publishing Division, 1994.

Christian Social Association. *Information Bulletin,* monthly. Warsaw.

Clissold, Kenneth. *The Wisdom of Spanish Mystics.* New York: New Directions, 1997.

Congar, Yves. *Je Crois en l'Esprit Saint,* Vol. III. Paris: Les Editions du Cerf, 1980.

———. *La Parole et le Souffle.* Collection 'Jesus et Jesus Christ', no. 20. Paris: Desclèe, 1984.

Crosson, F. J. "Phenomenology." *New Catholic Encyclopedia.* New York: McGraw-Hill, 1967.

"Cultura impregno per l'uomo. Atti del IV convegno sul Magistero Pontificio." *La Traccia* 4 (1984).

De Fiores, Stefano, S.M. *Itenerario spirituale di S. Luigi Maria de Montfort (1673–1716) nel periodo fino al sacerdozio (5 giugno 1700).* Marian Library Studies, n.s. 6. Dayton, OH: University of Dayton, 1974.

De Fiores, Stefano, S.M. and Salvatore Meo, O.S.M., Eds. *Nuovo Dizionario di Mariologia.* Milan: Edizioni Paoline, 1985.

De Montfort, Saint Louis-Marie Grignion. *Oeuvres complètes de Saint Louis-Marie Grignion de Montfort.* Paris: Éditions du Seuill, 1982.

―――. *God Alone: The Collected Writings of Saint Louis Mary de Montfort.* Bay Shore, NY: Montfort Publications, 1987.

Denziger, Henricus, and Adolfus Schonmetzer, S.J., Eds. *Enchiridion Symbolorum Definitionum et Declarationum de Rebus Fidei et Morum.* 32nd ed. Freiburg im Breisgau: Herder, 1963.

Dewar, Diana. *Saint of Auschwitz. The Story of Maximilian Kolbe.* London: Darton, Longman and Todd.

Documentos de la Conferencia del Episcopado Dominicano: 1955–1990. República Dominicana: Colección Quinto Centenario, Santo Domingo, 1990.

Dolan, Jay P. *The American Catholic Experience: A History from Colonial Times to the Present.* Notre Dame, IN: University of Notre Dame Press, 1992.

Du Roy, O. J. B. "Augustine, Saint" *New Catholic Encyclopedia* 1: 1041–1058. New York: McGraw Hill, 1967.

Flannery, Austin, O.P. *Vatican II: The Conciliar and Post Conciliar Documents.* Boston: Saint Paul Editions, 1992.

Flannery, Austin, Ed. *Dignitatis Humanae, Declaration on Religious Liberty. Documents of Vatican II* (December 7, 1965). Grand Rapids: William B. Eerdmans Publishing Company, 1975.

―――. *Gaudium et Spes, Pastoral Constitution on the Church. Documents of Vatican II* (November 21, 1964). Grand Rapids: William B. Eerdmans Publishing Company, 1975.

―――. *Lumen Gentium, Dogmatic Constitution on the Church. Documents of Vatican II* (November 21, 1964). Grand Rapids: William B. Eerdmans Publishing Company, 1975.

―――. *Presbyterorum Ordinis, Decree on the Ministry and Life of Priests. Documents of Vatican II.* (December 7, 1965). Grand Rapids: William B. Eerdmans Publishing Company, 1975.

Galot, Jean. *Christ De Notre Foi.* Louvain: Editions Sintal, 1986.

―――. *Christ, Qui Es-Tu?* Louvain: Editions Sintal, 1985.

Garrigou-Lagrange, Reginald. *Christian Perfection and Contemplation According to Saint Thomas and Saint John of the Cross.* Saint Louis: Herder, 1937.

―――. *The Theological Virtues.* Saint Louis: Herder, 1964.

Gramatowski, Wiktor and Zofia Wilinska. *Jan Pawel II: Bibliografic Polska 1978–1983.* Rome: Fundacja Jana Pawla II, Osrodek Dokumentacji Pontyficatu, 1987.

Gramatowski, Wiktor, Zofia Wilinska and Danuta Guzajewska. *Jan Pawel II: Bibliografia Polska 1984–1986.* Rome: Fundacja Jana Pawla II, Osrodek Dokumentacji Pontyficatu, 1991.

Insegnamenti di Giovanni Paolo II. Vatican City: Libreria Editrice Vaticana, 1979– .

Insegnamenti di Paolo VI (1963–1978). 15 vols. Vatican City: Libreria Editrice Vaticana, 1965–1979.

Kalser, Robert. *The Encyclical That Never Was.* London: Sheed & Ward, 1989.

Kant, I. *Critica della Ragion patrica.* Bari: 1966, 152.

———. *Critique of Practical Reason*, I, i, 3. Chicago: University of Chicago Press, 1949.

———. *Foundations of the Metaphysics of Morals*, II. Chicago: University of Chicago Press, 1949.

Koehler, Theodore, S.M. "Mary's Spiritual Maternity after the Second Vatican Council." *Marian Studies* 23 (1972): 39–68.

Kolbe, Saint Maximilian , O.F.M. Conv. *Gli Scritti di Massimiliano Kolbe: eroe di Oswiecim e Beato della Chiesa.* 3 vols. Trans. Cristoforo Zambelli. Florence: Citta di Vita, 1975–1978.

Laurentin, Rene. "The Magisterium of the Church on the Alliance of the Hearts of Jesus and Mary." Trans. Srs. Edita Telan, M.I.C., and Rachel de Mars, M.I.C., in *The Alliance of the Hearts of Jesus and Mary: The International Theological/Pastoral Conference, Manila Phillipines, November 30, December 1987, Texts and Documents*, 158–187. Manila: Bahay Maria, 1988.

———. "Mary and Womanhood in the Renewal of Christian Anthropology." *Marian Library Studies* 1: 77–95. Dayton, OH: University of Dayton, 1969.

———. *A Year of Grace with Mary: Rediscovering Her Presence and Her Role in Our Consecration.* Trans. Msgr. Michael J. Wrenn. Dublin: Veritas, 1987.

Mahoney, Roger. "The Teaching of Revelation." *L'Osservatore Romano* 32/33 (1991): 9.

Neuner, J., S.J., and J. Dupuis, S.J., eds. *The Christian Faith in the Doctrinal Documents of the Catholic Church.* New York: Alba House, 1982.

Papfava, Francesco, Ed. *The Sistine Chapel.* Vatican City: Musei Vaticani, 1992.

Paul VI. *Humanae Vitae, On Human Life.* Washington, D.C.: Office for Publishing and Promotion Services. United States Catholic Conference, 1968.

———. *Mary–God's Mother and Ours.* Boston: Saint Paul Editions, 1979.

Pius XII. "Munificentissimus Deus." *Selected Documents of His Holiness Pope Pius XII 1939–1958.* Washington, D.C.: National Catholic Welfare Conference.

———. *Mystici Coporis. The Mystical Body of Christ.* Washington, D.C.: National Catholic Welfare Conference, 1943.

Pontifical Council for the Family. *Marriage and the Family.* San Francisco: Ignatius Press, 1987.

Ratzinger, Joseph Cardinal. *Dogma y predicación.* Brescia: Queriniana, 1974.

———. *Turning Point for Europe?* San Francisco: Ignatius Press, 1994.

Ratzinger, Joseph Cardinal with Vittorio Messori. *The Ratzinger Report.* San Francisco: Ignatius Press, 1985.

Roschini, Gabriele M., O.S.M. *Maria Santissima nella storia della Salvezza.* 4 vols. Isola del Liri: Tipografia Editrice M. Pisani, 1969.

Sacrosanctum Oecumenicum Concilium Vaticanum II. *Constitutiones, Decreta, Declarationes.* Cura et studio Secretariae Generalis Concilii Oecumenici Vaticani II. Vatican City: Typis Polyglottis Vaticanis, 1974.

Santo Domingo Conclusions: New Evangelization, Human Development, Christian Culture. Fourth Conference of Latin American Bishops, October 12–28, 1992. Washington, D.C.: Secretariat, Bishops' Committee for the Church in Latin America, National Conference of Catholic Bishops, 1993.

Satini, Alceste. *Agostino Casaroli: Uomo del Dialogo.* Torino: Edizioni San Paolo, 1993.

Simon, Ulrich. *A Theology of Auschwitz.* London: SPCK, 1978.

Statistical Yearbook of the Church. Vatican City: Secretaria Status, Rationarium Generale Ecclesiae, 1991.

Styczen, Tadeusz, S.D.S. *Le encicliche di Giovanni Paolo II.* Milan: Mondadori, 1994.

Suenens, Léon Joseph Cardinal. *Ecumenism and Charismatic Renewal.* London: Darton, Longman and Todd, 1978.

Terelya, Josyp and Michael H. Brown. *Witness.* Milford: Faith Publishing Company, 1992.

Trasatti, Sergio and Arturo Mari. *Journey in Suffering.* Bergamo, Italy: Editrice Velar, 1981.

Vatican Council II: The Conciliar and Post-Conciliar Documents. Volumes 1 and 2. Northport, NY: Costello, 1992.

Index

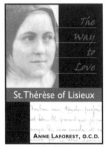
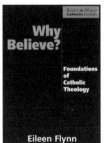